Praise for Eric Tyson

"Eric Tyson is doing something important - namely, helping people at all income levels to take control of their financial futures. This book is a natural outgrowth of Tyson's vision that he has nurtured for years. Like Henry Ford, he wants to make something that was previously accessible only to the wealthy accessible to middle-income Americans."

> — James C. Collins, coauthor of the national bestseller *Built to Last;* former Lecturer in Business, Stanford Graduate School of Business

"*Personal Finance For Dummies* is the perfect book for people who feel guilty about inadequately managing their money but are intimidated by all of the publications out there. It's a painless way to learn how to take control."

> — National Public Radio's *Sound Money*

"Eric Tyson . . . seems the perfect writer for a *...For Dummies* book. He doesn't tell you what to do or consider doing without explaining the why's and how's - and the booby traps to avoid - in plain English. . . . It will lead you through the thickets of your own finances as painlessly as I can imagine."

> — *Chicago Tribune*

"This book provides easy-to-understand personal financial information and advice for those without great wealth or knowledge in this area. Practitioners like Eric Tyson, who care about the well-being of middle-income people, are rare in today's society."

> — Joel Hyatt, founder, Hyatt Legal Services, one of the nation's largest general-practice personal legal service firms

"Worth getting. Scores of all-purpose money-management books reach bookstores every year, but only once every couple of years does a standout personal finance primer come along. *Personal Finance For Dummies,* by financial counselor and columnist Eric Tyson, provides detailed, action-oriented advice on everyday financial questions. . . . Tyson's style is readable and unintimidating."

> — Kristin Davis, *Kiplinger's Personal Finance Magazine*

"This is a great book. It's understandable. Other financial books are too technical and this one really is different."

> — Business Radio Network

More Bestselling For Dummies Titles by Eric Tyson

Investing For Dummies®

Wall Street Journal bestseller walks you through how to build wealth in stocks, real estate and small business as well as other investments.

Mutual Funds For Dummies®

This bestselling guide is now updated to include current fund and portfolio recommendations. Using the practical tips and techniques, you'll design a mutual fund investment plan suited to your income, lifestyle, and risk preferences.

Taxes For Dummies®

The complete, best-selling reference for completing your tax return and making tax-wise financial decisions year-round. Tyson co-authors this book with tax expert David Silverman.

Home Buying For Dummies®

America's #1 real estate book includes coverage of online resources in addition to sound financial advice from Eric Tyson and frontline real estate insights from industry veteran Ray Brown. Also available from America's best-selling real estate team of Tyson and Brown — *House Selling For Dummies* and *Mortgages For Dummies*.

Small Business For Dummies®

Take control of your future and make the leap from employee to entrepreneur with this enterprising guide. From drafting a business plan to managing costs, you'll profit from expert advice and real-world examples that cover every aspect of building your own business. Tyson co-authors this book with fellow entrepreneur Jim Schell.

Personal Finance
FOR
DUMMIES®
4TH EDITION

by Eric Tyson, MBA

WILEY

Wiley Publishing, Inc.

Personal Finance For Dummies®, 4th Edition

Published by
Wiley Publishing, Inc.
909 Third Avenue
New York, NY 10022
www.wiley.com

Copyright © 2003 by Eric Tyson

Published by Wiley Publishing, Inc., Indianapolis, Indiana

Published simultaneously in Canada

No part of this publication may be reproduced, stored in a retrieval system, or transmitted in any form or by any means, electronic, mechanical, photocopying, recording, scanning, or otherwise, except as permitted under Sections 107 or 108 of the 1976 United States Copyright Act, without either the prior written permission of the Publisher, or authorization through payment of the appropriate per-copy fee to the Copyright Clearance Center, 222 Rosewood Drive, Danvers, MA 01923, 978-750-8400, fax 978-646-8700. Requests to the Publisher for permission should be addressed to the Legal Department, Wiley Publishing, Inc., 10475 Crosspoint Blvd., Indianapolis, IN 46256, 317-572-3447, fax 317-572-4447, or e-mail permcoordinator@wiley.com

Trademarks: Wiley, the Wiley Publishing logo, For Dummies, the Dummies Man logo, A Reference for the Rest of Us!, The Dummies Way, Dummies Daily, The Fun and Easy Way, Dummies.com and related trade dress are trademarks or registered trademarks of Wiley Publishing, Inc., in the United States and other countries, and may not be used without written permission. All other trademarks are the property of their respective owners. Wiley Publishing, Inc., is not associated with any product or vendor mentioned in this book.

For general information on our other products and services or to obtain technical support, please contact our Customer Care Department within the U.S. at 800-762-2974, outside the U.S. at 317-572-3993, or fax 317-572-4002.

Wiley also publishes its books in a variety of electronic formats. Some content that appears in print may not be available in electronic books.

Library of Congress Cataloging-in-Publication Data:

Library of Congress Control Number: 2003105627

ISBN: 07645-2590-5

Manufactured in the United States of America

10 9 8 7 6 5 4 3 2

 is a trademark of Wiley Publishing, Inc.

About the Author

Eric Tyson first became interested in money more than three decades ago. After his father was laid off during the 1973 recession and received some retirement money from Philco-Ford, Eric worked with his dad to make investing decisions with the money. A couple of years later, Eric won his high school's science fair with a project on what influences the stock market. Dr. Martin Zweig, who provided some guidance, awarded Eric a one-year subscription to the Zweig Forecast, a famous investment newsletter. Of course, Eric's mom and dad share some credit with Martin for Eric's victory.

After toiling away for a number of years as a management consultant to Fortune 500 financial-service firms, Eric finally figured out how to pursue his dream. He took his inside knowledge of the banking, investment, and insurance industries and committed himself to making personal financial management accessible to us all.

Today, Eric is an internationally acclaimed and best-selling personal finance book author, syndicated columnist, and speaker. He has worked with and taught people from all financial situations, so he knows the financial concerns and questions of real folks just like you. Despite being handicapped by an M.B.A. from the Stanford Graduate School of Business and a B.S. in Economics and Biology from Yale University, Eric remains a master at "keeping it simple."

An accomplished personal finance writer, his "Investor's Guide" syndicated column, distributed by King Features, is read by millions nationally, and he was an award-winning columnist for the San Francisco Examiner. He is the author of five national best-selling financial books in the ...For Dummies series on personal finance, investing, mutual funds, home buying (co-author), and taxes (co-author). The latest edition of his best-selling book, *Personal Finance for Dummies* was awarded the Benjamin Franklin Award for Best Business Book of the Year.

Eric's work has been featured and quoted in hundreds of local and national publications including Newsweek, The Wall Street Journal, Los Angeles Times, Chicago Tribune, Forbes, Kiplinger's Personal Finance Magazine, Parenting, Money, Family Money, Bottom Line/Personal, and on NBC'S Today Show, ABC, CNBC, PBS Nightly Business Report, CNN, and FOX-TV, and on CBS national radio, NPR Sound Money, Bloomberg Business Radio, and Business Radio Network.

Dedication

This book is hereby and irrevocably dedicated to my family and friends, as well as to my counseling clients and customers, who ultimately have taught me everything that I know about how to explain financial terms and strategies so that all of us may benefit.

Author's Acknowledgments

Being an entrepreneur involves endless challenges, and without the support and input of my good friends and mentors Peter Mazonson, Jim Collins, and my best friend and wife, Judy, I couldn't have accomplished what I have.

I hold many people accountable for my perverse and maniacal interest in figuring out the financial services industry and money matters, but most of the blame falls on my loving parents, Charles and Paulina, who taught me most of what I know that's been of use in the real world.

I'd also like to thank Michael Bloom, Chris Dominguez, Maggie McCall, David Ish, Paul Kozak, Chris Treadway, Sally St. Lawrence, K.T. Rabin, Will Hearst III, Ray Brown, Susan Wolf, Rich Caramella, Lisa Baker, Renn Vera, Maureen Taylor, Jerry Jacob, Robert Crum, Duc Nguyen, and Maria Carmicino, and all the good folks at King Features for believing in and supporting my writing and teaching.

Many thanks to all the people who provided insightful comments on this book, especially financial planner Bill Urban with Bingham Osborn & Scarborough and Barton Francis, Mike van den Akker, Gretchen Morgenson, Craig Litman, Gerri Detweiler, Mark White, Alan Bush, Nancy Coolidge, and Chris Jensen.

And thanks to all the wonderful people at my publisher on the front line and behind the scenes, especially Kathy Cox, Marcia Johnson, Greg Pearson, and Elizabeth Rea.

Publisher's Acknowledgments

We're proud of this book; please send us your comments through our Dummies online registration form located at www.dummies.com/register/.

Some of the people who helped bring this book to market include the following:

Acquisitions, Editorial, and Media Development

Project Editor: Marcia L. Johnson

(Previous Editions: Kathy Cox, Wendy Hatch)

Acquisitions Editor: Kathy Cox

Copy Editor: Greg Pearson

Acquisitions Coordinator: Holly Grimes

Technical Editor: William R. Urban

Editorial Manager: Jennifer Ehrlich

Editorial Assistant: Elizabeth Rea

Cartoons: Rich Tennant, www.the5thwave.com

Production

Project Coordinator: Maridee Ennis

Layout and Graphics: Seth Conley, Carrie Foster, Joyce Haughey, LeAndra Hosier, Stephanie Jumper, Michael Kruzil, Jacque Schneider, Erin Zeltner

Proofreaders: John Greenough, Susan Moritz, Angel Perez, Carl Pierce, Kathy Simpson, Brian Walls

Indexer: Ty Koontz

Publishing and Editorial for Consumer Dummies

Diane Graves Steele, Vice President and Publisher, Consumer Dummies

Joyce Pepple, Acquisitions Director, Consumer Dummies

Kristin A. Cocks, Product Development Director, Consumer Dummies

Michael Spring, Vice President and Publisher, Travel

Brice Gosnell, Publishing Director, Travel

Suzanne Jannetta, Editorial Director, Travel

Publishing for Technology Dummies

Andy Cummings, Vice President and Publisher, Dummies Technology/General User

Composition Services

Gerry Fahey, Vice President of Production Services

Debbie Stailey, Director of Composition Services

Contents at a Glance

Introduction 1

Part I: Assessing Your Fitness and Setting Goals 7
Chapter 1: Improving Your Financial Fitness 9
Chapter 2: Setting and Achieving Goals 33

Part II: Saving More, Spending Less 59
Chapter 3: Determining Where Your Money Goes 61
Chapter 4: Conquering Debt and Credit Problems 73
Chapter 5: Reducing Your Spending 91
Chapter 6: Taming Taxes 119

Part III: Building Wealth through Investing 141
Chapter 7: Important Investment Concepts 143
Chapter 8: Choosing Your Investment Vehicles 171
Chapter 9: Investing in Mutual Funds 191
Chapter 10: Investing in Retirement Accounts 211
Chapter 11: Investing Outside Retirement Accounts 233
Chapter 12: Investing for Educational Expenses 247
Chapter 13: Investing in Real Estate 259

Part IV: Insurance: Protecting What You've Got 299
Chapter 14: Insurance: Getting What You Need at the Best Price 301
Chapter 15: Insurance on You: Life, Disability, and Health 317
Chapter 16: Covering Your Assets 341

Part V: Where to Go for More Help 355
Chapter 17: Working with Financial Planners 357
Chapter 18: Computer Money Management 381
Chapter 19: On Air and in Print 393

Part VI: The Part of Tens **401**
Chapter 20: Survival Guide for Ten Life Changes 403
Chapter 21: Ten Things More Important than Money 419

Glossary **423**
Index **439**

Table of Contents

Introduction 1

    Why This Book? 1
    What's New in This Edition 2
    Uses for This Book 3
    How This Book Is Organized 3
        Part I: Assessing Your Fitness and Setting Goals 4
        Part II: Saving More, Spending Less 4
        Part III: Building Wealth through Investing 4
        Part IV: Insurance: Protecting What You've Got 4
        Part V: Where to Go for More Help 5
        Part VI: The Part of Tens 5
        Glossary 5
    Icons Used in This Book 5

Part 1: Assessing Your Fitness and Setting Goals 7

Chapter 1: Improving Your Financial Fitness 9

    Targeting the Trouble Spots 9
        Talking money at home 11
        Teaching personal finance in schools 12
        Identifying unreliable sources of information 12
    Jumping over Real and Imaginary Hurdles 16
        Discovering the real hurdles holding you back 17
        Practicing good habits 18
    Common Financial Problems: You've Got Company 20
    Defining Bad Debt and Good Debt 22
    Knowing How Much Bad Debt Is Too Much 23
    Determining Your Financial Net Worth 25
        Financial assets 25
        Financial liabilities 26
        Your net worth calculation 26
        Interpreting your net worth results 28
    Savings Analysis 28
    Measuring Your Investing Knowledge 30
    Measuring Your Insurance Savvy 32

Chapter 2: Setting and Achieving Goals 33

   Creating Your Own Definition of "Wealth" 33

      Considering what money can't buy 34

      Managing the balancing act 35

   Prioritizing Your Savings Goals 37

      Knowing what's most important to you 38

      Valuing retirement accounts 38

      Dealing with competing goals 39

   Building Emergency Reserves 40

   Saving to Buy a Home or Business 41

   Funding Kids' Educational Expenses 42

   Saving for Big Purchases 42

   Preparing for Retirement 43

      Figuring what you need for retirement 44

      Understanding retirement building blocks .46

      Counting on Social Security 46

      Planning your personal savings/investment strategy 49

      Making the most of pensions 49

      Retirement planning worksheet 50

      Making up for lost time 52

      Overcoming objections to retirement accounts 54

Part II: Saving More, Spending Less *59*

Chapter 3: Determining Where Your Money Goes 61

   Examining the Roots of Overspending 61

      Access to credit 62

      Using credit cards 62

      Making minimum monthly payments 62

      Taking out car loans 63

      Bending to peer pressure 64

      Spending to feel good 64

      Becoming addicted to spending 64

      Trying to keep current 64

      Ignoring your financial goals when buying .65

      Wanting the best for your children 65

   Analyzing Your Spending 66

      Tracking your spending on paper 67

      Tracking your spending on the computer 70

   Growing Rich on Your Income: The Secret 72

Chapter 4: Conquering Debt and Credit Problems 73

Using Savings to Reduce Your Debt 74
    Understanding how you gain 74
    Discovering money to pay down consumer debts 75
Decreasing Debt When You Lack Savings 76
    Transferring balances to lower-interest-rate credit cards 76
    Cutting up your credit cards 77
    Discovering debit cards: The best of both worlds 78
Filing Bankruptcy 79
    Understanding bankruptcy benefits 80
    Coming to terms with bankruptcy drawbacks 81
    Choosing between Chapter 7 and 13 84
    Seeking bankruptcy advice 84
Ending the Spending-and-Debting Cycle 85
    Resisting the credit temptation 85
    Identifying and treating an addiction 86
Dealing with Credit Mistakes 87
    Obtaining a copy of your credit report 88
    Getting others to correct their mistakes 88
    Telling your side of the story 89

Chapter 5: Reducing Your Spending 91

Finding the Keys to Successful Spending 92
    Living within your means 92
    Looking for the best values 93
    Eliminating the fat from your spending 97
    Turning your back on consumer credit 98
Reducing Your Spending: Eric's Strategies 98
    Reducing food costs 100
    Saving on shelter 102
    Lowering your phone bills 104
    Cutting transportation costs 106
    Controlling clothing costs 109
    Repaying your debt 110
    Indulging responsibly in fun and recreation 110
    Personal care 112
    Paring down professional expenses 113
    Managing medical expenses 114
    Keeping an eye on insurance premiums 115
    Trimming your taxes 115
    Eliminating costly addictions 116

Chapter 6: Taming Taxes **119**

Understanding the Taxes You Pay 119
Recognizing the importance of your marginal tax rate 120
Defining taxable income 121
Trimming Employment Income Taxes 122
Contributing to retirement plans 123
Shifting some income 124
Increasing Your Deductions 124
Choosing standard or itemized deductions 125
Purchasing real estate 126
Trading consumer debt for mortgage debt 127
Contributing to charities 127
Remembering auto registration fees and state insurance 128
Deducting miscellaneous expenses 129
Deducting self-employment expenses 130
Reducing Investment Income Taxes 132
Fill up those retirement accounts 133
Invest in tax-free money market funds and bonds 133
Select other tax-friendly investments 134
Make your profits long-term 134
Getting Help from Tax Resources 135
IRS assistance 135
Preparation and advice guides 136
Software and Web sites 136
Professional hired help 136
Dealing with an Audit 138
Getting your act together 138
Surviving the day of reckoning 139

Part III: Building Wealth through Investing *141*

Chapter 7: Important Investment Concepts **143**

Establishing Your Goals 143
Understanding the Major Investment Flavors 144
Looking at lending investments 144
Exploring ownership investments 146
Shunning gambling instruments and behaviors 147
Understanding Investment Returns 148
Sizing Investment Risks 149
Comparing the risks of stocks and bonds 150
Focusing on the risks you can control 151
Discovering low-risk, high-return investments 152

Diversifying Your Investments 152
    Spreading it around: Asset allocation 154
    Allocating money for the long-term 155
    Sticking with your allocations: Don't trade 156
    Investing lump sums via dollar-cost averaging 157
Acknowledging Differences among Investment Firms 159
    Focusing on the best firms 160
    Places to consider avoiding 161
Experts Who Predict the Future 166
    Investment newsletters 166
    Investment gurus 167
Leaving You with Some Final Advice 169

Chapter 8: Choosing Your Investment Vehicles 171
Slow and Steady Investments 171
    Transaction/checking accounts 172
    Savings and money market accounts 172
    Bonds 173
Building Wealth with Ownership Vehicles 175
    Stocks 175
    Generating wealth with real estate 180
    Investing in small business 185
Off the Beaten Path: Investment Odds and Ends 188
    Precious metals 188
    Annuities 188
    Collectibles 189
    Life insurance with a cash value 189

Chapter 9: Investing in Mutual Funds 191
Understanding the Benefits of Mutual Funds 191
Exploring Various Fund Types 193
    Money market funds 194
    Bond funds 194
    Stock funds 195
    Balancing bonds and stocks: Hybrid funds 196
    U.S., international, and global funds 196
    Index funds 197
    Specialty (sector) funds 199
Selecting the Best Mutual Funds 200
    Reading prospectuses and annual reports 200
    Keeping costs low 201
    Evaluating historic performance 204
    Assessing fund manager and fund family reputations 204
    Rating tax-friendliness 205
    Determining your needs and goals 205

Deciphering Your Fund's Performance 206
Dividends 207
Capital gains 208
Share price changes 208
Following and Selling Your Funds 209

Chapter 10: Investing in Retirement Accounts 211
Looking at Types of Retirement Accounts 211
Employer-sponsored plans 212
Self-employment plans 215
Individual retirement accounts (IRAs) 218
Annuities: An odd investment 219
Allocating Your Money in Retirement Plans 221
Prioritizing retirement contributions 221
Setting up a retirement account 221
Allocating money when your employer selects
the investment options 222
Allocating money in plans you design 225
Transferring Retirement Accounts 228
Transferring accounts you control 229
Moving money from an employer's plan 231

Chapter 11: Investing Outside Retirement Accounts 233
Getting Started 234
Paying off high-interest debt 234
Taking advantage of tax breaks 235
Understanding Taxes on Your Investments 235
Fortifying Your Emergency Reserves 236
Bank and credit union accounts 236
Money market mutual funds 237
Investing Money for the Longer Term 240
Defining your time horizons 240
Allocating assets for the long haul 241
Bond funds 241
Certificates of deposit (CDs) 244
Stock funds 245
Annuities 245
Real estate 245
Small-business investments 245

Chapter 12: Investing for Educational Expenses 247
Figuring Out How the Financial Aid System Works 247
Treatment of retirement accounts 249
Treatment of money in the kids' names 250
Treatment of home equity and other assets 251

Strategizing to Pay for Educational Expenses 251
    Estimating college costs 253
    Setting realistic savings goals 253
    Tips for getting loans, grants, and scholarships 254
Investing Educational Funds 256
    Good investments: No-load mutual funds 256
    Bad investments 256
    Overlooked investments 257

Chapter 13: Investing in Real Estate **259**
Deciding Whether to Buy or Continue Renting 259
    Assessing your timeline 260
    Determining what you can afford to buy 260
    Calculating how much lenders will allow you to borrow ...261
    Comparing the cost of owning versus renting 263
    Considering the long-term costs of renting 266
Financing Your Home 267
    Understanding the two types of mortgages 268
    Choosing between fixed- and adjustable-rate mortgages ...268
    Shopping for fixed-rate mortgages 270
    Inspecting adjustable-rate mortgages (ARMs) 273
    Avoiding the down payment blues 276
    Comparing 15-year and 30-year mortgages 278
    Finding the best lender 280
    Increasing your approval chances 281
Finding the Right Property and Location 283
    Condo, town house, co-op, or detached home? 283
    Casting a broad net 284
    Finding out actual sale prices 284
    Researching the neighborhood and area 285
Working with Real Estate Agents 285
    Recognizing real estate agents' conflicts of interest ...286
    Looking for the right qualities in real estate agents ...287
Putting Your Deal Together 289
    Negotiating 101 289
    Inspecting before you buy 290
    Remembering title insurance and escrow fees 291
After You Buy 292
    Refinancing your mortgage 292
    Mortgage life insurance 294
    Is getting a reverse mortgage a good idea? 295
    Selling your house 296

Part IV: Insurance: Protecting What You've Got 299

Chapter 14: Insurance: Getting What You Need at the Best Price 301

Discovering My Three Laws of Buying Insurance 301
  Law I: Insure for the big stuff, not the small stuff 302
  Law II: Buy broad coverage 306
  Law III: Shop around and buy direct 308
Dealing with Insurance Problems 311
  Knowing what to do if you're denied coverage 311
  Getting your due on claims 313

Chapter 15: Insurance on You: Life, Disability, and Health 317

Providing for Your Loved Ones: Life Insurance 318
  Determining how much life insurance to buy 318
  Comparing term life insurance to cash value life insurance 320
  Making your decision 323
  Buying term insurance 324
  Getting rid of cash value life insurance 325
  Considering the purchase of cash value life insurance 326
Preparing for the Unpredictable: Disability Insurance 326
  Determining how much disability insurance you need 328
  Identifying other features you need in disability insurance 329
  Deciding where to buy disability insurance 330
Getting the Care You Need: Health Insurance 331
  Choosing the best health plan 331
  Buying health insurance 334
  Dealing with insurance denial 334
  Looking at retiree medical care insurance 336
Discovering the Most Overlooked Form of Insurance 338

Chapter 16: Covering Your Assets 341

Protecting Where You Live 341
  Dwelling coverage: The cost to rebuild 342
  Personal property coverage: For your things 342
  Liability insurance: Coverage for hurting others 343
  Flood and earthquake insurance: Protection from
    Mother Nature 344
  Deductibles: Your cost with a claim 345
  Special discounts 345
  Buying homeowner's or renter's insurance 345
Auto Insurance 101 346
  Bodily injury/property damage liability 346
  Uninsured or underinsured motorist liability 347
  Deductibles 348

Special discounts 348
Little-stuff coverage to skip 349
Buying auto insurance 350
Protecting Against Mega-Liability: Umbrella Insurance 350
You Can't Take It with You: Planning Your Estate 351
Wills, living wills, and medical powers of attorney 351
Avoiding probate through living trusts 352
Reducing estate taxes 353

Part V: Where to Go for More Help 355

Chapter 17: Working with Financial Planners 357
Alice in Financial-Planner Land 357
Alice's (mis)adventures 358
Learning from Alice's journey 359
Surveying Your Financial Management Options 362
Doing nothing 362
Doing it yourself 362
Hiring financial help 363
Deciding Whether to Hire a Financial Planner 365
How a good financial planner can help 366
Why financial planners aren't for everyone 367
The Frustrations of Finding Good Financial Planners 368
Regulatory problems 368
Recognizing financial planners' conflicts of interest 369
Finding a Good Financial Planner 373
Soliciting personal referrals 373
Seeking advisors through associations 375
Interviewing Financial Advisors: Asking the Right Questions 375
What percentage of your income comes from clients' fees
versus commissions from the products that you sell? 376
What percentage of fees paid by your clients is for
ongoing money management versus hourly
financial planning? 377
What is your hourly fee? 377
Do you also perform tax or legal services? 378
What work and educational experience qualifies
you to be a financial planner? 378
Have you ever sold limited partnerships?
Options? Futures? Commodities? 378
Do you carry liability (errors and omissions) insurance? 379
Can you provide references from clients with needs
similar to mine? 379

Will you provide specific strategies and product
recommendations that I can implement on
my own if I choose? 380
How is implementation handled? 380

Chapter 18: Computer Money Management 381

Surveying Software and Web Sites 381
Adding up financial software benefits 382
Treading carefully on the Web 383
Accomplishing Computer Money Tasks 385
Paying your bills and tracking your money 385
Planning for retirement 386
Preparing your taxes 388
Researching investments 388
Trading online 389
Reading and searching periodicals 390
Buying life insurance 390
Preparing legal documents 391

Chapter 19: On Air and in Print 393

Observing the Mass Media 393
Alarming or informing us? 394
Teaching what kind of values? 394
Worshipping prognosticating pundits 395
Rating Radio and Television Financial Programs 395
Learning to Surf the Internet 396
Navigating Newspapers and Magazines 397
Betting on Books 398

Part VI: The Part of Tens 401

Chapter 20: Survival Guide for Ten Life Changes 403

Starting Out: Your First Job 404
Changing Jobs or Careers 405
Getting Married 406
Buying a Home 408
Having Children 408
Starting a Small Business 412
Caring for Aging Parents 412
Divorcing 414
Receiving a Windfall 415
Retiring 416

Chapter 21: Ten Things More Important than Money 419
    Putting your family first 419
    Making and keeping friends 420
    Investing in your health 420
    Caring for kids 420
    Knowing your neighbors 421
    Appreciating what you do have 421
    Minding your reputation 421
    Continuing your education 422
    Having fun 422
    Solving social problems 422

Glossary *423*

Index *439*

Introduction

●●●

Welcome to *Personal Finance For Dummies,* 4th Edition. The publication of this edition marks the 10th anniversary of the 1st edition. More than 1.3 million copies of this book are in print, and as you can see from the quotes in the front of this edition, readers and reviewers alike were pleased with the previous editions. I was thrilled when the prior (3rd) edition won the Benjamin Franklin Award for Best Business Book of the Year in 2001.

However, I don't rest on my laurels. So the book you hold in your hands reflects more hard work and brings you the freshest material for addressing your personal financial quandaries.

Why This Book?

Many Americans are financially illiterate. If your knowledge is limited when it comes to your finances, it's probably not your fault. Personal Finance 101 is not offered in our schools — not in high school, and not even in the best colleges and graduate schools. It should be. (Of course, if it were, I wouldn't be able to write fun and useful books such as this — or maybe they would use this book in the course!)

People keep making the same common financial mistakes over and over — procrastinating and lack of planning, wasteful spending, falling prey to financial salespeople and pitches, failing to do sufficient research before making important financial decisions, and so on. This book, like a good friend, can whop you upside the head and keep you from falling into the same traps.

As unfair as it may seem, many of these traps await you when you seek help for your financial problems. The world is filled with biased and bad financial advice. As a practicing financial counselor, I see and hear about the consequences of poor advice. Of course, every profession has bad apples, but too many of the people calling themselves "financial planners" have conflicts of interest and an inadequate level of competence.

All too often, financial advice ignores the big picture and focuses narrowly on investing. Because money is not an end in itself but a part of your whole life, this book helps connect your financial goals and problems to the rest of your life. You need a broad understanding of personal finance to include all areas of your financial life: spending, taxes, saving and investing, insurance, and planning for major goals like education, buying a home, and retirement.

Even if you understand the financial basics, thinking about your finances in a holistic way can be difficult. Sometimes you're too close to the situation to be objective. Like the organization of your desk or files (or disorganization, as the case may be), your finances may reflect the history of your life more than they reflect a comprehensive plan for your future.

You're likely a busy person who doesn't have enough hours in the day to get things done. Thus, you want to know how to diagnose your financial situation quickly (and painlessly) and determine what you should do next. Unfortunately, after figuring out which financial strategies make sense for you, choosing specific financial products in the marketplace can be a nightmare. You have literally thousands of investment, insurance, and loan options to choose from. Talk about information overload!

To complicate matters even more, you probably hear about most products through advertising that can be misleading, if not downright false. Of course, some ethical and useful firms advertise, but so do those that are more interested in converting your hard-earned income and savings into their profits. And they may not be here tomorrow when you need them.

You want to know the best places to go for your circumstances, so I fill this book with specific, tried-and-proven product recommendations. I also suggest where to turn next if you need more information and help.

What's New in This Edition

To make solid financial decisions, you need up-to-date information and advice, and that's what this book provides. Every page in this book has been updated and freshened.

Here are some of the major updates you may notice as you peruse the pages of this book:

- Major, major tax law changes were enacted since the last edition was published. In addition to the coverage provided in Chapter 6, you can also find a discussion of how tax law changes affect recommended investment strategies in Chapters 7 through 12, and estate planning strategies in Chapter 16.

- Updated investment recommendations, especially in the area of mutual funds, throughout Part III.

✔ Added coverage of new options that can help you save and invest for college and other educational expenses.

✔ Revised recommendations for where to get the best insurance deals in Part IV.

✔ Expanded and updated coverage of money resources (especially online resources).

Uses for This Book

You can use this book in one of three ways:

✔ If you want to find out about a specific topic, such as getting out of high-interest consumer debt, planning for major goals, or investing, you can flip to that section and get answers quickly.

✔ If you want a crash course in personal finance, read this book cover-to-cover. Reading the whole book helps solidify major financial concepts and gets you thinking about your finances in a more comprehensive way.

✔ If you're tired of picking up scattered piles of bills, receipts, and junk mail every time the kids chase the cat around the den, you can use this book as a paperweight!

Seriously though, this book is basic enough to help a novice get his or her arms around thorny financial issues. But advanced readers will be challenged, as well, to think about their finances in a new way and identify areas for improvement. Check out the table of contents for a chapter-by-chapter run-down of what this book offers. You can also look up a specific topic in the index. Or you can turn the page and start at the beginning: Chapter 1.

How This Book Is Organized

This book is organized into six parts, with each covering a major area of your personal finances. The chapters within each part cover specific topics in detail. You can read each chapter and part without having to read what comes before, which is useful if you have better things to do with your free time. This book also makes for great reading anywhere you may be sitting for a length of time (perhaps the bathroom). You may be referred occasionally to somewhere else in the book for more details on a particular subject. Here is a summary of what you'll find in each part.

Part 1: Assessing Your Fitness and Setting Goals

This part explains how to diagnose your current financial health and explores common reasons for any missing links in your personal finance knowledge. We all have dreams and goals, so in this part, I also encourage you to think about your financial aspirations and figure out how much you should be saving if you want to retire someday or accomplish other important goals.

Part 11: Saving More, Spending Less

Most people don't have gobs of extra cash. Therefore, this part shows you how to figure out where all your dollars are going and tells you how to reduce your spending. Chapter 4 is devoted to helping you get out from under the burden of high-interest consumer debt (such as credit card debt). I also provide specifics for reducing your tax burden.

Part 111: Building Wealth through Investing

Earning and saving money is hard work, so you should be careful when it comes to investing what you have worked so hard to save (or waited so long to inherit!). In this part, I assist you with picking investments wisely and help you understand investment risks, returns, and a whole lot more. I explain all the major, and best, investment options. I recommend specific strategies and investments to use both inside and outside of tax-sheltered retirement accounts. I also discuss buying, selling, and investing in real estate, as well as other wealth-building investments.

Part 1V: Insurance: Protecting What You've Got

Insurance is an important part of your financial life. Unfortunately, for most people, insurance is a thoroughly overwhelming and dreadfully boring topic. But perhaps I can pique your interest in this esoteric topic by telling you that you're probably paying more than you should for insurance, and you probably don't have the right coverage for your situation. This part tells you all you ever wanted to know (okay, fine — all you *never* wanted to know but probably should know anyway) about how to buy the right insurance at the best price.

Part V: Where to Go for More Help

As you build your financial knowledge, more questions and issues may arise. In this part, I discuss where to go and what to avoid when you seek financial information and advice. I also discuss hiring a financial planner as well as investigating resources in print, on the air, and online.

Part VI: The Part of Tens

The chapters in this part can help you manage major life changes, survive tough financial times, and keep money in the proper perspective with the rest of your life.

Glossary

The world of money is filled with jargon, so you'll be happy to know that this book includes a comprehensive glossary of financial terms that are often tossed around but seldom explained.

Icons Used in This Book

This nerdy looking guy appears beside discussions that aren't critical if you just want to understand basic concepts and get answers to your financial questions. You can safely ignore these sections, but reading them can help deepen and enhance your personal financial knowledge. This stuff can also come in handy if you're ever on a game show, or if you find yourself stuck on an elevator with a financial geek.

This target flags strategy recommendations for making the most of your money (for example, paying off your credit card debt with your lottery winnings).

This icon highlights the best financial products in the areas of investments, insurance, and so on. These products can help you implement my strategy recommendations.

This icon points out information that's discussed elsewhere in the book or stuff you'll definitely want to remember.

This icon marks things to avoid and common mistakes people make when managing their finances.

This icon alerts you to scams and scoundrels that prey on the unsuspecting.

This icon tells you when you should consider doing some additional research. Don't worry — I explain what to look for and what to look out for.

Part I
Assessing Your Fitness and Setting Goals

The 5th Wave   By Rich Tennant

"I FIND IT EASIER TO SAY 'NO', IF I IMAGINE THEM SAYING, 'MOMMY, CAN I HAVE THE LATEST OVER-HYPED, OVER-PRICED, COMMERCIAL EXPLOITATION OF AN OBNOXIOUSLY ADORABLE CARTOON CHARACTER."

In this part . . .

1 discuss the concepts that underlie sensible personal financial management. You also find out why you didn't know all these concepts before now (and whom to blame). Here, you undergo a (gentle) financial physical exam to diagnose your current economic health. I also cover how to plan for and accomplish your financial goals.

Chapter 1

Improving Your Financial Fitness

In This Chapter

▶ Understanding and conquering obstacles to personal financial success

▶ Overcoming real and imagined financial hurdles

▶ Comprehending common money problems

▶ Understanding bad debt, good debt, and too much debt

▶ Determining assets, liabilities, and your (financial) net worth

▶ Calculating your rate of savings

▶ Assessing your investments and insurance

*W*e're barely acquainted, but I do know that you're not dumb. Real dummies don't read and educate themselves. And real dummies don't understand the value of investing in their education. Real dummies also can't deflate their egos enough to admit that they need help and guidance.

Here's what dumb is: Dumb is the crook who walked into a convenience store, put a $20 bill on the counter, and asked for change. When the cashier opened the register, the man pulled a gun and demanded all the cash. The thief took the loot — $15 — and fled, leaving his $20 bill on the counter. Or how about the criminal who robbed a person who lacked cash? The victim offered the assailant a check, which the assailant later attempted to cash at the bank, where — surprise, surprise — he was arrested. Both of these stories are true!

So you're most definitely not dumb! But you may not be literate when it comes to personal finances.

Targeting the Trouble Spots

Unfortunately, most Americans don't know how to manage their personal finances because they were never taught how to do so. Nearly all our high schools and colleges lack even one course that teaches this vital, lifelong-needed skill.

In the handful of schools that do offer a course remotely related to a personal finance class, the class is typically an economics course (and an elective at that). "Archaic theory is being taught and it doesn't do anything for the students as far as preparing them for the real world," says one high school principal I know. Having taken more than my fair share of economics courses in college, I understand the principal's concerns.

Some people are fortunate enough to learn the financial keys to success at home, from knowledgeable friends and good books like this one. Others either never learn the keys to financial success, or they learn them the hard way — by making lots of costly mistakes. The lack of proficiency in personal financial management causes not only tremendous anxiety but also serious problems. Consider the following sobering statistics:

- About 1.5 million personal bankruptcies are now filed in the United States annually. That's about one in every 80 households. So in the next eight years, nearly one in every ten households in the United States — the most affluent country in the world — will file bankruptcy.

- Studies show that fewer than 20 percent of baby boomers are saving adequately for retirement, and that one-quarter of the adults between the ages of 35 and 54 have not even *begun* to save for retirement.

- One out of every two marriages in America ends in divorce. Studies show that financial disagreement is one of the leading causes of marital discord. In a survey conducted by *Worth* magazine and the market research firm of Roper/Starch, couples admitted to fighting about money more than anything else (more than three times more often than they fight about their sex lives). And a staggering 57 percent of those surveyed agreed with the statement, "In every marriage, money eventually becomes the most important concern."

- Fewer than 10 percent of American adults understand a 401(k) well enough to explain it to someone else. Fewer than one in four can explain what a municipal bond is.

- In a Princeton Survey Research Associates investing basics test, approximately one-third of the people who took the quiz answered fewer than 50 percent of the questions correctly. These results are all the more stunning when you consider that the questions only offered two or three multiple choice answers as options!

- Nearly 80 percent of consumers do not know how the grace period on a credit card works. An even greater percentage doesn't understand that interest starts accumulating *immediately* for new purchases on credit cards with outstanding debts.

- Fifty-three percent of people who took a multiple choice investing quiz did not know that *total return* was the best measure of a mutual fund's performance.

The overall costs of personal financial illiteracy to our society are huge. The high rate of spending and low rate of saving in the United States leads to lower long-term economic growth and higher interest rates. Annually, billions of dollars are wasted through the purchase of inferior and inefficient financial products.

Talking money at home

I was fortunate that my parents taught and instilled in me the importance of personal financial management. Mom and Dad taught me a lot of things that have been invaluable throughout my life. Among the useful things my folks taught me were sound principles for earning, spending, and saving money. My parents had to know how to do these things, because they were raising a family of three children on (usually) one modest income. They knew the importance of making the most of what you have and of passing that vital skill on to your kids.

In many families, however, money is a taboo subject — parents don't level with their kids about the limitations, realities, and details of their budgets. Some parents I talk with believe that dealing with money is an adult issue, and that kids should be insulated from it so that they can enjoy being kids. In many families, kids may hear about money *only* when disagreements and financial crises bubble to the surface. Thus begins the harmful cycle of children having negative associations with money and financial management.

In other cases, parents with the best of intentions pass on their money-management habits. Unfortunately, some of those habits are bad habits. Now I'm not saying that you shouldn't listen to your parents. But in the area of personal finance, as in any other area, poor family advice can be problematic. Think about where your parents learned about money management, and then consider whether they had the time, energy, or inclination to research choices before making their decisions. For example, your parents may mistakenly think that banks are the best places for investing money. (You can find the best places for investing your money in Part III of this book.)

In still other cases, the parents have the right approach, but the kids go to the other extreme out of rebellion. For example, if your parents spent money carefully and thoughtfully, you may tend to do the opposite, such as buying yourself gifts the moment any extra money comes your way.

Although you and I can't change what the educational system and your parents did or didn't teach you about personal finances, you now have the ability to find out what you need to know to manage your finances. And if you have children of your own, I'm sure you'll agree that kids really are amazing.

Don't underestimate their potential or send them out into the world without the skills they need to be productive and happy adults. Buy them some good financial books when they head off to college or begin their first job.

Teaching personal finance in schools

Nancy Donovan teaches personal finance to her fifth-grade math class as a way to illustrate how math can be used in the real world. "Students choose a career, find jobs, and figure out what their taxes and take-home paychecks will be. They also have to rent apartments and figure out a monthly budget," says Donovan, adding, "Students like it and parents have commented to me how surprised they are with how much financial knowledge their kids can handle." Donovan also has her students invest $10,000 (play money) and then track the performance of their investments.

Urging our schools to teach the basics of personal finance is just common sense. We should be teaching our children about how to manage a household budget, about the importance of saving money for future goals, and about the consequences and dangers of overspending. Unfortunately, few schools offer classes like Nancy Donovan's. In most cases, the financial basics aren't taught at all.

Some people argue that teaching children financial basics is the job of parents. However, this well-meant sentiment is what we're relying on now, and for all too many, it isn't working. In some families, financial illiteracy is passed on from generation to generation.

We must recognize that education takes place in the home, on the streets, *and* in the schools. Therefore, schools must bear some responsibility for teaching this very important life skill. And with more and more teenage students holding down after-school jobs, teaching money-management know-how through the schools makes even more sense.

Lobby your schools! Make sure that financial basics are taught in schools at all levels. If you think that you're powerless to change the situation, you're mistaken. Many of the changes that were made to our education system started at the grassroots level.

Identifying unreliable sources of information

Some people are smart enough to realize that they're not financial geniuses. So they set out to take control of their finances by reading or consulting a financial advisor. Because the pitfalls are so numerous and the challenges so mighty when choosing an advisor, I devote Chapter 17 to the financial planning business and tell you what you need to know to avoid being fooled.

Reading is good. Reading is fundamental. But reading to find out how to manage your money can be dangerous if you're a novice. Misinformation can come from popular and seemingly reliable information sources, as I explain in the following sections.

Won't investment gurus make me rich?

One formerly best-selling personal finance book (*Wealth Without Risk* by Charles Givens) advises you to "Buy disability insurance only if you are in poor health or accident prone." Putting aside the minor detail that no insurance company (that's interested in making a profit) is going to issue you a disability policy *after* you fall into poor health, how do you know when you're going to be accident-prone? Because health problems and auto accidents cause many disabilities, you can't see disabilities coming unless your horoscope happens to warn you!

Consider the investment seminars by Wade Cook. These seminars lure you in by promising outrageous and unrealistic returns. The stock market has generated average annual returns of about 10 percent over the long-term. Cook, a former taxicab driver, promoted his seminars as follows: "A live, hands-on, do the deals, two-day intense course in making huge returns in the stock market. If you aren't getting 20% per month, or 300% annualized returns on your investments, you need to be there." (I guess I do — as does every investment manager and individual investor I know!)

Cook's get-rich-quick seminars, which cost more than $6,000, were so successful at attracting people, that his company went public in the late 1990s and generated annual revenues of more than $100 million.

Cook's "techniques" included trading in and out of stocks and options on stocks after short holding periods of weeks, days, or even hours. His trading strategies can best be described as techniques that are based upon technical analysis — that is, charting a stock's price movements and volume history, and then making predictions based on those charts.

The perils of following an approach that advocates short-term trading with the allure of high profits are numerous:

- You're going to rack up enormous brokerage commissions.

- On those occasions where your short-term trades produce a profit, you pay high ordinary income tax rates rather than the far lower capital gains rate for investments held more than 12 months.

- ✔ You're not going to make big profits — quite the reverse. You're going to underperform the market averages if you stick with this approach.

- ✔ You're going to make yourself a nervous wreck. This type of trading is gambling, not investing. Get sucked up in it and you'll lose more than money — you may also lose the love and respect of your family and friends.

"The past history of stock prices cannot be used to predict the future in any meaningful way. Technical strategies are usually amusing, often comforting, but of no real value," says Burton Malkiel, a Princeton University business professor and author of the investment classic, *A Random Walk Down Wall Street.*

If Cook's followers were indeed earning the 300 percent annual returns his seminars claim to help you achieve, any investor starting with just $10,000 would vault to the top of the list of the world's wealthiest people (ahead of Bill Gates and Warren Buffett) in just 11 years!

Understanding how undeserving investment gurus get popular

You may be wondering how Charles Givens and Wade Cook became so popular despite the obvious flaws in their advice. Givens made the most of his talent for working the media and his great self-promotion through seminars. One of the problems with the mass media is that hucksters like Givens can get good coverage and publicity. Many members of the media are themselves financially illiterate. And they love a good story. So Givens got all sorts of free publicity, getting quoted in the press and invited to appear on a number of national programs, such as *The Today Show, Oprah, Donahue,* and *Larry King Live.*

Thousands of people went to seminars conducted by Givens, partly because of the credibility Givens built through media appearances. As has now been well documented by some of those same members of the media, many unsuspecting investors were sold commission-laden products, including risky limited partnerships, through his organization.

Consider the case of Helen Giszczak, a 69-year-old retired secretary. She invested nearly two-thirds of her modest life savings in limited partnerships, which she said were described to her by Givens as "probably the most conservative investments we know of." But some of her limited partnerships ended up in bankruptcy, while the others lost much of their value.

Helen Giszczak appeared on the *Donahue* show with John Allen, an investment broker turned securities lawyer who helped her sue Givens's organization to get her money back. After a lengthy dialogue with Giszczak and Allen, Phil Donahue asked Helen how a smart person like her could get sucked in like that. She replied, "He was on your show and Oprah's. You gave him credibility. You gave him free advertising."

Wade Cook promoted his seminars through infomercials and other advertising, including radio ads on respected news stations. The high stock market returns of the 1990s brought greed back into fashion. My experience has been that you see more of this greed near market tops than you do near market bottoms.

The attorneys general of numerous states sued Cook's company and sought millions of dollars in consumer refunds. The suits alleged that the company lied about its investment track record (not a big surprise — this company claimed that you'd make 300 percent per year in stocks!).

Cook's company settled the blizzard of state and Federal Trade Commission (FTC) lawsuits against his firm by agreeing to accurately disclose its trading record in future promotions and give refunds to customers who were misled by past inflated return claims.

According to a news report by Bloomberg News, Cook's firm disclosed that it lost a whopping 89 percent of its own money trading during the last reporting year. As Deb Bortner, director of the Washington State Securities Division and president of the North American Securities Administrators Association observed, "Either Wade is unable to follow his own system, which he claims is simple to follow, or the system doesn't work."

Don't assume that someone with something to sell, who is getting good press and running lots of ads, is going to take care of you. That "guru" may just be good at press relations and self-promotion. Certainly, talk shows and the media at large can and do provide useful information on a variety of topics, but you need to be aware that bad eggs sometimes turn up. These bad eggs may not always smell bad upfront. In fact, they may hoodwink people for many years before finally being exposed.

Pandering to advertisers

Thousands of publications and media outlets — newspapers, magazines, Web sites, radio, television, and so on — dole out personal financial advice and perspectives. Although many of these "service providers" collect revenue from subscribers, virtually all are dependent — in some cases, fully dependent (especially on the Internet, radio, and television) — on advertising dollars. Although advertising is a necessary part of capitalism, advertisers can taint and, in some cases, dictate the content of what you read, listen to, and view.

Consider this case from a nonfinancial publication — *Modern Bride* magazine. *Harper's* magazine got ahold of an apologetic letter (which it humorously entitled "To Love, Honor And Obey Our Advertisers") that *Bride's* fashion advertising director sent to the magazine's advertisers. Here's an excerpt:

"*Bride's* recommends that its readers (your customers) negotiate price, borrow a slip or petticoat, and compare catalog shoe prices, and tells its readers that the groom's tuxedo may be free. It is difficult to understand why *Bride's* was compelled to publish this information. With 57 years of publishing experience and support to the bridal industry, *Bride's* could and should have been more sensitive to the retailers that it purports to serve. All of us in the bridal business must concentrate on projecting full-service bridal retailing in a positive light."

I don't find it difficult to understand why the writer of the criticized *Bride's* article revealed cost-saving strategies to its readers — she was trying to give them useful information and advice! Now, revealing letters like this one are hard to come by, so how can you, a consumer of financial information, separate the good publications from the advertiser-biased publications? After writing and working for a number of publications, and observing the workings of even more, I've developed some ideas on the subject.

First, consider how dependent a publication or media outlet is on advertising. I find that "free" publications, radio, and television are the ones who most often create conflicts of interest by pandering to advertisers. (All three derive all of their revenue from advertising.) Much of what is on the Internet is advertiser-driven, as well. Many of the investing sites on the Internet cater to offering advice about individual stocks. Interestingly, such sites derive much of their revenue from online brokerage firms seeking to recruit customers who are foolish enough to believe that selecting their own stocks is the best way to invest. (See Part III for more information about your investment options.)

Next, as you read various publications, watch TV, or listen to the radio, note how consumer-oriented these media are. Do you get the feeling that they're looking out for your interests? Or are they primarily creating an advertiser-friendly broadcast or publication? For example, if lots of auto manufacturers advertise, does the media outlet ever tell you how to save money when shopping for a car, or the importance of buying a car within your means?

Jumping over Real and Imaginary Hurdles

Perhaps you know that you should be living within your means, buying and holding sound investments for the long term, and securing proper insurance coverage. However, you can't bring yourself to do these things. We all know how difficult it is to break detrimental habits that have been practiced for many years. The temptation to spend money lurks everywhere you turn. Ads show attractive and popular people enjoying the fruits of their labors — a new car, an exotic vacation, and a lavish home.

Maybe you felt deprived by your tightwad parents as a youngster, or maybe you're bored with life and you like the adventure of buying new things. If only you could hit it big on one or two investments, you think, you could get rich quick and do what you really want with your life. As for disasters and catastrophes, well, those things happen to other people, not to you. Besides, you'll probably have advance warning of pending problems, so you can prepare accordingly.

Your emotions and temptations can get the better of you. Certainly, part of successfully managing your finances involves coming to terms with your shortcomings and the consequences of your behaviors. If you don't, you may end up enslaved to a dead-end job so that you can keep feeding your spending addiction. Or you can spend more time with your investments than you do with your family and friends. Disasters and catastrophes can happen to anyone at any time.

Discovering the real hurdles holding you back

A variety of personal and emotional hurdles can get in the way of making the best financial moves. As I discuss earlier in this chapter, a lack of financial knowledge (which stems from a lack of personal financial education) can stand in the way of making good decisions.

However, I've seen some people get caught in the psychological trap of blaming something else for their financial problems. For example, some people believe that all our adult problems can be traced back to our childhood and how we were raised. Behaviors ranging from substance abuse and credit card addiction to sexual infidelity are supposedly caused by our roots.

I don't want to diminish the negative impact particular backgrounds can have on some people's tendency to make the wrong choices during their lives. Exploring your personal history can certainly yield clues to what makes you tick. That said, we are adults making choices and engaging in behaviors that affect ourselves as well as others. We shouldn't blame our parents for our own inability to plan for our financial futures, live within our means, and make sound investments.

Some people also have a common tendency to blame their financial short-comings on not earning more income. Such people believe that if they only earned more income, their financial (and personal) problems would melt away.

My experience working and speaking with people from diverse economic backgrounds has taught me that achieving financial success — and more importantly, personal happiness — has virtually nothing to do with how much income a person makes but rather with what she makes of what she does have. I know financially wealthy people who are emotionally poor even though they have all the material goods they want. Likewise, I know people who are quite happy, contented, and emotionally wealthy even though they're struggling financially.

Americans — even those who have not had an "easy" life — should be able to come up with numerous things to be happy about and grateful for: a family who loves them; friends who laugh at their stupid jokes; the freedom to catch a movie or play, or read a good book; a great singing voice, sense of humor, or a full head of hair; or the fact that they live in a country not at war with any other country.

Financially speaking, Americans are pretty spoiled. Two-thirds of the people in the world have a standard of living that is a mere 20 percent of the U.S. average. Think about that. In other words, the average American is five times better off financially than two out of every three people in the world.

Practicing good habits

After you understand the basic concepts and know where to buy the best financial products when you need them, you'll soon see that managing your personal finances well is not much more difficult than other things you do regularly, like tying your shoelaces and getting to and from work each day.

Regardless of your income, you can make your dollars stretch farther if you practice good financial habits and avoid mistakes. In fact, the lower your income, the more important it is that you make the most of your income and savings (because you don't have the luxury of falling back on your next fat paycheck to bail you out).

More and more industries are subject to global competition, and you need to be on your financial toes now more than ever. Job security is on the wane. Layoffs and retraining for new jobs are on the increase. Putting in 20 or 30 years for one company and retiring with the gold watch and lifetime pension are becoming as rare as never having problems with your computer.

Speaking of company pensions, odds are increasing that you work for an employer that has you save toward your own retirement rather than provide a pension for you. Not only do you need to save the money, you must also decide how to invest it.

Managing your personal finances involves much more than just managing and investing money. It also includes making all the pieces of your financial life fit together. It means lifting yourself out of financial illiteracy. Like planning a vacation, managing your personal finances means formulating a plan for making the best use of your limited time and dollars. (I discuss common financial problems in the next section.)

Intelligent personal financial strategies have little to do with your gender, ethnicity, or marital status. We all need to manage our finances wisely. Some aspects of financial management become more or less important at different points in your life, but for the most part, the principles remain the same for all of us.

Knowing the right answers isn't enough. You have to practice good financial habits just as you practice other good habits, such as brushing your teeth. Don't be overwhelmed. As you read this book, make a short list of your financial marching orders and then start working away. Throughout this book, I highlight ways you can overcome temptations and keep control of your money rather than let your emotions and money rule you.

You probably don't like being made to feel stupid or told that you're doing something wrong. And what you do with your money is a quite personal and confidential matter. I endeavor not to be paternalistic in this book, but to provide guidance and advice that is in your best interest. You don't have to take it all — pick what works best for you and understand the pros and cons of your options. But from this day forward, please don't make the easily avoidable mistakes or overlook the sound strategies that I discuss throughout this book.

If you're young, congratulations for being so forward-thinking as to realize the immense value of investing in your personal financial education. You'll reap the rewards for decades to come. But even if you're not so young, you surely have many years to make the most of the money you currently have, the money you're going to earn, and even the money you may inherit!

Throughout our journey together, I hope to challenge and even change the way you think about money and about making important personal financial decisions — and sometimes even about the meaning of life. No, I'm not a philosopher, but I do know that money — for better but more often for worse — is connected to many other parts of our lives.

Common Financial Problems: You've Got Company

How financially healthy are you? You may already know the bad news. Or perhaps things aren't quite as bad as they seem.

When was the last time you sat down surrounded by all your personal and financial documents and took stock of your overall financial situation, including reviewing your spending, savings, future goals, and insurance? If you're like most people, you've either never done this exercise, or you did so a long time ago.

Financial problems, like many medical problems, are best detected early (clean living doesn't hurt, either). Here are some common personal financial problems I've seen in my work as a financial counselor:

- **Not planning.** Human beings were born to procrastinate. That's why we have deadlines — and deadline extensions. Unfortunately, you may have no explicit deadlines with your overall finances. You can allow your credit card debt to accumulate, or you can leave your savings sitting in lousy investments for years. You can pay higher taxes, leave gaps in your retirement and insurance coverage, and overpay for financial products. Of course, planning your finances isn't as much fun as planning a vacation, but doing the former can help you take more of the latter.

- **Overspending.** The average American saves less than 5 percent of his or her after-tax income (in contrast to those in other industrialized countries, where the savings rate is two to three times that in America). Simple arithmetic helps you determine that savings is the difference between what you earn and what you spend (assuming that you're not spending more than you're earning!). To increase your savings, you either have to work more (yuck!), know a wealthy family who wants to leave its fortune to you, or spend less. For most of us, the thrifty approach is the key to building savings and wealth.

- **Buying with consumer credit.** Even with the benefit of today's lower interest rates, carrying a balance month-to-month on your credit card or buying a car on credit means that even more of your future earnings are going to be earmarked for debt repayment. Buying on credit encourages you to spend more than you can really afford.

- **Delaying saving for retirement.** Most people say that they want to retire by their mid-60s or sooner. But in order to accomplish this goal, most people need to save a reasonable chunk (around 10 percent) of their incomes starting sooner rather than later. The longer you wait to start saving for retirement, the harder it will be to reach your goal. And you'll pay much more in taxes to boot if you don't take advantage of the tax benefits of investing through particular retirement accounts.

✔ **Falling prey to financial sales pitches.** Great deals that can't wait for a little reflection or a second opinion are often disasters waiting to happen. A sucker may be born every minute, but a slick salesperson is born every second! Steer clear of those who pressure you to make decisions, promise you high investment returns, and lack the proper training and experience to help you.

✔ **Not doing your homework.** To get the best deal, you need to shop around, read reviews, and get advice from disinterested, objective third parties. You need to check references and track records so that you don't hire incompetent, self-serving, or fraudulent financial advisors. But with all the different financial products available, making informed financial decisions has become an overwhelming task. I do a lot of the homework for you with the recommendations in this book. I also explain what additional research you need to do and how to go about doing it.

✔ **Making decisions based on emotion.** You're most vulnerable to making the wrong moves financially after a major life change (a job loss or divorce, for example) or when you feel under pressure. Maybe your investments plunged in value. Or perhaps a recent divorce has you fearing that you won't be able to afford to retire when you planned, so you pour thousands of dollars into some newfangled financial product. Take your time and keep your emotions out of the picture. In Chapter 20, I discuss how to approach major life changes with an eye to determining what changes you may need to make to your financial picture.

✔ **Not separating the wheat from the chaff.** In any field in which you're not an expert, you run the danger of following the advice of someone who you think is an expert but really isn't. This book shows you how to separate the financial fluff from the financial facts. If you look in the mirror, you see the person who is best able to manage your personal finances. Educate and trust yourself!

✔ **Exposing yourself to catastrophic risk.** You're vulnerable if you and your family don't have insurance to pay for financially devastating losses. People without a savings reserve and support network can end up homeless. Many people lack sufficient insurance coverage to replace their income. Don't wait for a tragedy to strike to find out whether you have the right insurance coverages.

✔ **Focusing too much on money.** Placing too much emphasis on making and saving money can warp your perspective on what's important in life. Money is not the first or even second priority in happy people's lives. Your health, relationships with family and friends, career satisfaction, and fulfilling interests should be more important.

Most problems can be fixed over time with changes in your behavior. (That's what the rest of the book is all about.)

The rest of this chapter guides you through a *financial physical* to help you detect problems with your current financial health. But don't get depressed and dwell on your "problems." View them for what they are — opportunities for improving your financial situation. In fact, the more areas for improvement that you can identify, the greater the potential you have to build real wealth and accomplish your financial and personal goals.

Defining Bad Debt and Good Debt

Why do you borrow money? Usually, you borrow money because you don't have enough to buy something you want or need — like a college education. If you want to buy a four-year college education, you can easily spend $100,000 or more. Not too many people have that kind of spare cash. So borrowing money to finance part of that cost enables you to buy the education.

How about a new car? A trip to your friendly local car dealer shows you that a new set of wheels will set you back around $15,000 or more. Although more people may have the money to pay for that than, say, the college education, what if you don't? Should you finance the car the way you finance the education?

The auto dealers and bankers who are eager to make you an auto loan say that you deserve and can afford to drive a nice, new car, and they tell you to borrow away.

I say, *"NO! NO! NO!"*

Why do I disagree with the auto dealers and lenders? For starters, I'm not trying to sell you a car or loan from which I derive a profit! More importantly, there's a *big* difference between borrowing for something that represents a long-term investment and borrowing for short-term consumption.

If you spend, say, $1,500 on a vacation, the money is gone. Poof! You may have fond memories and even some Kodak moments, but you have no financial value to show for it. "But," you say, "vacations replenish my soul and make me more productive when I return. In fact, the vacation more than pays for itself!"

Great. I'm not saying that you shouldn't take a vacation. By all means, take one, two, three, or as many as you can afford yearly. But that's the point — *take what you can afford.* If you have to borrow money in the form of an outstanding balance on your credit card for many months in order to take the vacation, you *can't afford* it.

I refer to debt incurred for consumption as *bad debt,* because such debt is harmful to your long-term financial health.

You'll be able to take many more vacations during your lifetime if you save the cash in advance. If you get into the habit of borrowing and paying all that interest for vacations, cars, clothing, and other consumer items, you'll spend more of your future income paying back the debt and interest, leaving you with *less* money for vacations and all your other goals.

The relatively high interest rates banks and other lenders charge for bad debt is one of the reasons why you have less money when using such debt. Money borrowed through credit cards, auto loans, and other types of consumer loans not only carries a relatively high interest rate but it's also not tax-deductible.

 I'm not saying that you should never borrow money and that all debt is bad. Good debt, such as that used to buy real estate and small businesses, is generally available at lower interest rates than bad debt and is usually tax-deductible. If well managed, these investments may also increase in value. Borrowing to pay for educational expenses can also make sense. Education is generally a good long-term investment, because it can increase your earning potential.

Knowing How Much Bad Debt Is Too Much

Calculating how much debt you have relative to your annual income is a useful way to size up your debt load. Ignore, for now, good debt — the loans you may owe on real estate, a business, an education, and so on. I'm focusing on bad debt, the higher-interest debt used to buy items that depreciate in value.

For example, suppose that you earn $30,000 per year. Between your credit cards and an auto loan, you have $15,000 of debt. In this case, your bad debt represents 50 percent of your annual income.

```
   bad debt
annual income   =   bad debt danger ratio
```

The financially healthy amount of bad debt is zero. (Not everyone agrees with me. One major U.S. credit card company says — in its "educational" materials, which it gives to schools to teach students about supposedly sound financial management — that carrying consumer debt amounting to 10 to 20 percent of your annual income is just fine.)

When your *bad debt danger ratio* starts to push beyond 25 percent, it can spell real trouble. Such high levels of high-interest consumer debt on credit cards and auto loans is like cancer. As with cancer, the growth of the debt can snowball and get out of control unless something significant intervenes. If you have consumer debt beyond 25 percent of your annual income, see Chapter 4 to find out how to get out of debt.

How much good debt is acceptable? The answer varies. The key question is: Are you able to save sufficiently to accomplish your goals? In the "Savings Analysis" section, later in this chapter, I help you figure out how much you're actually saving, and in Chapter 2, I help you determine what you should be saving to accomplish your goals. Take a look at Chapter 13 to find out how much mortgage debt is appropriate to take on when buying a home.

Avoid borrowing money for consumption (bad debt) — for spending on things that decrease in value and eventually become financially worthless, such as cars, clothing, vacations, and so on. Borrow money only for investments (good debt) — for purchasing things that retain and hopefully increase in value over the long term, such as an education, real estate, or your own business.

Playing the credit card float

Given what I have to say about the vagaries of consumer debt, you may think that I'm always against using credit cards. Actually, I have credit cards, and I use them — but I pay my balance in full each month. Besides the convenience credit cards offer me — in not having to carry around extra cash and checks — I receive another benefit: I have free use of the bank's money extended to me through my credit card charges. (Some cards offer other benefits, such as frequent flyer miles. Also, purchases made on credit cards may be contested if the seller of the product or service doesn't stand behind what it sells.)

When you charge on a credit card that does not have an outstanding balance carried over from the prior month, you typically have several weeks (known as the *grace period*) from the date of the charge to the time when you must pay your bill. Financial types call this *playing the float*. Had you paid for this purchase by cash or check, you would have had to shell out the money sooner.

If you have difficulty saving money, and plastic tends to burn holes through your budget, forget the float game. You're better off not using credit cards. The same applies to those who pay their bills in full but spend more because it's so easy to do so with a piece of plastic.

Determining Your Financial Net Worth

Your financial net worth is an important barometer of your monetary health. Your net worth indicates your capacity to accomplish major financial goals, such as buying a home, retiring, and withstanding unexpected expenses or loss of income.

Your financial net worth has absolutely, positively *no* relationship to your worth as a human being. This is not a test. You don't have to compare your number with your neighbor's. Financial net worth is not the scorecard of life.

Your *net worth* is your financial assets minus your financial liabilities.

```
Financial Assets - Financial Liabilities = Net Worth
```

Financial assets

A *financial asset* is worth real money or is something you can convert to hard dollars that you can use to buy things now or in the future.

Financial assets generally include the money you have in bank accounts, stocks, bonds, and mutual fund accounts (see Part III, which deals with investments). Money that you have in retirement accounts (including those with your employer) and the value of any businesses or real estate that you own are also included.

I generally recommend that you exclude your personal residence when figuring your financial assets. Include your home only if you expect to someday sell it or otherwise live off the money you now have tied up in it (perhaps by taking out a reverse mortgage, which I discuss in Chapter 13). If you plan on someday tapping into the *equity* (the difference between the market value and any debt owed on the property) in your home, add that portion of the equity that you expect to use to your list of assets.

Assets also include your future expected Social Security benefits and pension payments (if your employer has such a plan). These assets are usually quoted in dollars per month rather than in a lump sum value. I explain in a moment how to account for these monthly benefits when tallying your financial assets.

Personal property such as your car, clothing, stereo, and wine collection does *not* count as a financial asset. I know that adding these things to your assets makes your assets *look* larger (and some financial software packages and publications encourage you to list these items as assets), but you can't live off them unless you sell them.

Financial liabilities

To arrive at your financial net worth, you must subtract your *financial liabilities* from your assets.

Liabilities include loans and debts outstanding, such as credit card and auto loan debts. When figuring your liabilities, include money you borrowed from family and friends (unless you're not gonna pay it back — I won't tell). Include mortgage debt on your home as a liability *only* if you include the value of your home in your asset list. Be sure to also include debt owed on other real estate — no matter what.

Your net worth calculation

Table 1-1 provides a place for you to figure your financial assets. Go ahead and write in the spaces provided, unless you plan to lend this book to someone and you don't want to put your money situation on display.

Important note: See Table 2-1 in Chapter 2 to estimate your Social Security benefits.

Table 1-1	Your Financial Assets
Account	*Value*
Savings and investment accounts (including retirement accounts):	
Example: Bank savings account	$5,000
_____	$_____
_____	$_____
_____	$_____
_____	$_____
_____	$_____
_____	$_____
Total =	$_____

Account	Value
Benefits earned that pay a monthly retirement income:	
Employer's pensions	$_____ / month
Social Security	$_____ / month
	× 240*
Total =	$_____
Total Financial Assets (add the two totals) =	$_____

* To convert benefits that will be paid to you monthly into a total dollar amount, and for purposes of simplification, assume that you will spend 20 years in retirement. (Ah, think of two decades of lolly-gagging around — vacationing, harassing the kids, spoiling the grandkids, starting another career, or maybe just living off the fat of the land.) As a shortcut, multiply the benefits that you'll collect monthly in retirement by 240 (12 months per year times 20 years). Inflation may reduce the value of your employer's pension if it doesn't contain a cost-of-living increase each year in the same way that Social Security does. Don't sweat this now — you can take care of it in the section on planning for retirement in Chapter 2.

Now comes the potentially depressing part — figuring out your debts and loans in Table 1-2.

Table 1-2	Your Financial Liabilities
Loan	**Balance**
Example: Gouge 'Em Bank Credit Card	$4,000
_____	$_____
_____	$_____
_____	$_____
_____	$_____
_____	$_____
_____	$_____
Total Financial Liabilities =	$_____

Now you can subtract your liabilities from your assets to figure your net worth in Table 1-3.

Table 1-3	Your Net Worth
Find	*Write It Here*
Total Financial Assets (from Table 1-1)	$_____
Total Financial Liabilities (from Table 1-2)	– $_____
Net Worth =	$_____

Interpreting your net worth results

Your net worth is important and useful only to you and your unique situation and goals. What seems like a lot of money to a person with a simple lifestyle may seem like a pittance to a person with high expectations and a desire for an opulent lifestyle.

In Chapter 2, you can crunch some more numbers to determine your financial status more precisely for such goals as retirement planning. I also discuss saving toward other important goals in that chapter. In the meantime, if your net worth (excluding expected monthly retirement benefits such as those from Social Security and pensions) is negative or less than half your annual income, take notice. You have lots of company — in fact, you're with the majority of Americans. If you're in your 20s, and you're just starting to work, a low net worth is less concerning. Getting rid of your debts — the highest-interest ones first — is the most important thing. Then you need to build a safety reserve equal to three to six months of living expenses. You should definitely find out more about getting out of debt, reducing your spending, and developing tax-wise ways to save and invest your future earnings.

Savings Analysis

How much money have you actually saved in the past year? By savings, I mean the amount of new money you added to your nest egg, stash, or whatever you like to call it.

Most people don't know or have only a vague idea of the rate at which they're saving money. The answer may sober, terrify, or pleasantly surprise you. In order to calculate your savings over the past year, you need to calculate your net worth as of today *and* as of one year ago.

The amount you actually saved over the past year is equal to the change in your net worth over the past year — in other words, your net worth today minus your net worth from one year ago. I know it may be a pain to find statements showing what your investments were worth a year ago, but bear with me; it's a useful exercise.

If you own your home, ignore this in the calculations. (You can consider the extra payments you make to pay off your mortgage principal faster as new savings.) And don't include personal property, such as your car, computer, clothing, and so on, with your assets.

When you have your two figures, plug them into Step 1 of Table 1-4. If you're anticipating the exercise and are already subtracting your net worth of a year ago from what it is today in order to determine your rate of savings, your instincts are correct, but the exercise is not quite that simple. You need to do a few more calculations in Step 2 of Table 1-4. Why? Well, counting the appreciation of the investments you've owned over the past year as savings wouldn't be fair. Suppose that you bought 100 shares of a stock a year ago at $17 per share, and now the value is at $34 per share. Your investment increased in value by $1,700 during the past year. Although you'd be the envy of your friends at the next party if you casually mentioned your investments, the $1,700 of increased value is not really savings. Instead, it represents appreciation on your investments, so you must remove this appreciation from the calculations.

Note: Just so you know, I'm not unfairly penalizing you for your shrewd investments — you also get to add back the decline in value of your less-successful investments.

Table 1-4		Your Savings Rate over the Past Year	
Step 1: Figuring your savings.			
Today		*One Year Ago*	
Savings & investments	$_____	Savings & investments	$_____
– Loans & debts	$_____	– Loans & debts	$_____
= Net worth today	$_____	= Net worth 1 year ago	$_____
Step 2: Correcting for changes in value of investments you owned during the year.			
Net worth today		$_____	
– Net worth 1 year ago		$_____	
– Appreciation of investments (over past year)		$_____	
+ Depreciation of investments (over past year)		$_____	
= Savings rate		$_____	

If all this calculating gives you a headache, you get stuck, or you just hate crunching numbers, try the intuitive, seat-of-the-pants approach: Save a regular portion of your monthly income. You can save it in a separate savings or retirement account.

How much do you save in a typical month? Get out the statements for accounts you contribute to or save money in monthly. It doesn't matter if you're saving money in a retirement account that you can't access — money is money.

Note: If you save, say, $200 per month for a few months, and then you spend it all on auto repairs, you're not really saving. If you contributed $3,000 to an individual retirement account (IRA), for example, but you depleted money that you had from long ago (in other words, it wasn't saved during the past year), you should not count the $3,000 IRA contribution as new savings.

You should be saving at least 5 to 10 percent of your annual income for longer-term financial goals such as retirement. If you're not, be sure to read Chapter 5 to find out how to reduce your spending so that you can increase your savings.

Measuring Your Investing Knowledge

Congratulations! If you stuck with me from the beginning of this chapter, you completed the hardest part of your financial physical. The physical is a whole lot easier from here on in!

Regardless of how much or how little money you have invested in banks, mutual funds, or other types of accounts, you want to invest your money in the wisest way possible. Knowing the rights and wrongs of investing is vital to your long-term financial well-being. Few people have so much extra money that they can afford major or frequent investing mistakes.

Answering "yes" or "no" to the following questions can help you determine how much time you need to spend with my "Investing Crash Course" in Part III, which focuses on investing. *Note:* The more "no" answers you reluctantly scribble, the more you need to find out about investing, and the faster you should turn to Part III.

_____ Do you understand the investments you currently hold?

_____ Is the money that you'd need to tap in the event of a short-term emergency in an investment where the principal does not fluctuate in value?

_____ Do you know what marginal income-tax bracket (combined federal and state) you're in, and do you factor that in when choosing investments?

_____ For money outside of retirement accounts, do you understand how these investments produce income and gains, and whether these types of investments make the most sense from the standpoint of taxes?

_____ Do you have your money in different, diversified investments that aren't dependent on one or a few securities or one type of investment (that is, bonds, stocks, U.S. investments, real estate, and so on)?

_____ Is the money that you're going to need for a major expenditure in the next few years invested in conservative investments rather than in riskier investments such as stocks or pork bellies?

_____ Is the money that you have earmarked for longer-term purposes (more than five years) invested to produce returns that are well ahead of inflation?

_____ If you currently invest in or plan to invest in individual stocks, do you understand how to evaluate a stock, including reviewing the company's balance sheet, income statement, business strategy, competitive position, price-earnings ratio versus its peer group, and so on?

_____ If you work with a financial advisor, is that person compensated in a way that minimizes potential conflicts of interest in the strategies and investments he or she recommends?

Making and saving money is not a guarantee of financial success but rather a prerequisite. If you don't know how to choose sound investments that meet your needs, you'll more than likely end up throwing money away, which leads to the same end result as never having earned and saved it in the first place. Worse still, you won't be able to derive any enjoyment from spending the lost money on things that you perhaps need or want. Turn to Part III to discover the best ways to invest; otherwise, you may wind up spinning your wheels working and saving.

Measuring Your Insurance Savvy

In this section, you must deal with the prickly subject of protecting your assets and yourself with *insurance*. (The following questions help you get started.) If you're like most people, reviewing your insurance policies and coverages is about as much fun as a root canal. Open wide!

_____ Do you understand the individual coverages, protection types, and amounts of each insurance policy you have?

_____ Does your current insurance protection make sense given your current financial situation (as opposed to your situation when you bought the policies)?

_____ If you wouldn't be able to make it financially without your income, do you have adequate long-term disability insurance coverage?

_____ If you have family members who are dependent on your continued income, do you have adequate life insurance coverage to replace your income should you die?

_____ Do you buy insurance through discount brokers, fee-for-service advisors, and companies that sell directly to the public (bypassing agents)?

_____ Do you carry enough liability insurance on your home, car (including umbrella/excess liability), and business to protect all your assets?

_____ Have you recently (in the last year or two) shopped around for the best price on your insurance policies?

_____ Do you know whether your insurance companies have good track records when it comes to paying claims and keeping customers satisfied?

That wasn't so bad, was it? If you answered "no" more than once or twice, don't feel dumb — more than nine out of ten people make major mistakes when buying insurance. Find your insurance salvation in Part IV. If you answered "yes" to all the preceding questions, you can spare yourself from reading Part IV, but bear in mind that many people need as much help in this area as they do in other aspects of personal finance.

Chapter 2

Setting and Achieving Goals

In This Chapter

▶ Defining your own happiness

▶ Establishing and prioritizing your financial goals

▶ Saving for a rainy day, a real estate purchase, a small business, or educational needs

▶ What you need to get through retirement, and ways to make up for lost time

*I*n my work as a financial counselor, I always asked new clients what their short- and long-term personal and financial goals were. Quite a large portion of people reported that reflecting on this question was incredibly valuable, because they hadn't considered it for a long time — if ever.

In this chapter, I help you dream about what you want to get out of life. Although my expertise is in personal finance, I wouldn't be doing my job if I didn't get you to consider your nonfinancial goals and how money fits into the rest of your life goals. So before I jump into how to establish and save toward common financial goals, I want to take a moment to discuss how you think about making and saving money, and how to best fit your financial goals into the rest of your life.

Creating Your Own Definition of "Wealth"

Pick up just about any major financial magazine or newspaper, or scan stories on the Internet, and you'll quickly see our culture's obsession with financial wealth. The more money financial executives, movie stars, or professional athletes make and have, the more publicity and attention they seem to get. In fact, many publications go as far as ranking those people who earn the most or have amassed the greatest wealth!

I'm frankly perplexed at why many of the most affluent and highest-income earners maintain workaholic schedules despite being married and having kids. From what I observe, our society seems to define "wealth" as the following:

- ✔ Fat paychecks

- ✔ Huge investment account balances

- ✔ The ability to hire full-time employees to raise your children

- ✔ Being too busy at your career to maintain friendships or take an interest in your neighbors, community, or important social problems

- ✔ The freedom to be unfaithful and dump your spouse when you're no longer pleased with him or her

Considering what money can't buy

Recall the handful of moments in your life that you wouldn't trade for anything. Odds are, those moments don't include the time you bought a car or found a designer sweater that you liked. The old saying is true: The most enjoyable and precious things of value in your life can't be bought.

The following statement should go without saying, but I must say it, because too many people act as if it weren't so: Money can't buy happiness. It's tempting to think that if you could only make 10 or 20 percent more money, you'd be happier. You'd have more money to travel, eat out, and buy that new car you've been eyeing, right? Not so. A great deal of thoughtful research suggests that little relationship exists between money and happiness.

"Wealth is like health: Although its absence can breed misery, having it is no guarantee of happiness," summarizes Dr. David Myers, professor of psychology at Michigan's Hope College, in his book *The Pursuit of Happiness: Discovering the Pathway to Fulfillment, Well-Being, and Enduring Personal Joy* (Avon Books). (This guy has it good! Imagine studying happiness for a living.)

Despite cheap air travel, VCRs, compact discs, microwaves, computers, voice mail, and all the other stuff that's supposed to make our lives easier and more enjoyable, Americans aren't any happier than they were four decades ago. According to research conducted by the National Opinion Research Center, in 1957, 35 percent of Americans said that they were "very happy," whereas now, two generations later, fewer say the same. These unexpected results occur even though incomes, after adjusting for inflation, have more than doubled during that time.

As Dr. Myers observes in *The Pursuit of Happiness,* ". . . if anything, to judge by soaring rates of depression, the quintupling of the violent crime rate since 1960, the doubling of the divorce rate, and the tripling of the teen suicide rate, we're richer and less happy."

What is your relationship to money?

Over the years in my work as a financial counselor, I've come to find that how a person relates to and feels about money has a great impact on how good he is at managing his money and making important financial decisions. For example, knowing that you have a net worth of –$13,200 because of credit card debt is useful, but it's probably not enough information for you to do something constructive about your problem. A logical next step would be to examine your current spending and take steps to reduce your debt load.

Although I cover practical solutions to common financial quandaries later in this book, I also discuss the more touchy-feely side of money. For example, some people who continually rack up consumer debt have a spending addiction. Other people who jump in and out of investments and follow them like a hawk have psychological obstacles that prevent them from holding investments.

And then you have those somewhat philosophical and psychological issues relating to money and the meaning of life. Saving more money and increasing your net worth isn't always the best approach. In my work, I've come across numerous people who attach too much significance to personal wealth accumulation and neglect important human relationships in their pursuit of more money. Some retirees have a hard time loosening the purse springs and actually spending some of the money they worked so hard to save for their golden years.

Balancing your financial goals with other important life goals is key to your happiness. What's the point, for example, of staying in a well-paying, admired profession if you don't care for the work and you're mainly doing it for the financial rewards? Life is too short and precious for you to squander away your days.

So, as you read through the various chapters and sections of this book, please consider your higher life goals and purposes. What are your nonfinancial priorities (family, friends, causes), and how can you best accomplish your goals with the financial resources you do have?

Managing the balancing act

Believe it or not, some people save too much. In my financial counseling practice, I certainly saw plenty of people who fell into that category. If making and saving money is a good thing, then the more the better, right?

Well, take the admittedly extreme case of Anne Scheiber, who, on a modest income, started saving at a young age, allowing her money to compound in wealth-building investments such as stocks over many years. As a result, she was able to amass $20 million before she passed away at the age of 101.

Scheiber lived in a cramped studio apartment and never used her investments. She didn't even use the interest or dividends — she lived solely on her Social Security benefits and the small pension from her employer. Scheiber was extreme in her frugality and obsessed with her savings. As reported by James Glassman in the *Washington Post,* "She had few friends . . . she was an unhappy person, totally consumed by her securities accounts and her money."

Most people, myself included, wouldn't choose to live and save the way that Scheiber did. She saved for the sake of saving: no goal, no plan, no reward for herself. Saving should be a means to an end, not something that makes you mean to the end.

Even those who are saving for an ultimate goal can become consumed by their saving habits. I see some people pursuing higher-paying jobs and pinching pennies in order to retire early. But sometimes they make too many personal sacrifices today while chasing after some vision of their lives tomorrow. Others get consumed by work and then don't notice or understand why their family and friends feel neglected.

Another problem with seeking to amass wealth is that tomorrow may not come. Even if all goes according to plan, will you know how to be happy when you're not working if you spend your entire life making money? More importantly, who will be around to share your leisure time? One of the costs of an intense career is time spent away from friends and family. You may indeed realize your goal of retiring early, but you may be putting off too much living today in expectation of living tomorrow.

As Charles D'Orleans said in 1465, "It's very well to be thrifty, but don't amass a hoard of regrets."

Of course, at the other extreme are spendthrifts who live only for today. A friend of mine once said, "I'm not into delayed gratification." Shop 'til you drop seems to be the motto of this personality type. "Why bother saving when I might not be here tomorrow?" reasons this type of person.

The danger of this approach is that tomorrow may come after all, and most people don't want to spend all their tomorrows working for a living. The earlier neglect of saving, however, may make it necessary for you to work when you're older. And if for some reason you can't work, and you have little money to live on, much less live enjoyably, the situation can be tragic. The only difference between a person without any savings or access to credit and some homeless people is a few months of unemployment.

Making and saving money is like eating food. If you don't eat enough, you may suffer. If you eat too much, the overage may go to waste or make you overweight. The right amount, perhaps with some extra to spare, affords you a healthy, balanced, peaceful existence. Money should be treated with respect and acknowledged for what it is — a means to an end, and a precious resource that shouldn't be thoughtlessly squandered and wasted.

As Dr. David Myers, whom I introduce earlier in this chapter, says: "Satisfaction isn't so much getting what you want as wanting what you have. There are two ways to be rich: one is to have great wealth, the other is to have few wants." Find ways to make the most of the money that does pass through your hands, and never lose sight of all that is far more important than money.

Prioritizing Your Savings Goals

Most people I know have financial goals. The rest of this chapter discusses the most common financial goals and how to work toward accomplishing them.

- ✔ **Becoming part of the landed gentry.** Renting and dealing with landlords can be a financial and emotional drag, so most folks want to buy into the American dream and own some real estate — the most basic of which is to own your own home.

- ✔ **Retiring.** No, retiring does not imply sitting on a rocking chair watching the world go by while hoping that some long lost friend, your son's or daughter's family, or the neighborhood dog comes by to visit. *Retiring* is a catch-all term for discontinuing full-time work or perhaps not even working for pay at all.

- ✔ **Educating the kids.** No, all those diaper changes, late-night feedings, and trips to the zoo aren't enough to get junior out of your house and into the real world as a productive, self-sufficient adult. You may want to help your children get a college education — unfortunately, that can cost a truckload of dough.

- ✔ **Owning your own business.** Many employees want to face the challenges and rewards that come with being the boss. The primary reason that most people continue to dream without actually plunging into their own small businesses is that they lack the money to do so. Although many businesses don't require gobs of start-up cash, almost all require that you withstand a substantial reduction in your income during the early years.

Because each of us is different, we can have goals (other than those in the previous list) that are unique to our own situation. Accomplishing such goals almost always requires saving money. As one of my favorite Chinese proverbs says, "Do not wait until you are thirsty to dig a well." In other words, don't wait to save money until you're ready to accomplish a personal or financial goal!

Knowing what's most important to you

Unless you earn really big bucks or have a large family inheritance to fall back on, your personal and financial desires will probably outstrip your resources. Thus, you must prioritize your goals if you want to accomplish them.

One of the biggest mistakes I see people make is rushing into financial decisions without considering what's really important to them. Because many of us get caught up in the responsibilities of our daily lives, we often never have time for reflection.

As a result of my experience counseling and teaching many people about better personal financial management, I can tell you that the people who accomplish their goals aren't necessarily smarter or higher-income earners than those who don't. People who identify their goals and then work toward them are the ones who accomplish their goals.

Valuing retirement accounts

Where possible, you should try to save and invest in accounts that offer you a tax advantage. This is precisely what retirement accounts offer you. These accounts — known by such enlightening acronyms and names as 401(k), 403(b), SEP-IRAs, Keoghs, and so on — offer tax breaks to people of all economic means. (You can find the details of the different types of retirement accounts in Chapter 10.) Consider the following advantages to investing in retirement accounts:

- ✔ **Contributions are usually tax-deductible.** Retirement accounts should really be called *tax-reduction accounts*. If they were, people might be more excited about contributing to them. For many, avoiding higher taxes is the motivating force that opens the account and starts the contributions.

  By putting money in a retirement account, you not only plan wisely for your future but you also get an immediate financial reward: lower taxes — and lower taxes mean more money available for saving and investing. Retirement account contributions are generally not taxed at either the federal or state income tax levels until withdrawal (but they are still subject to social security and Medicare taxes when earned). If you're paying, say, 35 percent between federal and state taxes (refer to Chapter 6 to determine your tax bracket), a $5,000 contribution to a retirement account will lower your taxes by $1,750.

- ✔ **Returns on your investment compound over time without taxation.** After you put money into a retirement account, any interest, dividends, and appreciation add to your account without being taxed. Of course, there's no such thing as a free lunch — these accounts don't allow for complete tax avoidance. Yet you can get a really great lunch at a discount — you get to defer taxes on all of the accumulating gains and profits until you withdraw the money down the road. Thus, more money is working for you over a longer period of time. (The newer Roth IRA that I discuss in Chapter 10 offers no upfront tax breaks but does allow future tax-free withdrawal of investment earnings.)

✔ In some company retirement accounts, companies match a portion of your own contributions. Thus, in addition to tax breaks, you get free extra money courtesy of your employer!

Dealing with competing goals

Unless you enjoy paying higher taxes, why would you save money outside of retirement accounts? The reason is that some financial goals are not easily achieved by saving in retirement accounts. Also, retirement accounts have caps on the amount you can contribute annually.

Avoiding retirement account early withdrawal penalties

You can find ways to avoid the early withdrawal penalties that the tax gods normally apply.

Suppose that you read this book at a young age, develop sound financial habits early, and save enough to retire before age 59½. In this case, you can take money out of your retirement account without triggering penalties (which are normally 10 percent of the amount withdrawn for federal income tax plus whatever your state levies). The IRS allows you to withdraw money before 59½ if you do so in equal, annual installments based on your life expectancy. The IRS (this is slightly chilling) even has a little table that allows you to look up your life expectancy.

You can now also make penalty-free withdrawals from Individual Retirement Accounts for either a first-time home purchase (limit of $10,000) or higher educational expenses for you, your spouse, your children, or your grandchildren.

The other conditions under which you can make penalty-free early withdrawals from retirement accounts are not as enjoyable: If you have major medical expenses (exceeding 7.5 percent of your income) or a disability, you may be exempt from the penalties under certain conditions.

If you get into a financial pinch while you're still employed, be aware that some company retirement plans allow you to borrow against your cash balance. This tactic is like loaning money to yourself — the interest payments go back into your account.

If you lose your job and withdraw retirement account money simply because you need it to live on, the penalties do apply. However, if you're not working, and you're earning so little income that you need to raid your retirement account, you surely fall into a low tax bracket. The lower income taxes you pay (when compared to the taxes you would have paid on that money had you not sheltered it in a retirement account in the first place) should make up for most or all of the penalty.

If you're accumulating money for a down payment on a home or to start or buy a business, for example, you'll probably need to save that money outside of a retirement account. Why? Because if you withdraw funds from retirement accounts before age 59½, and you're not retired, you not only have to pay income taxes on the withdrawals but you also generally have to pay *early withdrawal penalties* — 10 percent of the withdrawn amount in federal tax and whatever your state charges. (See the sidebar, "Avoiding retirement account early withdrawal penalties," for exceptions to this rule.)

Because you're constrained by your financial resources, you must prioritize your goals. Before funding your retirement accounts and racking up those tax breaks, read on to consider your other goals.

Building Emergency Reserves

No one can predict the future. You simply have no reliable way to tell what may happen with your job, health, or family. Because you don't know what the future holds, preparing for the unexpected is financially wise. Even if you're the lucky sort who sometimes finds $5 bills on street corners, you can't control the sometimes chaotic world in which we live.

Conventional wisdom says that you should have approximately six months of living expenses put away for an emergency. This particular amount may or may not be right for you, because it depends, of course, on how expensive the emergency is. Why six months, anyway? And where should you put it? Unfortunately, no hard and fast rules exist. How much of an emergency stash you need depends on your situation.

I recommend saving the following emergency amounts under differing circumstances (in Chapter 11, I recommend good places to invest this money):

✔ **Three months' living expenses** if you have other accounts, such as a 401(k), or family members and close friends that you can tap for a short-term loan. This minimalist approach makes sense when you're trying to maximize investments elsewhere (for example, in retirement accounts), or you have stable sources of income (employment or otherwise).

✔ **Six months' living expenses** if you don't have other places to turn for a loan, or you have some instability in your employment situation or source of income.

✔ **Up to one year's living expenses** if your income fluctuates wildly from year to year, or if your profession involves a high risk of job loss and it could take you a long time to find another job, and you don't have other places to turn for a loan.

Don't buy cash value life insurance plans

Life insurance salespeople are often eager to sell you *cash value life insurance policies,* which combine life insurance protection with a type of savings account. A salesperson may very well try to sucker you into buying a cash value life insurance policy as a savings vehicle for accomplishing goals such as retiring or paying for a child's educational costs. Don't fall for this sales trap.

Cash value life insurance policies give you no immediate tax deduction. By contrast, a retirement savings plan such as a 401(k), 403(b), SEP-IRA, or Keogh allows you to deduct your contributions from your taxable income. When you don't have access to these plans, you're better off saving and investing through an IRA or annuity plan (both are detailed in Chapter 10).

Most people should buy term life insurance. (See Chapter 15 for more details.) Because agents earn far larger commissions selling cash value policies, they usually push those policies.

In the event that your only current source of emergency funds is a high-interest credit card, you should first save at least three months' worth of living expenses in an accessible account before funding a retirement account or saving for other goals.

Saving to Buy a Home or Business

When you're starting out financially, deciding whether to save money to buy a home or to put money into a retirement account presents a dilemma. In the long run, owning your own home is a wise financial move. On the other hand, saving sooner for retirement makes achieving your goal easier.

Presuming both goals are important to you, you should be saving towards both buying a home *and* for retirement. If you're eager to own a home, you can throw all your savings toward achieving that goal and temporarily put your retirement savings on hold. Save for both purposes simultaneously if you're not in a rush.

You may be able to have your cake and eat it too if you work for an employer that allows borrowing against retirement account balances. You can save money in the retirement account and then borrow against it for the down payment of a home. Be careful, though. Retirement account loans typically must be paid back within a set number of years (check with your employer), or immediately if you quit or lose your job. As I mention earlier in this chapter, you're also allowed to make penalty-free withdrawals of up to $10,000 from Individual Retirement Accounts toward a first-time home purchase.

When saving money for starting or buying a business, most people encounter the same dilemma they face when deciding to save to buy a house: If you fund your retirement accounts to the exclusion of earmarking money for your small-business dreams, your entrepreneurial aspirations may never become a reality. Generally, I advocate hedging your bets by saving some money in your tax-sheltered retirement accounts as well as some toward your business venture. As I discuss in Part III, an investment in your own small business can produce great rewards, so you may feel comfortable focusing your savings on your own business.

Funding Kids' Educational Expenses

Wanting to provide for your children's future is perfectly natural. But doing so before you've saved adequately toward your own goals can be a major financial mistake. The college financial-aid system effectively penalizes you for saving money outside of retirement accounts, and penalizes you even more if the money is invested in the child's name.

It may sound selfish, but you need to take care of *your* future first. You should first take advantage of saving through your tax-sheltered retirement accounts before you set aside money in custodial savings accounts for your kids. This practice isn't selfish — do you really want to have to leech off your kids when you're old and frail, because you didn't save any money for yourself?

See Chapter 12 for a complete explanation of how to save for educational expenses.

Saving for Big Purchases

If you want to buy a car, a canoe, or a plane ticket to France, do not, I repeat, *do not* buy such things with *consumer credit* (that is, carrying debt month-to-month to finance the purchase on a credit card or auto loan). As I explain in Chapter 4, cars, boats, vacations, and the like are consumer items, not investments that build wealth, such as real estate or small businesses. A car begins to depreciate the moment you drive it off the sales lot. A plane ticket to France is worthless the moment you arrive back home. (I know your memories will be priceless, but they won't pay the bills.)

Paying for high-interest consumer debt can cripple your ability not only to save for long-term goals like retirement or a home but also to make major purchases in the future. Interest on consumer debt is exorbitantly expensive — up to 18 percent for most credit cards. When contemplating the purchase of a consumer item on credit, add up the total interest you end up paying on your debt and call it the price of instant gratification.

Don't deny yourself gratification; just learn how to delay it. Get into the habit of saving for your larger consumer purchases to avoid paying for them over time with high-interest consumer credit. When saving up for a consumer purchase such as a car, a money market account or short-term bond fund (see Chapter 11) is a good place to store your short-term savings.

Preparing for Retirement

Many people toil away at work, dreaming about a future in which they can stop the daily commute and grind; get out from under that daily deluge of faxes, voice mails, and e-mails; and do what they want, when they want. People often assume that this magical day will arrive either on their next true day off or when they retire or win the lottery — whichever comes first.

I've never cared much for the term *retire*. This word seems to imply idleness or the end of usefulness to society. But if retirement means not having to work at a job (especially one you don't enjoy) and having financial flexibility and independence, then I'm all for it.

Being able to retire sooner rather than later is part of the American dream. But this idea has some obvious problems. First, you set yourself up for disappointment. If you want to retire by your mid-60s (when Social Security kicks in), you'll need to save enough money to support yourself for 20 years, maybe longer. Two decades is a long time to live off your savings. You're going to need a good-sized chunk of money — more than most people realize. The earlier you hope to retire, the more money you need to set aside, and the sooner you have to start saving — unless you plan to work part-time in retirement to earn more income!

Many of the people I speak to say that they do want to retire, and most say "the sooner, the better." Yet more than half of Americans between the ages of 18 and 34, and a quarter of those aged 35 to 54, have not begun to save for retirement. When I asked one of my middle-aged counseling clients, who had saved little for retirement, when he would like to retire, he deadpanned, "Sometime before I die." If you're in this group (and even if you're not), determine where you stand financially regarding retirement. If you're like most working people, you need to increase your savings rate for retirement.

Don't neglect nonfinancial preparations for retirement

Investing your money is just one (and not even the most important) aspect of preparing for your retirement. In order to enjoy the lifestyle that your retirement savings will provide you, you need to invest energy into other areas of your life, as well.

✔ Few things are more important than your health. Without your health, enjoying the good things in life can be hard. Unfortunately, many people are not motivated to care about their health until after they discover problems. By then, it may be too late.

Although exercising regularly, eating a balanced and nutritious diet, and avoiding substance abuse can't guarantee you a healthful future, these good habits go a long way toward preventing many of the most common causes of death and debilitating disease. Regular medical exams also are important in detecting problems early.

✔ In addition to your physical health, be sure to invest in your psychological health. People live longer and have happier and healthier lives when they have a circle of family and friends around them for support.

Unfortunately, many people become more isolated and lose regular contact with business associates, friends, and family members as they grow older.

Happy retirees tend to stay active, getting involved in volunteer organizations and new social circles. They may travel to see old friends or younger relatives who may be too busy to visit them.

Treat retirement life like a bubbly, inviting hot tub set at 102 degrees. You want to ease yourself in nice and slow; jumping in hastily can take most of the pleasantness out of the experience. Abruptly leaving your job without some sort of plan for spending all that free time is an invitation to boredom and depression. Everyone needs a sense of purpose and a sense of routine. Establishing hobbies, volunteer work, or a sideline business while gradually cutting back your regular work schedule can be a terrific way to ease into retirement.

Lower yourself into the tub slowly. Take some time to get used to the temperature change. Ahhh . . . nice, isn't it?

Figuring what you need for retirement

If you hope to someday reduce the time you spend working or cease working altogether, you'll need sufficient savings to support yourself. Many people — particularly young people and those who don't work well with numbers — underestimate the amount of money needed to retire. To figure out how much you should be saving per month to achieve your retirement goals, you need to crunch a few numbers. (Don't worry — this number-crunching should be easier than doing your taxes.)

Luckily for you, you don't have to start cold. Studies show how people typically spend money before and during retirement. Most people need about 70 to 80 percent of their pre-retirement income throughout retirement to maintain their standard of living. For example, if your household earns $40,000 per year before retirement, you're likely to need $28,000 to $32,000 (70 to 80 percent of $40,000) per year during retirement to live the way you're accustomed to living. The 70 to 80 percent is an average. Some people may need more simply because they have more time on their hands to spend their money. Others adjust their standard of living and live on less.

You, of course, are not average in any way — you're unique! So how do you figure out what you're going to need? The simplest method for estimating what you need is for me to tell you what percentage you need. (I know we've only known each other a short time, but I'm going to offer some friendly counseling.) The following three profiles provide a rough estimate of the percentage of your pre-retirement income you're going to need during retirement. Pick the one that most accurately describes your situation. If you fall between two descriptions, pick a percentage that fits in between the two.

To maintain your standard of living in retirement

- ✔ You need **65 percent of your pre-retirement income** if you

    • save a large amount (15 percent or more) of your annual earnings

    • are a high-income earner

    • will own your home free of debt by the time you retire

    • do not anticipate leading a lifestyle in retirement that reflects your current high income

    If you're an especially high-income earner who lives well beneath your means, you may be able to do just fine with even less than 65 percent. Try picking an annual dollar amount or percentage of your current income that will allow the kind of retirement lifestyle you desire.

- ✔ You need **75 percent of your pre-retirement income** if you

    • save a reasonable amount (5 to 14 percent) of your annual earnings

    • will still have some mortgage debt or a modest rent to pay by the time you retire

    • anticipate having a standard of living in retirement that is comparable to what you have today

- ✔ You need **85 percent of your pre-retirement income** if you

    • save little or none of your annual earnings (less than 5 percent)

    • will have a significant mortgage payment or sizeable rent to pay in retirement

    • anticipate wanting or needing to maintain your current lifestyle throughout retirement

Of course, you can use a more precise approach to figure out how much you need per year in retirement. Be forewarned, though, that this more personalized method is far more time-consuming, and because you're making projections into an uncertain future, it may not be any more accurate than the simple method I explain earlier in this section. If you're data-oriented, you may feel comfortable tackling this method: You need to figure out where you're spending your money today (worksheets are available in Chapter 3) and then work up some projections for your expected spending needs in retirement (the information in Chapter 18 may help you, as well).

Understanding retirement building blocks

Did you play with Lego blocks or Tinkertoys when you were a child? You start by building a foundation on the ground, and then you build up. Before you know it, you're creating bridges, castles, and panda bears. Although preparing financially for retirement isn't exactly like playing with blocks, the concept is the same: You need a basic foundation so that your necessary retirement reserves can grow.

If you've been working steadily, you may already have a good foundation, even if you haven't been actively saving toward retirement. In the pages ahead, I walk you through the probable components of your future retirement income and show you how to figure how much you should be saving to reach particular retirement goals.

Counting on Social Security

Social Security is the Rodney Dangerfield of U.S. government programs. According to polls, nearly half of American adults under the age of 35, and more than a third of those between the ages of 35 and 49, think that Social Security benefits will not be available by the time they retire.

Contrary to widespread cynicism, Social Security should be available when you retire, no matter how old you are today. In fact, Social Security is one of the sacred cow political programs. Imagine what would happen to the group of politicians that voted not to pay any more benefits!

If you think that you can never retire because you don't have any money saved, I'm happy to inform you that you're probably wrong. You likely have some Social Security. But Social Security is generally not enough to live on comfortably.

Social Security is intended to provide you with a subsistence level of retirement income for the basic necessities: food, shelter, and clothing. Social Security is not intended to be your sole source of income. Few people could maintain their current lifestyles without supplementing Social Security with personal savings and company retirement plans.

How much will I get from Social Security?

Table 2-1 shows the approximate size of your expected monthly allowance from Social Security. The first column gives your average *yearly employment earnings* (in today's dollars) on which you pay Social Security taxes. The second column contains the approximate *monthly benefit amount* (in today's dollars) that you'll receive when eligible for full benefits.

Note: The benefit amounts in Table 2-1 are for an individual income earner. If you're married, and one of you doesn't work for pay, the nonworking spouse collects 50 percent of what the working spouse collects. Working spouses are eligible for either individual benefits or half of their spouse's benefits — whichever amount is greater.

Table 2-1	Your Expected Social Security Benefits
Annual Earnings	*Approximate Monthly Benefit (Value in Today's Dollars)*
$10,000	$535
$20,000	$725
$30,000	$920
$40,000	$1,110
$50,000	$1,290
$60,000	$1,480
$70,000	$1,570
$80,000+	$1,660

How much work makes me eligible?

To be eligible to collect Social Security benefits, you need to have worked a minimum number of quarters. If you were born after 1928, you need 40 quarters of work credits to qualify for Social Security retirement benefits.

More Social Security details

When the Social Security system was created in the 1930s, its designers underestimated how long people would live in retirement (the Roosevelt administration must have included a lot of young people). Thanks to scientific advances and improved medical care, life expectancies have risen substantially since that time. As a result, many of today's retirees get back far more than they paid into the system.

The age at which you can start collecting full benefits has been increased, and it may be increased again. In the "good old days" (prior to changes made in Social Security regulations in 1983), you could collect full Social Security payments at age 65, assuming you were eligible. This rule no longer holds true. If you were born before 1938, you're still eligible to collect full Social Security benefits at age 65. If you were born in 1960 or after, you have to wait until age 67 for full benefits. If you were born between 1938 and 1959, full benefits are payable to you at age 66 (plus or minus some number of months, depending on the year you were born).

These regulations may seem unfair, but they're necessary for updating the system to fit with the realities of our increased longevity, large federal budget deficits, and aging baby boomers. Without changes, the Social Security system may collapse, because it will be fed by a relatively small number of workers while supporting large numbers of retirees.

In addition to paying for retirement-income checks for retirees, your Social Security taxes also help fund disability insurance for you, survivor income insurance for your financial dependents, and Medicare (the health insurance program for retirees).

The amount of Social Security benefits you receive in retirement depends on your average earnings during your working years. Don't worry about the fact that you probably earned a lot less many years ago. The Social Security benefits calculations increase your older earnings to account for the lower cost of living and wages in prior years.

If for some reason you work only the first half of a year or only during summer months, don't despair. You don't need to work part of every quarter to get a quarter's credit. You get credits based on the income you earn during the year. As of this writing, you get the full four quarters credited to your account if you earn $3,560 or more in a year. (In earlier years, folks got one quarter's credit for each actual calendar quarter in which they earned $50.) To get 40 quarters of coverage, you basically need to work (at least portions of) ten years.

To get credits, your income must be reported and you must pay taxes on it (including Social Security tax). In other words, you and those you employ encounter problems when you neglect to declare income or you pay people under the table — you may be cheating yourself, or others, out of valuable benefits.

To get a more precise handle on your Social Security benefits, call the Social Security Administration at 800-772-1213 and ask for Form 7004, which allows you to receive a record of your reported earnings and an estimate of your Social Security benefits. (You can also visit the Social Security Administration

Web site at www.ssa.gov.) Or you can just wait by your mailbox — the government now annually mails a personal Social Security Statement that includes estimates of the benefits you and your family members may qualify for. (Check your earnings record, because occasional errors do arise and — surprise — they usually aren't in your favor.)

Planning your personal savings/investment strategy

Money you're saving toward retirement can include money under the mattress as well as money in a retirement account such as an Individual Retirement Account (IRA), 401(k), or similar plan (see Chapter 10). You may have also earmarked investments in nonretirement accounts for your retirement.

Equity (the difference between the market value less any mortgage balances owed) in rental real estate can be counted toward your retirement, as well. Deciding whether to include the equity in your primary residence (your home) is trickier. If you don't want to count on using this money in retirement, don't include it when you tally your stash. You may want to count a portion of your home equity in your total assets for retirement. Many people sell their homes when they retire and move to a cheaper region of the country, move closer to family, or downsize to a more manageable household. And increasing numbers of older retirees are tapping their homes' equity through reverse mortgages.

Making the most of pensions

Pension plans are a benefit offered by some employers — mostly larger organizations and government agencies. Even if your current employer doesn't offer a pension, you may have earned pension benefits through a previous job.

The plans I'm referring to are known as *defined-benefit plans.* With these plans, you qualify for a monthly benefit amount to be paid to you in retirement based on your years of service for a specific employer.

Although each company's plan differs, all plans calculate and pay benefits based on a formula. A typical formula might credit you with 1.5 percent of your salary for each year of service (full-time employment). For example, if you work ten years, you earn a monthly retirement benefit worth 15 percent of your monthly salary.

Pension benefits can be quite valuable. In the better plans, employers put away the equivalent of 5 to 10 percent of your salary to pay your future pension. This money is not quoted as part of your salary — it's in addition to your salary. You never see it in your paycheck, and it isn't taxed. The employer puts this money away in an account for your retirement.

To qualify for pension benefits, you don't have to stay with an employer long enough to receive the 25-year gold watch. Under current government regulations, employees must be fully *vested* (entitled to receive full benefits based on years of service upon reaching retirement age) after five years of full-time service.

Defined-benefit pension plans are becoming rare for two major reasons:

- They are costly for employers to maintain. Many employees don't understand how these plans work and why they're so valuable, so companies don't get mileage out of their pension expenditures — employees don't see the money, so they don't appreciate how generous the company is being.

- Most of the new jobs being generated in the U.S. economy are with small companies that typically don't offer these types of plans.

More employers are offering plans like 401(k)s, in which employees elect to save money out of their own paychecks. Known as *defined-contribution plans,* these plans allow you to save toward your retirement at your own expense rather than at your employer's expense. (To encourage participation in defined-contribution plans, some employers "match" a portion of their employees' contributions.) More of the burden and responsibility of investing for retirement falls on your shoulders with 401(k) and similar plans, so it's important to understand how these plans work. Most people are ill-equipped to know how much to save and how to invest the money. The retirement planning worksheet in the next section should help get you started with figuring out the amount you need to save. (Part III shows you how to invest.)

Retirement planning worksheet

Now that you've toured the components of your future retirement income, I want you to take a shot at tallying where you stand in terms of retirement preparations. Don't be afraid to do this exercise — it's not difficult, and you may find that you're not in such bad shape. I even explain how to catch up if you find that you're behind in saving for retirement.

Note: The following worksheet (Table 2-2) and the Growth Multiplier (Table 2-3) assume that you're going to retire at age 66 and that your investments will produce an annual rate of return that is 4 percent higher than the rate of inflation. (For example, if inflation averages 3 percent, this table assumes that you will earn 7 percent per year on your investments.)

Table 2-2	Retirement Planning Worksheet	
1. Annual retirement income needed in today's dollars (see earlier in this chapter).	$_____ / year	
2. Annual Social Security (see Table 2-1).	–$_____ / year	
3. Annual pension benefits (ask your benefits department). Multiply by 60% if your pension won't increase with inflation during retirement.	–$_____ / year	
4. Annual retirement income needed from personal savings (subtract lines 2 and 3 from line 1).	=$_____ / year	
5. Savings needed to retire at age 66 (multiply line 4 by 15).	$_____	
6. Value of current retirement savings.	$_____	
7. Value of current retirement savings at retirement (multiply line 6 by Growth Multiplier in following minitable).	$_____	
8. Amount you still need to save (line 5 minus line 7).	$_____	
9. Amount you need to save per month (multiply line 8 by Savings Factor in following minitable).	$_____ / month	

To get a more precise handle on where you stand in terms of retirement planning (especially if you'd like to retire earlier than your mid-60s), call T. Rowe Price at 800-638-5660 and ask for the company's retirement planning booklets. You can also turn to Chapter 18, where I recommend retirement planning software and Web sites that can ease your number-crunching burdens.

Table 2-3	Growth Multiplier	
Your Current Age	*Growth Multiplier*	*Savings Factor*
26	4.8	.001
28	4.4	.001
30	4.1	.001
32	3.8	.001
34	3.5	.001
36	3.2	.001
38	3.0	.002

(continued)

Table 2-3 *(continued)*

Your Current Age	Growth Multiplier	Savings Factor
40	2.8	.002
42	2.6	.002
44	2.4	.002
46	2.2	.003
48	2.0	.003
50	1.9	.004
52	1.7	.005
54	1.6	.006
56	1.5	.007
58	1.4	.009
60	1.3	.013
62	1.2	.020
64	1.1	.041

Making up for lost time

If the amount you need to save per month to reach your retirement goals seems daunting, don't despair. All is not lost. Here are my top recommendations for making up for lost time.

✔ **Question your spending.** You have two ways to boost your savings: Earn more money or cut your spending (or do both). Most people don't spend their money nearly as thoughtfully as they earn it. Refer to Chapter 5 for suggestions and strategies for reducing your spending.

✔ **Be more realistic about your retirement age.** If you extend the age at which you plan to retire, you get a double financial benefit: You're earning and saving money for more years, and you're spending your nest egg over fewer years. Of course, if your job is making you crazy, this option may not be too appealing. Try to find work that makes you happy, and consider working, at least part-time, during the early years typically considered the retirement years.

✔ **Use your home equity.** The prospect of tapping the cash in your home can be troubling. After getting together the down payment, you probably worked for many years to pay off that sucker. You're delighted not to have to mail a mortgage payment to the bank anymore. But what's the use of owning a house free of mortgage debt when you lack sufficient retirement reserves? All the money that's tied up in the house can be used to help increase your standard of living in retirement.

You have a number of ways to tap your home's equity. You can sell your home and either move to a lower-cost property or rent an apartment. Tax laws allow you to realize up to $250,000 in tax-free profit from the sale of your house ($500,000 if you're married). Another option is a *reverse mortgage,* where you get a monthly income check as you build a loan balance against the value of your home. The loan is paid when your home is finally sold. (See Chapter 13 for more information about reverse mortgages.)

✔ **Get your investments growing.** The faster the rate at which your money grows and compounds, the less you need to save each year to reach your goals. Earning just a few extra percentage points per year on your investments can dramatically slash the amount you need to save. The younger you are, the more powerful the effect of compounding interest. For example, if you're in your mid-30s, and your investments appreciate 6 percent per year (rather than 4 percent) faster than the rate of inflation, the amount you need to save each month to reach your retirement goals drops by about 40 percent!

✔ **Turn a hobby into supplemental retirement income.** Even if you've earned a living in the same career over many decades, you have skills that are portable and can be put to profitable use. Pick something you enjoy and are good at, develop a business plan, and get smart about how to market your services and wares (check out the latest edition of *Small Business For Dummies* from Wiley Publishing, which I co-wrote with veteran entrepreneur Jim Schell). Remember, as people get busier, more specialized services are created to support their hectic lives. A demand for quality, homemade goods of all varieties also exists. Be creative! You never know — you may wind up profiled in a business publication!

✔ **Invest in a tax-wise way.** By investing in a tax-wise fashion, you can boost the effective rate of return on your investments without taking on additional risk. Many people don't save and invest money in a way that minimizes their taxes.

Direct your savings into tax-favored retirement accounts such as a 401(k) plan. With these accounts, you generally get an immediate tax deduction for your contribution. (Accounts such as the newer Roth IRA don't offer the upfront tax break, but they do allow for a tax-free withdrawal of investment earnings in the future.) For a typical person, a third or more of your contribution represents money you would have had to pay in federal and state income taxes. This money works for you, rather than for the government, in the years ahead, and your investment compounds over the years without taxation.

As for money outside of tax-sheltered retirement accounts, if you're in a relatively high tax bracket, you may earn more by investing in tax-free investments and other vehicles that minimize highly taxed distributions. (I discuss tax-friendly investments and retirement accounts in detail in Chapter 10.)

✔ **Take a look at jobs that offer retirement plans.** When you're evaluating employers, cash is usually king. As long as the position includes health insurance, most people are concerned only about the salary. But having access to a retirement savings plan is a valuable benefit. Even more beneficial is a pension plan, which pays you a monthly retirement benefit based on your years of service (a completely pain-free way to build wealth for retirement). If you're lucky enough to have choices, check out these plans when considering a job offer.

✔ **Think about inheritances.** Although you should never count on an inheritance to support your retirement, you may inherit money someday. If you want to see what impact an inheritance has on your retirement calculations, simply add a conservative estimate of the amount you expect to inherit to your current total savings in Table 2-2.

Overcoming objections to retirement accounts

Despite all the great tax benefits of investing through retirement accounts, many people aren't jumping at the opportunity to take advantage of them. Each of us has unique priorities. Maybe you're saving for a home purchase or paying off student loans. Some reasons for not taking advantage of retirement accounts, however, stem from a lack of knowledge and understanding. The following sections cover the objections to contributing to tax-favored accounts that I hear most frequently. Some of these objections can be overcome, whereas others are legitimate reasons for not funding retirement accounts.

Retirement's a long way away

When you're in your 20s or 30s, age 65 seems like the distant future. For many people, warning bells don't stimulate thoughts about one's golden years until middle age.

Delaying the age at which you start to sock away money is usually a financial mistake. The sooner you start to save, the less painful it is to save each year, because your contributions have more years to compound. For each decade you procrastinate, the percentage of your earnings that you should save to meet your goals approximately doubles. For example, if saving 5 percent per year in your early 20s would get you to your retirement goal, waiting until your 30s may mean that you have to sock away 10 percent, waiting until your 40s may mean that you have to save 20 percent, and so on.

When should you start saving for retirement? Ideally, you should start saving a small portion of your employment earnings with your first paycheck. Start your kids' saving habits while they're young!

Only losers who don't know how to have fun save for retirement

Some people really believe this statement. But I also know "losers" who don't save for retirement and still don't know how to have a good time (none of my counseling clients and friends, of course).

This attitude is just a rationalization. The reality is that if you manage your finances efficiently and start working toward your goals sooner, you can spend more and have more fun in the long run. Besides, who says spending all your money is the only way to have fun?

There are greener investment pastures elsewhere

Some people find retirement accounts boring and believe that they can get a better return in the real estate market. Rental real estate can appreciate in value and produce increasing rental income over the years. Investing in real estate is a legitimate reason for not maximizing retirement plan contributions.

Although real estate provides some tax breaks, you need to also consider its drawbacks:

- While you accumulate the down payment, you may pay higher income taxes if you're sacrificing contributions to retirement accounts that are tax-deductible.

- Rental real estate produces income that is taxable and is added to all your other income during the year, which may push you into a higher tax bracket. Even if the extra real estate income doesn't push you into a higher tax bracket, this income is taxable immediately at the ordinary income tax rates rather than deferred for many years.

In a retirement account, the earnings continue to compound without taxation, and you decide when you want to start drawing on the money.

You may be able to invest in what you want and gain tax relief, too. Many types of investments — stocks, bonds, mutual funds, precious metals, and even real estate — can be held in retirement accounts. (See Chapter 10 for more details.)

I have no money left over to save

The more you spend, the less you're able to fund retirement accounts. Thus, the extra taxes that you pay because you can't afford retirement account contributions are an additional cost of overspending today. So if you can reduce your expenditures (refer to Chapter 5), you can more easily meet your retirement goals. You'll have more money to contribute to retirement accounts, and you'll save on your taxes, too!

In some cases, people have a pile of money invested outside of tax-sheltered retirement accounts that's not earmarked for specific future needs. They may use all of their monthly employment income to meet their ongoing living expenses. As a result, they believe that they can't afford to save in a retirement account.

If you believe that you can't afford to save in a retirement account because you spend all of your income on living expenses, you're compartmentalizing your finances. Look at the big picture. For example, what if you save $300 per month through your tax-deductible retirement plan? Suppose that doing so reduces your taxes by $100 and therefore really costs you only $200 a month. You then can take $200 from your savings outside the retirement account and put it toward living expenses.

What you're effectively doing is transferring your savings from outside retirement accounts to inside a retirement account. You're not really saving new money, but you're getting terrific tax savings by playing this perfectly legal investing shell game. Just be careful not to drain your emergency savings reserve down too far.

I love my job and will work forever

Are you one of those people who loves his or her work? Do you feel that because you don't plan to retire, you don't need to amass a pile of money to live on for 20-plus years? If so, you can get away with saving a lot less than your eager-to-retire friends.

You may not, however, be *able* to work at your current job forever. What if you lose your job? What if something happens to your health? You can't assume that you will always be able to work — plan ahead for these what-ifs.

I've saved enough already

Congratulations! This is the single best excuse for not saving more for retirement. If you have a lot of money outside of tax-sheltered retirement accounts, you may still want to contribute to retirement accounts for the tax benefits.

Part II
Saving More, Spending Less

The 5th Wave   By Rich Tennant

@RICHTENNANT

"I bought a software program that should help us monitor and control our spending habits, and while I was there, I picked up a few new games, a couple of screen savers, 4 new mousepads, this nifty pull out keyboard cradle...."

In this part . . .

1 show you how to identify where your hard-earned dollars are going. I detail numerous ways to make those dollars go toward helping you build up your savings rather than go toward wasteful spending. What? You're buried in debt with little to show for it? Well, it's never too late to start digging out. Here you find out how to reduce your debt burden. I also devote an entire chapter to discussing taxes and how to legally minimize them, because too much of your money may be going to pay taxes.

Chapter 3

Determining Where Your Money Goes

. . . .

In This Chapter

▶ Understanding the roots of overspending

▶ Assessing your spending

▶ Finding the road to salvation

. . . .

*I*f you're like most people, you must live within your means in order to accomplish your financial goals. This requires spending less than you earn and then taking your "savings" and hopefully investing it intelligently.

Many folks earn just enough to make ends meet. And some can't even do that; they simply spend more than they make. The result of such spending habits is, of course, an accumulation of debt — witness the U.S. government and its six trillion dollars' worth of debt accumulation.

No matter what your financial dreams are, you need to save and invest (unless you plan on winning the lottery or gaining a large inheritance). To put yourself in a position that allows you to start saving, you need to take a close look at your spending habits.

Examining the Roots of Overspending

Most of the influences in society encourage you to spend; credit is so widely and easily available. Think about it. More often than not, you're referred to as a *consumer* in the media and in the hallowed halls of our government. You're not referred to as a person, a citizen, or a human being.

Here are some of the adversaries you're up against as you attempt to control your spending.

Access to credit

As you probably already know, spending your money is easy. Thanks to innovations like ATM machines and credit cards, your money is always available for spending, 24 hours a day, 365 days a year (except during leap years, when your money is available 366 days a year). Every little outlet in the mall is pitching its own credit card, including the gas station across the street and the convenience store down the road. It certainly won't surprise me when those two little kids on my block start taking credit cards at their lemonade stand. I can hear it now: "We take Visa, Mr. Tyson, but we don't take American Express."

Sometimes it may seem as though lenders are trying to give away money by making credit so easily available. But this free money is a dangerous illusion. When it comes to consumer debt (credit cards, auto loans, and the like), lenders aren't giving away anything except the opportunity for you to get in over your head, rack up high interest charges, and delay your progress toward your financial and personal goals.

Credit is most dangerous when you make consumption purchases you can't afford in the first place.

Using credit cards

The modern day bank credit card was invented by Bank of America near the end of the baby boom. The credit industry has been booming along with the boomers ever since.

If you pay your bill in full every month, credit cards offer a convenient way to buy things with an interest-free, short-term loan. But if you carry your debt over from month to month at high interest rates, credit cards encourage you to live beyond your means. Credit cards make it easy and tempting to spend money that you don't have.

 If you have a knack for charging up a storm and spending more than you should with those little pieces of plastic, only one solution exists: Get rid of your credit cards. Put scissors to the plastic. Go cold turkey. You can function without them. (See the next chapter for details on how to live without credit cards.)

Making minimum monthly payments

 You'll never get your credit card debt paid off if you keep charging on your card and making only the minimum monthly payment. Interest continues to pile up on your outstanding debt. Paying only the minimum monthly payment is like using a paper cup to bail water from a sinking boat with a basketball-sized hole in its bottom.

Taking out car loans

Walking onto a car lot and going home with a new car that you could never afford if you had to pay cash is easy. The dealer gets you thinking in terms of monthly payments that sound small when compared to what that four-wheeler is *really* gonna cost you. Auto loans are easy for just about anyone to get (except maybe a recently paroled felon).

Suppose that you're tired of driving around in your old clunker. The car is battle-scarred and boring, and you don't like to be seen in it. Plus, the car is likely to need more repairs in the months ahead. So off you go to your friendly local car dealer.

You start looking around at all the shiny, new cars and then — like the feeling you experience when spotting a water fountain on a scorching hot day — there it is: the replacement for your old clunker. This new car is sleek and clean, and it has A/C, stereo, and power everything.

Before you have an opportunity to read the fine print on the sticker page on the side window, the salesperson moseys on up next to you. He gets you talking about how nice the car is, the weather, or anything but the sticker price of that car.

"How," you begin to think to yourself, "can this guy afford to spend time with me without knowing if I can afford this thing?" After a test drive and more talk about the car, the weather, and your love life (or lack thereof) comes your moment of truth.

The salesperson, it seems, doesn't care about how much money you have. Whether you have lots of money or very little money, it doesn't matter. Either way, it's no problem!

The car is only $299 a month.

"That price isn't bad," you think. Heck, you were expecting to hear that the car costs at least 20 grand. Before you know it, the dealer runs a credit report on you and has you sign a few papers, and minutes later you're driving home — the proud owner of a new car.

 The dealer wants you to think in terms of monthly payments because the cost *sounds* so cheap: $299 for a car. But, of course, that's $299 per month, every month, for many, many months. You're gonna be payin' forever — after all, you just bought a car that cost a huge chunk (perhaps 100 percent or more) of your yearly take-home income!

But it gets worse. What does the total sticker price come to when interest charges are added in? (Even if interest charges are low, you may still be buying a car with a sticker price you can't afford.) And what about insurance, registration, and maintenance over the seven or so years that you'll own the car? Now you're probably up to more than a year's worth of your income. Ouch! (See Chapter 5 for info on how to spend what you can afford on a car.)

Bending to peer pressure

You go out with some friends to dinner, a ballgame, or a show. Try to remember the last time one of you said, "Let's go someplace (or do something) cheaper. I can't afford to spend this much."

On the one hand, you don't want to be a stick in the mud. But on the other hand, some of your friends have more money than you do — and the ones who don't may be running up debt fast.

Spending to feel good

Life is full of stress, obligations, and demands. "I work hard," you say, "And darn it, I deserve to indulge!" Especially after your boss took the credit for your last great idea or blamed you for his last major screwup. So you buy something expensive or go to a fancy restaurant. Feel better? You won't when the bill arrives. And the more you spend, the less you save, and the longer you'll be stuck working for jerks like your boss!

Becoming addicted to spending

Just as people can become addicted to alcohol, tobacco, television, and the Internet, some people also become addicted to the high they get from spending. A number of psychological causes for spending addiction can be identified, with some relating to how your parents handled money and spending. (And you thought you identified all the problems you can blame on mom and dad!)

If your spending and debt problems are chronic, Debtors Anonymous — a 12-step support group program patterned after Alcoholics Anonymous — can help. See Chapter 4 for more information.

Trying to keep current

You just have to see the latest hit movie, wear the latest designer clothes, or get the new, super-improved, oversized tennis racquet with shock absorbers, double-wishbone suspension, and polyxylitol handgrips. All your friends are getting one, so you'd better get one, too. Right?

Wrong. Besides, many new technologies or products don't live up to their billing. Be smart. Wait until a product is proven and you can afford it.

Ignoring your financial goals when buying

When was the last time you heard someone say that he decided to forego a purchase because he was saving for retirement or a home purchase? It doesn't happen often, does it? Just dealing with the here-and-now and forgetting your long-term needs and goals is tempting. This mindset leads people to toil away for too many years in jobs they dislike.

Living for today has its virtues: Tomorrow *may* not come. But odds are good that it will. Will you still feel the same way about today's spending decisions tomorrow? Or will you feel guilty that you again failed to stick to your goals?

If you haven't set any goals yet, you may not know how much you should be saving. Chapter 2 helps you kick-start the planning and saving process.

Wanting the best for your children

For children, many of the best things in life are free, just as they are for you. Junior can live without the latest $100 sneakers. Later on in life, your children will thank you for teaching them that they don't need everything they see in ads: Better to pass on sound judgment and wise thriftiness than the worship of material goods.

Education can cost good money. However, education experts — my wife is one of them — are the first to dissuade you of the assumption that you're doing the best for your children when you spend lots of money to live in a town with a supposedly top-of-the-line school district or fund the tuition of a costly private school education. If you aren't home enough to take care of your children's other wants and needs, even the best education won't help your children succeed in life.

Education begins in (and is best done in) the home. I see some parents spend so much time running around and working to afford all the supposedly best things for their kids, that they neglect to spend *time* and get involved with them — the most important ingredient to their children's long-term happiness and success.

Analyzing Your Spending

Washing your face, brushing your teeth, and exercising regularly are good habits. Spending less than you earn and saving enough to meet your future financial objectives are the financial equivalents of these habits.

Despite relatively high incomes compared with the rest of the world, most Americans have a hard time saving a good percentage of their incomes. Why? Because we spend too much — often far more than is necessary.

The first step to saving more of the income that you work so hard for is to figure out where that income typically gets spent. The spending analysis in the next section helps you determine where your income is going.

You should do the spending analysis if any of the following apply to you:

- You aren't saving enough money to meet your financial goals. (If you're not sure whether this is the case, please see Chapter 2.)

- You feel as though your spending is out of control, or you don't really know where all your income goes.

- You're anticipating a significant life change (for example, marriage, leaving your job to start a business, having children, retiring, and so on).

If you're already a good saver, you may not need to complete the spending analysis. If you're saving enough to accomplish your goals, I don't see much value in continually tracking your spending. You already established the good habit — saving. Tracking exactly where you spend your money month after month is *not* the good habit. As long as you're saving enough, I say who cares where the leftover money is being spent! (You may still benefit from perusing my smarter spending recommendations in Chapter 5.)

The immediate goal of a spending analysis is to figure out where you're typically spending your money. The long-range goal is to establish a good habit: Maintaining a regular, automatic savings routine.

Notice the first four letters in the word *analysis*. (You may never have noticed, but I feel the need to bring it to your attention.) Knowing where your money is going each month is useful. Making changes in your spending behavior and cutting out the fat so that you can save more money and meet your financial goals is terrific. But you may make yourself and those around you miserable if you try to be anal-retentive about documenting precisely where you're spending every single dollar and cent.

Remember: Saving what you need to achieve your goals is what matters most.

Tracking your spending on paper

Doing a spending analysis is a little bit like being a detective. Your goal is to reconstruct the crime of spending. You probably have some major clues at your fingertips or piled somewhere on the desk or table where you plop yourself down to pay bills.

Unless you keep meticulous records that detail every dollar you spend, you won't have perfect information. Don't sweat it! A number of available sources should allow you to reconstruct where you've been spending the bulk of your money. To get started, get out your

- ✔ Recent pay stubs
- ✔ Tax returns
- ✔ Checkbook register or canceled checks
- ✔ Credit and charge card bills

Ideally, you want to assemble the documents needed to track one year's (12 months'), spending. But if your spending patterns don't fluctuate greatly from month to month (or if your dog ate some of the old bills), you can reduce your data gathering to one six-month period, or to every second or third month for the past year. If you take a major vacation or spend a large amount on gifts during certain months of the year, make sure that you include these months in your analysis.

Purchases made with cash are the hardest to track, because they don't leave a paper trail. Over the course of a week or perhaps even a month, you *could* keep a record of everything you buy with cash. Tracking cash can be an enlightening exercise, but it can also be a hassle. If you're lazy like I sometimes am or you lack the time and patience, try *estimating.* Think about a typical week or month — how often do you buy things with cash? For example, if you eat lunch out four days a week, paying around $6 a shot, that's about $100 a month. You may also want to try adding up all the cash withdrawals from your checking account statement and then working backwards to try to remember where you spent the cash.

Try to separate your expenditures into as many useful and detailed categories as possible. Table 3-1 gives you a suggested format — you can tailor it to fit your needs. Remember, if you lump too much of your spending into broad, meaningless categories like *Other,* you'll end up right back where you started: wondering where all the money went. (**Note:** When completing the tax section in Table 3-1, you should report the total tax you paid for the year as tabulated on your annual income tax return — and take the total Social Security and Medicare taxes paid from your end-of-year paystub — rather than the tax withheld or paid during the year.)

Table 3-1	Detailing Your Spending	
Category	*Monthly Average ($)*	*Percent of Total Gross Income (%)*
Taxes, taxes, taxes (income)		_____
FICA (Social Security & Medicare)	_____	
Federal	_____	
State and local	_____	
The roof over your head		_____
Rent	_____	
Mortgage	_____	
Property taxes	_____	
Gas/electric/oil	_____	
Water/garbage	_____	
Phone	_____	
Cable TV & Internet	_____	
Gardener/housekeeper	_____	
Furniture/appliances	_____	
Maintenance/repairs	_____	
Food, glorious food		_____
Supermarket	_____	
Restaurants and take-out	_____	
Getting around		_____
Gasoline	_____	
Maintenance/repairs	_____	
State registration fees	_____	
Tolls and parking	_____	
Bus or subway fares	_____	
Style		_____
Clothing	_____	
Shoes	_____	

Category	Monthly Average ($)	Percent of Total Gross Income (%)
Jewelry (watches, earrings)	_____	
Dry cleaning	_____	
Debt repayments (excluding mortgage)		_____
Credit/charge cards	_____	
Auto loans	_____	
Student loans	_____	
Other	_____	
Fun stuff		_____
Entertainment (movies, concerts)	_____	
Vacation and travel	_____	
Gifts	_____	
Hobbies	_____	
Subscriptions/memberships	_____	
Pets	_____	
Other	_____	
Personal care		_____
Haircuts	_____	
Health club or gym	_____	
Makeup	_____	
Other	_____	
Personal business		_____
Accountant/attorney/financial advisor	_____	
Other	_____	
Health care		_____
Physicians and hospitals	_____	
Drugs	_____	
Dental and vision	_____	
Therapy	_____	

(continued)

Table 3-1 *(continued)*

Category	Monthly Average ($)	Percent of Total Gross Income (%)
Insurance		_____
Homeowner's/renter's	_____	
Auto	_____	
Health	_____	
Life	_____	
Disability	_____	
Umbrella liability	_____	
Educational expenses		_____
Tuition	_____	
Books	_____	
Supplies	_____	
Children		_____
Day care	_____	
Toys	_____	
Child support	_____	
Charitable donations	_____	_____
Other		_____
_____	_____	
_____	_____	
_____	_____	
_____	_____	
_____	_____	

Tracking your spending on the computer

Numerous software programs can assist you with paying bills and tracking your spending. The main advantage of using software is that you can continually track your spending as long as you keep entering the information. These software packages can even help speed up the check-writing process (after you figure out how to use them, which is not always an easy thing to do).

But you don't need a computer and fancy software to pay your bills and figure out where you're spending money. Many people I know give up entering data into the software after a few months. If tracking your spending is what you're after, you need to enter information from the bills you pay by check and the expenses you pay by credit card and cash.

Like home exercise equipment and exotic kitchen appliances, such software often ends up in the consumer graveyard.

Paper, pencil, and a calculator work just fine for tracking your spending.

If you want to try computerizing your bill payments and expense tracking, I recommend the best software packages in Chapter 18.

Don't waste time on financial administration

Tom is the model of financial organization. His financial documents are neatly organized into color-coded folders. Every month, he enters all his spending information into his computer. He even carries a notebook to detail his cash spending so that every penny is accounted for.

Tom also balances his checkbook, "to make sure that everything is in order." He can't remember the last time his bank made a mistake, but he knows someone who once found a $50 error.

If you spend seven hours per month balancing your checkbook and detailing all your spending (as Tom does), you may be wasting nearly two weeks' worth of time per year — the equivalent of two-thirds of your vacation time if you take three weeks annually.

Suppose that, every other year, you're "lucky" enough to find a $100 error the bank made in its favor. If you spend just three hours per month tracking your spending and balancing your checkbook to discover this glitch, you'll be spending 72 hours over two years to find a $100 mistake. Your hourly pay: a wafer-thin $1.39 per hour. You can make more flipping burgers at a burger joint. (**Note:** If you make significant-sized deposits or withdrawals, make sure that you capture them on your statement.)

To add insult to injury, you may not have the desire and energy to do the more important stuff after working a full week and doing all your financial and other chores. Your big personal financial picture — establishing goals, choosing wise investments, securing proper insurance coverage — may continue to be shoved to the back burner. As a result, you may lose thousands of dollars annually. Over the course of your adult life, this amount could translate into tens or even hundreds of thousands of lost dollars.

Tom, for example, didn't know how much he should be saving to meet his retirement goals. He didn't review his employer's benefit materials, so he didn't understand his insurance and retirement plan options. He knew that he paid a lot in taxes, but he wasn't sure how to reduce his taxes.

You want to make the most of your money. Unless you truly enjoy dealing with money, you need to prioritize the money activities you work on. Time is limited and life is short. Working harder on financial administration doesn't earn you bonus points. The more time you spend dealing with your personal finances, the less time you have available to gab with friends, watch a good movie, read a good novel, and do other things you really enjoy.

(continued)

(continued)

Don't get me wrong — nothing is inherently wrong with balancing your checkbook. In fact, if you regularly bounce checks because you don't know how low your balance is, the exercise may save you a lot in returned check fees. However, if you keep enough money in your checking account so that you don't have to worry about the balance reaching $0.00, or if you have overdraft protection, balancing your checkbook is probably a waste of your valuable time, even if your hourly wages aren't lofty. I haven't balanced mine in years (but please don't tell my bank — it might start making some "mistakes" and siphoning money out).

If you're busy, consider ways to reduce the amount of time you spend on mundane financial tasks like bill paying. Many companies, for example, allow you to pay your monthly bills electronically via your bank checking account or your credit card. (Don't use this option unless you pay your credit card bill in full each month.) The fewer bills you have to pay, the fewer separate checks and envelopes you must process each month. That translates into more free time and less paper cuts!

Growing Rich on Your Income: The Secret

As a financial counselor, I've worked with people who bring in tiny incomes, people who have incomes of hundreds of thousands of dollars or more, and everyone in between. At every income level, people fall into one of the following three categories:

- People who spend more than they earn (accumulating debt)
- People who spend all that they earn (saving nothing)
- People who save 2, 5, 10, or even 20 percent (or more!)

I've seen $30,000 earners who save 20 percent of their income ($6,000), $60,000 earners who save just 5 percent ($3,000), and people earning well into six figures annually who save nothing or accumulate debt.

Suppose that you currently earn $40,000 per year and spend all of it. You may wonder, "How can I save money?"

Good question!

Rather than knock yourself out at a second job or hustle for that next promotion, you may want to try living below your income — in other words, spend less than you earn. (I know spending less than you earn is hard to imagine, but you can do it.) Consider that for every discontented person earning and spending $40,000 per year, someone else is out there making do on $35,000.

A great many people live on less than you make. If you spend as they do, you can save and invest the difference.

Chapter 4

Conquering Debt and Credit Problems

- -

In This Chapter

▶ Using your savings to lower your debt

▶ Getting out of debt when you don't have savings

▶ Understanding the pros and cons of filing bankruptcy

▶ Halting your spending and debting

▶ Handling credit problems

- -

*W*hen debt is used for investing in your future, I call it *good debt* (see Chapter 1). Borrowing money to pay for an education, buy real estate, or invest in a small business is like eating foods rich in calcium for strong bones or eating fruits and vegetables for their vitamins.

But accumulating *bad debt* (consumer debt) by buying things like new living room furniture or a new car that you really can't afford is like living on a diet of sugar and caffeine: a quick fix with little nutritional value. Borrowing on your credit card to afford that vacation to Cabo is costly and detrimental to your long-term financial health.

In this chapter, I help you battle the increasing problem of consumer debt. Getting rid of your bad debts may be even more difficult than giving up the junk foods you love. But in the long run, you'll be glad you did; you'll be financially healthier and emotionally happier. And after you get rid of your high-cost consumer debts, make sure that you practice the best way to avoid future credit problems: *Don't borrow with bad debt.*

Before you decide which debt reduction strategies make sense for you, you first must consider your overall financial situation and assess your alternatives. (Strategies for reducing your current spending — which help you free up more cash to pay down your debts — are discussed in the next chapter.)

Using Savings to Reduce Your Debt

Many people build a psychological brick wall between their savings and investment accounts and their debt accounts. By failing to view their finances holistically, they simply fall into the habit of looking at these accounts individually. The thought of putting a door in that big brick wall doesn't occur to them.

Understanding how you gain

When you use savings to pay down debts, it may seem like you're losing money, but you're actually gaining money. Although your savings and investments may be earning decent returns, odds are that the interest you're paying on your consumer debts is higher.

Paying off consumer loans on a credit card at, say, 12 percent is like finding an investment with a guaranteed return of 12 percent — *tax-free*. You would actually need to find an investment that yielded even more — around 18 percent — to net 12 percent after paying taxes in order to justify not paying off your 12 percent loans. The higher your tax bracket (see Chapter 6), the higher the return you need on your investments to justify keeping high-interest consumer debt.

If you have the savings to pay off high-interest credit card and auto loans, do so. Sure, you diminish your savings, but you also reduce your debts. You benefit financially because the interest on your savings is far less than the interest accruing on your consumer debt. Make sure you pay off the loans with the highest interest rates first.

Even if you think that you're an investment genius and you can earn more on your investments, swallow your ego and pay down your consumer debts anyway. In order to chase that higher potential return from investments, you need to take substantial risk. You *may* earn more investing in that hot stock tip or that bargain real estate located on a toxic waste site, but more than likely, you won't.

If you use your accessible savings to pay down consumer debts, be careful to leave yourself enough of an emergency cushion. (In Chapter 2, I tell you how to determine how large of an emergency reserve you should have.) You want to be in a position to withstand an unexpected large expense or temporary loss of income. On the other hand, if you use savings to pay down credit card debt, you can run your credit card balances back up in a financial pinch (unless your card gets canceled), or you can turn to a family member or wealthy friend for a low-interest loan.

Discovering money to pay down consumer debts

Have you ever reached into the pocket of an old winter parka and found a rolled-up $20 bill you forgot you had? Stumbling across some forgotten funds is always a pleasant experience. But before you root through all your closets in search of stray cash to help you pay down that nagging credit card debt, check out some of these financial jacket pockets you may have overlooked:

- ✔ **Borrow against your cash value life insurance policy.** If you were approached by a life insurance agent, he or she probably sold you a cash value policy because it pays high commissions to insurance agents. Or perhaps your parents bought one of these policies for you when you were a little gremlin. Borrow against the cash value to pay down your debts. (*Note:* You may want to consider discontinuing your cash value policy altogether — see Chapter 15 for more details.)

- ✔ **Sell investments held outside of retirement accounts.** Maybe you have some shares of stock or a Treasury bond gathering dust in your safety deposit box. Consider cashing in these investments to pay down your loan balances. Just be sure to consider the tax consequences of selling these investments. If possible, only sell those investments that won't generate a big tax bill.

- ✔ **Borrow against the equity in your home.** If you're a homeowner, you may be able to tap into your home's *equity,* which is the difference between the property's market value and outstanding loan balance. You can generally borrow against real estate at a lower interest rate and get a tax deduction to boot.

- ✔ **Borrow against your employer's retirement account.** Check with your employer's benefits department to see if you can borrow against your retirement account balance. The interest rate is usually reasonable. Be careful, though — if you leave your job (or if you're asked to leave), you'll have to repay the loan within only 60 days. Also recognize that you'll miss out on investment returns on the money borrowed.

- ✔ **Borrow from friends and family.** They know you, love you, realize your shortcomings, and — heck — probably won't be as cold-hearted as some bankers I know. Money borrowed from family members can have strings attached, of course. Treating the obligation seriously is important. To avoid misunderstandings, write up a simple agreement listing the terms and conditions of the loan. Unless your family members are like the worst bankers I know, you'll probably get a fair interest rate, and your family will have the satisfaction of helping you out — just don't forget to pay them back.

Decreasing Debt When You Lack Savings

If you lack savings to throw at your consumer debts, not surprisingly, you have some work to do. If you're currently spending all your income (and more!), you need to figure out how you can decrease your spending (see Chapter 5 for lots of great ideas) and/or increase your income. In the meantime, you need to slow the growth of your debt.

Transferring balances to lower-interest-rate credit cards

Different credit cards charge different interest rates. Why in the world should you pay 14, 16, or 18 percent (or more) when you can pay less? The credit card business has become quite competitive. Gone are the days where all banks charge 18 percent or more for VISA and MasterCard.

Until you get your debt paid off, make it more difficult for your debt to grow. You may be able to slow the growth of your debt by reducing the interest rate you're paying. Here are sound ways to do that:

- **Apply for a lower-rate credit card.** If you're earning a decent income, you're not too burdened with debt, and you have a clean credit record, qualifying for lower-rate cards is relatively painless. Some persistence (and clean-up work) may be required if you have income and debt problems or nicks in your credit report. After you're approved for a new, lower-interest-rate credit card, you can simply transfer your outstanding balance from your higher-rate card.

   Among the banks with consistently low-interest-rate credit cards, I like AFBA Industrial Bank (800-776-2265), which offers a no-annual-fee card with a 4.9 percent interest rate. (**Note:** After the introductory period, the future interest rate is set at a minimum of 11.4 percent, but it can be higher — the rate is determined by adding 2.9 percent to the so-called prime interest rate.)

- **Call the bank(s) that issued your current high-interest-rate credit card(s) and say that you want to cancel your card(s) because you found a competitor that offers no annual fee and a lower interest rate.** Your bank may choose to match the terms of the "competitor" rather than lose you as a customer.

- **While you're paying down your credit card balance(s), stop making new charges on cards that have outstanding balances.** Many people don't realize that interest starts to accumulate *immediately* when they carry a balance. *You have no grace period* — the 20-odd days you normally have to pay your balance in full without incurring interest charges — if you carry a credit card balance month to month.

1.9 percent interest rate credit cards!

Avoid getting lured into applying for a credit card that hypes an extremely low interest rate. One such card advertises a 1.9 percent rate, but you have to dig into the fine print for the rest of the story.

First, any card that offers such a low interest rate will only honor that rate for a short period of time — in this case, six months. After six months, the interest rate skyrockets to nearly 15 percent.

But wait, there's more. Make just one late payment or exceed your credit limit, and the company raises your interest rate to 19.8 percent and slaps you with a $29 fee for each such infraction. If you want a cash advance on your card, you get socked with a fee equal to 3 percent of the amount advanced. (During the economic slowdown in the early 2000s, some banks were even advertising 0 percent interest rates — although that rate generally applied only to balances transferred from another card, and such cards were subject to all of the other vagaries discussed in this sidebar.)

Now I'm not saying that everyone should avoid this type of card. Such a card may make sense for you if you want to transfer an outstanding balance and then pay off that balance within a matter of months, cancel the card, and avoid getting socked with the high fees on the card.

If you hunt around for a low-interest-rate credit card, be sure to check out all the terms and conditions. Start by reviewing the uniform rates and terms disclosure, which details the myriad fees and conditions. Also, be sure that you understand how the future interest rate is determined on cards that charge variable interest rates.

Cutting up your credit cards

If you have a pattern of living beyond your means by buying on credit, get rid of the culprit — the credit card, that is. To kick the habit, a smoker needs to toss *all* the cigarettes, and an alcoholic needs to get rid of *all* the booze. Cut up *all* of your credit cards and call the issuers of the cards to cancel your accounts. And when you buy consumer items such as cars and furniture, do not apply for E-Z credit.

The world worked fine back in the years B.C. (Before Credit). Think about it: Just a couple of generations ago, credit cards didn't even exist. People paid with cash and checks — imagine that! You *can* function without buying anything on a credit card. In certain cases, you may need a card as collateral — like when you rent a car. When you bring back the rental car, however, you can pay with cash or check. Leave the card at home in the back of your sock drawer or freezer, and pull (or thaw) it out only for the occasional car rental.

If you can trust yourself, keep a separate credit card *only* for new purchases that you know you can absolutely pay in full each month. No one needs three, five, or ten credit cards! You can live with one (and actually none), given the wide acceptance of most cards. Count 'em up, including retail store and gas cards, and get rid of 'em. Retailers such as department stores and gas stations just love to give you their cards. Not only do these cards charge outrageously high interest rates but they also duplicate VISA and MasterCard. Virtually all retailers accept VISA and MasterCard. More credit lines mean more temptation to spend what you can't afford.

If you decide to keep one widely accepted credit card instead of getting rid of them all, be careful. You may be tempted to let debt accumulate and roll over for a month or two, starting up the whole horrible process of running up your consumer debt again. Rather than keeping one credit card, consider getting a debit card.

Discovering debit cards: The best of both worlds

Credit cards are the main reason today's consumers are buying more than they can afford. So logic says that one way you can keep your spending in check is to stop using your credit cards. But in a society that's used to flashing the widely accepted VISA and MasterCard plastic for purchases, changing habits is hard. And you may be legitimately concerned that carrying your checkbook or cash can be a hassle or costly if you're mugged.

Debit cards truly offer the best of both worlds. The beauty of the debit card is that it offers you the convenience of making purchases with a piece of plastic without the temptation or ability to run up credit card debt. Debit cards keep you from spending money you don't have and help you live within your means.

A debit card looks just like a credit card with either the VISA or MasterCard logo. The big difference between debit cards and credit cards is that, as with checks, debit card purchase amounts are deducted electronically from your checking account within days. (Bank ATM cards are also debit cards; however, if they lack a VISA or MasterCard logo, bank ATM cards are accepted by far fewer merchants.)

If you switch to a debit card, and you keep your checking account balance low and don't ordinarily balance your checkbook, you may need to start balancing it. Otherwise, you may face unnecessary bounced check charges.

Here are some other differences between debit and credit cards:

- If you pay your credit card bill in full and on time each month, your credit card gives you free use of the money you owe until it's time to pay the bill; debit cards take the money out of your checking account almost immediately. (Note that some credit cards charge a fee even if you pay your balance in full each month. You didn't think the banks would let you use the float forever, did you?)

✔ Credit cards make it easier for you to dispute charges for problematic merchandise through the issuing bank. Most banks allow you to dispute charges for up to 60 days after purchase and will credit the disputed amount to your account pending resolution. Most debit cards offer a much shorter window, typically less than one week, for making disputes.

Because moving your checking account can be a hassle, see if your current bank offers VISA or MasterCard debit cards. If your bank does not offer one, shop among the major banks in your area, which are more likely to offer the cards. Because such cards come with checking accounts, make sure that you do some comparison shopping between the different account features and fees.

A number of investment firms offer VISA or MasterCard debit cards with their asset management accounts. These investment firm "checking accounts" not only can help you break the credit card overspending habit but they may also get you thinking about saving and investing your money. One drawback of these accounts is that most of them require fairly hefty minimum initial investment amounts — typically $5,000 to $10,000. Among brokerages with competitive investment offerings and prices are TD Waterhouse (800-934-4448; www.tdwaterhouse.com), Vanguard (800-992-8327; www.vanguard.com), and Muriel Siebert (800-872-0711; www.siebertnet.com).

Filing Bankruptcy

For consumers in over their heads, the realization that their monthly income is increasingly exceeded by their bill payments is usually a traumatic one. In many cases, years can pass before drastic measures like filing bankruptcy are considered. Both financial and emotional issues come into play in one of the most difficult and painful, yet potentially beneficial, decisions.

When Helen, a mother of two and a sales representative, contacted attorney Harry Orr, her total credit card debt equaled her annual gross income. As a result of her crushing debt load, she could not meet her minimum monthly credit card payments. Rent and food gobbled up most of her earnings. What little was left over went to the squeakiest wheel.

Creditors were breathing down Helen's back. "I started getting calls from collection departments at home and work — it was embarrassing," relates Helen. Helen's case is typical in that credit card debt was the prime cause of her bankruptcy. "If credit card debt didn't exist, I wouldn't have a job," says bankruptcy attorney Harry Orr.

Helen's case is typical in other regards. Her debt accumulated over a number of years. Helen, a former homeowner with a Master's degree from a prestigious university, had good credit until a couple of years before. After getting a divorce, Helen rented an apartment with her two children while holding down a job. Unfortunately, she was laid off when her employer encountered tough times.

At first, bills to her dentist and doctor went unpaid. When Helen went into business for herself, she used her credit cards for office furniture and other start-up expenses. "I would have done more corner cutting, but the credit cards were easily available cash and allowed me to think in terms of monthly payments," says Helen.

As the debt load grew (partly exacerbated by the high interest rates on the cards), more and more purchases got charged — from the kids' clothing to repairs for the car. Finally, after running out of cash, she had to take a large cash advance on her credit cards to pay for rent and food.

Despite trying to work out lower monthly payments to keep everyone happy, most of the banks to which Helen owed money were inflexible. "When I asked one bank's VISA department if it preferred that I declare bankruptcy because it was unwilling to lower my monthly payment, the representative said yes," Helen says. After running out of options, Helen filed personal bankruptcy.

Understanding bankruptcy benefits

Every year, about 1.5 million American households (that's about 1 in every 80 households) file personal bankruptcy.

With bankruptcy, certain types of debts can be completely eliminated or *discharged*. Debts that typically can be discharged include credit card, medical, auto, utilities, and rent. Debts that may *not* be canceled generally include child support, alimony, student loans, taxes, and court-ordered damages (for example, drunk driving settlements). Helen was an ideal candidate for bankruptcy because her debts (credit cards) were dischargeable.

Helen also met another important criterion — her level of high-interest consumer debt relative to her annual income was high (100 percent). When this ratio (discussed in Chapter 1) exceeds more than 25 percent, filing bankruptcy may be your best option.

Eliminating your debt also allows you to start working toward your financial goals. Depending on the amount of debt you have outstanding relative to your income, you may need a decade or more to pay it all off. In Helen's case, at the age of 48, she had no money saved for retirement, and she was increasingly unable to spend money on her children.

What you can keep if you file bankruptcy

In every state, you can retain certain property and assets when you file for bankruptcy. You may be surprised to discover that in some states, you can keep your home regardless of its value! Most states, though, allow you to protect a certain amount of home equity.

Additionally, you're allowed to retain some other types and amounts of personal property and assets. For example, most states allow you to retain household furnishings, clothing, pensions, and money in retirement accounts. So don't empty your retirement accounts or sell off personal possessions to pay debts unless you're absolutely sure that you won't be filing bankruptcy.

Filing bankruptcy offers not only financial benefits but emotional benefits, as well. "I was horrified at filing, but it is good to be rid of the debts and collection calls — I should have filed six months earlier. I was constantly worried. When I saw homeless families come to the soup kitchen where I sometimes volunteer, I thought that someday that could be me and my kids," said Helen.

Coming to terms with bankruptcy drawbacks

Filing bankruptcy, needless to say, has a number of drawbacks. First, bankruptcy appears on your credit report for up to ten years, so you will have difficulty obtaining credit, especially in the years immediately following your filing.

However, if you already have problems on your credit report (because of late payments or a failure to pay previous debts), the damage has already been done. And, without savings, you're probably not going to be making major purchases (such as a home) in the next several years anyway.

If you do file bankruptcy, getting credit in the future is still possible. You may be able to obtain a *secured credit card,* which requires you to deposit money in a bank account equal to the credit limit on your credit card. Of course, as I advocate earlier in this chapter, you'll be better off without the temptation of any credit cards and better served with a debit card. Also know that if you can hold down a stable job, most creditors will be willing to give you loans within a few years of your filing bankruptcy. Almost all lenders ignore bankruptcy after five to seven years.

Biased advice at CCCS

Every year, hundreds of thousands of debt-burdened consumers seek "counseling" from the more than 1,000 Consumer Credit Counseling Service (CCCS) offices. Unfortunately, people like Leona Davis find that the service doesn't always work the way it is pitched.

Davis, whose family racked up significant debt due largely to unexpected medical expenses and a reduction in her income, found herself in trouble with too much debt. So she turned to CCCS, which she heard about through its advertising and marketing materials.

CCCS markets itself as a "nonprofit community service." Davis, like many others I know who have used CCCS, found that the "service" was not objective. After her experience with CCCS, Davis feels that a more appropriate name for this organization would be the Credit Card Collection Agency.

Unbeknownst to Davis and most of the other people who use CCCS is the fact that about 85 percent of CCCS's funding comes from the fees that creditors pay. CCCS collects fees on a commission basis — just as collection agencies do!

CCCS's strategy is to place those who come in for help on their "debt management program." Under this program, counselees like Davis agree to pay a certain amount per month to CCCS, which in turn parcels out the money to the various creditors. The debt management program usually ignores other non-credit-card debts that the counselees may have: in Davis's case, a mortgage and outstanding medical bills.

Because of Davis's tremendous outstanding consumer debt (it exceeded her annual income) and the fact that she didn't receive budgeting help from CCCS to plan her current expenses, her repayment plan was doomed to failure.

Davis managed to make 10 months' worth of payments, largely because she raided a retirement account for $28,000. Unfortunately, Davis was never told by CCCS that if she filed bankruptcy (which she ultimately needed to do), she would be able to keep her retirement money.

But Davis's CCCS counselor never discussed the bankruptcy option. "I received no counseling. Real counselors take the time to understand your situation and offer options. I was offered one solution, a forced payment plan," says Davis.

Others who have consulted CCCS, including one of my research assistants who, undercover, visited a CCCS office to seek advice, confirm that CCCS has a cookie-cutter approach to dealing with debt. CCCS typically recommends that debtors go on a repayment plan that has the consumer pay 3 percent of each outstanding loan balance to CCCS, which in turn pays the money to creditors.

Unable to keep up with the enormous monthly payments, Davis finally turned to an attorney and filed for bankruptcy — but not before she had unnecessarily lost thousands of dollars because of CCCS's one-sided approach to debt problems.

Although CCCS's promotional materials and counselors aren't shy about highlighting the drawbacks to bankruptcy, CCCS's counselors are reluctant to discuss the negative impact of signing up for a CCCS debt payment plan. Davis's CCCS counselor never told her that restructuring her credit card payments would tarnish her credit report. The counselor my researcher met with also neglected to mention this important fact. When asked, the counselor was evasive about the debt "management" program's impact on his credit report.

Another drawback of bankruptcy is that it costs money. I know this seems terribly unfair. You're already in financial trouble — that's why you're filing bankruptcy! Nevertheless, filing bankruptcy may set you back anywhere from several hundred dollars to $1,000 in court filing and legal fees.

And, finally, most people find that filing bankruptcy causes emotional stress. Admitting that your personal income can't keep pace with your debt obligations is a painful thing to do. Although filing bankruptcy clears the decks of debt and gives you a fresh financial start, feeling a profound sense of failure (and sometimes shame) is common. Despite the increasing incidence of bankruptcy, bankruptcy filers are reluctant to talk about it with others, including family and friends.

Another part of the emotional side of filing bankruptcy is that you must open your personal financial affairs to court scrutiny and court control during the several months it takes to administer a bankruptcy. A court-appointed bankruptcy trustee oversees your case and tries to recover as much of your property as possible to satisfy the *creditors* — those to whom you owe money.

Some people also feel that they're shirking responsibility by filing for bankruptcy. One client I worked with should have filed, but she couldn't bring herself to do it. She said, "I spent that money, and it's my responsibility to pay it back."

Most banks make gobs and gobs of money from their credit card businesses. As a former consultant who worked in the industry, I can tell you that credit cards are one of the most profitable lines of business for banks. If you don't believe me, consider that, at a banking conference sponsored by the investment bank Salomon Brothers, CEO John Reed referred to the credit card business for banks as a "high-return, low-risk" business. Now you know why your mailbox is always filled with solicitations for more cards.

So if you file for bankruptcy, don't feel bad about not paying back the bank. The nice merchants from whom you bought the merchandise have already been paid. *Charge-offs* — the banker's term for taking the loss on debt that you discharge through bankruptcy — are the banker's cost, which is another reason why the interest rate is so high on credit cards, and why you shouldn't borrow on credit cards.

Choosing between Chapter 7 and 13

You can file one of two forms of personal bankruptcy:

- ✔ **Chapter 7** allows you to discharge or cancel certain debts. Chapter 7 bankruptcy makes the most sense when you have significant debts that you're legally allowed to cancel. (See "Understanding bankruptcy benefits," earlier in this chapter, for details on which debts can be canceled, or discharged.)

- ✔ **Chapter 13** comes up with a repayment schedule that requires you to pay your debts over several years. Chapter 13 stays on your credit record (just like Chapter 7), *but it doesn't eliminate debt,* so its value is limited — usually to dealing with debts like taxes that can't be discharged through bankruptcy. Chapter 13 can keep creditors at bay until a repayment schedule is worked out in the courts.

Seeking bankruptcy advice

Be careful where you get advice about whether to file for bankruptcy. Many people make the mistake of turning to and solely trusting bankruptcy attorneys or Consumer Credit Counseling Services (CCCS).

Attorneys who earn a legal fee from bankruptcy filings have a conflict of interest. All things being equal, bankruptcy attorneys are inclined to — you guessed it — *recommend bankruptcy,* because it generates their fees.

Hiring a bankruptcy attorney makes sense when you have major assets (such as a home) to protect. Attorney fees can easily exceed anywhere from several hundred dollars to over $1,000 for complicated cases.

CCCS faces the opposite conflict. CCCS describes itself as a nonprofit educational service that helps consumers who are in debt. Although it's true that CCCS has some well-intentioned employees, it's also true that CCCS is funded by credit-card issuers. Therefore, CCCS counselors aren't likely to recommend bankruptcy. (See the "Biased advice at CCCS" sidebar for more info about CCCS biases.)

If you want to find out more about the pros, cons, and details of filing for bankruptcy, pick up a copy of *Bankruptcy: Is It the Right Solution to Your Debt Problems?* by Robin Leonard (Nolo Press). If you're comfortable with your decision to file, and you think that you can complete the paperwork, you may be able to do it yourself. *How to File for Chapter 7 Bankruptcy,* by attorneys Elias, Renauer, Leonard, and Michon (Nolo Press), comes with all the necessary filing forms. Hiring a paralegal typing service to prepare the forms, which can be a cost-effective way to get help with the process if you don't need heavy-duty legal advice, is an intermediate approach. To find a paralegal typing service in your area, check your local yellow pages under "Paralegals."

Ending the Spending-and-Debting Cycle

Regardless of how you deal with paying off your debt, you're in real danger of falling back into old habits. Backsliding happens not only to people who file bankruptcy but also to those who use savings or home equity to eliminate their debt. This section speaks to that risk and tells you what to do about it.

Resisting the credit temptation

Getting out of debt can be challenging, but I have confidence that you can do it with this book by your side and me as your guide. In addition to the ideas I discuss earlier in this chapter (such as eliminating all your credit cards and getting a debit card), the following list provides some additional tactics you can use to limit the influence credit cards hold over your life:

- **Reduce your credit limit.** If you're not going to take the advice I give you earlier in this chapter and get rid of all of your credit cards or secure a debit card, be sure to keep a lid on your credit card's credit limit (the maximum balance allowed on your card). Just because your bank keeps raising your credit limit to reward you for being such a profitable customer, you don't have to accept the increase. Call your credit-card service's toll-free phone number and lower your credit limit to a level you're comfortable with.

- **Replace your credit card with a charge card.** A *charge card* (such as the American Express Card) requires you to pay your balance in full each billing period. You have no credit line or interest charges. Of course, spending more than you can afford to pay when the bill comes due is possible. But you'll be much less likely to overspend if you know you have to pay in full monthly.

- **Never buy on credit anything that depreciates in value.** Meals out, cars, clothing, and shoes all depreciate in value. Never buy these things on credit. Borrow money only for sound investments — education, real estate, or your own business, for example.

- **Think in terms of total cost.** Everything sounds cheaper in terms of monthly payments — that's how salespeople entice you into buying things you can't afford. Take a calculator along, if necessary, to tally up the sticker price, interest charges, and upkeep. The total cost will scare you. *It should.*

✔ **Stop the junk mail avalanche.** Look at your daily mail — I bet half of it is solicitations and mail-order catalogs. You can save some trees and time sorting junk mail by removing yourself from most mailing lists. To remove your name from mailing lists, write to the Direct Marketing Association, Mail Preference Service, P.O. Box 282, Carmel, NY 10512 (you can register through their Web site at `www.dmaconsumers.org/consumerassistance.html`, but you have to pay a $5 fee to do so). To remove your name from the major credit reporting agency lists that are used by credit card solicitation companies, call 888-567-8688. Also, be sure to tell any credit card companies you keep cards with that you want your account marked to indicate that you do not wish to have any of your personal information shared with telemarketing firms.

✔ **Limit what you can spend.** Go shopping with a small amount of cash and no plastic or checks. That way, you can only spend what little cash you have with you!

Identifying and treating an addiction

No matter how hard they try to break the habit, some people become addicted to spending and accumulating debt. It becomes a chronic problem that starts to interfere with other aspects of their lives. Financial problems can lead to problems at work and with family and friends.

Debtors Anonymous (DA), which was officially started in 1976, is a nonprofit organization that provides support (primarily through group meetings) to people trying to break their debt accumulation and spending habits. DA is modeled after the 12-step Alcoholics Anonymous (AA) program.

Like AA, Debtors Anonymous works with people from all walks of life and socioeconomic backgrounds. You can find people who are financially on the edge, $100,000-plus income earners, and everybody in between at DA meetings. Even former millionaires join the program.

DA has a simple questionnaire that helps determine whether you're a problem debtor. If you answer "yes" to at least 8 of the following 15 questions, you may be developing or already have a compulsive spending and debt accumulation habit:

1. Are your debts making your home life unhappy?

2. Does the pressure of your debts distract you from your daily work?

3. Are your debts affecting your reputation?

4. Do your debts cause you to think less of yourself?

5. Have you ever given false information in order to obtain credit?

6. Have you ever made unrealistic promises to your creditors?

7. Does the pressure of your debts make you careless when it comes to the welfare of your family?

8. Do you ever fear that your employer, family, or friends will learn the extent of your total indebtedness?

9. When faced with a difficult financial situation, does the prospect of borrowing give you an inordinate feeling of relief?

10. Does the pressure of your debts cause you to have difficulty sleeping?

11. Has the pressure of your debts ever caused you to consider getting drunk?

12. Have you ever borrowed money without giving adequate consideration to the rate of interest you're required to pay?

13. Do you usually expect a negative response when you're subject to a credit investigation?

14. Have you ever developed a strict regimen for paying off your debts, only to break it under pressure?

15. Do you justify your debts by telling yourself that you are superior to the "other" people, and when you get your "break," you'll be out of debt?

To find a Debtors Anonymous (DA) support group in your area, check your local phone directory (in the "Business" section) or visit the DA Website at www.debtorsanonymous.org. You can write to DA's national headquarters for meeting locations in your area and a literature order form at the following address: Debtors Anonymous General Service Office, P.O. Box 920888, Needham, MA 02492-0009. You can also contact the DA's national headquarters by phone at 781-453-2743.

Dealing with Credit Mistakes

You may not know it (or care), but you probably have a personal credit report. Creditors generally examine your credit report before granting you a loan or credit line.

Many people don't realize that they have a blemish on their credit report until they are turned down for a loan or questioned by the creditor about the glitch. For example, when I applied for my first mortgage, I discovered a minor wart on my own credit report.

Although dealing with credit report problems takes up some of your time, it isn't difficult if you know what to do and what not to do.

Obtaining a copy of your credit report

If you're turned down for rental housing, employment, or a loan because of derogatory information on your credit report, most states require the prospective lender or the credit reporting bureaus to give you a copy of the report.

If you're applying for a mortgage or other major loan, most lenders will give you a copy of your credit report if you simply ask. And why shouldn't they if you're paying them to obtain the copy!

Reading a credit report is a challenge, given all the abbreviations and jargon, so I recommend that, in addition to getting the report, you ask the lender what specific information on the report led to the denial of credit.

Getting others to correct their mistakes

If you obtain your credit report and find a boo-boo on it that you don't recognize as being your mistake or fault, do *not* assume that the information is correct. Credit reporting bureaus and the creditors who report credit information to these bureaus often make mistakes.

You hope and expect that, if a credit bureau has negative and incorrect information in your credit report and you bring the error to their attention, they will graciously and expeditiously fix the mistake. If you believe that, you're the world's greatest optimist; perhaps you also believe that you won't have to wait in line at the department of motor vehicles, post office, or your local bank at noon on payday.

"Credit repair" firms

On late-night television and in the backs of newspapers and magazines, you may see ads for credit repair companies that claim to fix your credit report problems. In the worst cases I've seen, these firms charge outrageous amounts of money and don't come close to fulfilling their marketing hype.

If you have legitimate glitches on your credit report, credit repair firms can't make the glitches disappear. Hope springs eternal, however — some people would like to believe that their credit problems can be fixed.

Remember — if your problems are fixable, you can fix them yourself, and you don't need to pay a company big bucks to do it.

Odds are you're going to have to make some phone calls or write a letter or two to fix the problems on your credit report. Here's how most errors that aren't your fault are corrected:

✔ **The credit problem is someone else's.** A surprising number of personal credit report glitches are the result of someone else's negative information getting on your credit report. If the bad information on your report is completely foreign-looking to you, tell the credit bureau and explain that you need more information because you don't recognize the creditor.

✔ **The creditor made a mistake.** Creditors make mistakes, too. You need to write or call the creditor to get them to correct the erroneous information that they sent to the credit bureau. Phoning first usually works best. (The credit bureau should be able to tell you how to reach the creditor if you don't know how.) If necessary, follow up with a letter.

Whether you speak with a credit bureau or an actual lender, make notes of your conversations. If representatives say that they can fix the problem, get their names and extensions and follow up with them if they don't deliver as promised. If you're ensnared in bureaucratic red tape, escalate the situation by speaking with a department manager. By law, bureaus are required to respond to a request to fix a credit error within 30 days — hold the bureau accountable!

Telling your side of the story

With a minor credit infraction, some lenders may simply ask for an explanation. I had a credit report glitch that was the result of being away for several weeks and missing the payment due date for a couple of small bills. When my proposed mortgage lender saw my late payments, all I had to do was provide a written explanation.

You and a creditor may not see eye to eye on a problem, and the creditor may refuse to budge. If that's the case, credit bureaus are required by law to allow you to add a 100-word explanation to your credit file.

Chapter 5

Reducing Your Spending

• •

In This Chapter

▶ The keys to successful spending

▶ Proven techniques for reducing your spending

• •

I know a highly paid professional man (whom I'll call Bart) who lived in one of the most prestigious communities in America. He owned his own business, drove top-of-the-line cars outfitted with all the latest toys and gadgets, and belonged to the most expensive country club in the area. The problem was, however, that he was a workaholic. In fact, he seemed to be a workaholic in order to support his spending habits. Over time, his wife tired of the life they were leading and filed for divorce. Bart called me for a consultation soon after his divorce was finalized. He looked beaten and depressed. He said that he needed help making some financial decisions, but what he appeared to need more than anything else was a good, long vacation and some personal counseling.

At the other end of the spending extreme was Justin, a young man in his mid-20s who, like Bart, was well-educated and intelligent. Justin lived a Spartan lifestyle even though he lived in the same costly metropolitan area as Bart. Justin took a leave from his work to sail partway around the world with some friends. He was passionate about music; he played in a band outside of work and found time to produce a CD. Justin spent little money, yet he was happy.

Too often, movies and the media portray people who make more money and have more toys as being happier and more powerful than people who don't have these things, but in my experience, I have come across far more Barts than Justins. In part because of his high income, Bart took no interest in learning how to spend smarter — as a result, he had little savings to show for all his earnings. Justin, by contrast, viewed spending well beneath his means as a welcome challenge and a means to an end. The better use he made of his money, the more freedom he felt he had.

No matter where you are or where you go today, you're bombarded with advertising and spending temptations. Therefore, I'm not surprised to find that so many people could spend their money more wisely than they currently do.

Telling people how and where to spend their money is a risky undertaking, because most people like to spend money and hate to be told what to do. You'll be glad to hear that I'm *not* going to tell you exactly where you must cut your spending. I'm simply going to give you numerous strategies that have worked for other people. The final decision for what to cut rests solely with you. Only you can decide what's important to you and what's dispensable — should you cut out your weekly poker games, or cut back on your shoe collection?

I assume throughout these recommendations that you value your time. Therefore, I'm not going to tell you to scrimp and save by doing things like cutting open a tube of toothpaste so that you can use every last bit of it. And I won't tell you to have your spouse do your ironing to reduce your dry-cleaning bills — no point in having extra money in the bank if your significant other walks out on you!

The fact that you're busy all the time may be part of the reason why you spend money the way you do. Therefore, the recommendations in this chapter focus on methods that produce significant savings but don't involve a lot of time. In other words, these strategies provide bang for the buck.

Finding the Keys to Successful Spending

For most people, spending money is a whole lot easier and more fun than earning it. Far be it from me to tell you to stop having fun and turn into a penny-pinching, stay-at-home miser. Of course you can spend money. But there's a world of difference between spending money *carelessly* and spending money *wisely.*

If you spend too much and spend unwisely, you put pressure on your income and your future need to continue working. Savings dwindle, debts may accumulate, and you can't achieve your financial goals.

If you dive into details too quickly, you may miss the big picture. So before I jump into the specific areas where you can trim your budget, I give you my four overall keys to successful spending. These four principles run through most of the recommendations I provide in this chapter.

Living within your means

Spending too much is a *relative* problem. Two people can each spend $40,000 per year yet still have drastically different financial circumstances. How? Suppose that one of them earns $50,000 annually, while the other makes $35,000. The $50,000 income earner saves $10,000 each year. The $35,000 wage earner, on the other hand, accumulates $5,000 of new debt (or spends that amount from prior savings). Spend within your means.

Don't let the spending habits of others dictate your spending habits. Certain people — and you know who they are — bring out the big spender in you. Do something else with them besides shopping and spending. If you can't find any other activity to share with them, try shopping with limited cash and no credit cards. That way, you can't overspend on impulse.

How much you can safely spend while still working toward your financial goals depends on what your goals are and where you are financially. Chapter 2 assists you with figuring how much you should be saving and what you can afford to spend to accomplish your financial goals.

Looking for the best values

You can find high quality and low cost in the same product. Conversely, paying a high price is no guarantee that you're getting high quality. Cars are a good example. Whether you're buying a subcompact, a sports car, or a luxury four-door sedan, some cars are more fuel-efficient and cheaper to maintain than rivals that carry the same sticker price.

When you evaluate the cost of a product or service, you need to think in terms of total, long-term costs. Suppose that you're comparing the purchase of two used cars: the Solid Sedan, which costs $11,995, and the Clunker Convertible, which weighs in at $9,995. On the surface, the convertible appears to be cheaper. However, the price that you pay for a car is but a small portion of what that car ultimately costs you. If the convertible is costly to operate, maintain, and insure over the years, it could end up costing you much more than the sedan would have. Sometimes paying more upfront for a higher-quality product or service ends up saving you money in the long run.

People who sell particular products and services may initially appear to have your best interests at heart when they steer you toward buying something that isn't costly. However, you may be in for a rude awakening when you discover the ongoing service, maintenance, and other fees you face in the years ahead. Salespeople are generally trained to pitch you a lower-cost product if you indicate that's what you're after.

I urge you to be especially careful when you shop on the Internet for the supposed purpose of saving money. You won't have much difficulty finding relatively low advertised prices on the Internet. However, many people overlook shipping costs, the cost of their computer equipment, and monthly Internet service fees when weighing how great a deal they're really getting online. Also, what about the possibility that you're not going to be happy with the product after it's delivered? You'll probably be stuck with paying the shipping costs back to the online retailer, which you hope is still in business, not to mention the hassle and inconvenience of returning the product.

Don't waste money on brand names

You don't want to compromise on quality, especially in the areas where quality is important to you. But you also don't want to be duped into believing that brand-name products are better or worth a substantially higher price. Be suspicious of companies that spend gobs on image-oriented advertising. Why? Because heavy advertising costs many dollars, and, as a consumer of those companies' products and services, you pay for all that advertising.

All successful companies advertise their products. Advertising is cost-effective and good business if it brings in enough new business. But you need to consider the products and services and the claims that companies make.

Does a cola beverage really taste better if "It's the real thing" or "The choice of a new generation?" Consider all the silly labels and fluffy marketing of beers. Blind taste testing demonstrates little if any difference between the expensive brand name products and the cheaper, less heavily advertised ones.

Now, if you can't live without your Coca-Cola or Pepsi, and you think that these products are head and shoulders above the rest, drink them to your heart's content. But question the importance of the name and image of the products you buy. Companies spend a lot of money creating and cultivating an image, which has zero impact on how their products taste or perform.

Branding is used in many fields to sell overpriced, mediocre products and services to consumers. Take the lowly can of paint. Tests show some differences among different brands of paint. However, when you can buy high-quality paints for about $20 a gallon, do you really think that a $100 can of paint blessed with the name of Ralph Lauren or Martha Stewart is that much better?

D/L Laboratories, a testing firm, compared these $100-per-gallon snooty paints to $20-per-gallon high-quality alternatives and found little difference — or at least no difference that was worth paying for. In fact, one of the "gourmet" paints splattered more, had a less uniform sheen, didn't cover the surface as well, was more prone to run when applied, and emitted a high level of volatile organic compounds! Some other snooty brands didn't fare much better. As people in the trade can tell you (thanks to computer-based matching), if you find a particular color of paint you like in a highbrow line, match it in a high-quality but far less costly line.

Consumer Reports is a reputable publication that evaluates products and services based on quality and performance, not brand image. Consult it on major consumer purchases.

Getting your money back

Take a look around your home for items you never use. Odds are you have some (maybe even many). Returning such items to their retail origin can be cathartic; it also reduces your home's clutter and puts more money in your pocket.

Also, think about the last several times you bought a product or service and didn't get what was promised. What did you do about it? Most people do nothing and let the derelict company off the hook. Why? Here are some common explanations for this type of behavior:

- ✔ **Low standards.** We've come to expect shoddy service and merchandise because of the common lousy experiences we've had.

- ✔ **Conflict avoidance.** Most people shun confrontation. It makes us tense and anxious, and it churns our stomachs.

- ✔ **Hassle aversion.** Most companies don't make it easy for complainers to get their money back or obtain satisfaction. To get restitution from some companies, you need the tenacity and determination of a pit bull.

You can increase your odds of getting what you expect for your money by doing business with companies that

- ✔ **Have fair return policies.** Don't purchase any product or service until you understand the company's return policy. Be especially wary of buying from companies that either charge hefty "restocking" fees for returned merchandise or simply don't allow returns at all. Reputable companies offer full refunds and don't make you take store credit (although taking credit is fine if you're sure that you'll use it soon, and you're sure that the company will still be around).

- ✔ **Can provide good references.** Suppose that you're going to install a fence on your property, and, as a result, you're going to be speaking with fencing contractors for the first time. You can sift out many inferior firms by asking each contractor that you interview for at least three references from people in your local area who have had a fence installed in the past year or two.

- ✔ **Are committed to the type of product or service they provide.** Suppose that your chosen fencing contractor does a great job, and now that you're in the market for new gutters on your home, the contractor says that he does gutters, too. Although the path of least resistance would be for you to simply hire the same contractor for your gutters, you should inquire about how many gutters the contractor has installed and also interview some other firms that specialize in such work. Because your fencing contractor may have only done a handful of gutter jobs, he may not know as much about such work.

Following these guidelines can greatly diminish your chances of having unhappy outcomes with products or services you buy. And here's another important tip: Whenever possible, pay with a credit card. Doing so enables you to dispute a charge within 60 days and gives you more leverage for getting your money back.

Recognizing the Better Business Bureau's conflicts of interest

The Better Business Bureau (BBB) states that its mission is "to promote and foster the highest ethical relationship between businesses and the public." The reality of the typical consumer's experience of dealing with the BBB doesn't live up to the BBB's marketing.

"They don't go after local established businesses — they are funded by these same businesses. The BBB certainly has a good public relations image, better than what is warranted. They don't do all that much for consumers," says consumer advocate Ralph Nader.

"It's a business trade organization and each local BBB is basically independent like a franchise. By and large, when somebody has a problem with a company and they fill out a complaint form with the BBB, if the company is a member of the BBB, there's ample evidence that consumers often end up not being satisfied. The BBB protects their members," says John Bear, an author of consumer advocacy books, including *Send This Jerk the Bedbug Letter: How Companies, Politicians, and the Mass Media Deal With Complaints & How to Be a More Effective Complainer* (Ten Speed Press).

Particularly problematic among the BBB's pro-business practices are the company reports the BBB keeps on file. The BBB will consider a legitimate complaint satisfactorily resolved even though you're quite unhappy and the company is clearly not working to satisfy the problems for which it is responsible.

Bear also cites examples of some truly troubling BBB episodes. In one case, he says that a diploma mill company called Columbia State University was being run in Louisiana, and the business was a member of the local BBB. "When complaints started coming in, the BBB's response was always that the company met their standards and that the complaints were resolved. The reality was that the complaints weren't satisfactorily resolved and it took about two years until complaints reached into the hundreds for the BBB to finally cancel the diploma mill's membership and give out a bland statement about complaints. Two months later, the FBI raided the company. Millions of consumers' dollars were lost because the BBB didn't do its job," says Bear.

The President of a South Florida BBB (the fifth largest in the country, according to Bear) was ultimately imprisoned for taking bribes from companies in exchange for maintaining favorable reports on file.

The truth about the BBB is unfortunate, because as state consumer protection agencies are being cut back and dissatisfied consumers are being shunted to the BBB, more people are in for unsatisfactory experiences with an organization that does not go to bat for them.

If you find that you're not able to make progress when trying to get compensation for a lousy product or service, here's what I recommend that you do:

✔ **Document.** Taking notes whenever you talk to someone at a company can help you validate your case down the road, should problems develop. However, how realistic is it for any of us to take notes every time we buy a product or service? Obviously, the bigger the purchase and the more you have at stake, the more carefully you should document what you've been promised. In many cases, though, you probably won't start carefully noting each conversation until a conflict develops. Keep copies of companies' marketing literature, because such documents often make promises or claims that companies fail to live up to in practice.

✔ **Escalate.** Some front-line employees either aren't capable of resolving disputes or lack the authority to do so. No matter what the cause, speak with a department supervisor and continue escalating from there. If you're still not making progress, lodge a complaint to whatever state regulatory agency (if any) oversees such companies. Also, be sure to tell your friends and colleagues not to do business with the company (and let the company know that you're doing this until your complaint is resolved to your satisfaction). Also consider contacting a consumer help group — these groups are typically sponsored by broadcast or print media in metropolitan areas. They can be helpful in resolving disputes or shining adverse publicity on disreputable companies or products.

✔ **Litigate.** If all else fails, consider taking the matter to small claims court if the company continues to be unresponsive. (Depending on the amount of money at stake, this tactic may be worth your time.) The maximum dollar limit that you may recover varies by state, but you're usually limited to a few thousand dollars. For larger amounts than those allowed in small claims court in your state, you can, of course, hire an attorney and pursue the traditional legal channels — although you may end up throwing away more of your time and money. Mediation and arbitration are generally a better option than following through on a lawsuit.

Eliminating the fat from your spending

If you want to reduce your overall spending by, say, 10 percent, you can just cut all of your current expenditures by 10 percent. Or you can reach your 10-percent goal by cutting some categories a lot and others not at all. You need to set priorities and make choices about where you want and don't want to spend your money.

What you spend your money on is sometimes a matter of habit rather than a matter of what you really want or value. For example, some people shop at whatever stores are close to them; they never bother to look elsewhere.

Eliminating fat doesn't necessarily mean cutting back on your purchases. You save money by buying in bulk. Some stores specialize in selling larger packages or quantities of a product at a lower price, because they save money on the packaging and handling. And even though that 20-pound bag of rice means more cash upfront than the little box of Uncle Ben's, every meal that you make from the 20-pound bag will be a great deal cheaper than a meal out of the little box. (If you're single, shop with a friend and split the bulk purchases.)

Turning your back on consumer credit

As I discuss in Chapters 3 and 4, buying items that depreciate — such as cars, clothing, and vacations — on credit is hazardous to your long-term financial health. Buy only what you can afford today. If you're going to be forced to carry a debt for months or years on end, you can't really afford what you're buying on credit today.

Without a doubt, *renting-to-own* is the most expensive way to buy. Here's how it works. You see a huge ad blaring "$12.95 for a DVD player!"

Well, the ad has a big hitch: That's $12.95 per week, for many weeks. When all is said and done (and paid), buying a $200 DVD player through a rent-to-own store costs a typical buyer more than $750!

Welcome to the world of rent-to-own stores, which offer cash-poor consumers the ability to lease consumer items and, at the end of the lease, an option to buy.

If you think that paying an 18-percent interest rate on a credit card is expensive, consider this: The effective interest rate charged on many rent-to-own purchases exceeds 100 percent; in some cases, it may be 200 percent or more! Renting-to-own makes buying on a credit card look like a great deal.

I'm not sharing this information with you to encourage you to buy on credit cards, but to point out what a rip-off renting-to-own is. Such stores prey on cashless consumers who either can't get credit cards or don't understand how expensive renting-to-own really is.

Consumer credit is expensive, and it reinforces a bad financial habit: spending more than you can afford.

Reducing Your Spending: Eric's Strategies

As you read through the following strategies for reducing your spending, please keep in mind that some of these strategies will make sense for you and some of them won't. Start your spending reduction plan with the strategies that come easily. Work your way through them. Keep a list of the options that are more challenging for you — ones that may require more of a sacrifice but be workable if necessary to achieve your spending and savings goals.

TIP

Budgeting to save more money

When most people hear the word *budgeting,* they usually think unpleasant thoughts — and, like dieting, rightfully so. But budgeting can help you move from knowing how much you spend on various things to successfully reducing your spending.

The first step in the process of budgeting, or planning your future spending, is to analyze where your current spending is going (refer to Chapter 3). After you do that, calculate how much more you'd like to save each month. Then comes the hard part: deciding where to make cuts in your spending.

Suppose that you're currently not saving any of your monthly income, and you want to save 10 percent. If you can save and invest money through a tax-sheltered retirement account, such as an employer's 401(k) or 403(b), or a self-employed plan, such as an SEP-IRA or Keogh, you don't actually need to cut your spending by 10 percent to reach a savings goal of 10 percent (of your gross income).

When you contribute money to a tax-deductible retirement account, you reduce your federal and state taxes. If you're a moderate-income-earner paying, say, 35 percent in federal and state taxes on your marginal income, you actually only need

to reduce your spending by 6.5 percent to save 10 percent. The "other" 3.5 percent of the savings comes from the lowering of your taxes. (The higher your tax bracket, the less you need to cut your spending to reach a particular savings goal.)

So to boost your savings rate to 10 percent, go through your current spending category by category until you come up with enough proposed cuts to reduce your spending by 6.5 percent. Make your cuts in the areas that will be the least painful and where you're getting the least value from your current level of spending. (If you don't have access to a tax-deductible retirement account, budgeting still involves the same process or assessment and makes cuts in various spending categories.)

Another method of budgeting involves starting completely from scratch rather than examining your current expenses and making cuts from that starting point. Ask yourself how much you'd like to spend on different categories. The advantage of this approach is that it doesn't allow your current spending levels to constrain your thinking. You'll likely be amazed at the discrepancies between what you think you should be spending and what you actually are spending in certain categories.

No matter which of the ideas in this chapter you choose for yourself, rest assured that keeping your budget lean and mean pays enormous dividends. After you implement a spending reduction strategy, you'll reap the benefits for years to come. Take a look at Figure 5-1: For every $1,000 that you shave from your annual spending (that's just $83 per month), check out how much more money you'll have down the road. (This chart assumes that you invest your new-found savings in a tax-favored retirement account, you average 10 percent per year returns on your investments, and you're in a moderate combined federal and state tax bracket of 35 percent — see Chapter 6 for information on tax brackets.)

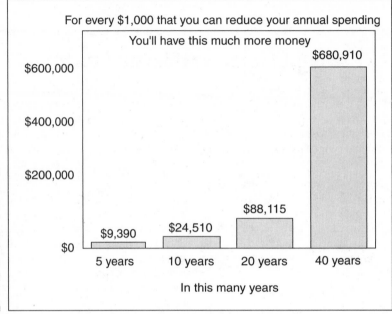

For every $1,000 that you can reduce your annual spending

You'll have this much more money

Figure 5-1:
Reducing your spending can yield large investment sums.

In this many years

Reducing food costs

Stopping eating is one way to reduce your food expenditures. However, this method tends to make you weak and dizzy, so it's probably not a viable long-term strategy. The following culinary strategies will keep you on your feet — and perhaps even improve your health — and help you save money.

Joining a wholesale superstore

Superstores such as Costco and Sam's Club enable you to buy groceries in bulk at wholesale prices. And, contrary to popular perception, you *don't* have to buy 1,000 rolls of toilet paper at once — just 24.

I performed price comparisons between wholesale superstores and retail grocery stores, and found that wholesalers charge about 30 to 40 percent less for the exact same stuff — all without the hassle of clipping coupons or hunting for which store has the best price on crackers this month! (At these discount prices, you only need to buy about $100 per year to recoup Costco and Sam's Club's membership fees, which start at $30 per year.)

In addition to saving you lots of money, buying in bulk requires fewer shopping trips. You'll have more supplies around your humble abode — so you'll have less need to eat out (which is costly) or make trips (wasted time and gasoline) to the local grocer, who may be really nice but charges the most.

Mom was right about eating those vegetables

Not only is meat expensive, but it's also coming under increasing scrutiny as being bad for your health. In a landmark report entitled "The Surgeon General's Report on Nutrition and Health" (produced under former U.S. Surgeon General C. Everett Koop, M.D.), reliance on a meat- and dairy-based diet — with its fat and cholesterol — was found to be the cause of the majority of premature deaths in the United States. In fact, five out of the top ten causes of death — heart disease, certain types of cancer, stroke, diabetes, and arteriosclerosis — are caused largely by Americans' poor diets.

In developing countries that are poorer economically than the United States, people eat mainly grains, beans, and vegetables, and have significantly lower rates of heart disease and diet-related cancers, such as cancer of the prostate and colon.

Meat is expensive, so the less meat you eat, the more money you save. Even if you choose to merely reduce your meat consumption rather than eliminate it, you can still save significant dough. If you decide to eliminate meat from your diet, make changes in your diet gradually. I gave up beef, pork, and lamb, but I still eat some chicken, fish, and low-fat dairy products.

Besides saving you money and bolstering your health, vegetarian diets are also friendlier to the environment. Raising cattle requires a great deal more land and water than does growing vegetables. Here's a tidbit sure to liven up a dull cocktail party conversation: Livestock also produce a great deal of flatulence, which adds more methane to the atmosphere. One-hundred-million tons of the world's annual methane emissions — 20 percent of the total — are from cattle!

Perishables run the risk of living up to their name, so don't buy what you can't use. Repackage bulk packs into smaller quantities and store them in the freezer if possible. If you're single, shop with a friend or two and split the order.

Be careful when you shop at the warehouse clubs — you may be tempted to buy things you don't really need. These stores carry all sorts of items, including wide-screen TVs, computers, furniture, clothing, complete sets of baseball cards, and giant canisters of M&Ms and biscotti — so beware! Try not to make impulse purchases, and be especially careful when you have kids in tow.

To find a superstore near you, check your local phone directory. You can also find a Costco store near you by visiting the Costco Web site at www.costco.com or calling 800-774-2678. Sam's Club is on the Internet at www.samsclub.com.

Eating out frugally

Eating meals out and getting takeout can be timesavers, but they rack up big bills if done too often and too lavishly. Eating out is a luxury — think of it as hiring someone to shop, cook, and clean up for you. Of course, some people either hate to cook or don't have the time, space, or energy to do much in the kitchen. If this sounds like you, choose restaurants carefully and order from the menu selectively. Here are a couple of tips for eating out:

- **Avoid beverages, especially alcohol.** Most restaurants make big profits on beverages. Drink water instead. (Water is healthy for you, and it reduces the likelihood that you'll want a nap after a big meal.)

- **Order vegetarian.** Vegetarian dishes generally cost less than meat-based entrees (and they're generally healthier for you).

I don't want to be a killjoy. I'm not saying that you should live on bread and water. You can have dessert — heck, have some wine, too! Just try not to eat dessert with every meal. Try eating appetizers and dessert at home, where they're a lot less expensive (especially if you follow my advice on shopping for food).

Saving on shelter

Housing and all the costs associated with it (utilities, furniture, appliances, and, if you're a homeowner, maintenance and repairs) can gobble a large chunk of your monthly income. I'm not suggesting that you live in an igloo or teepee (even though they're probably less costly), but people often overlook common opportunities to save money in this category.

Reducing rental costs

Rent can take up a sizable chunk of your monthly take-home pay. Many people consider rent to be a fixed and inflexible part of their expenses, but it's not. Here are some things you can do to cut down your rental costs:

- **Move to a lower-cost rental.** Of course, a lower-cost rental may not be as nice — it may be smaller, lack a private parking spot, or be located in a less popular area. Remember that the less you spend renting, the more you can save toward buying your own place. Just be sure to factor in all the costs of a new location, including the possible higher commuting costs.

- **Share a rental.** Living alone has some benefits, but financially speaking, it's a luxury. If you rent a larger place with roommates, your rental costs will go way down, and you'll get more home for your rental dollars. You have to be in a sharing mood, though. Roommates can be a hassle at times, but they can also be a plus — you get to meet all sorts of new people, and you have someone else to blame when the kitchen's a mess.

- **Negotiate your rental increases.** Every year, like clockwork, your landlord bumps up your rent by a certain percentage. If your local rental market is soft or your living quarters are deteriorating, stand up for yourself! You have more leverage and power than you probably realize. A smart landlord doesn't want to lose good tenants who pay rent on time. Filling vacancies takes time and money. State your case: You've been a responsible tenant, and your research shows comparable rentals going for less. Crying "poor" may help, too. At the very least, if you can't stave off the rent increase, maybe you can wrangle some improvements to the place.

✔ **Buy rather than rent.** Purchasing your own place can be costly, yes, but in the long run, owning should be cheaper than renting, and you'll have something to show for it in the end. If you purchase real estate with a 30-year fixed-rate mortgage, your mortgage payment (which is your biggest ownership expense) remains constant. Only your property taxes, maintenance, and insurance costs are exposed to the vagaries of inflation.

As a renter, your entire monthly housing cost can rise with increases in the cost of living (unless you're the beneficiary of a rent-controlled apartment). See Chapter 13 to find out how to buy real estate, even if you're short on cash.

Reducing homeowner expenses

As every homeowner knows, houses suck up money. You should be especially careful to watch your money in this area of your budget.

✔ **Know what you can afford.** Don't make the mistake of overspending when buying a home. Whether you're on the verge of buying your first home or trading up to a more costly property, crunch some realistic numbers before you jump. When too little money is left over for your other needs and wants — such as taking trips, eating out, enjoying hobbies, or saving for retirement — your new dream house may become a financial prison.

Calculate how much you can afford to spend monthly on a home by figuring your other needs first. (Doing the exercises in Chapter 3, about where you're spending your money, and Chapter 2, about saving for retirement, will help you calculate the amount you can afford.)

Although real estate can be a good long-term investment, you can end up pouring a large portion of your discretionary dollars into your home. In addition to decorating and remodeling, some people feel the need to trade up to a bigger home every few years. Of course, after they're in their new home, the remodeling and renovation cycle simply begins again, which costs even more money. Appreciate what you have, and remember that homes are for living in, not museums for display. If you have children, why waste a lot of money on expensive furnishings that take up valuable space and require you to constantly nag your kids to tread carefully? And don't covet — the world will always have people with bigger houses and more toys than you.

✔ **Rent out a room.** Because selling your home to buy a less expensive place can be a big hassle, consider taking in a tenant to reduce your housing expenses. Check out the renter thoroughly: Get references, run a credit report, and talk about ground rules and expectations before sharing your space. Don't forget to check with your insurance company to see whether your homeowner's policy needs adjustments to cover potential liability from renting.

✔ **Refinance your mortgage.** This step may seem like common sense, but surprisingly, many people don't keep up-to-date on mortgage rates. If interest rates are lower than they were when you obtained your current mortgage, you may be able to save money by refinancing (see Chapter 13 for more information).

✔ **Appeal your property-tax assessment.** If you bought your property during a period when housing prices were higher in your area than they are now, you may be able to save money by appealing your assessment. Also, if you live in a region of the country where your assessment is based upon how the local assessor valued the property (rather than what you paid for your home), your home may be over-assessed. Check with your local assessor's office for the appeals procedure you need to follow. You generally have to prove that your property is worth less today than it was when you bought it, or that the assessor incorrectly valued your property. In the first case, an appraiser's recent evaluation of your property will do — you may already have one if you refinanced your mortgage recently. In the latter case, review how the assessor valued your property compared with similar ones nearby — mistakes happen.

✔ **Reduce utility costs.** Sometimes you have to spend money to save money. Old refrigerators, for example, can waste a lot of electricity. Insulate to save on heating and air-conditioning bills. Install water flow regulators in shower heads and toilet bowls. When planting your yard, don't select water-guzzling plants, and keep your lawn area reasonable. Even if you don't live in an area susceptible to droughts, why waste water (which isn't free) unnecessarily? Recycle — recycling means less garbage, which translates into lower trash bills and benefits the environment by reducing landfill.

Lowering your phone bills

Thanks to increased competition and technology, telephoning costs are falling. If you haven't looked for lower rates recently, you're probably paying more than you need to for quality phone service. Unfortunately, shopping among the many service providers is difficult. Plans come with different restrictions, minimums, and bells and whistles. Here are my recommendations for saving on your phone bills:

- ✔ **Look at your phone company's other calling plans.** You may have to switch companies to reduce your bill, but I find that many people can save significantly with their current phone company simply by getting onto a better calling plan. So, before you spend hours shopping around, contact your current local and long distance providers and ask them which of their calling plans offer the lowest cost for you based on the patterns of your calls.

- ✔ **Get help when shopping for other providers.** Two useful sources are Consumer Reports (800-234-1645; www.consumerreports.org) and Telecommunications Research & Action Center, or TRAC (www.trac.org).

The cell phone business is booming. And while being able to make calls from wherever you are can be enormously convenient, you can spend a lot of money for service given the myriad of extra charges. On the other hand, if you're able to take advantage of the free minutes many plans offer (on weekends, for example), a good cell phone service can save you money. Here's how to get your money's worth from cell phone service:

- ✔ **Question the need for a cell phone.** Okay, I realize that this is a risky point to be raising for those cell phone addicts among us. If you enjoy having a cell phone to use during downtime when commuting or for emergency purposes, I won't try to talk you out of your cell phone. However, many people really don't have a need for a cell phone.

- ✔ **Shop around.** Make sure that you sign up with the best calling plan and carrier given your typical usage. Telebright and TRAC (see previous list) can also help you research wireless phone services. Reputable carriers allow you to test out their service. They also offer full refunds if you're not satisfied after a week or two of service.

Are satellite television and unlimited Internet access making our lives better?

At the risk of exposing my age, I can tell you how much simpler things were when I was growing up. I remember being able to choose among three national television channels and a handful of local channels. Now, many cable and satellite services offer hundreds of channels. And, of course, you can surf millions of Web sites for one monthly fee.

While I enjoy choices and convenience as much as the next person, I also see the detrimental impact these technologies are having on

our families' lives. As it is, most families struggle to find quality time together given their work obligations, long school days, and various other activities. At home, all of these technology choices and options compete for attention and often pull families apart. The cost for all these services and gadgets adds up, leading to a continued enslavement to our careers.

Err on the side of keeping your life simple. Doing so costs less, reduces stress, and allows for more time for the things that really do matter in life.

Sending a thoughtful letter is usually cheaper, more appreciated, and longer lasting than placing a phone call. Just block out an hour, grab a pen and paper, and rediscover the lost art form of letter writing. Formulating your thoughts on paper can be clarifying and therapeutic, as well. Computer users may find that they can also save money by sending e-mail.

Cutting transportation costs

America is a car-driven society. In most other countries, cars are a luxury. More than 90 percent of the people in the rest of the world can't afford a new car. If more people in the United States thought of cars as a luxury, Americans might have far fewer financial problems (and accidents). Cars not only pollute the air and clog the highways but they also cost you a bundle. Purchasing a quality car and using it wisely can save you money. Using other transportation alternatives can also help save you money.

Contrary to advertising slogans, cars are not built to last — car manufacturers don't want you to stick with the same car year after year. New models are constantly introduced with new features and styling changes. Getting a new set of wheels every few years is an expensive luxury.

Don't try to keep up with the Joneses as they show off their new cars every year — for all you know, they're running themselves into financial ruin just trying to impress you. Let your neighbors admire you for your thriftiness and wisdom instead.

Research before you buy a car

When you buy a car, you don't just pay the initial sticker price: You also have to pay for gas, insurance, registration fees, maintenance, and repairs. Don't compare simple sticker prices; think about the total, long-term costs of car ownership.

Speaking of total costs, remember that you're also trusting your life to the car. With about 40,000 Americans killed in auto accidents annually (about half of which are caused by drunk drivers), safety should be an important consideration, as well. Air bags, for example, may save your life. The National Highway Traffic Safety Administration Web site (www.nhtsa.gov) has lots of crash test data, as well as information on other car safety issues.

Consumer Reports publishes a number of useful buying guides for new and used cars. You find *Consumer Reports* on the Internet at www.consumer reports.org. For you data jocks, *The Complete Car Cost Guide,* which is published by Intellichoice (800-227-2665; www.intellichoice.com), is packed with information about all categories of ownership costs, warranties, and dealer costs. The guide rates new cars based on total ownership costs. But can you *really* afford a new car?

Buy your car with cash

The main reason people end up spending more than they can afford on a car is that they finance the purchase. As I discuss in Part I, you should avoid borrowing money for consumption purchases, especially for items that depreciate in value (like cars). A car is most definitely *not* an investment.

When buying a car, leasing is generally more expensive than borrowing money. Leasing is like a long-term car rental. We all know how well rental cars get treated — well, leased cars are treated just as well, which is one of the reasons why leasing is so costly.

Unfortunately, the practice of leasing cars or buying them on credit is increasingly becoming the norm in our society. This approach is certainly attributable to a lot of the misinformation that's spread by car dealers and, in some cases, the media. Consider the magazine article entitled "Rewards of Car Leasing." The article claims that leasing is a great deal when compared to buying. Ads for auto dealers advertising auto leasing were placed next to the article. The magazine, by the way, is *free* to subscribers — which means that 100 percent of its revenue comes from advertisers such as auto dealers. Also be aware that, because of the influence of advertising (and ignorance), leasing is widely endorsed on Web sites that purport to provide information on cars.

Replace high-cost cars

Maybe you realized by now that your car is too expensive to operate because of insurance, gas, and maintenance costs. Or maybe you bought too much car — people who lease or borrow money to buy a car frequently buy a far more expensive car than they can realistically afford.

Dump your expensive car and get something more financially manageable. The sooner you switch, the more money you'll save. Getting rid of a car on a lease is a challenge, but it can be done. I had one client who, when he lost his job and needed to slash expenses, convinced the dealer (by writing a letter to the owner) to take the leased car back.

Keep cars to a minimum

I've seen households that have one car per person — four people, four cars! Some people have a "weekend" car that they use only on days off! For most households, maintaining two or more cars is an expensive extravagance. Try to find ways to make do with fewer cars.

You can move beyond the confines of owning a car by either carpooling or riding buses or trains to work. Some employers give incentives for taking public transit to work, and some cities and counties offer assistance for setting up vanpools or carpools along popular routes. By leaving the driving to someone else, you can catch up on reading or just relax on the way to and from work. You also help reduce pollution.

But I can't buy a new car with cash!

"Come on, Eric," you may be thinking, "how can I and most wage earners today afford to buy a new car with cash — who has that kind of dough sitting around?"

Some people feel that it's unreasonable of me to expect them to use cash to buy a new car. After all, many publications effectively endorse and encourage loaning and leasing to buy a car. Of course, these same publications also derive great advertising revenue from auto dealers and lenders. (Coincidence? I think not.)

I'm a reasonable kind of guy. So believe me when I say that I'm trying to look out for your best long-term financial interests. Please consider the following:

✔ If you lack sufficient cash to buy a new car, I say "DON'T BUY A NEW CAR!" Most of the world's population can't even afford a car, let alone a new one! Buy a car that you can afford — which for most people is a used one.

✔ Don't fall for the rationalization that says buying a used car means lots of maintenance, repair expenses, and problems. Do your homework and buy a good quality used car. That way, you can have the best of both worlds. A good used car costs less to buy and, thanks to lower insurance costs, less to operate.

✔ A fancy car is not needed to impress people for business purposes. Some people I know say that they absolutely must drive a nice, brand-spanking-new car to set the right impression for business purposes. I'm not going to tell you how to manage your career, but I will ask you to consider that if clients and others see you driving an expensive new car, they may think that you spend money wastefully or you're getting rich off of them!

When you're considering the cost of living in different areas, don't forget to factor in commuting costs. One advantage of living close to work, or at least close to public transit systems, is that you may be able to make do with fewer cars (or no car at all) in your household.

Buy commuter passes

In many areas, you can purchase train, bus, or subway passes to help reduce the cost of commuting. Many toll bridges also have booklets of tickets that you can buy at a discount. Some booths don't advertise that they offer these plans — maybe as a strategy to help keep revenues up. Some areas even allow before-tax dollars to be withheld from your paycheck to buy commuter passes.

Buy regular unleaded gas

A number of studies have shown that "super-duper-ultrapremium" gasoline is not worth the extra expense. But make sure that you buy gasoline that has an octane rating recommended for your vehicle. Paying more for the higher octane "premium" gasoline just wastes money. Your car won't run better; you just pay more for gas. Fill up your tank when you're on a shopping trip to the warehouse wholesalers (discussed earlier in this chapter). These superstores are usually located in lower-cost areas, so the gas is often cheaper there, too. Also, don't use credit cards to buy your gas if you have to pay a higher price to do so.

Service your car regularly

Sure, servicing your car (for example, changing the oil every 5,000 miles) costs money, but it saves you dough in the long run by extending the operating life of your car. Servicing your car also reduces the chance that your car will crap out in the middle of nowhere, which requires a humongous towing charge to a service station. Stalling on the freeway during peak rush hour and having thousands of angry commuters stuck behind you is even worse.

Controlling clothing costs

Given the amount of money that some people spend on clothing and related accessories, I've come to believe that people in nudist colonies must be great savers! But you probably live among the clothed mainstream of society, so here's a short list of economical ideas:

- ✔ **Avoid clothing that requires dry cleaning.** When you buy clothing, try to stick with cottons and machine-washable synthetics rather than wools or silks that require dry cleaning. Check labels before you buy clothing.

- ✔ **Don't chase the latest fashions.** Fashion designers and retailers are constantly working to tempt you to buy more. Don't do it. Ignore publications that pronounce this season's look. In most cases, you simply don't need to buy racks of new clothes or an entire new wardrobe every year. If your clothes are not lasting at least ten years, you're probably tossing them before their time or buying clothing that isn't very durable.

  Fashion, as defined by what people wear, changes quite slowly. In fact, the classics don't ever go out of style. If you want the effect of a new wardrobe every year, store last year's purchases away next year and then bring them out the year after! Or rotate your clothing inventory every third year. Set your own fashion standards. Buy basic, and buy classic — if you let fashion gurus be your guide, you'll end up with the biggest wardrobe in the poorhouse.

- ✔ **Minimize accessories.** Shoes, jewelry, handbags, and the like can gobble large amounts of money. Again, how many of these accessory items do you really need? The answer is probably very few, because each one should last many years.

Go to your closet or jewelry box and tally up the loot. What else could you have done with all that cash? Do you see things you regret buying or forgot you even had? Don't make the same mistake again. Have a garage sale if you have a lot of stuff that you don't want.

Repaying your debt

In Chapter 4, I discuss strategies for reducing the cost of carrying consumer debt. The *best* way to reduce the costs of such debt is to avoid it in the first place when you're making consumption purchases. You can avoid consumer debt by eliminating your access to credit or by limiting your purchase of consumer items to what you can pay off each month. Remember, only borrow for long-term investments (see Chapter 1 for more information).

Don't keep a credit card that charges you an annual fee, especially if you pay your balance in full each month. Many no-fee credit cards exist — and some even offer you a benefit for using them:

- ✔ Discover Card (800-347-2683) rebates up to 1 percent of purchases in cash.
- ✔ GM Card (800-846-2273) gives credits worth 5 percent of your charges that can be used toward the purchase of most GM-manufactured vehicles.
- ✔ AFBA (800-776-2265).
- ✔ USAA Federal Savings (800-922-9092).

You should consider the cards in the previous list only if you pay your balance in full each month, because no-fee cards typically levy high interest rates for balances carried month-to-month. The small rewards that you earn really won't do you much good if they're negated by interest charges.

If you have a credit card that charges an annual fee, try calling the company and saying that you want to cancel the card because you can get a competitor's card without an annual fee. Many banks will agree to waive the fee on the spot. Some require you to call back yearly to cancel the fee — a hassle that can be avoided by getting a true no-fee card.

Some cards that charge an annual fee and offer credits toward the purchase of a specific item, such as a car or airline ticket, may be worth your while if you pay your bill in full each month and charge $10,000 or more annually. *Note:* Be careful — you may be tempted to charge more on a card that rewards you for more purchases. Spending more than you would otherwise in order to rack up bonuses defeats the purpose of the credits.

Indulging responsibly in fun and recreation

Having fun and taking time out for R and R can be money well spent. But when it comes to fun and recreation, financial extravagance can wreck an otherwise good budget.

Using thrift with gifts

Think about how you approach buying gifts throughout the year — especially during the holidays. I know people who spend so much on their credit cards during the December holidays, that it takes them until late spring or summer to pay their debts off!

Although I don't want to deny your loved ones gifts from the heart — or you the pleasure of giving them — spend wisely. Homemade gifts are less costly to the giver and may be dearer to recipients. Many children actually love durable, classic, basic toys. If the TV commercials dictate your kids' desires, it may be time to toss the TV or set better rules for what the kids are allowed to watch.

Some people forget their thrifty shopping habits when gift buying, perhaps because they don't like to feel cheap when buying a gift. As with other purchases you make, paying careful attention to where and what you buy can save you significant dollars. Don't make the mistake of equating the value of a gift with its dollar cost.

And here's a good suggestion for getting rid of those old, unwanted gifts. One of the most entertaining and memorable holiday parties I've ever attended involved a "white elephant" gift exchange: Everyone brought a wrapped, unwanted gift from the past and exchanged it with someone else. After the gifts were opened, trading was allowed. (Just be sure not to bring a gift that was given to you by any of the exchange participants!)

Entertainment

If you adjust your expectations, entertainment doesn't have to cost a great deal of money. Many movies, theaters, museums, and restaurants offer discount prices on certain days and times.

Cultivate some interests and hobbies that are free or low-cost. Visiting with friends, hiking, reading, and playing sports can be good for your finances as well as your health.

Vacations

For many people, vacations are a luxury. For others, regular vacations are essential parts of their routine. Regardless of how you recharge your batteries, remember that vacations are not investments, so you shouldn't borrow through credit cards to finance your travels. After all, how relaxed will you feel when you have to pay all those bills?

Try taking shorter vacations that are closer to home. Have you been to a state or national park recently? Take a vacation at home, visiting the sights in your local area. Great places that you've always wanted to see but haven't visited for one reason or another are probably located within 200 miles of you. Or you may want to just block out some time and do what my cats do: Take lots of naps and relax around your home.

If you do travel a long way to a popular destination, travel during the off-season for the best deals on airfares and hotels. Keep an eye out for discounts and "bought-but-unable-to-use" tickets advertised in your local paper. The *Consumer Reports Travel* newsletter and numerous Web sites such as www.priceline.com, www.expedia.com, and www.travelocity.com can help you find low-cost travel options, as well. Senior citizens generally qualify for special fares at most airlines — ask the airline what programs it offers.

Also, be sure to shop around, even when working with a travel agent. Travel agents work on commission, so they may not work hard to find you the best deals. Tour packages, when they meet your interests and needs, can also save you money. If you have flexible travel plans, courier services can cut your travel costs significantly (but make sure that the company is reputable).

Personal care

You have to take care of yourself, but as with anything else, you can find ways to do it that are expensive, and you can find ways that save you money.

- ✔ **Hair care.** Going bald is one way to save money in this category. I'm working on this one myself. In the meantime, if you have hair to be trimmed, a number of no-frills, low-cost hair-cutting joints can do the job. Supercuts is one of the larger hair care chains. You may insist that your stylist is the only one who can manage your hair the way you like it. At the prices charged by some of the trendy hair places, you have to really adore what they do to justify the cost. Consider going periodically to a no-frills stylist for maintenance after getting a fabulous cut at a more expensive place. If you're daring, you can try getting your hair cut at a local training school. For parents of young children, buying a simple-to-use home haircutting electric shaver (such as Wahl's) can be a great time and money saver — no more agonizing trips with little ones to have their hair cut by a "stranger." The kit pays for itself after just two to three haircuts!

- ✔ **Other personal-care services.** As long as we're on the subject of outward beauty, I have to say that, in my personal opinion, the billions spent annually on cosmetics are largely a waste of money (not to mention all the wasted time spent applying and removing it). Women look fine without makeup. (In most cases, they look better.) And having regular facials, pedicures, and manicures can add up quickly.

- ✔ **Health club expenses.** Money spent on exercise is almost always money well spent. But you don't have to belong to a trendy club to receive the benefits of exercise. If you belong to a gym or club for the social scene (whether for dating or business purposes), you have to judge whether it's worth the cost.

Low-cost exercise facilities are everywhere — look for them anywhere you see children and young adults. Local schools, colleges, and universities often have tennis courts, running tracks, swimming pools, basketball courts, and exercise rooms, and they may provide instruction, as well. Community centers offer fitness programs and classes, too. Metropolitan areas that have lots of health clubs undoubtedly have the widest range of options and prices. ***Note:*** When figuring the cost of membership, be sure to factor in the cost of travel to and from the clubs, and any parking costs (and the realistic likelihood of going there regularly to work out).

Don't forget that healthy exercise can be done indoors or out, free of charge. Isn't biking in the park at sunset more fun than pedaling away on a stationary bike, anyway? You may want to buy some basic gym equipment for use at home. Be careful though: Lots of rowing machines and free weights languish in a closet after their first week at home.

Paring down professional expenses

Accountants, lawyers, and financial advisors can be worth their expense if they're good. But be wary of professionals who create or perpetuate work and have conflicts of interest with their recommendations.

Look for value in the publications to which you subscribe

Everyone has a favorite and not-so-favorite publication. Some people don't realize how much they spend on publications, partly because they never tally up the cost.

Take *The New York Times,* for example. (Actually, consider not taking it.) At $9.30 per week in the New York Metro area and $11.50 per week elsewhere, you pay a whopping $483 or $598 per year! Most areas have decent newspapers that cost a fraction of these amounts. You can also keep up with news and events through weekly news magazines such as *Newsweek* — which costs just $43 per year.

Free publications are often driven by advertisers, so I don't encourage you to load up on them. But take a close look at the total amount you spend on publications and how much each one costs. Keep the ones that you're getting sufficient value from and cancel the rest. You can always read them at your local library.

If you took the money that you're spending on *The New York Times,* for example, and invested it in a retirement account that earns a mere 10 percent per year, in 25 years you'd have about $71,000 (New York metro subscribers) or about $90,000 (everyone else in the country)! And this example assumes that the subscription prices won't increase every year, which they always do. After seeing these figures, you'd really have to feel that you're getting good value from *The New York Times* to keep subscribing!

Make sure that you get organized before meeting with a professional for tax, legal, or financial advice. Do some background research to evaluate their strengths and biases. Set goals and estimate fees in advance so that you know what you're getting yourself into.

Computer and printed resources (see Chapters 18 and 19) can be useful, low-cost alternatives to hiring professionals.

Managing medical expenses

Health care is a big topic nowadays. The cost of health care is going up fast. Your health insurance — if you have health insurance, that is — probably covers most of your health-care needs. (Chapter 15 explains how to shop for health insurance.) But many plans require you to pay for certain expenses out of your own pocket.

Medical care and supplies are like any other services and products — prices and quality vary. And medicine in the United States, like any other profession, is a business. A conflict of interest exists whenever the person recommending treatment benefits financially from providing that treatment. Many studies have documented some of the unnecessary surgeries and medical procedures that have resulted from this conflict of interest.

Remember to shop around when seeking health insurance. Don't take any one physician's advice as gospel. Always get a second opinion for any major surgery. Most health insurance plans, out of economic self-interest, require a second opinion anyway.

Therapy can be useful and even lifesaving. Have a frank talk with your therapist about how much total time and money you can expect to spend and what kind of results you can expect to receive. As with any professional service, a competent therapist will give you a straight answer if he or she is looking out for your psychological *and* financial well-being.

Alternative medicine (holistic, for example) is gaining attention because of its focus on preventive care and the treatment of the whole body or person. Although alternative medicine can be dangerous if you're in critical condition, alternative treatment for many forms of chronic pain or disease may be worth investigating. Alternative medicine may lead to better *and* lower-cost health care.

If you have to take certain drugs on an ongoing basis and pay for them out-of-pocket, ordering through a mail-order company can bring down your costs and help make refilling your prescriptions more convenient. Your health plan should be able to provide more information about this option.

Examine your employer's benefit plans. Take advantage of being able to put away a portion of your income before taxes to pay for out-of-pocket health care expenses. Make sure that you pay close attention to the "use it or lose it" provisions of each plan.

Keeping an eye on insurance premiums

Insurance is a vast minefield. In Part IV, I explain the different types of coverage, suggest what to buy and avoid, and detail how to save on policies. The following list explains the most common ways people waste money on insurance.

> ✔ **Keeping low deductibles.** The *deductible* is the amount of a loss that must come out of your pocket. For example, if you have an auto insurance policy with a $100 collision deductible, and you get into an accident, you pay for the first $100 of damage and your insurance company picks up the rest. Low deductibles, however, translate into much higher premiums for you. In the long run, you save money with a higher deductible, even when factoring in the potential for greater out-of-pocket costs to you when you do have a claim. Insurance should protect you from economic disaster. Don't get carried away with a really high deductible, which can cause financial hardship if you have a claim and lack savings.
>
> If you have a lot of claims, you won't come out ahead with lower deductibles, because your insurance premiums will escalate. Plus, low deductibles mean more claim forms to file for small losses (creating more hassle). Filing an insurance claim is usually not an enjoyable or quick experience.
>
> ✔ **Covering small potential losses or unnecessary needs.** You shouldn't buy insurance for anything that won't be a financial catastrophe if you have to pay for it out of your own pocket. Although the postal service isn't per-fect, insuring inexpensive gifts sent in the mail is not worth the price. Buying dental or home warranty plans, which also cover relatively small potential expenditures, doesn't make financial sense for the same reason. And, if no one is dependent on your income, you don't need to buy life insurance either. (Who will be around to collect when you're gone?)
>
> ✔ **Failing to shop around.** Rates vary *tremendously* from insurer to insurer. In Part IV, I recommend the best companies to call for quotes and other cost saving strategies.

Trimming your taxes

Taxes are probably one of your largest — if not *the* largest — expenditures. (So why is it last here? Read on to find out.)

Retirement savings plans are one of the best and simplest ways to reduce your tax burden. (I explain more about retirement savings plans in Chapter 10.) Unfortunately, most people can't take full advantage of these plans, because they spend everything they make. So not only do they have less savings but they also pay higher income taxes — a double whammy.

I've attended many presentations where a fast-talking investment guy in an expensive suit lectures about the importance of saving for retirement and explains how to invest your savings. Yet details and tips about finding the money to save (the hard part for most people) are left to the imagination.

In order to take advantage of the tax savings that come through retirement savings plans, you must first spend less than you earn. Only then can you afford to contribute to these plans. That's why the first part of this chapter is all about strategies to reduce your spending.

Reduced sales tax is another benefit of spending less and saving more. When you buy most consumer products, you pay sales tax. Therefore, when you spend less money and save more in retirement accounts, you reduce your income *and* sales taxes. (See Chapter 6 for detailed tax-reduction strategies.)

Eliminating costly addictions

Human beings are creatures of habit. We all have habits we wish we didn't have, and breaking those habits can be very difficult. Costly habits are the worst. The following tidbits may nudge you in the right direction toward breaking your own financially-draining habits.

✔ **Kick the smoking habit.** Despite the decline in smoking over the past few decades, about one in four Americans still smoke. The smokeless tobacco habit, which also causes long-term health problems, is on the increase. Americans spend more than $50 billion annually on tobacco products — that's a staggering $1,000 per year per tobacco user. The increased medical costs and the costs of lost work time are even greater, as they're estimated at more than $50 billion every year. Of course, if you continue to smoke, you may eliminate the need to save for retirement.

Check with local hospitals for smoking-cessation programs. The American Lung Association (check your local phone directory) also offers Freedom from Smoking clinics around the country. The National Cancer Institute (800-422-6237, or 800-4CANCER) and the Office on Smoking and Health at the Centers for Disease Control (1600 Clifton Road, Atlanta, GA 30333; phone 770-488-5703) offer free information guides that contain effective methods for stopping smoking.

✔ **Stop abusing alcohol and other drugs.** Nearly one million Americans seek treatment annually for alcoholism or drug abuse. These addictive behaviors, like spending, transcend all educational and socioeconomic lines in our society. Even so, studies have demonstrated that only one in seven alcohol or drug abusers seek help. Three of the ten leading causes of death — cirrhosis of the liver, accidents, and suicides — are associated with excessive alcohol consumption.

The National Clearinghouse for Alcohol and Drug Information (800-729-6686) can refer you to local treatment programs such as Alcoholics Anonymous. It also provides pamphlets and other literature about the various types of substance abuse. The National Substance Abuse Information and Treatment Hotline (800-662-4357, or 800-662-HELP) can refer you to local drug treatment programs. It provides literature as well.

✔ **Don't gamble.** The house *always* comes out ahead in the long run. Why do you think so many governments run lotteries? Because governments make money on people who gamble, that's why.

Casinos, horse and dog racetracks, and other gambling establishments are sure long-term losers for you. So, too, is the short-term trading of stocks, which isn't investing but gambling. Getting hooked on the dream of winning is easy and tempting. And sure, occasionally you win a little bit (just enough to keep you coming back). Every now and then, a few folks win a lot. But your hard-earned capital mostly winds up in the pockets of the casino owners.

If you gamble just for the entertainment, take only what you can afford to lose. Gamblers Anonymous (213-386-8789; www.gamblersanonymous.org) helps those for whom gambling has become an addiction.

Chapter 6

Taming Taxes

In This Chapter

▶ Understanding the baffling tax system

▶ Reducing employment income taxes

▶ Discovering ways to increase your deductions

▶ Lowering investment income taxes

▶ Preparing your return with help from tax resources

▶ Handling an audit notice

*Y*ou pay a lot of money in taxes — probably more than you realize. Believe it or not, few people know just how much they pay in taxes each year. Most people remember only whether they received a refund or owed money on their return. But when you file your tax return, all you're doing is settling up with tax authorities over the amount of taxes you paid during the year versus the total tax that you owe based on your income and deductions.

Understanding the Taxes You Pay

Some people feel lucky when they get a refund, but all a refund really indicates is that you overpaid in taxes during the year. You should have had this money in your own account all along. If you're consistently getting big refunds, you need to pay less tax throughout the year. (Fill out a simple tax form, the W-4, to determine how much you should be paying in taxes throughout the year. You can obtain a W-4 through your employer's payroll department. If you're self-employed, you can obtain Form 1040-ES by calling the IRS at 800-TAX-FORM [800-829-3676], or visiting its Web site at www.irs.gov.)

Instead of focusing on whether you're going to get a refund when you complete your annual tax return, you *should* be focusing on the *total* taxes you pay. To find out the *total* taxes you pay, you need to get out your federal and state tax returns. On each of those returns is a line that shows the *total tax:* This is line 61 on the most recent federal 1040 returns. If you add up the totals from your federal and state tax returns, you'll probably see one of your largest expenses.

The goal of this chapter is to help you legally and permanently reduce the total taxes you pay. Understanding the tax system is the key to reducing your tax burden — if you don't, you'll surely pay more taxes than necessary. Your tax ignorance can lead to mistakes, which can be costly if the IRS and state government catch your underpayment errors. With the proliferation of computerized information and data tracking, discovering mistakes has never been easier.

The tax system, like other public policy, is built around incentives to encourage *desirable* behavior and activity. Home ownership, for example, is considered desirable because it encourages people to take more responsibility for maintaining buildings and neighborhoods. Clean, orderly neighborhoods are often the result of home ownership. Therefore, the government offers all sorts of tax perks, which I discuss later in this chapter, to encourage people to buy homes.

Not all people follow the path the government encourages — after all, it's a free country. However, the *fewer* desirable activities you engage in, the more you pay in taxes. If you understand the options, you can choose the ones that meet your needs as you approach different stages of your financial life.

Recognizing the importance of your marginal tax rate

When it comes to taxes, *not all income is treated equally.* This fact is far from self-evident. If you work for an employer and earn a constant salary during the course of a year, a steady and equal amount of federal and state taxes is deducted from each paycheck. Thus, it appears as though all that earned income is being taxed equally.

In reality, however, you pay less tax on your first dollars of earnings and more tax on your *last* dollars of earnings. For example, if you're single, and your taxable income (a term I define in the next section) totals $40,000 during 2003, you pay federal tax at the rate of 10 percent on the first $7,000 of taxable income, 15 percent on income between $7,000 and $28,400, and 25 percent on income from $28,400 up to $40,000.

Table 6-1 gives federal tax rates for singles and married households filing jointly.

Table 6-1	2003 Federal Income Tax Brackets and Rates	
Singles Taxable Income	*Married-Filing-Jointly Taxable Income*	*Federal Tax Rate (Bracket)*
$0–$7,000	$0–$14,000	10%
$7,000–$28,400	$14,000–$56,800	15%
$28,400–$68,800	$56,800–$114,650	25%
$68,800–$143,500	$114,650–$174,700	38%
$143,500–$311,950	$174,700–$311,950	33%
Over $311,950	Over $311,950	35%

Your *marginal tax rate* is the rate of tax you pay on your *last,* or so-called *highest,* dollars of income. In the example of a single person with taxable income of $40,000, that person's federal marginal tax rate is 25 percent. In other words, she effectively pays 25 percent federal tax on her last dollars of income — those dollars in excess of $28,400.

Marginal tax rates are a powerful concept. Your marginal tax rate allows you to quickly calculate the additional taxes you'd have to pay on additional income. Conversely, you can delight in quantifying the amount of taxes you save by reducing your taxable income, either by decreasing your income or by increasing your deductions.

As you're probably already painfully aware, you pay not only federal income taxes but also state income taxes — that is, unless you live in one of the handful of states (Alaska, Florida, Nevada, South Dakota, Texas, Washington, or Wyoming) that have no state income tax. *Note:* Some states, such as New Hampshire, do not tax employment but do tax other income, such as income from investments.

Your *total marginal rate* includes your federal *and* state tax rates.

You can look up your state tax rate in your current state income tax preparation booklet.

Defining taxable income

Taxable income is the amount of income on which you actually pay income taxes. (In the sections that follow, I explain strategies for reducing your taxable income.) The following reasons explain why you don't pay taxes on your total income:

Alternative minimum tax (say what?)

You may find this hard to believe, but a second tax system actually exists (as if the first tax system wasn't already complicated enough). This second system may raise your taxes even higher than they would normally be. I'll explain while you reach for some aspirin.

Over the years, as the government grew hungry for more revenue, taxpayers who slashed their taxes by claiming lots of deductions or exclusions from taxable income came under greater scrutiny. So the government created a second tax system — the alternative minimum tax (AMT) — to ensure that those with high deductions or exclusions pay at least a certain percentage of taxes on their incomes.

If you have a lot of deductions or exclusions from state income taxes, real estate taxes, certain types of mortgage interest, and passive investments (for example, rental real estate), you may fall prey to AMT. You may also get tripped up by AMT if you exercise certain types of stock options.

AMT restricts you from claiming certain deductions and requires you to add back in income that is normally tax-free (like certain municipal-bond interest). So you have to figure your tax under the AMT system and under the other system, and then pay whichever amount is higher. I hope that aspirin is starting to kick in.

- ✔ **Not all income is taxable.** For example, you pay federal tax on the interest you earn on a bank savings account but not on the interest you earn from municipal bonds. (As discussed later in this chapter, some income, such as from stock dividends and long-term capital gains, is taxed at lower rates.)

- ✔ **You get to subtract deductions from your income.** Some deductions are available just for being a living, breathing human being. In 2003, single people get an automatic $4,750 standard deduction, and married couples filing jointly get $9,500. (People over age 65 and those who are blind get a slightly higher deduction.) Other expenses, such as mortgage interest and property taxes, are deductible in the event that these so-called itemized deductions exceed the standard deductions. When you contribute to qualified retirement plans, you also effectively get a deduction.

Trimming Employment Income Taxes

You're supposed to pay taxes on income you earn from work. Countless illegal ways are available to reduce your employment income — for example, not reporting it — but if you use them, you can very well end up paying a heap of penalties and extra interest charges on top of the taxes you owe. And you may even get tossed in jail. Because I don't want you to serve jail time or lose even more money by paying unnecessary penalties, this section focuses on the *legal* ways to reduce your taxes.

Contributing to retirement plans

A retirement plan is one of the few painless and completely legal ways to reduce your taxable employment income. Besides reducing your taxes, retirement plans help you build up a nest egg so that you don't have to work for the rest of your life.

You can deduct money from your taxable income by tucking it away in employer-based retirement plans, such as 401(k) or 403(b) accounts, or self-employed retirement plans, such as SEP-IRAs or Keoghs. If your combined federal and state marginal tax rate is 35 percent, and you contribute $1,000 to one of these plans, you reduce your federal and state taxes by $350. Do you like the sound of that? How about this: Contribute another $1,000, and your taxes drop *another* $350 (as long as you're still in the same marginal tax rate). And when your money is inside a retirement account, it can compound and grow without taxation.

Cutting back on expenses to fund retirement accounts

Many people miss this great opportunity for reducing their taxes because they *spend* all (or too much) of their current employment income and, therefore, have nothing (or little) left to put into a retirement account. If you're in this predicament, you need to reduce your spending before you can contribute money to a retirement plan. (Chapter 5 explains how to decrease your spending.)

If your employer doesn't offer the option of saving money through a retirement plan, see whether you can drum up support for it. Lobby the benefits and human resources departments. If they resist, you may want to add this to your list of reasons for considering another employer. Many employers offer this valuable benefit, but some don't. Some company decision-makers either don't understand the value of these accounts or feel that they're too costly to set up and administer.

If your employer doesn't offer a retirement savings plan, individual retirement account (IRA) contributions may or may not be tax-deductible, depending on your circumstances. You should first exhaust contributions to the previously mentioned tax-deductible accounts. Chapter 10 can help you determine whether you should contribute to an IRA, what type you should contribute to, and whether your IRA contributions are tax-deductible.

Funding retirement accounts and special tax credits

Married couples filing jointly with adjusted gross incomes (AGIs) of less than $50,000, and single taxpayers with an AGI of less than $25,000, can earn a new tax credit for retirement account contributions. This credit, which is detailed in Table 6-2, is a percentage of the first $2,000 contributed (or $4,000 on a joint return). The credit is not available to those under the age of 18, full-time students, or people who are claimed as dependents on someone else's tax return.

Table 6-2	Special Tax Credit for Retirement Plan Contributions	
Single Taxpayers Adjusted Gross Income	**Married Couples Filing Jointly Adjusted Gross Income**	**Tax Credit for Retirement Account Contributions**
$0 to $15,000	$0 to $30,000	50%
$15,001 to $16,250	$30,001 to $32,500	20%
$16,251 to $25,000	$32,501 to $50,000	10%

Shifting some income

Income shifting, which has nothing to do with money laundering, is a more esoteric tax-reduction technique that's an option only to those who can control *when* they receive their income.

For example, suppose that your employer tells you in late December that you're eligible for a bonus. You're offered the option to receive your bonus in either December or January. If you're pretty certain that you'll be in a higher tax bracket next year, you should choose to receive your bonus in December.

Or suppose that you run your own business, and you think that you'll be in a lower tax bracket next year. Perhaps you plan to take time off to be with a newborn or take an extended trip. You can send out some invoices later in the year so that your customers won't pay you until January, which falls in the next tax year.

Increasing Your Deductions

Deductions are amounts you subtract from your income after totaling your taxable income and before calculating the tax you owe. To make things more complicated, the IRS gives you two methods for determining your total deductions. The good news is that you get to pick the method that leads to greater deductions — and hence, lower taxes.

Choosing standard or itemized deductions

The first method for figuring deductions requires no thinking or calculating. If you have a relatively uncomplicated financial life, taking the so-called standard deduction is generally the better option. Earning a high income, renting your house or apartment, and lacking unusually large expenses from medical bills, moving expenses, charitable contributions, or loss due to theft or catastrophe are not symptoms of a simple tax life.

As I mention earlier in this chapter, single folks qualify for a $4,750 standard deduction, and married couples filing jointly get a $9,500 standard deduction in 2003. If you're 65 or older, or blind, you get a slightly higher standard deduction.

Itemizing your deductions on your tax return is the other method for determining your allowable deductions. This method is definitely more of a hassle, but if you can tally up more than the standard amounts noted in the preceding section, itemizing will save you money. Use Schedule A of IRS Form 1040 for summing up your itemized deductions.

Many of the categories on Schedule A — such as line 10, which reads "Home mortgage interest and points reported to you on Form 1098" — are reasonably self-evident. (If you own your home and have a mortgage, your bank should send you Form 1098 early in the new year. This form tells you how much deductible mortgage interest you paid.)

Organize your deductions

Locating Form 1098 and all the other scraps of paper you need when you're completing your tax return can be a hassle. Setting up a filing system can be a big timesaver:

✔ **One receptacle.** If you have limited patience for setting up neat file folders, and you lead an uncomplicated financial life (that is, you haven't saved receipts throughout the year), you can confine your filing to January and February. During those months, you receive tax summary statements on wages paid by your employer (Form W-2), investment income (Form 1099), and home mortgage interest (Form 1098) in the mail. Label a folder with something easy to remember ("2003 Taxes" is a brilliant choice) and dump these papers and your tax booklet into it. When you're ready to crunch numbers, you'll have everything you need to complete the form.

✔ **Many receptacles.** Organizing the bills you pay into individual folders during the entire year is a more thorough approach. This method is essential if you own your own business and need to tabulate your expenditures for office supplies each year. No one is going to send you a form totaling your office expenditures for the year — you're on your own.

> ✓ **Software as a receptacle.** Software programs can help organize your tax information during the year and save you time and accounting fees come tax-preparation time. See Chapter 18 for more information about tax and financial software.

The following sections explain the most *overlooked* deductions and deduction strategies. Some are listed on Schedule A, and others appear on Form 1040.

Shift or bunch deductions

When you total your itemized deductions on Schedule A, and the total is lower than the standard deduction, you should take the standard deduction. This total is worth checking each year, because you may have more deductions in some years, and itemizing may make sense.

Because you can control when you pay particular expenses that are eligible for itemizing, you can *shift* or *bunch* more of them into the select years where you have enough deductions to take advantage of itemizing. Suppose, for example, that you're using the standard deduction this year because you don't have many itemized deductions. Late in the year, though, you become certain that you're going to be buying a home next year. With mortgage interest and property taxes to write off, you also know that you can itemize next year. Shifting and collecting as many deductible expenses as possible into next year then makes sense. For example, if you typically make more charitable contributions in December because of the barrage of solicitations you receive when you're in the giving mood, you may want to write the checks in January rather than in December.

When you're sure that you're not going to have enough deductions in the current year to itemize, try to shift as many expenses as you can into the next tax year.

Purchasing real estate

When you buy a home, you can claim two big ongoing expenses of home ownership — your property taxes and the interest on your mortgage — as deductions on Schedule A. You're allowed to claim mortgage interest deductions for a primary residence (where you actually live) and on a second home for mortgage debt totaling $1,000,000 (and a home equity loan of up to $100,000).

You can also deduct the full amount of your property taxes, even if you live in a multimillion-dollar mansion. What a deal!

In order to buy real estate, you need to first collect a down payment, which requires maintaining a lid on your spending. See Part I for help with prioritizing and achieving important financial goals.

Trading consumer debt for mortgage debt

When you own real estate, you haven't borrowed the maximum, and you've run up high-interest consumer debt, you may be able to trade one debt for another. You may be able to save on interest charges by refinancing your mortgage or taking out a home equity loan, and pulling out extra cash to pay off your credit card, auto loan, or other costly credit lines. You can usually borrow at a lower interest rate for a mortgage and get a tax deduction as a bonus, which lowers the effective borrowing cost further. Consumer debt, such as that on auto loans and credit cards, is not tax-deductible.

This strategy involves some danger. Borrowing against the equity in your home can be an addictive habit. I've seen cases where people run up significant consumer debt three or four times and then refinance their home the same number of times over the years to bail themselves out.

An appreciating home creates the illusion that excess spending isn't really costing you. But debt is debt, and all borrowed money has to be repaid. In the long run, you wind up with greater mortgage debt, and paying it off takes a bigger bite out of your monthly income. Refinancing and establishing home equity lines cost you more in terms of loan application fees and other charges (points, appraisals, credit reports, and so on).

At a minimum, the continued expansion of your mortgage debt handicaps your ability to work toward other financial goals. In the worst case, easy access to borrowing encourages bad spending habits that can lead to bankruptcy or foreclosure on your debt-ridden home.

Contributing to charities

You can deduct contributions to charities if you itemize your deductions. For example, most people know that when they write a check for $50 to their favorite church or college, they can deduct it. *Note:* Make sure that you get a receipt for contributions of $250 or more, because a canceled check is no longer sufficient documentation for the IRS.

Many taxpayers overlook the fact that you can also deduct expenses for work you do with charitable organizations. For example, when you go to a soup kitchen to help prepare and serve meals, you can deduct your transportation costs. You just need to keep track of your bus fares or driving mileage.

You also can deduct the fair market value (which can be determined by looking at the price of similar merchandise in thrift stores) of donations of clothing, household appliances, furniture, and other goods to charities. (Many charities will even drive to your home to pick up the stuff.) Find out whether organizations such as the Salvation Army, Goodwill, or others are interested in your donation. Just make sure that you keep some documentation — write up an itemized list and get it signed by the charity. Consider taking pictures of your more valuable donations. You can even donate securities and other investments to charity. In fact, donating an appreciated investment gives you a tax deduction for the full market value of the investment and eliminates your need to pay tax on the (unrealized) profit.

Remembering auto registration fees and state insurance

If you don't currently itemize, you may be surprised to discover that your state income taxes can be itemized. When you pay a fee to the state to register and license your car, you can itemize the expenditure as a deduction (on Schedule A, line 7, "Personal Property Taxes"). The IRS allows you to deduct the part of the fee that relates to the value of your car. The state organization that collects the fee should be able to tell you what portion of the fee is deductible. (Some states detail on the invoice what portion of the fee is tax-deductible.)

Bad news — limitations on deductions

If you're a high-income earner, tax laws limit the amount of itemized deductions you may subtract when calculating your taxable income. You have to reduce your total itemized deductions by 3 percent of your income above $139,500.

Here's how it works: Say that your income is $159,900, and your total itemized deductions come to $30,000. Because your income exceeds $139,500 by $20,000, you have to reduce your itemized deductions by $600 ($20,000 × 3 percent). Even though you started with itemized deductions of $30,000, you can deduct only $29,400.

Of course, given a large enough income and low enough total deductions, the 3 percent rule threatens to wipe out all your deductions. Don't worry. The IRS has benevolently set a limit on the amount that your deductions can be reduced — no more than 80 percent. So if we take the preceding example but boost your income to $1 million, you still get to deduct $6,000, because your $30,000 in deductions can't be reduced by more than $24,000 ($30,000 × 80 percent).

If you're in this high-income category and your spirits are down, here's a little consolation (and something to make it all a little more complicated). Not all of your deductions are subject to the 3 percent rule: Medical and dental expenses, investment interest, casualty and theft losses, and gambling losses are all exempt.

Knowing this 3 percent rule and all of its nuances is important if you're a high-income earner, because it can affect some of your financial decisions. The 3 percent rule raises your effective tax rate and may encourage you, for example, to spend less on a home or pay off your mortgage faster, because you don't merit a full deduction.

Several states have state disability insurance funds. If you pay into these funds (check your W-2), you can deduct your payments as state and local income taxes on line 5 of Schedule A. You may also claim a deduction on this line for payments you make into your state's unemployment compensation fund.

Deducting miscellaneous expenses

A number of so-called *miscellaneous expenses* are deductible on Schedule A. Most of these expenses relate to your job or career, and the management of your finances:

- **Educational expenses.** You may be able to deduct the cost of tuition, books, and travel to and from classes if your education is related to your career. Specifically, you can deduct these expenses if your course work improves your work skills. Courses the law or your employer requires you to take to maintain your position are deductible. Continuing education classes for professionals may also be deductible. *Note:* Educational expenses that allow you to move into a new field or career are not deductible.

- **Job searches and career counseling.** After you obtain your first job, you may deduct legitimate costs related to finding another job within your field. For example, suppose that you're a chef in a steakhouse in Chicago, and you decide that you want to do stir fry in Los Angeles. You take a crash course in vegetarian cooking and then fly to L.A. a couple of times for interviews. You can deduct the cost of the course and your trips — *even if you don't change jobs.* And if you hire a career counselor to help you figure everything out, you can deduct that cost as well. On the other hand, if you're burned out on cooking, and you decide that you want to become a professional volleyball player in L.A., that's a new career. You may get a better tan, but you won't generate deductions from changing jobs.

- **Expenses related to your job that aren't reimbursed.** When you pay for your own subscriptions to trade journals to keep up with your field or buy a new desk and chair to ease back pain, you can deduct these costs. If your job requires you to wear special clothes or a uniform, you can write off the cost of purchasing and cleaning these clothes, as long as they aren't suitable for wearing outside of work. When you buy a computer for use outside the office at your own expense, you may be able to deduct the cost if the computer is for the convenience of your employer, is a condition of your employment, and is used more than half the time for business. Union dues and membership fees for professional organizations are also deductible.

✔ **Investment and tax-related expenses.** Investment and tax-advisor fees are deductible, as are subscription costs for investment-related publications. Accounting fees for preparing your tax return or conducting tax planning during the year are deductible; legal fees related to your taxes are also deductible. If you purchase a home computer to track your investments or prepare your taxes, you can deduct that expense, too.

When you deduct miscellaneous expenses, you get to deduct only the amount that exceeds 2 percent of your AGI (adjusted gross income). AGI is your total wage, interest, dividend, and all other income minus retirement account contributions, self-employed health insurance, alimony paid, and losses from investments.

Deducting self-employment expenses

When you're self-employed, you can deduct a multitude of expenses from your income before calculating the tax you owe. If you buy a computer or office furniture, you can deduct those expenses. (Sometimes they need to be gradually deducted or *depreciated* over time.) Salaries for your employees, office supplies, rent or mortgage interest for your office space, and phone expenses are also generally deductible.

Many self-employed folks don't take all the deductions they're eligible for. In some cases, people simply aren't aware of the wonderful world of deductions. Others are worried that large deductions will increase the risk of an audit. Spend some time finding out more about tax deductions; you'll be convinced that taking full advantage of your eligible deductions makes sense and saves you money.

The following are common mistakes made by people who are their own bosses:

✔ **Being an island unto yourself.** When you're self-employed, going it alone is usually a mistake when it comes to taxes. You must educate yourself to make the tax laws work for rather than against you. Hiring tax help is well worth your while. (See "Professional hired help," later in this chapter, for info on hiring tax advisors.)

✔ **Making administrative tax screw-ups.** As a self-employed individual, you're responsible for the correct and timely filing of all taxes owed on your income and employment taxes on your employees. You need to make estimated tax payments on a quarterly basis. And if you have employees, you also need to withhold taxes from each paycheck they receive, and make timely payments to the IRS and the appropriate state authorities. In addition to federal and state income tax, you also need to withhold and send in Social Security and any other state or locally mandated payroll taxes.

To pay taxes on your income, use Form 1040-ES. This form, along with instructions, can be obtained from the IRS (call 800-TAX-FORM, or 800-829-3676). The form comes complete with an estimated tax worksheet and the four payment coupons you need to send in with your quarterly tax payments. If you want to find the rules for withholding and submitting taxes from employees' paychecks, ask the IRS for Form 941 and Form 940, which is for unemployment insurance. And unless you're lucky enough to live in a state with no income taxes, you need to call for your state's estimated income tax package. Another alternative is to hire a payroll firm, such as Paychex, to do all this drudgery for you.

✔ **Failing to document expenses.** When you pay with cash, following the paper trail for all the money you spent can be hard for you to do (and for the IRS, in the event you're ever audited). At the end of the year, how are you going to remember how much you spent for parking or client meals if you fail to keep a record? How will you survive an IRS audit without proper documentation? For purchases under $75, you don't need a receipt as proof, but you do need a system or written record of your daily petty cash purchases. Most pocket calendars or daily organizers include ledgers that allow you to track these small purchases. If you aren't that organized, at least get a receipt for cash transactions and stash them in a file folder in your desk. Or keep receipts in envelopes labeled with the month and year.

✔ **Choosing the wrong business entity.** When you set up your own business, you can structure its legal and tax organization in a variety of ways. A *corporation* is a separate legal entity from you, the individual. For example, if you're incorporated, and a customer slips on a stray banana peel at your office, the customer can sue your company, but he can't go after your personal assets. Incorporating makes more sense if you have employees or customers visit your office, or if you do business with many vendors.

Incorporating is not always the right answer. For professional service providers such as self-employed attorneys, physicians, or tax advisors, incorporating isn't necessarily useful as protection against professional negligence suits related to their work. *Professional liability insurance* is the answer for these folks. Check with the professional associations in your field for information on insurers who offer such policies.

✔ **Failing to fund a retirement plan.** You should be saving money toward retirement anyway, and you can't beat the tax break. People who are self-employed are allowed to save a substantial portion of their net income on an annual basis. To find out more about SEP-IRAs, Keoghs, and other retirement plans, see Chapter 10.

✔ **Failing to use numbers to help manage business.** If you're a small-business owner who doesn't track her income, expenses, staff performance, and customer data on a regular basis, your tax return may be the one and only time during the year when you take a financial snapshot of your business. After you go to all the time, trouble, and expense to file your tax return, make sure that you reap the rewards of all your work: Use those numbers to help analyze and manage your business.

Some bookkeepers and tax preparers can provide you with management information reports on your business from the tax data they compile for you. Just ask! Software packages can also help. See "Software and Web sites," later in this chapter, for my recommendations.

✔ **Failing to pay family help.** If your children, spouse, or other relatives help with some aspect of your business, consider paying them for the work. Besides showing them that you value their work, this practice may reduce your family's tax liability. For example, children are usually in a lower tax bracket than you are. So by shifting some of your income to your child, you cut your tax bill.

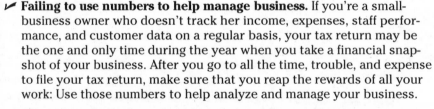

Reducing Investment Income Taxes

You don't need to worry about taxes for investments that you hold in *tax-sheltered* retirement accounts — IRAs and 401(k) plans, for example. This money is generally not taxed until you actually withdraw funds from the retirement account.

The distributions and profits on investments that you hold outside of tax-sheltered retirement accounts are exposed to taxation when you receive them. Interest, dividends, and profits (called *capital gains*) from the sale of an investment at a price that is higher than the purchase price are all taxed.

Taxes on investment income should be of concern to you if you're in a relatively high tax bracket. If you're in the 28 percent or higher federal bracket (refer to Table 6-1), make sure that you pay attention to the rest of this section.

If you're in the 25 percent federal tax bracket, the following strategies may or may not help you reduce your investment income taxes. Pay close attention to the issues that increase or decrease the benefits of following each of the strategies.

If you're in the 10 or 15 percent federal bracket, you can probably skip this section. You may sit quietly at your desk and amuse yourself until the rest of the class is finished.

Although this section explains some of the best methods for reducing the taxes on investments exposed to taxation, Chapter 11 discusses how and where to invest money held outside of tax-sheltered retirement accounts.

Fill up those retirement accounts

Taking advantage of opportunities to direct money into retirement accounts gives you two possible tax benefits. First, your contributions to the retirement account may be immediately tax-deductible (see Chapter 10 for details). Second, the distributions and growth of the investments in the retirement accounts aren't generally taxed until withdrawal.

As I explain later in this chapter, certain distributions from non-retirement accounts do receive favorable tax treatment.

Invest in tax-free money market funds and bonds

When you're in a high enough tax bracket, you may find that you come out ahead with tax-free investments. Tax-free investments pay investment income, which is exempt from federal tax, state tax, or both. (See Part III for details.)

Tax-free investments yield less than comparable investments that produce taxable income. But because of the difference in taxes, the earnings from tax-free investments *can* end up being greater than what you're left with from taxable investments.

Tax-free money market funds can be a better alternative to bank savings accounts (where interest is subject to taxation). Likewise, tax-free bonds are intended to be longer-term investments that pay tax-free interest, so they may be a better investment option for you than bank certificates of deposit, Treasury bills and bonds, and other investments that produce taxable income. (See Chapter 11 for specifics on which tax-free investments may be right for your situation.)

Select other tax-friendly investments

Too often, when selecting investments, people mistakenly focus on past rates of return. We all know that the past is no guarantee of the future. But choosing an investment with a reportedly high rate of return without considering tax consequences is an even worse mistake. What you get to keep — after taxes — is what matters in the long run.

For example, when comparing two similar funds, most people prefer a fund that averages returns of 14 percent per year to one that earns 12 percent per year. But what if the 14-percent-per-year fund forces you to pay a lot more in taxes? What if, after factoring in taxes, the 14-percent-per-year fund nets just 9 percent, while the 12-percent-per-year fund nets an effective 10 percent return? In such a case, you'd be unwise to choose a fund solely on the basis of the higher (pre-tax) reported rate of return.

I call investments that appreciate in value and don't distribute much in the way of taxable income *tax friendly*. (Some in the investment business use the term *tax efficient*.) See Chapter 9 for more information on tax-friendly stocks and stock mutual funds.

Real estate is one of the few areas with privileged status in the tax code. In addition to deductions allowed for mortgage interest and property taxes, you can depreciate rental property to reduce your taxable income. *Depreciation* is a special tax deduction allowed for the gradual wear and tear on rental real estate. When you sell investment real estate, you may be eligible to conduct a tax-free exchange when buying a so-called replacement rental property. See Chapter 13 for a crash course in real estate.

Make your profits long-term

As I discuss in Part III, when you buy growth investments such as stocks and real estate, you should do so for the long-term — ideally 10 or more years. The tax system rewards your patience with lower tax rates on your profits.

When you're able to hold on to an investment (outside of a retirement account) such as a stock, bond, or mutual fund for more than one year, you get a tax break if you sell that investment at a profit. Specifically, your profit is taxed under the lower capital gains tax rate schedule.

If you're in the 25 percent or higher federal income tax bracket, you pay just 15 percent of your long-term capital gains' profit in federal taxes. (The 2003 tax bill also similarly reduced the tax rate on stock dividends.) If you're in the

10 or 15 percent federal income tax brackets, the long-term capital gains tax rate is just 5 percents (and is actually scheduled to fall to 0 percent in 2008).

Getting Help from Tax Resources

All sorts of ways to prepare your tax return exist. Which approach makes sense for you depends on the complexity of your situation and your knowledge of taxes.

Regardless of which approach you use, you should be taking financial moves during the year to reduce your taxes. By the time you actually file your return in the following year, it's often too late for you to take advantage of many tax-reduction strategies.

IRS assistance

If you have a simple, straightforward tax return, filing it on your own using only the IRS instructions is fine. This approach is as cheap as you can get. The main costs are time, patience, photocopying expenses (you should always keep a copy for your files), and postage for mailing the completed tax return.

IRS publications don't have Tip or Warning icons. And the IRS has been known to give wrong information from time to time. When you call the IRS with a question, be sure to take notes about your conversation to protect yourself in the event of an audit. Date your notes and include the name and identification number of the tax employee you talked to, the questions you asked, and the employee's responses. File your notes in a folder with a copy of your completed return.

In addition to the standard instructions that come with your tax return, the IRS offers some free (actually, paid for with your tax dollars) and some-times useful booklets. Publication 17, *Your Federal Income Tax,* is designed for individual tax-return preparation. Publication 334, *Tax Guide for Small Businesses,* is for (you guessed it) small-business tax-return preparation. These publications are more comprehensive than the basic IRS instructions. Call 800-TAX-FORM (or 800-829-3676) to request these booklets, or visit the IRS Web site at www.irs.gov.

Preparation and advice guides

Books about tax preparation and tax planning that highlight common problem areas and are written in clear, simple English are invaluable. They supplement the official instructions not only by helping you complete your return correctly but also by showing you how to save as much money as possible. Consider picking up a copy of the latest edition of *Taxes For Dummies,* coauthored by yours truly and David J. Silverman (Wiley Publishing).

Software and Web sites

If you have access to a computer, good tax-preparation software can be helpful. TaxCut and TurboTax are programs that I have reviewed and rated as the best. If you go the software route, I highly recommend having a good tax advice book by your side.

For you Websurfers, the Internal Revenue Service Web site (www.irs.gov) is among the better Internet tax sites, believe it or not. The Tax and Accounting Sites Directory at www.taxsites.com is another good Web site with links to many other useful tax sites.

Professional hired help

Competent tax preparers and advisors can save you money — sometimes more than enough to pay their fees — by identifying tax-reduction strategies you may overlook. They can also help reduce the likelihood of an audit, which can be triggered by blunders. Mediocre and lousy tax preparers, on the other hand, may make mistakes and not be aware of sound ways to reduce your tax bill.

Tax practitioners come with varying backgrounds, training, and credentials. The four main types of tax practitioners are preparers, enrolled agents (EAs), Certified Public Accountants (CPAs), and tax attorneys. The more training and specialization a tax practitioner has (and the more affluent his clients), the higher his hourly fee usually is. Fees and competence vary greatly. If you hire a tax advisor, and you're not sure of the quality of work performed and the soundness of the advice, try getting a second opinion.

Preparers

Preparers generally have the least amount of training of all the tax practitioners, and a greater proportion of them work part-time. As with financial planners, no national regulations apply to preparers, and no licensing is required.

Preparers are appealing because they're relatively inexpensive — they can do most basic returns for around $100 or so. The drawback of using a preparer is that you may hire someone who doesn't know much more than you do.

Preparers make the most sense for folks who have relatively simple financial lives, who are budget minded, and who hate doing their own taxes. If you're not good about hanging onto receipts, or you don't want to keep your own files with background details about your taxes, you should definitely shop around for a tax preparer who's committed to the business. You may need all that stuff someday for an audit, and many tax preparers keep and organize their clients' documentation rather than return everything each year. Also, going with a firm that is open year-round may be a safer option (some small shops are open only during tax season) in case tax questions or problems arise.

Enrolled agents (EAs)

A person must pass IRS scrutiny in order to be called an *enrolled agent.* This license allows the agent to represent you before the IRS in the event of an audit. Continuing education is also required; the training is generally longer and more sophisticated than it is for a typical preparer.

Enrolled agents' fees tend to fall between those of a preparer and a CPA. Returns that require a few of the more common schedules (such as Schedule A for deductions and Schedule B for interest and dividends) shouldn't cost more than a couple hundred dollars to prepare.

EAs are best for people who have moderately complex returns and don't necessarily need complicated tax-planning advice throughout the year (although some EAs provide this service, as well). You can get names and telephone numbers of EAs in your area by contacting the National Association of Enrolled Agents (NAEA). You can call the NAEA at 800-424-4339, or visit its Web site at www.naea.org.

Certified public accountants (CPAs)

Certified public accountants go through significant training and examination before receiving the CPA credential. In order to maintain this designation, a CPA must also complete a fair number of continuing education classes every year.

CPA fees vary tremendously. Most charge $100+ per hour, but CPAs at large companies and in high-cost-of-living areas tend to charge somewhat more.

If you're self-employed and/or you file lots of other schedules, you may want to hire a CPA. But you don't need to do so year after year. If your situation grows complex one year and then stabilizes, consider getting help for the perplexing year and then using preparation guides, software, or a lower-cost preparer or enrolled agent in the future.

Tax attorneys

Tax attorneys deal with complicated tax problems and issues that usually have some legal angle. Unless you're a super-high-income earner with a complex financial life, hiring a tax attorney to prepare your annual return is prohibitively expensive. In fact, many tax attorneys don't prepare returns as a normal practice.

Because of their level of specialization and training, tax attorneys tend to have the highest hourly billing rates — $200 to $300+ per hour is not unusual.

Dealing with an Audit

On a list of real-life nightmares, most people would rank tax audits right up there with root canals, rectal exams, and court appearances. Many people are traumatized by audits because they feel like they're on trial and being accused of a crime. Take a deep breath and don't panic.

You may be getting audited simply because a business that reports tax information on you, or someone at the IRS, made an error regarding the data on your return. In the vast majority of cases, the IRS conducts its audit by corresponding with you through the mail.

Audits that require you to schlep to the local IRS office are the most feared type of audit. In these cases, about 20 percent of such audited returns are left unchanged by the audit — in other words, the taxpayer didn't end up owing more money. In fact, if you're the lucky sort, you may be one of the 5 percent of folks who actually gets a refund because the audit finds a mistake in your favor!

Unfortunately, you'll most likely be one of the roughly 75 percent of audit survivors who end up owing more tax money. The amount of additional tax that you owe in interest and penalties hinges on how your audit goes.

Getting your act together

Preparing for an audit is sort of like preparing for a test at school. The IRS will let you know which sections of your tax return it wants to examine.

The first decision you face when you get an audit notice is whether to handle it yourself or hire a tax advisor to represent you. Hiring representation may help you save time, stress, and money.

If you normally prepare your own return, and you're comfortable with your understanding of the areas being audited, handle the audit yourself. When the amount of tax money in question is small when compared to the fee you'd pay the tax advisor to represent you, self-representation is probably your best option. However, if you're likely to turn into a babbling, intimidated fool, and you're unsure of how to present your situation, hire a tax advisor to represent you. (See "Professional hired help," earlier in this chapter, for information about whom to hire.)

If you decide to handle the audit yourself, get your act together sooner rather than later. Don't wait until the night before to start gathering receipts and other documentation. You may need to contact others to get copies of documents you can't find.

You need to document and be ready to speak only about the areas the audit notice says are being investigated. Organize the various documents and receipts into folders. You want to make it as easy as possible for the auditor to review your materials. *Don't* show up, dump shopping bags full of receipts and paperwork on the auditor's desk, and say, "Here it is — *you* figure it out."

Whatever you do, *don't ignore your audit request letter.* The IRS is the ultimate bill-collection agency. And if you end up owing more money (the unhappy result of most audits), the sooner you pay, the less interest and penalties you'll owe.

Surviving the day of reckoning

Two people with identical situations can walk into an audit and come out with very different results. The loser can end up owing much more in taxes and have the audit expanded to include other parts of the return. The winner can end up owing less tax money.

Here's how to be a winner in your tax audit:

✔ **Treat the auditor as a human being.** This advice may be obvious, but it isn't practiced by taxpayers very often. You may be resentful or angry about being audited. You may be tempted to gnash your teeth and tell the auditor how unfair it is that an honest taxpayer like you had to spend hours getting ready for this. You may feel like ranting and raving about how the government wastes too much of your tax money, or that the party in power is out to get you. Bite your tongue.

Believe it or not, most auditors are decent people just trying to do their job. They are well aware that taxpayers don't like seeing them. Don't suck up, either — just relax and be yourself. Behave as you would around a boss you like — with respect and congeniality.

✔ **Stick to the knitting.** Your audit is for discussing *only* the sections of your tax return that are in question. The more you talk about other areas or things that you're doing, the more likely the auditor will probe into other items. Don't bring documentation for parts of your return that aren't being audited. Besides creating more work for yourself, you may be opening up a can of worms that doesn't need to be opened. Should the auditor inquire about areas that aren't covered by the audit notice, politely say that you're not prepared to discuss those other issues and that another meeting should be scheduled.

✔ **Don't argue when you disagree.** State your case. When the auditor wants to disallow a deduction or otherwise increase the taxes you owe, and you disagree with him, state once why you don't agree with his assessment. If the auditor won't budge, don't get into a knock-down, drag-out confrontation. He or she may not want to lose face and is inclined to find additional tax money — that's the auditor's job. *Remember:* When necessary, you can plead your case with several people who work above your auditor. If this method fails, and you still feel wronged, you can take your case to tax court.

✔ **Don't be intimidated.** Most auditors are not tax geniuses. The work is stressful — being in a job where people dislike seeing you is not easy. Turnover is quite high. Thus, many auditors are fairly young, just-out-of-school types who majored in something like English, history, or sociology. They may know less about tax and financial matters than you do. The basic IRS tax boot camp that auditors go through doesn't come close to covering all the technical details and nuances in the tax code. So you may not be at such a disadvantage in your tax knowledge after all, especially if you work with a tax advisor (most tax advisors know more about the tax system than the average IRS auditor).

Part III
Building Wealth through Investing

The 5th Wave   By Rich Tennant

"I read about investing in a company called UniHandle Ohio, but I'm uneasy about a stock that's listed on the NASDAQ as UhOh."

In this part . . .

I lay out the basics of investing and show you how to choose your investments wisely. Earning and saving are hard work, so you need to be careful where you invest the fruits of your labor. This part is where you find out the real story on such things as stocks, bonds, mutual funds, the differences between investing in retirement and non-retirement accounts, how to invest for college, and how to buy a home.

Chapter 7

Important Investment Concepts

In This Chapter

▶ Determining your investment goals

▶ Major types of investments

▶ Expected investment returns and risks

▶ Understanding diversification and asset allocation

▶ The different types of investment firms

▶ Investment gurus and their prognostications

*M*aking wise investments doesn't have to be complicated. However, many investors get bogged down in the morass of the thousands of investment choices out there. This chapter helps you grasp the important, "bigger picture" issues that will help you ensure that your investment plan meshes with your needs and the realities of the investment marketplace.

Establishing Your Goals

Before you select a specific investment, you should first determine your investment needs and goals. Why are you saving this pile of money? What are you going to use it for? You don't need to earmark every dollar, but you should set some major objectives. Setting objectives is important because the expected use of the money helps you determine how long it's going to be invested. And that, in turn, helps you determine which investments to choose.

The risk level of your investments should factor in your time frame *and your comfort level.* Investing in high-risk vehicles doesn't make sense if you're going to spend all your profits on stress-induced medical bills. For example, suppose you've been accumulating money for a down payment on a home you want to buy in a few years. You can't afford much investment risk with that money. You're going to need that money sooner rather than later. Putting that money in the stock market, then, is probably not a wise move. As I discuss later in this chapter, the stock market can drop a lot in a year or over several consecutive years. So stocks are probably too risky a place to invest money you plan to use soon.

Perhaps you're saving toward a longer-term goal, such as retirement, that is 20 or 30 years away. In this case, you're in a position to make riskier investments, because your holdings have more time to bounce back from temporary losses or setbacks. You may want to consider investing in growth investments, such as stocks, in a retirement account that you leave alone for 20 years or longer. You can tolerate year-to-year volatility in the market — you have time on your side. If you haven't yet done so, take a tour through Chapter 2, which helps you contemplate and establish your financial goals.

Understanding the Major Investment Flavors

For most people, jumping right into picking a particular investment is the fun and exciting part of investing. Perhaps you're tired of thinking about where to invest and watching others make profits while you sit on the sidelines. You may have an idea about where you want to invest after doing some reading or watching some entertaining investment-type tout investments on television or online. Or maybe Uncle Louie is whispering in your ear that he's gonna get you in on the ground floor of a great new opportunity — a real sure thing.

Looking at lending investments

For a moment, forget all the buzzwords, jargon, and product names you've heard tossed around in the investment world — in many cases, they're only meant to obscure what an investment really is and to hide the hefty fees and commissions. Imagine a world with only two investment flavors — chocolate and vanilla ice cream (or low-fat, nondairy frozen dessert for you health-minded folks).

The investment world is really just as simple. You have only two major investment choices: You can be a lender or an owner.

You're a *lender* when you invest your money in a bank certificate of deposit (CD), a treasury bill, or a bond issued by a company like General Motors, for example. In each case, you lend your money to an organization — a bank, the federal government, or GM. You're paid an agreed-upon rate of interest for lending your money. The organization also promises to have your original investment (the *principal*) returned to you on a specific date.

Getting paid all of the interest in addition to your original investment (as promised) is the best that can happen with a lending investment. Given that the investment landscape is littered with carcasses of failed investments, this is not a result to take for granted.

The worst that can happen with a lending investment is that you don't get everything you're promised. Promises can be broken under extenuating circumstances. When a company goes bankrupt, for example, you can lose all or part of your original investment.

Another risk associated with lending investments is that, even though you get what you were promised, the ravages of inflation may make your money worth less — it has less purchasing power than you thought it would. Back in the 1960s, for example, high-quality companies issued long-term bonds that paid approximately 4 percent interest. At the time, buying a long-term bond seemed like a good deal, because the cost of living was increasing by only 2 percent per year.

When inflation rocketed to 6 percent and higher, those 4 percent bonds didn't seem so attractive. The interest and principal didn't buy nearly the amount they did years earlier when inflation was lower. Table 7-1 shows the reduction in the purchasing power of your money at varying rates of inflation after just ten years.

Table 7-1	Reduction in Purchasing Power Due to Inflation
Inflation Rate	*Reduction in Purchasing Power after 10 Years*
6 percent	−44 percent
8 percent	−54 percent
10 percent	−61 percent

Some conservative-minded investors make the common mistake of thinking that they are diversifying their long-term investment money by buying several bonds, some CDs, and an annuity. The problem, however, is that all these investments pay a relatively low fixed rate of return that is exposed to the vagaries of inflation.

A final drawback to lending investments is that you don't share in the success of the organization to which you lend your money. If the company doubles or triples in size and profits, your principal and interest rate don't double or triple in size along with it; they stay the same. Of course, such success should ensure that you get your promised interest and principal.

Exploring ownership investments

You're an *owner* when you invest your money in an asset, such as a company or real estate, that has the ability to generate earnings or profits. Suppose that you own 100 shares of Gap stock. With hundreds of millions of shares of stock outstanding, Gap is a mighty big company — your 100 shares represent a tiny piece of it.

What do you get for your small slice of Gap? As a stockholder, you share in the profits of a company in the form of annual dividends and an increase (you hope) in the stock price if the company grows and becomes more profitable. Of course, you receive these benefits if things are going well. If Gap's business declines, your stock may be worth less (or even worthless!).

Real estate is another one of my favorite financially rewarding and time-honored ownership investments. Real estate can produce profits when it is rented out for more than the expense of owning the property or sold at a higher price than what you paid for it. I know numerous successful real estate investors (myself included) who have earned excellent long-term profits.

The value of real estate depends not only on the particulars of the individual property but also on the health and performance of the local economy. When companies in the community are growing and more jobs are being produced at higher wages, real estate often does well. When local employers are laying people off and excess housing is sitting vacant because of previous overbuilding, rent and property values are likely to fall.

Many Americans have also built substantial wealth through small business. According to *Forbes* magazine, more of the United States' (and the world's) wealthiest individuals have built their wealth through their stake in small businesses than through any other vehicle. Small business is the engine that drives much of our economic growth. Although firms with fewer than 20 employees account for about one-quarter of all employees, such small firms were responsible for nearly half of all new jobs created in the past two decades.

You can participate in small business in a variety of ways. You can start your own business, buy and operate an existing business, or simply invest in promising small businesses. In the chapters ahead, I explain each of these major investment types in detail.

Shunning gambling instruments and behaviors

Although investing is often risky, it's not gambling — at least not the way I advocate investing. *Gambling* is putting your money into schemes that are sure to lose you money over time. That's not to say that everyone loses or that you lose every time you gamble. However, the deck is stacked against you. The house wins most of the time.

Horse racing tracks, gambling casinos, and lotteries are set up to pay out 50 to 60 cents on the dollar. The rest goes to profits and the administration of the system — don't forget that these are businesses. Sure, your chosen horse may win a race or two, but in the long run, you're almost guaranteed to lose about 40 to 50 percent of what you bet. Would you put your money in an "investment" where your expected return was –40 percent?

Forsake futures, options, and other derivatives

Futures, options, and commodities are *derivatives*, or financial investments whose value is derived from the performance of another security such as a stock or bond.

You may have heard the radio ad from the firm Fleecem, Cheatem, and Leavem, advocating that you buy heating oil futures because the cold weather months lead to the use of more heating oil. You call the firm and are impressed by the smooth-talking vice president who spends so much time with little ol' you. His logic makes sense, and he spent a lot of time with you, so you send him a check for $10,000.

Buying futures isn't much different from blowing $10,000 at the craps tables in Las Vegas. Futures prices depend on short-term, highly volatile price movements. As with gambling, you occasionally win when the market moves the right way at the right time. But in the long run, you're gonna lose. In fact, you can lose it all.

Options are as risky as futures. With options, you're betting on the short-term movements of a specific security. If you have inside information (such as knowing in advance when a major corporate development is going to occur), you can get rich. But don't forget one minor detail — insider trading is illegal. You may end up in the slammer.

Honest brokers who help their clients invest in stocks, bonds, and mutual funds will tell you the truth about commodities, futures, and options. A former broker I know who worked for Merrill Lynch and Salomon Smith

Barney for 12 years told me, "I had one client who made money in options, futures, or commodities, but the only reason he came out ahead was because he was forced to pull money out to close on a home purchase just when he happened to be ahead. The commissions were great for me, but there's no way a customer will make money in them." Remember these words if you're tempted to gamble with futures, options, and the like.

Futures and options are not always used for speculation and gambling. Some sophisticated professional investors use them to hedge, or actually reduce risk of, their broad investment holdings. Even the supposed professionals fail to get good results when using them in this fashion. You, the individual investor, should steer clear of futures and options.

Ditch daytrading

Daytrading — which is the rapid buying and selling of securities online — is a newer and equally foolish vehicle for individual investors to pursue. Placing trades via the Internet is far cheaper than the older methods of trading (such as telephoning a broker), but the more you trade, the more trading costs eat into your investment capital.

Frequent trading also increases your tax bill as profits realized over short periods of time are taxed at your highest possible tax rate (see Chapter 6). You can certainly make some profits when daytrading. However, over an extended period of time, you'll inevitably underperform the broad market averages. In those rare instances where you may do a little better than the market averages, it's rarely worth the time and personal sacrifices that you and your family and friends endure.

Understanding Investment Returns

The previous sections describe the difference between ownership and lending investments, and help you distinguish gambling and speculation from true investments. "That's all well and good," you say, "but how do I choose which type of investments to put my money into? How much can I make, and what are the risks?"

Good questions. I'll start with the returns you *might* make. I say "might" because I'm looking at history, and history is a record of the past. Using history to predict the future — especially the near future — is dangerous. History may repeat itself, but not always in exactly the same fashion, and not necessarily when you expect it to.

During this past century, ownership investments such as stocks and real estate returned around 10 percent per year, handily beating lending investments such as bonds (around 5 percent) and savings accounts (roughly 4 percent) in the investment performance race. Inflation has averaged 3 percent per year.

If you already know that the stock market can be risky, you may be wondering why investing in stocks is worth the anxiety and potential losses. Why bother for a few extra percent per year? Well, over many years, a few extra percent per year can really magnify the growth of your money (see Table 7-2). The more years you have to invest, the greater the difference a few percent makes in your returns.

Table 7-2	The Difference a Few Percent Makes	
At This Rate of Investment Return on $10,000	*You'll Have This Much in 25 Years*	*You'll Have This Much in 40 Years*
4% (savings account)	$26,658	$48,010
5% (bond)	$33,863	$70,400
10% (stocks and real estate)	$108,347	$452,592

Investing is not a spectator sport. You can't earn good returns on stocks and real estate if you keep your money in cash on the sidelines. If you invest in growth investments such as stocks and real estate, don't chase one new investment after another trying to beat the market average returns. *The biggest value is to be in the market, not to beat it.*

Sizing Investment Risks

Many investors have a simplistic understanding of what risk means and how to apply it to their investment decisions. For example, when compared to the yo-yo motions of the stock market, a bank savings account may seem like a less risky place to put your money. Over the long term, however, the stock market usually beats the rate of inflation, while the interest rate on a savings account does not. Thus, if you're saving your money for a long-term goal like retirement, a savings account can be a "riskier" place to put your money.

Before you invest, ask yourself these three questions:

- ✔ "What am I saving and investing this money for? In other words, what's my goal?"
- ✔ "What is my timeline for this investment — when will I use this money?"
- ✔ "What is the historical volatility of the investment I'm considering, and does that suit my comfort level and timeline for this investment?"

After you answer these questions, you'll have a better understanding of *risk*, and you'll be able to match your savings goals to their most appropriate investment vehicles. In Chapter 2, I help you consider your savings goals and timeline. I address investment risk and returns in the sections that follow.

Comparing the risks of stocks and bonds

Given the relatively higher historic returns I mention for ownership investments in the previous section, some people think that they should put all of their money in stocks and real estate. So what's the catch?

Investments with a potential for higher returns carry greater risks. Risk and return go hand in hand. If you're not willing to accept more risk, you're not going to be able to achieve higher rates of return.

The risk with ownership investments is the short-term fluctuations in their value. During the last century, stocks declined, on average, by more than 10 percent (in one particular year) every five years. Drops in stock prices of more than 20 percent occurred, on average, once every ten years. Real estate prices suffer similar periodic setbacks.

Therefore, in order to earn those generous long-term returns from ownership investments like stocks and real estate, you must be willing to tolerate volatility. You absolutely should not put all your money in the stock or real estate market. You should not invest your emergency money or money you expect to use within the next five years in such volatile investments.

The shorter the time period that you have for holding your money in an investment, the less likely that growth-oriented investments like stocks will beat out lending-type investments like bonds. Table 7-3 illustrates the historical relationship between stock and bond returns based on number of years held.

Table 7-3	Stocks versus Bonds
Number of Years Investment Held	*Likelihood of Stocks Beating Bonds*
1	60%
5	70%
10	80%
20	91%
30	99%

Some types of bonds have higher yields than others, but the risk-reward relationship remains intact. A bond generally pays you a higher rate of interest when it has a

- ✔ Lower credit rating — to compensate for the higher risk of default and the higher likelihood of losing your investment
- ✔ Longer-term maturity — to compensate for the risk that you'll be unhappy with the bond's set interest rate if the market level of interest rates moves up

Focusing on the risks you can control

I always asked students in my personal finance class to write down what they would like to learn. Here's what one student had to say: "I want to learn what to invest my money in now as the stock market is overvalued and interest rates are about to go up, so bonds are dicey and banks give lousy interest — HELP!"

This student recognizes the risk of price fluctuations in her investments, but she also seems to believe, like too many people, that you can predict what's going to happen. How does *she* know that the stock market is overvalued, and why hasn't the rest of the world figured it out? How does *she* know that interest rates are about to go up, and why hasn't the rest of the world figured that out, either?

 When you invest in stocks and other growth-oriented investments, you must accept the volatility of these investments. Invest the money that you have earmarked for the longer-term in these vehicles. Minimize the risk of these investments through diversification. Don't buy just one or two stocks; buy a number of stocks. Later in this chapter, I discuss what you need to know about diversification.

Discovering low-risk, high-return investments

Despite what professors teach in the nation's leading business and finance graduate school programs, low-risk investments that almost certainly will lead to high returns are available. I can think of at least four such investments:

✔ **Paying off consumer debt.** If you're paying 10, 14, or 18 percent interest on an outstanding credit card or other consumer loan, pay it off before investing. To get a comparable return through other investment vehicles (after the government takes its share of your profits), you'd have to start a new career as a loan shark. If, between federal and state taxes, you're in a 33 percent tax bracket, and you're paying 12 percent interest on consumer debt, you'd need to annually earn a whopping 18 percent on your investments pre-tax to justify not paying off the debt. Good luck!

When your only source of funds for paying off debt is a small emergency reserve equal to a few months' living expenses, paying off your debt may involve some risk. Only tap into your emergency reserves if you have a backup source — for example, the ability to borrow from a willing family member or against a retirement account balance.

✔ **Investing in your health.** Eat healthy, exercise, and relax.

✔ **Investing in friends and family.** Invest time and effort in improving your relationships with loved ones.

✔ **Investing in personal and career development.** Pick up a new hobby, improve your communication skills, or read widely. Take an adult education course or go back to school for a degree. Your investment should lead to greater happiness and perhaps even higher paychecks.

Diversifying Your Investments

Diversification is one of the most powerful investment concepts. It refers to saving your eggs (or investments) in different baskets.

Diversification requires you to place your money in different investments with returns that are not completely correlated. This is a fancy way of saying that when some of your investments are down in value, odds are that others are up in value.

To decrease the chances of all of your investments getting clobbered at the same time, you must put your money in different types of investments, such as bonds, stocks, real estate, and small business. (I cover all these investments and more in Chapter 8.) You can further diversify your investments by investing in domestic as well as international markets.

Within a given class of investments such as stocks, investing in different types of stocks that perform well under various economic conditions is important. For this reason, *mutual funds,* which are diversified portfolios of securities such as stocks or bonds, are a highly useful investment vehicle. When you buy into a mutual fund, your money is pooled with the money of many others and invested in a vast array of stocks or bonds.

You can look at the benefits of diversification in two ways:

✔ Diversification reduces the volatility in the value of your whole portfolio. In other words, your portfolio can achieve the same rate of return that a single investment can provide, with less fluctuation in value.

✔ Diversification allows you to obtain a higher rate of return for a given level of risk.

Keep in mind that no one, no matter whom he works for or what credentials he has, can guarantee returns on an investment. You can do good research and get lucky, but no one is free from the risk of losing money. Diversification allows you to hedge the risk of your investments. See Figures 7-1, 7-2, and 7-3 to get an idea of how diversifying can reduce your risk. (The figures in these charts are adjusted for inflation.) Notice that different investments did better during different time periods. Because the future can't be predicted, diversifying your money into different investments is safer. (In the 1990s, stocks appreciated greatly, and bonds did pretty well, too, while gold and silver did poorly. In the early 2000s, stocks did poorly while bonds and precious metals did well.)

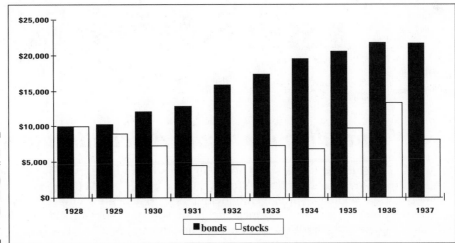

Figure 7-1:
Value of
$10,000
invested
from
1928-1937.

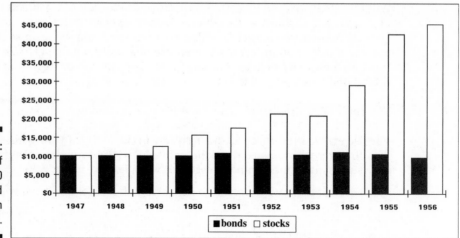

Figure 7-2:
Value of
$10,000
invested
from
1947-1956.

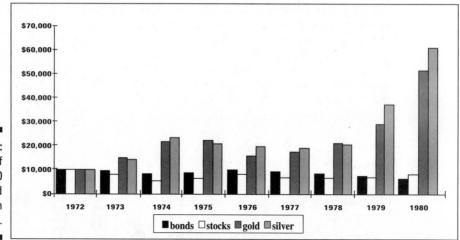

Figure 7-3:
Value of
$10,000
invested
from
1972-1980.

Spreading it around: Asset allocation

Asset allocation refers to how you spread your investing dollars among different investment options (stocks, bonds, money market accounts, and so on). Before you can intelligently decide how to allocate your assets, you need to ponder a number of issues, including your present financial situation, your goals and priorities, and the pros and cons of various investment options.

Although stocks and real estate offer attractive long-term returns, they can sometimes suffer significant declines. Thus, these investments are not suitable for money that you think you may want or need to use within, say, the next five years.

Money market and bond investments are good places to keep money that you expect to use soon. Everyone should have a reserve of money — about three to six months' worth of living expenses in a money market fund — that they can access in an emergency. Shorter-term bonds or bond mutual funds can serve as a higher-yielding, secondary emergency cushion. (Refer to Chapter 2 for more on emergency reserves.)

Bonds can also be useful for some longer-term investing for diversification purposes. For example, when investing for retirement, placing a portion of your money in bonds helps buffer stock market declines. The remaining chapters in this part of the book detail your various investment options and tell you how to select those that best meet your needs.

Allocating money for the long-term

Investing money for retirement is a classic long-term goal that most of us have. Your current age and the number of years until you retire are the biggest factors to consider when allocating money for long-term purposes. The younger you are and the more years you have before retirement, the more comfortable you should be with growth-oriented (and more volatile) investments, such as stocks and investment real estate.

One useful guideline for dividing or allocating your money between longer-term-oriented growth investments such as stocks and more-conservative lending investments such as bonds is to subtract your age from 100 (or 120 if you want to be aggressive) and invest the resulting percentage in stocks. You then invest the remaining amount in bonds.

For example, if you're 30 years old, you invest from 70 (100 – 30) to 90 (120 – 30) percent in stocks. The portion left over — 10 to 30 percent — is invested in bonds.

Table 7-4 lists some guidelines for allocating long-term money. All you need to figure out is how old you are and the level of risk you're comfortable with.

Table 7-4	Allocating Long-Term Money	
Your Investment Attitude	*Bond Allocation (%)*	*Stock Allocation (%)*
"Play it safe"	= Age	= 100 – age
"Middle-of-the-road"	= Age – 10	= 110 – age
"Aggressive"	= Age – 20	= 120 – age

For example, if you're the conservative sort who doesn't like a lot of risk but recognizes the value of striving for some growth and making your money work harder, you're a *middle-of-the-road* type. Using Table 7-4, if you're 40 years old, you may consider putting 30 percent (40 – 10) in bonds and 70 percent (110 – 40) in stocks.

In most employer retirement plans, mutual funds are the typical investment vehicle. If your employer's retirement plan includes more than one stock mutual fund as an option, you may want to try discerning which options are best by using the criteria I outline in Chapter 9. In the event that all your retirement plan's stock fund options are good, you can simply divide your stock allocation equally among the choices.

When one or more of the choices is an international stock fund, consider allocating a percentage of your stock fund money to overseas investments: at least 20 percent for *play-it-safe* investors, 25 to 35 percent for *middle-of-the-road* investors, and as much as 35 to 50 percent for *aggressive* investors.

If the 40-year-old middle-of-the-roader from the previous example is investing 70 percent in stocks, about 25 to 35 percent of the stock fund investments (which works out to be about 18 to 24 percent of the total) can be invested in international stock funds.

Historically, most employees haven't had to make their own investing decisions with retirement money. Pension plans, in which the company directs the investments, were more common in previous years. It's interesting to note that in a typical pension plan, companies choose to allocate the majority of money to stocks (about 60 percent), with a bit less placed in bonds (about 35 percent) and other investments. For more information on investing in retirement accounts, see Chapter 10.

Sticking with your allocations: Don't trade

The allocation of your investment dollars should be driven by your goals and desire to take risk. As you get older, gradually scaling back on the riskiness (and therefore growth potential) of your portfolio generally makes sense.

Don't tinker with your portfolio daily, weekly, monthly, or even annually. (Every three to five years or so, you may want to rebalance your holdings to get your mix to a desired asset allocation, as discussed in the previous section.) You should not engage in trading with the hopes of buying into a hot investment and selling your losers. Jumping onto a "winner" and dumping a "loser" may provide some short-term psychological comfort, but in the long-term, such an investment strategy can produce below-average returns.

When an investment gets front-page coverage and everyone is talking about its stunning rise, it's definitely time to take a reality check. The higher the value of an investment rises, the greater the danger that it's overpriced. Its next move may be downward. Don't follow the herd.

During the late 1990s, many technology stocks (especially Internet) had spectacular rises, thus attracting a lot of attention. Just because the U.S. economy is increasingly becoming technology-based, it doesn't mean that any price you pay for a technology stock is fine. Some investors who neglected to do basic research and bought into the attention-grabbing, high-flying technology stocks lost 80 percent or more of their investments in the early 2000s — ouch!

Conversely, when things look bleak, giving up hope is easy — who wants to be associated with a loser? However, investors who panic and sell after a major decline miss out on a tremendous buying opportunity.

Many people like buying everything from clothing to cars to ketchup on sale — yet whenever the stock market has a clearance sale, most investors stampede for the exits instead of snatch up great buys. Demonstrate your courage; don't follow the herd. After all, lemmings die because they follow the herd. (By the way, how is it that lemmings aren't extinct?)

Investing lump sums via dollar-cost averaging

When you have a large chunk of cash to invest — whether you received it from an accumulation of funds over the years, an inheritance, or a recent windfall from work you've done — you may have a problem deciding what to do with it. Many people, of course, would like to have your problem. (You're not complaining, right?) You want to invest your money, but you're a bit skittish, if not outright terrified, at the prospect of investing the lump of money all at once.

If the money is residing in a savings or money market account, you may feel like it's wasting away. You want to put it to work! My first words of advice are "Don't rush." Nothing is wrong with earning a small return in a money market account. (See Chapter 11 for my recommendations of the best money funds.) Remember that a money market fund beats the heck out of rushing into an investment in which you may lose 20 percent or more. I sometimes get calls from people in a state of near panic. Typically, these folks have CDs coming due, and they feel that they must decide exactly where they want to invest the money in the 48 hours before the CD matures.

Keeping your investing wits during uncertain times

During times like the early 2000s, some investors abandon the stock market for good. That's why the rebound from a severe bear market — and the down stock market cycle that began in 2000 has been the worst in magnitude and duration in decades — takes time to develop. While some people who have been burned badly learn that they're not cut out for stock investing, the rest of us should take stock of our investing approaches and adjust our practices and expectations.

In the early 2000s, the stock market began falling — with some growth stocks, especially technology stocks, plunging like stocks do in a depression. Layoffs mounted, and September 11th undermined consumer confidence. Then the general public learned that some major companies — Enron, WorldCom, and Global Crossing — pulled the wool over investors' eyes with shady accounting techniques that artificially inflated earnings. Concern about further terrorist attacks, smallpox, and war with Iraq (and perhaps other nations) hung like dark storm clouds on the horizon.

I see many similarities between the early 2000s and the early 1970s, when a multitude of problems (that could not have been predicted) unfolded. The early '70s saw record trade and budget deficits, inflation was rearing its ugly head, and we had the invasion of Cambodia, the Arab oil embargo, gas lines, and that period's Arab-Israeli conflict — the Yom Kippur War. United States Vice President Agnew resigned over the exposure of his personal income tax evasion and acceptance of bribes while working in Maryland's government.

Then news of Watergate broke, and Nixon's impeachment hearings began. After flirting with the 1,000 level since 1966, the Dow Jones Industrial Average plunged below 600 after Nixon resigned in 1974. Many investors soured on stocks and swore off the market forever. That reaction was unfortunate, because even with the recent, severe stock market decline, stocks are still 15-fold higher today than they were back in 1974.

Don't let a poor string of events sour you on stock investing. History has repeatedly proven that continuing to buy stocks during down markets increases your long-term returns. Throwing in the towel is the worst thing you can do in a slumping market. And don't waste your time trying to find a way to beat the system. Buy and hold a diversified portfolio of stocks. Remember that the financial markets reward investors for accepting risk and uncertainty.

Take a deeeep breath. You have absolutely no reason to rush into an important decision. Tell your friendly banker that, when the CD matures, you want to put the proceeds into the bank's highest-yielding savings or money market account. That way, your money continues to earn interest while you buy yourself some breathing room.

One approach to investing is called dollar-cost averaging (DCA). With DCA, you invest your money in equal chunks on a regular basis — such as once a month — into a diversified group of investments.

For example, if you have $60,000 to invest, you can invest $2,500 per month until it's all invested, which takes a couple of years. The money that's awaiting future investment isn't lying fallow. You keep it in a money market account so that it can earn a bit of interest while waiting its turn.

The attraction of DCA is that it allows you to ease into riskier investments instead of jumping in all at once. If the price of the investment drops after some of your initial purchases, you can buy some later at a lower price. If you dump all your money into the "sure win" investment all at once, and then it drops like a stone, you'll be kicking yourself for not waiting. (The flip side of DCA is that, when your investment of choice appreciates in value, you may wish that you had invested your money faster.)

Another possible drawback of DCA is that you may get cold feet as you continue to pour money into an investment that's dropping in value. Many people who are attracted to DCA because they fear that they may buy before a price drop end up bailing out of what feels like a sinking ship.

DCA can also cause headaches with your taxes when the time comes to sell investments held outside retirement accounts. When you buy an investment at many different times and prices, the accounting becomes muddied as you sell blocks of the investment.

DCA is most valuable when the money you want to invest represents a large portion of your total assets and you can stick to a schedule. Make DCA automatic so that you're less likely to chicken out should the investment fall after your initial purchases. Most of the investment firms I recommend in the next few chapters provide automatic exchange services.

Acknowledging Differences among Investment Firms

Thousands of firms sell investments and manage money. Banks, mutual fund companies, securities brokerage firms, and even insurance companies all vie for your hard-earned dough.

Just to make matters more complicated, each industry plays in the others' backyards. You can find mutual fund companies that offer securities brokerage, insurance firms that are in the mutual fund business, and mutual fund companies that offer banklike accounts and services. You benefit somewhat from all this competition and one-stop shopping convenience. On the other hand, some firms are novices at particular businesses, and they count on the fact that many people shop by brand-name recognition.

Focusing on the best firms

Make sure that you do business with a firm that

- ✔ **Offers the best value investments in comparison to their competitors.** Value is the combination of performance and cost. Given the level of risk that you're comfortable with, you want investments that offer higher rates of return, but you don't want to have to pay a small fortune for them. Commissions, management fees, maintenance fees, and other charges can turn a high-performance investment into a mediocre or poor one.

- ✔ **Employs representatives who do not have an inherent self-interest in steering you into a particular type of investment.** This criterion has nothing to do with whether an investment firm hires polite, well-educated, or well-dressed people. The most important factor is the way the company compensates its employees. If the investment firm's personnel are paid on commission, pass on that firm. Give preference to investing firms that don't tempt their employees to push one investment over another in order to generate more fees.

No-load (commission-free) mutual fund companies

Mutual funds are an ideal investment vehicle for most investors. *No-load mutual fund companies* are firms through which you can invest in mutual funds without paying sales commissions. In other words, every dollar you invest goes to work in the mutual funds you choose — nothing is siphoned off to pay sales commissions. See Chapter 9 for details on investing in mutual funds.

Discount brokers

In one of the most beneficial changes for investors in this century, the Securities and Exchange Commission (SEC) deregulated the retail brokerage industry on May 1, 1975. Prior to this date, investors were charged fixed commissions when they bought or sold stocks, bonds, and other securities. In other words, no matter which brokerage firm an investor did business with, the cost of the firm's services was set (and the level of commissions was high). After the 1975 deregulation, brokerage firms could then charge people whatever their little hearts desired.

Competition inevitably resulted in more and better choices. Many new brokerage firms (that did not do business the old way) opened. They were dubbed *discount brokers* because the fees they charged customers were substantially lower than what brokers charged under the old fixed-fee system.

Even more important than saving customers money, discount brokers established a vastly improved compensation system that greatly reduced conflicts of interest. Discount brokers generally pay the salaries of their brokers. The term *discount broker* is actually not an enlightening one. It's certainly true that this new breed of brokerage firm saves you lots of money when you invest. You can easily save 50 to 80 percent through the major discount brokers. But these firms' investments are not "on sale" or "second-rate." Discount brokers are simply brokers without major conflicts of interest. Of course, like any other for-profit enterprise, they're in business to make money, but they're much less likely to steer you wrong for their own benefit.

Be careful of discount brokers selling load mutual funds. (I discuss the reasons why you should shun these brokers in Chapter 9.)

Places to consider avoiding

The worst places to invest are those that charge you a lot, have mediocre- or poor-performing investments, and have major conflicts of interest. The prime conflict of interest arises when investment firms pay their brokers commissions on the basis of what and how much they sell. The result: The investment firms sell lots of stuff that pays fat commissions, and they *churn,* or cause a rapid turnover of, your account. (Because each transaction has a fee, the more you buy and sell, the more money they make.)

Some folks who call themselves *financial planners* or *financial consultants* work on commission. In addition to working at the bigger brokerage firms, many of them belong to so-called *broker-dealer networks,* which provide back-office support and investment products to sell. When a person claiming to be a financial planner or advisor is part of a broker-dealer network, odds are quite high that you're dealing with an investment salesperson. See Chapter 17 for more background on the financial planning industry and questions to ask an advisor you're thinking about hiring.

Commissions and their impact on human behavior

Investment products bring in widely varying commissions. The products that bring in the highest commissions tend to be the ones that money-hungry brokers push the hardest.

Table 7-5 lists the commissions that you pay and that come out of your investment dollars when you work with brokers, financial consultants, and financial planners who work on commission.

Table 7-5	Investment Sales Commissions	
Investment Type	*Average Commission on $20,000 Investment*	*Average Commission on $100,000 Investment*
Annuities	$1,400	$7,000
Initial public offerings (new stock issue)	$1,000	$5,000
Limited partnerships	$1,800	$9,000
Load mutual funds	$1,200	$6,000
Options and futures	$2,000+	$10,000+

Besides the fact that you can never be sure that you're getting an unbiased recommendation from a salesperson working on commission, you're wasting money unnecessarily. All good investments can be bought on a *no-load* (commission-free) basis. No-load mutual funds are a good example of an investment that can be purchased without paying a commission.

When you're unsure about an investment product that's being pitched to you (and even when you *are* sure), ask for a copy of the prospectus. In the first few pages, check out whether the investment includes a commission (also known as a *load*). While salespeople can hide behind obscure titles such as vice president or financial consultant, a prospectus must detail whether the investment carries a commission.

Investment salespeople's conflicts of interest

Financial consultants (also known as stockbrokers), financial planners, and others who sell investment products can have enormous conflicts of interest when recommending strategies and specific investment products. Commissions and other financial incentives can't help but skew the advice of even the most earnest and otherwise well-intentioned salespeople.

What to do when you're fleeced by a broker

You can't sue a broker just because you lose money on that person's investment recommendations. However, if you have been the victim of one of the following cardinal financial sins, you may have some legal recourse:

✔ **Misrepresentation and omission.** If you were told, for example, that a particular investment guarantees returns of 15 percent per year, and then the investment ends up plunging in value by 50 percent, you were misled. Misrepresentation can also be charged if you're sold an investment with hefty commissions after you were originally told that it was commission-free.

✔ **Unsuitable investments.** Retirees who need access to their capital are often advised to invest in limited partnerships (or LPs, discussed in Chapter 8) for safe, high yields. The yields on most LPs end up being anything but safe. LP investors have also discovered how *illiquid* (or not readily converted into cash) their investments are — some can't be liquidated for up to ten years or more.

✔ **Churning.** If your broker or financial planner is constantly trading your investments, odds are that his or her weekly commission check is benefiting at your expense.

✔ **Rogue elephant salespeople.** When your planner or broker buys or sells without your approval or ignores your request to make a change, you may be able to collect for losses caused by these actions.

Two major types of practitioners — securities lawyers and arbitration consultants — stand ready to help you recover your lost money. You can find securities lawyers by looking under "Attorneys — Securities" in the Yellow Pages or calling your local bar association for referrals. Arbitration consultants can be found in the phone book under "Arbitrators." If you come up dry, try contacting business writers at a major newspaper in your area or at your favorite personal finance magazine. These sources may be able to give you names and numbers of folks they know.

Most lawyers and consultants work on a *contingency-fee* basis — they get a percentage of damages (about 20 to 40 percent of the amount collected). They also often ask for an upfront fee, ranging from several hundred to several thousands of dollars, to help them cover their expenses and time. If they take your case and lose, they generally keep the upfront money. Securities lawyers are usually a more expensive option.

You may want to go to *arbitration* — an agreement you made (probably without realizing it) when you set up an account to work with the broker or planner. Arbitration is usually much quicker, cheaper, and easier than going to court. You can even choose to represent yourself. Both sides present their case to a panel of three arbitrators. The arbitrators then make a decision that neither side can squabble over or appeal.

If you decide to prepare for arbitration by yourself, the nonprofit American Arbitration Association can send you a package of background materials to help with your case. Check your phone directory for a local branch, or contact the association's headquarters (335 Madison Avenue, 10th Floor, New York, NY 10017-4605; phone 800-778-7879; Web site www.adr.org).

Numerous conflicts of interest can damage your investment portfolio. The following are the most common conflicts to watch out for:

- **Pushing higher-commission products.** As I discuss earlier in this chapter, commissions on investment products vary tremendously. Products like limited partnerships, commodities, options, and futures are at the worst end of the spectrum for you (and the best end of the spectrum for a salesperson). Investments such as no-load mutual funds and treasury bills that are 100 percent commission-free are at the best end of the spectrum for you (and therefore, the worst end of the spectrum for a salesperson).

  Surprisingly, commission-based brokers and financial planners don't have to give you the prospectus (where commissions are detailed) before you buy a financial product that carries commissions (as with a load mutual fund). In contrast, commission-free investment companies, such as no-load mutual fund companies, must send a prospectus before taking a mutual fund order. Commission-based investment salespeople should also be required to provide a prospectus and disclose any commissions upfront and in writing before making a sale. I suppose that if they were actually required to follow these guidelines, more people would choose to buy investments elsewhere — and politicians might start telling the truth!

- **Recommending active trading.** Investment salespeople often advise you to trade frequently into and out of different securities. They usually base their advice on current news events or an analyst's comments on the security. Sometimes these moves are valid, but more often they're not. In extreme cases, brokers trade on a monthly basis. By the end of the year, they've churned through your entire portfolio. Needless to say, all these transactions cost you big money in trading fees.

  Diversified mutual funds (discussed in Chapter 9) make more sense for most people. You can invest in mutual funds free of sales commissions. Besides saving money on commissions, you earn better long-term returns by having an expert money manager work for you.

- **Failing to recommend investing through retirement plans.** If you're not taking advantage of retirement savings plans (see Chapter 10), you may be missing out on valuable tax benefits. The initial contributions to most retirement plans are tax-deductible, and your money compounds without taxation over the years. An investment salesperson is not likely to recommend that you contribute to your employer's retirement plan — a 401(k) for example. Such contributions cut into the money you have available to invest with your friendly salesperson.

  If you're self-employed, salespeople are somewhat more likely to recommend that you fund a retirement plan, because they can set up such plans for you. You're better off setting up a retirement plan through a no-load mutual fund company (see Chapters 9 and 10).

✔ **Pushing high-fee products.** Many of the brokerage firms that used to sell investment products only on commission (for example, Prudential, Merrill Lynch, Smith Barney Shearson, and so on) moved into fee-based investment management. This change is an improvement for investors because it reduces some of the conflicts of interest caused by commissions.

On the other hand, these brokers charge extraordinarily high fees (which are usually quoted as a percentage of assets under management) on their managed investment (or wrap) accounts. For more on wrap accounts, see the "Wrap (or managed) accounts" sidebar in this chapter.

BEWARE

Wrap (or managed) accounts

Wrap accounts (which are also referred to as managed accounts) are all the rage among commission-based brokerage firms. These accounts go by a variety of names, but they are all similar in that they charge a fixed percentage of the assets under management to invest your money through money managers.

Wrap accounts can be poor investments because their management expenses may be extraordinarily high — up to 3 percent per year (some even higher) of assets under management. Remember that, in the long haul, stocks can return about 10 percent per year before taxes. So if you're paying 3 percent per year to have your money managed in stocks, 30 percent of your return (before taxes) is siphoned off. But don't forget — because the government sure won't — that you pay a good chunk of money in taxes on your 10 percent return as well. So the 3 percent wrap actually ends up depleting 40 to 50 percent of your after-tax profits!

The best no-load (commission-free) mutual funds offer investors access to the nation's best investment managers for a fraction of the cost of wrap accounts. You can invest in dozens of top-performing funds for an annual expense of 1 percent per year or less. Some of the best fund companies offer excellent funds for a cost as low as 0.2 to 0.5 percent (see Chapter 9).

You may be told, in the marketing of wrap accounts, that you're getting access to investment managers who don't normally take money from small-fry investors like you. Not a single study shows that the performance of money managers has anything to do with the minimum account they handle. Besides, no-load mutual funds hire many of the same managers who work at other money management firms.

You also may be told that you'll earn a higher rate of return, so the extra cost is worth it. "You could have earned 18 to 25 percent per year," they say, "had you invested with the 'Star of Yesterday' investment management company." The key word here is "had." History is history. Many of yesterday's winners become tomorrow's losers or mediocre performers.

You also need to remember that, unlike mutual funds, whose performance records are audited by the SEC, wrap account performance records may include marketing hype. Showing only the performance of selected accounts — those that performed the best — is the most common ploy.

Valuing brokerage research

Brokerage firms and the brokers who work for them frequently argue that their research is better. With their insights and recommendations, they say, you'll do better and "beat the market averages."

Wall Street analysts are often overly optimistic when it comes to predicting corporate profits. If analysts were simply inaccurate or bad estimators, you'd expect that they'd sometimes underestimate and, at other times, overestimate companies' earnings. The discrepancy identifies yet another conflict of interest among many of the brokerage firms.

Brokerage firm analysts are reluctant to write a negative report about a company, because the firms these analysts work for also solicit companies to issue new stock to the public. What better way to display your potential for selling shares at a high price to the public than by showing how much you believe in certain companies and writing glowing reports about their future prospects?

Brokerage analysts have great difficulty being objective. *Investment banking* (the business of helping companies sell new securities) can't objectively be done by companies supposedly evaluating and rating the same securities for the investing public.

Experts Who Predict the Future

Believing that you can increase your investment returns by following the prognostications of certain gurus is a common mistake that some investors make. Many of us may want to believe that some experts can predict the future of the investment world. Believing in gurus makes it easier to accept the risk you know you're taking when trying to make your money grow. The sage predictions that you read in an investment newsletter or hear from an "expert" who is repeatedly quoted in financial publications make you feel protected — sort of like Linus and his security blanket.

Investment newsletter subscribers and guru followers would be better off buying a warm blanket instead — it has a lot more value and costs a whole lot less! No one can predict the future. If they could, they would be so busy investing their own money and getting rich that they wouldn't have the time and desire to share their secrets with you.

Investment newsletters

Many investment newsletters purport to time the markets, telling you exactly the right time to get into and out of certain stocks or mutual funds (or the financial markets in general). Such an approach is doomed to failure in the long run. By failure, I mean that this approach is not going to beat the tried-and-true strategy of buy and hold.

I see people paying hundreds of dollars annually to subscribe to all sorts of market-timing and stock-picking newsletters. One client of mine, an attorney, subscribed to several newsletters. When I asked him why, he said that their marketing materials claimed that if you followed their advice, you would make a 20 percent per year return on your money. But in the four years that Ken had followed their advice, he actually *lost* money, despite appreciating financial markets overall.

Before you ever consider subscribing to any investment newsletter, examine its historic track record. The newsletter's marketing materials typically hype the supposed returns that the publication's recommendations have produced. Sadly, newsletters seem to be able to make lots of bogus claims without suffering the timely wrath of securities regulators.

Don't get predictive advice from newsletters. If newsletter writers were so smart about the future of financial markets, they'd be making lots more money as money managers. The only types of investment newsletters and periodicals that you should consider subscribing to are those that offer research and information rather than predictions. I discuss the investment newsletters that fit the bill in the subsequent investment chapters.

Investment gurus

Investment gurus come and go. Some of them get their 15 minutes of fame on the basis of one or two successful predictions that someone in the press remembers (and makes famous). A classic example is a former market analyst at Shearson named Elaine Garzarelli.

Ms. Garzarelli became famous for predicting the stock market's plummet in the fall of 1987. Garzarelli's fund, Smith Barney Shearson Sector Analysis, was established just before the crash. Supposedly, Garzarelli's indicators warned her to stay out of stocks, which she did, and in doing so, she saved her fund from the plunge.

Shearson, being a money-minded brokerage, quickly motivated its brokers to sell shares in Garzarelli's fund. In addition to her having avoided the crash, it didn't hurt that Shearson brokers were being rewarded with a hefty 5 percent sales commission for selling her fund. By the end of 1987, investors had poured nearly $700 million into this fund.

In 1988, Garzarelli's fund was the worst-performing fund among funds investing in growth stocks. From 1988 to 1990, Garzarelli's fund underperformed the

Standard & Poor 500 average by about 43 percent! In 1987 — the year of the crash — Garzarelli outperformed the S&P 500 by about 26 percent. So the amount she saved her investors by avoiding the crash was lost — along with more — in the years that followed. In fact, Garzarelli's performance was so dismal in the years following the crash, that Shearson eventually fired her.

Despite her poor long-term track record, Garzarelli is still quoted as a market soothsayer. She now manages money privately and hawks investment newsletters. The following marketing hype, promoting her newsletter, recently appeared in a mailed brochure entitled "The Garzarelli Edge."

> "The proven, scientific system that has produced compounded yearly gains of 20.2% since 1982!"

> "Elaine Garzarelli has called every major turn in the Dow since 1982."

Now, if these comments were true, why did Garzarelli's investment fund perform so poorly, and why did Shearson fire her in the mid-1990s following numerous years of inaccurate predictions and the dismal performance of her mutual fund? I also find it humorous that the 20.2 percent return was reportedly "audited by a Big-6 accounting firm." Down in the fine print, however, it says, "Audit Pending." I bet it's still pending — probably with the same folks who audited Enron's financials (and went under)!

Every year, new gurus emerge. All it seems to take to leap into guru status these days is one right call or one good stock pick. In the mid- to late-1990s, for example, prognosticators who recommended one of the high-flying technology stocks were nearly vaulted to instant guru status as the stocks continued climbing.

Pundits who pitched investing in Presstek and Iomega attracted fairly large followings as these stocks seemed to defy gravity and rationale valuations while they rocketed ever skyward. Like Ms. Garzarelli, however, these stocks and their promoters were brought back to reality during the late-1990s when the stocks plummeted by more than 65 percent.

And, like other high-flying stocks and the pundits made famous by them, many investors weren't attracted to invest in Presstek and Iomega until nearly everybody was talking about them. By then, those stocks were peaking, and investors who bought them got clobbered.

Herb Greenberg, a former business writer for the *San Francisco Chronicle*, held a stock market contest. The contest was won by a group of 13-year-olds, because they put most of their money into Iomega while it was still heading up. Does this mean that these 13-year-olds are investing geniuses to whom we should look for guidance on the next hot stock? Of course not. Treat other pundits who happened to guess right the same way.

Commentators and experts who publish predictive newsletters and are interviewed in the media can't predict the future. Ignore the predictions and speculations of self-proclaimed gurus and investment soothsayers. The few people who have a slight leg up on everyone else aren't going to share their investment secrets — they're too busy investing their own money! If you have to believe in something to offset your fears, believe in good information and proven investment managers. And don't forget the value of optimism, faith, and hope — regardless of *what* or *whom* you believe in!

Leaving You with Some Final Advice

I cover a lot of ground in this chapter. In the remaining chapters in this part, I detail different investment choices and accounts, and how to build a champion portfolio! Before you move on, here are several other issues to keep in mind as you make important investing choices:

✔ **Don't invest based on sales solicitations.** Companies that advertise and solicit prospective customers aggressively with tactics such as telemarketing offer some of the worst financial products with the highest fees. Companies with great products don't have to reach their potential customers this way. Of course, all companies have to do some promotion. But the companies with the best investment offerings don't have to use the hard-sell approach; they get plenty of new business through the word-of-mouth recommendations of satisfied customers.

✔ **Don't invest in what you don't understand.** The mistake of not understanding the investments you purchase usually follows from the preceding no-no — buying into a sales pitch. When you don't understand an investment, odds are good that it won't be right for you. Slick-tongued brokers (who may call themselves financial consultants, advisors, or planners) who earn commissions based on what they sell can talk you into inappropriate investments. Before you invest in anything, you should know its track record, its true costs, and how liquid it is.

✔ **Minimize fees.** Avoid investments that carry high sales commissions and management expenses (usually disclosed in a prospectus). Virtually all investments today can be purchased without a salesperson. Besides paying unnecessary commissions, the bigger danger in investing through a salesperson is that you may be directed to a path that's not in your best interests. Management fees create a real drag on investment returns. Not surprisingly, higher-fee investments, on average, perform worse than alternatives with lower fees. High ongoing management fees often go toward lavish offices, glossy brochures, and skyscraper salaries, or toward propping up small, inefficient operations. Do you want your hard-earned dollars to support either of these types of businesses?

✔ **Pay attention to tax consequences.** Even if you never become an investment expert, you're smart enough to know that the more money you pay in taxes, the less you have for investing and playing with. See Chapter 10 for how retirement accounts can help boost your investment returns. For investments outside retirement accounts, you need to match the types of investments to your tax situation (see Chapter 11).

Chapter 8

Choosing Your Investment Vehicles

- -

In This Chapter

▶ "Safe" investments: bank and money market accounts and bonds

▶ Investments to grow on: stocks, real estate, and small business

▶ Oddball investments: precious metals, annuities, collectibles, and life insurance

- -

*I*n the investment world, you can place your money in many different types of investment vehicles. Decent investment vehicles work their way methodically around the racetrack, rarely deterred but also never at a fast rate. The best investment vehicles make their way through the course at a rapid clip, only occasionally slowed by a bump or detour. The worst investment vehicles sputter in fits and starts, and sometimes crash and burn in a flaming heap.

Which vehicle you choose for your investment journey depends on where you're going, how fast you want to get there, and what risks you're willing to take along the way. If you haven't yet read Chapter 7, please do so now. In it, I cover a number of investment concepts, such as the difference between lending and ownership investments, that will enhance your ability to choose among the common investment vehicles I discuss in this chapter.

Slow and Steady Investments

Everyone should have some money riding in stable, safe investment vehicles. For example, money that you have earmarked for your short-term bills, both expected and unexpected, should have two seat belts on in the back seat of a Volvo family sedan. Likewise, if you're saving money for a home purchase within the next few years, you certainly don't want to risk that money on the roller coaster of the stock market.

The investment vehicles that follow are appropriate for money you don't want to put at great risk.

Transaction/checking accounts

Transaction/checking accounts are best used for depositing your monthly income and paying for your expenditures. If you want to have unlimited check-writing privileges and access to your money with an ATM card, checking accounts at local banks are often your best bet. Make sure that you shop around for accounts that don't ding you $1 here for the use of an ATM machine, and $10 there for a low balance.

With interest rates as low as they are now, you want to focus on avoiding monthly service charges rather than chasing after a checking account with a slightly higher interest rate. Some banks, for example, do not require you to maintain a minimum balance to avoid a monthly service charge when you direct deposit your paychecks.

You can generally get a better checking account deal at a credit union or a smaller bank. Because you can easily obtain cash through ATM outlets in supermarkets and other retail stores, you may not need to do business with Big City Bank, which has branch offices at every intersection.

In any event, you should only keep enough money in the account for your monthly bill payment needs. If you consistently keep more than a few thousand dollars in a checking account, get the excess out. You can earn more in a savings or money market account, which I describe in the following section.

Some folks (myself included) don't have a bank checking account. How do they do that? They have discount brokerage accounts that allow unlimited check-writing within a money market fund. (See Chapter 9 for recommended firms; also see my discussion in Chapter 18 about paying your bills via your computer and through other automatic means.)

Savings and money market accounts

Savings accounts are available through banks; money market funds are available through mutual fund companies. Savings accounts and money market funds are nearly identical, except that money market funds generally pay a better rate of interest. The interest rate paid to you, also known as the *yield,* fluctuates over time, depending on the level of interest rates in the overall economy. (Note that some banks offer money market *accounts,* which are basically like savings accounts and should not be confused with money market mutual *funds.*)

The federal government backs bank savings accounts with Federal Deposit Insurance Corporation (FDIC) insurance. Money market funds are not insured. You shouldn't give preference to a bank account just because your investment (principal) is insured. In fact, your preference should lean toward money market funds, because the better ones are higher yielding than the better bank savings accounts. And money market funds offer check writing and other easy ways to access your money.

Money market funds are closely regulated by the U.S. Securities and Exchange Commission. Hundreds of billions of dollars of individuals' and institutions' money are invested in hundreds of money market funds. The industry has never caused an individual to lose even a penny of principal.

Money market funds are extremely safe — many are guaranteed or backed by a federal government agency. The risk difference versus a bank account is nil. General purpose money market funds invest in safe, short-term bank certificates of deposit, U.S. Treasuries, and *corporate commercial paper* (short-term debt), which is issued by the largest and most credit-worthy companies.

Money market fund investments can exist only in the most credit-worthy securities and must have an average maturity of less than 120 days. In the unlikely event that an investment in a money market fund's portfolio goes sour, the mutual fund company that stands behind the money market fund will almost certainly cover the loss.

If the lack of insurance on money market funds still spooks you, select a money market fund that invests exclusively in U.S. government securities, which are virtually risk-free because they're backed by the full strength and credit of the federal government (as is the FDIC insurance system). These types of accounts typically pay less interest (usually ¼ percent less, although the interest is free of state income tax).

Bonds

When you invest in a bond, you effectively lend your money to an organization. When a bond is issued, it includes a specified maturity date at which time the principal will be repaid. Bonds are also issued at a particular interest rate, or what's known as a *coupon.* This rate is fixed on most bonds. So, for example, if you buy a five-year, 6 percent bond issued by Home Depot, you're lending your money to Home Depot for five years at an interest rate of 6 percent per year. Bond interest is usually paid in two equal, semi-annual installments.

The value of a bond generally fluctuates with changes in interest rates. For example, if you're holding a bond issued at 6 percent, and rates increase to 8 percent on comparable, newly issued bonds, your bond decreases in value. (Why would anyone want to buy your bond at the price you paid if it yields just 6 percent, and 8 percent can be obtained elsewhere?)

The overused certificate of deposit

A *certificate of deposit* (CD) is another type of bond that is issued by a bank. With a CD, as with a real bond, you agree to lend your money to an organization (in this case, a bank) for a predetermined number of months or years. Generally, the longer you agree to lock up your money, the higher the interest rate you receive.

With CDs, you pay a penalty for early withdrawal. If you want your money back before the end of the CD's term, you get whacked with the loss of a number of months' worth of interest. CDs also don't tend to pay very competitive interest rates. You can usually beat the interest rate on shorter-term CDs (those that mature within a year or so) with the best money market mutual funds, which offer complete liquidity without any penalty.

Some bonds are tied to variable interest rates. For example, you can buy bonds that are adjustable-rate mortgages, on which the interest rate can fluctuate. As an investor, you're actually lending your money to a mortgage borrower — indirectly, you're the banker making a loan to someone buying a home.

Bonds differ from one another in the following major ways:

- The type of institution to which you are lending your money

  With municipal bonds, you lend your money to the state government; with Treasuries, you lend your money to the federal government; with GNMAs (Ginnie Maes), you lend your money to a mortgage holder (GNMA); and with corporate bonds, you lend your money to a corporation

- The credit quality of the borrower to whom you lend your money

  This refers to the probability that the borrower will pay you the interest and return your principal as agreed.

- The length of maturity of the bond

  Bonds generally mature within 30 years. Short-term bonds mature within a few years, intermediate bonds within 3 to 10 years, and long-term bonds within 30 years. Longer-term bonds generally pay higher yields but fluctuate more with changes in interest rates.

Bonds are rated by major credit-rating agencies for their safety, usually on a scale where AAA is the highest possible rating. For example, high-grade corporate bonds (AAA or AA) are considered the safest (that is, most likely to pay you back). Next in safety are general bonds (A or BBB), which are still safe but just a little less so. Junk bonds (rated BB or lower), popularized by Michael Milken, are actually not all that junky; they're just lower in quality and have a slight (1 or 2 percent) probability of default.

Some bonds are *callable,* which means that the lender can decide to pay you back earlier than the previously agreed-upon date. This event usually occurs when interest rates fall and the lender wants to issue new, lower-interest-rate bonds to replace the higher-rate bonds outstanding. To compensate you for early repayment, the lender typically gives you a small premium or bonus over what the bond is really worth.

Building Wealth with Ownership Vehicles

The three best legal ways to build wealth are to invest in stocks, real estate, and small business. I found this to be true from observing many clients and other investors, and from my own personal experiences.

Stocks

Stocks, which represent shares of ownership in a company, are the most common ownership investment vehicle. When companies *go public,* they issue shares of stock that people like you and I can purchase on the major stock exchanges, such as the New York Stock Exchange, the American Stock Exchange, and NASDAQ (National Association of Securities Dealers Automated Quotation system), or the over-the-counter market.

As the economy grows, and companies grow with it and earn greater profits, stock prices generally follow suit. Stock prices don't move in lockstep with earnings, but over the years, the relationship is pretty close. In fact, the *price-earnings ratio* — which measures the level of stock prices relative to (or divided by) company earnings — of U.S. stocks has averaged approximately 15 during this century (although it's tended to be higher during periods of low inflation). A price-earnings ratio of 15 simply means that stock prices per share, on average, are selling at about 15 times those companies' earnings per share.

Companies that issue stock (called *publicly held* companies) include automobile manufacturers, computer software producers, fast food restaurants, hotels, magazine and newspaper publishers, supermarkets, wineries, zipper manufacturers, and everything in between! By contrast, some companies are *privately held,* which means that they have elected to have their stock owned by senior management (and sometimes a small number of affluent outside investors). Privately held companies' stocks do not trade on a stock exchange, so folks like you and me can't buy stock in such firms.

International stocks

Not only can you invest in company stocks that trade on the U.S. stock exchanges, but you can also invest in stocks overseas. Aside from folks with business connections abroad, why would the average citizen want to invest in stocks overseas?

I can give you several reasons. First, many investing opportunities exist overseas. If you look at the total value of all stocks outstanding worldwide, the value of U.S. stocks is less than half the total.

Another reason for investing in international stocks is that, when you confine your investing to U.S. securities, you miss a world of opportunities, not only because of business growth available in other countries but also because you get the opportunity to diversify your portfolio even further. International securities markets don't move in tandem with U.S. markets. During various U.S. stock market drops, some international stock markets drop less, while others actually rise in value.

Some people hesitate to invest in overseas securities for silly reasons. One column I came across in a big city paper was entitled "Plenty of Pitfalls in Foreign Investing: Timing is all in earning a decent return." The piece went on to say, "But as with sex, commuting and baseball, timing is everything in the stock market." Smart stock market investors know better than to try to time their investments. The piece also ominously warned, "Foreign stock markets have been known to evaporate overnight." I wish I could say the same for the jobs of some bone-headed financial journalists!

Others are concerned that overseas investing hurts the U.S. economy and contributes to a loss of American jobs. I have some counter-arguments. First, if you don't profit from the growth of economies overseas, someone else will. If there is money to be made, Americans may as well be there to participate. Profits from a foreign company are distributed to all stock-holders, no matter where they live. Dividends and stock price appreciation know no national boundaries.

Also, you must recognize that you already live in a global economy — making a distinction between U.S. and non-U.S. companies is no longer appropriate. Many companies that are headquartered in the United States also have overseas operations. Some U.S. firms derive a large portion of their revenue from their international divisions. Conversely, many firms based overseas also have U.S. operations. An increasing number of companies are worldwide operations. You don't get the full benefit of international investing by buying just large multinational companies headquartered in the United States. The overseas diversification advantage is obtained by investing in companies that trade on foreign exchanges.

Companies differ in what industry or line of business they're in and also in size. In the financial press, you often hear companies referred to by their *market capitalization,* which is the value of their outstanding stock (the number of total shares multiplied by the market price per share). When describing the sizes of companies, Wall Street has done away with such practical adjectives as *big* and *small,* and replaced them with expressions like *large cap* and *small cap* (where *cap* stands for *capitalization*). Such is the language of financial geekiness.

Investing in the stock market involves occasional setbacks and difficult moments (just like raising children or going mountain climbing), but the overall journey should be worth the effort. Over the past two centuries, the U.S. stock market has produced an annual average rate of return of about 10 percent. However, the market, as measured by the Dow Jones Industrial Average, fell more than 20 percent during 16 different periods in the 20th century. On average, these periods of decline lasted less than two years. So if you can withstand a temporary setback over a few years, the stock market is a proven place to invest for long-term growth.

You can invest in stocks by making your own selection of individual stocks or by letting a mutual fund manager (discussed in Chapter 9) do it for you.

Discovering the relative advantages of mutual funds

Efficiently managed mutual funds offer investors of both modest and substantial means low-cost access to high-quality money managers. Mutual funds span the spectrum of risk and potential returns, from nonfluctuating money market funds (which are similar to savings accounts) to bond funds (which generally pay higher yields than money market funds but fluctuate with changes in interest rates) to stock funds (which offer the greatest potential for appreciation but also the greatest short-term volatility).

For investors, mutual funds make better sense than individual securities. To illustrate, imagine the following scenario: You just bought your first home. It's an older, lived-in property with neon-yellow carpets that have accumulated 20-plus years of food spills and pet accidents. You want to tear out the yucky old carpet and install hardwood floors.

Imagine that you can either redo your flooring work yourself or pay a contractor just $200 to do it for you. You'd go with the contractor if you could hire him this cheaply. The only type of person who would choose to go it alone is someone who really enjoys this type of work. You're not going to be able to do a faster, better job than a full-time contractor if you do a decent job searching for a good one.

You should use this same line of thinking when considering how to invest in stocks and bonds. Investing in individual securities should be done only by those who really enjoy doing it. Mutual funds, if properly selected, are a low-cost, quality way to hire professional money managers.

Over the long haul, you're not going to beat full-time professional managers who are investing in the securities of the same type and risk level. As with hiring a contractor, you need to do your homework to find a good money manager. Chapter 9 is devoted to mutual funds.

Investing in individual stocks

My experience is that plenty of people choose to invest in individual securities because they think that they're smarter or luckier than the rest. I don't know you personally, but it's safe to say that, in the long run, your investment choices aren't going to outperform those of a full-time investment professional.

I notice a distinct difference between the sexes on this issue. Perhaps because of the differences in how people are raised, testosterone levels, or whatever, men tend to have more of a problem swallowing their egos and admitting that they're better off not selecting their own individual securities. Maybe the desire to be a stock picker is genetically linked to not wanting to ask for directions!

You should generally avoid investing in individual stocks. Success is difficult to attain, and the drawbacks and pitfalls are numerous:

- ✔ **You'll have to spend a significant amount of time doing research.** When you're considering the purchase of an individual security, you should know a lot about the company in which you're thinking about investing. Relevant questions to ask about the company include: What products does it sell? What are its prospects for future growth and profitability? How much debt does the company have? You need to do your homework not only before you make your initial investment but also on an ongoing basis for as long as you hold the investment. Research takes your valuable free time and sometimes costs money.

  Don't fool yourself or let others with a vested interest fool you into believing that picking and following individual companies and their stocks is simple, requires little time, and is far more profitable than investing in mutual funds.

- ✔ **Your emotions will probably get in your way.** Analyzing financial statements, corporate strategy, and competitive position requires great intellect and insight. However, those skills aren't nearly enough. Will you have the stomach to hold on after what you thought was a sure-win stock plunges 50 percent while the overall stock market holds steady or even climbs? Will you have the courage to dump such a stock if your new research suggests that the plummet is the beginning of the end rather than just a big bump in the road? When your money is on the line, emotions often kick in and undermine your ability to make sound long-term decisions. Few people have the psychological constitution to outfox the financial markets.

- ✔ **You're less likely to diversify.** Unless you have tens of thousands of dollars to invest in different stocks, you probably can't cost-effectively afford to develop a diversified portfolio. For example, when you're investing in stocks, you need to hold companies in different industries, different companies within an industry, and so on. By not diversifying, you unnecessarily add to your risk.

✔ **You'll face accounting and bookkeeping hassles.** When you invest in individual securities outside retirement accounts, you must report that transaction on your tax return every time you sell a specific security. Even if you pay someone else to complete your tax return, you still have the hassle of keeping track of statements and receipts.

Of course, you may find some people (with a vested interest) who try to convince you that picking your own stocks and managing your own portfolio of stocks is easy and more profitable than investing in, say, a mutual fund. In my experience, such stock-picking cheerleaders fall into at least one of the following categories:

✔ **Newsletter writers.** Whether in print or on a Web site, you can find plenty of pundits who pitch the notion that professional money managers are just overpaid buffoons, and that you can handily trounce the pros with little investment of your time by simply putting your money into the pundits' stock picks. Of course, what these self-anointed gurus are really selling is either an ongoing print newsletter (which can run upwards of several hundred dollars per year) or your required daily visitation of their advertising-stuffed Web sites. How else will you be able to keep up with their announced buy-and-sell recommendations? These supposed experts want you to be dependent on continually following their advice. Of course, you may be wondering, "Hey, if these pundits were such geniuses at picking the best stocks, why aren't they making piles of money just investing rather than selling their supposed brilliant insights on the cheap?" Go to the head of the class and don't waste your time and money following such pundits' picks! (I discuss investment newsletters in Chapter 7 and Web sites in Chapter 18.)

✔ **Book authors.** Go into any bookstore with a decent-sized investing section and you'll find plenty of books claiming that they can teach you a stock-picking strategy for beating the system. Never mind the fact that the author has no independently audited track demonstrating his success! In Chapter 19, I present examples of such hucksters, including one investment group whose book publisher was successfully sued over hyping and distorting the group's actual investment success.

✔ **Stockbrokers.** Some brokers steer you toward individual stocks for several reasons that benefit the broker and not you. First, as I discuss in Chapter 7, the high commission brokerage firms can make handsome profits for themselves by getting you to buy stocks. Secondly, brokers can use changes in the company's situation to encourage you to then sell and buy different stocks, generating even more commissions. Lastly, as with newsletter writers, this whole process forces you to be dependent on the broker, leaving you broker!

Individual stock dividend reinvestment plans

Many corporations allow existing shareholders to reinvest their dividends in more shares of stock without paying brokerage commissions. In some cases, companies allow you to make additional cash purchases of more shares of stock, also commission-free.

In order to qualify, you must first generally buy some shares of stock through a broker (although some companies allow the initial purchases to be made directly from them). Ideally, you should purchase these initial shares through a discount broker to keep your commission burden as low as possible. Some investment associations also have plans that allow you to buy one or just a few shares to get started.

I'm not enamored of these plans, because this type of investing is generally available and cost-effective for investments held outside retirement accounts. You typically need to complete a lot of paperwork to invest in a number of different companies' stock. Life is too short to bother with these plans for this reason alone.

Finally, even with those companies that do sell stock directly without charging an explicit commission like a brokerage firm, you pay plenty of other fees. Many plans charge an upfront enrollment fee, fees for reinvesting dividends, and another fee when you want to sell.

Researching individual stocks can be more than a full-time job, and if you choose to take this path, remember that you'll be competing against the professionals who do so on a full-time basis. If you derive pleasure from picking and following your own stocks, or you want an independent opinion of some stocks you currently own, the best research reports are available from the Value Line Investment Survey. This superb publication provides concise, user-friendly, single-page summaries of thousands of stocks. Libraries with good business sections often carry this publication. You can order a 10-week trial by calling Value Line at 800-833-0046. I also recommend that you limit your individual stock-picking to no more than 20 percent of your overall investments.

Generating wealth with real estate

Over the generations, real estate owners and investors have enjoyed rates of return comparable to those produced by the stock market, thus making real estate another time-tested method for building wealth. However, like stocks, real estate goes through good and bad performance periods. Most people who make money investing in real estate do so because they invest over many years.

Buying your own home is the best place to start investing in real estate. The *equity* (the difference between the market value of the home and the loan owed on it) in your home that builds over the years can become a significant part of your net worth. Among other things, this equity can be tapped into to help finance other important money and personal goals such as retirement, college, and starting or buying a business.

Throughout your adult life, owning a home should be less expensive than renting a comparable home. The reason: As a renter, your housing costs are fully exposed to inflation (unless you're the beneficiary of a rent-controlled apartment). As a homeowner, the bulk of your housing costs — your monthly mortgage — is not exposed to inflation if you finance your home purchase with a fixed-rate mortgage. And your mortgage interest and property tax costs are generally deductible expenses for tax purposes. You can also make substantial tax-free profits when you sell your home. See Chapter 13 to discover the best ways to buy and finance real estate.

Real estate: Not your ordinary investment

Besides providing solid rates of return, real estate also differs from most other investments in several other respects. Here's what makes real estate unique as an investment:

- ✔ **Usability.** You can't live in a stock, bond, or mutual fund (although I suppose you could glue together a substantial fortress with all the paper these companies fill your mailbox with each year). Real estate is the only investment you can use (living in or renting out) to produce income.

- ✔ **Land is in limited supply.** Last time I checked, the percentage of the Earth occupied by land wasn't increasing. And because humans like to reproduce, the demand for land and housing continues to grow. Consider the areas that have the most expensive real estate prices in the world — Hong Kong, Tokyo, Hawaii, San Francisco, and Manhattan. In these densely populated areas, virtually no new land is available for building new housing.

- ✔ **Zoning shapes potential value.** Local government regulates the zoning of property, and zoning determines what a property can be used for. In most communities these days, local zoning boards are against big growth. This position bodes well for future real estate values. Also know that, in some cases, a particular property may not have been developed to its full potential. If you can figure out how to develop the property, you can reap large profits.

- ✔ **Leverage.** Real estate is also different from other investments because you can borrow a lot of money to buy it — up to 80 to 90 percent or more of the value of the property. This borrowing is known as exercising *leverage:* With only a small investment of 10 to 20 percent down, you're able to purchase and own a much larger investment. When the value of your real estate goes up, you make money on your investment and on all the money you borrowed. (In case you're curious, you can leverage non-retirement-account stock and bond investments through margin borrowing. However, you have to make a much larger "down payment" — about double to triple when compared with buying real estate.)

For example, suppose that you plunk down $20,000 to purchase a property for $100,000. If the property appreciates to $120,000, you make a profit of $20,000 (on paper) on your investment of just $20,000. In other words, you make a 100 percent return on your investment. But leverage cuts both ways. If your $100,000 property decreases in value to $80,000, you actually lose (on paper) 100 percent of your original $20,000 investment, even though the property value only drops 20 percent in value.

✔ **Hidden values.** In an *efficient market,* the price of an investment accurately reflects its true worth. Some investment markets are more efficient than others because of the large number of transactions and easily accessible information. Real estate markets can be inefficient at times. Information is not always easy to come by, and you may find an ultramotivated or uninformed seller. If you're willing to do some homework, you may be able to purchase a property below its fair market value (perhaps by as much as 10 to 20 percent).

Just as with any other investment, real estate has its drawbacks. For starters, buying or selling a property generally takes time and significant cost. Also, holding a property typically costs a good deal of ongoing money. When you're renting property, you discover firsthand the occasional headaches of being a landlord. And, especially in the early years of rental property ownership, the property's expenses may exceed the rental income, producing a net cash drain.

The best real estate investment options

Although real estate is in some ways unique, it's also like other types of investments in that prices are driven by supply and demand. You can invest in homes or small apartment buildings and then rent them out. In the long run, investment-property buyers hope that their rent income and the value of their properties will increase faster than their expenses.

When selecting real estate for investment purposes, remember that local economic growth is the fuel for housing demand. In addition to a vibrant and diverse job base, you want to look for limited supplies of both existing housing and land on which to build. When you identify potential properties in which you may want to invest, run the numbers to understand the cash demands of owning the property and the likely profitability. See Chapter 13 for help determining the costs of real estate ownership.

Comparing real estate and stocks

Real estate and stocks have historically produced comparable returns. Deciding between the two depends less on the performance of the markets than on you and your situation. Consider the following major issues when deciding which investment may be better for you:

✔ The first and most important question to ask yourself is whether you're cut out to handle the responsibilities that come with being a landlord. Real estate is a time-intensive investment. Investing in stocks can be time-intensive as well, but it doesn't have to be if you use professionally managed mutual funds (see Chapter 9).

✔ An often-overlooked drawback to investing in real estate is that you earn no tax benefits while you're accumulating your down payment. Retirement accounts such as 401(k)s, SEP-IRAs, Keoghs, and so on (see Chapter 10) give you an immediate tax deduction as you contribute money to them. If you haven't exhausted your contributions to these accounts, consider doing so before chasing after investment real estate.

✔ Ask yourself which investments you have a better understanding of. Some folks feel uncomfortable with stocks and mutual funds because they don't understand them. If you have a better handle on what makes real estate tick, you have a good reason to consider investing in it.

✔ Figure out what will make you happy. Some people enjoy the challenge that comes with managing and improving rental property; it can be a bit like running a small business. If you're good at it, and you have some good fortune, you can make money and derive endless hours of enjoyment.

Although few will admit it, some real estate investors get an ego rush from a tangible display of their wealth. Sufferers of this "edifice complex" can't obtain similar pleasure from a stock portfolio detailed on a piece of paper (although others have been known to boast of their stock-picking prowess).

When you want to invest directly in real estate, residential housing — such as single-family homes or small multi-unit buildings — may be a straightforward and attractive investment for you. Buying properties close to "home" offers the advantage of allowing you to more easily monitor and manage what's going on. The downside is that you'll be less diversified — more of your investments will be dependent on your local economy.

If you don't want to be a landlord — one of the biggest drawbacks of investment real estate — consider investing in real estate through real estate investment trusts (REITs). *REITs* are diversified real estate investment companies that purchase and manage rental real estate for investors. A typical REIT invests in different types of property, such as shopping centers, apartments, and other rental buildings. You can invest in REITs either by purchasing them directly on the major stock exchanges or by investing in a real estate mutual fund (see Chapter 9) that invests in numerous REITs.

The worst real estate investments

Not all real estate investments are good; some aren't even real investments. The bad ones are characterized by burdensome costs and problematic economic fundamentals:

✔ **Limited partnerships.** You should avoid limited partnerships (LPs) sold through brokers and financial consultants. LPs are inferior investment vehicles. They're so burdened with high sales commissions and ongoing management fees that deplete your investment, that you can do better elsewhere. The investment salesperson who sells you such an investment stands to earn a commission of up to 10 percent or more — so only 90 cents of each dollar gets invested. Each year, LPs typically siphon off another several percent for management and other expenses. Most partnerships have little or no incentive to control costs. In fact, they have a conflict of interest that forces them to charge more to enrich the managing partners.

Unlike a mutual fund, you can't vote with your dollars. If the partnership is poorly run and expensive, you're stuck. LPs are *illiquid* (readily convertible into cash without a substantial loss). You can't access your money until the partnership is liquidated, typically seven to ten years after you buy in.

Brokers who sell LPs often tell you that, while your investment is growing at 20 percent or more per year, you get handsome dividends of 8 percent or so per year. Many of the yields on LPs have turned out to be bogus. In some cases, partnerships propped up their yields by paying back investors' principals (without telling them, of course). As for returns — well — most LP investors of a decade ago are lucky to have half their original investment left. The only thing limited about a limited partnership is its ability to make you money.

✔ **Time shares.** Time shares are another nearly certain money loser. With a time share, you buy a week or two of ownership, or usage, of a particular unit (usually a condominium in a resort location) per year. If, for example, you pay $8,000 for a week (in addition to ongoing maintenance fees), you're paying the equivalent of more than $400,000 for the whole unit, when a comparable unit nearby may sell for only $150,000. The extra markup pays the salespeople's commissions, administrative expenses, and profits for the time share development company.

People usually get enticed into buying a time share when they're enjoying a vacation someplace. They're easy prey for salespeople who want to sell them a souvenir of the trip. The "cheese in the mousetrap" is an offer of something free (for example, a free night's stay in a unit) for going through the sales presentation.

If you can't live without a time share, consider buying a used one. Many previous buyers, who more than likely have lost a good chunk of money, are trying to dump their shares (which should tell you something). In this case, you may be able to buy a time share at a fair price. But why commit yourself to taking a vacation in the same location and building at the same time each year? Many time shares let you trade your weeks for other times and other places; however, doing so is a hassle — you're charged an extra fee, and your choices are usually limited to time slots that other people don't want (that's why they're trading them!).

✔ **Second homes.** The weekend getaway is a sometimes romantic notion and an extended part of the so-called American dream — a place you can escape to a couple of times a month. When your vacation home is not in use, you may be able to rent it out and earn some income to help defray the expense of keeping it up.

If you can realistically afford the additional costs of a second (or vacation) home, I'm not going to tell you how to spend your extra cash. But please don't make the all-too-common mistake of viewing a second home as an investment. The way most people use them, they're not. Most second-homeowners seldom rent out their property — they typically do so 10 percent or less of the time. As a result, second homes are usually money drains.

The supposed tax benefits are part of the attraction of a second home. Even when you qualify for some or all of them, tax benefits only partially reduce the cost of owning a property. In some cases, the second home is such a cash drain, that it prevents its owners from contributing to and taking advantage of tax-deductible retirement savings plans.

If you aren't going to rent out a second home most of the time, ask yourself whether you can afford such a luxury. Can you accomplish your other financial goals — saving for retirement, paying for the home in which you live, and so on — with this added expense? Keeping a second home is more of a consumption than an investment decision. Few people can afford more than one home.

Investing in small business

With what type of investment have more people built great wealth? If you said the stock market or real estate, you're wrong. The answer is small business. You can invest in small business by starting one yourself (and thus finding yourself the best boss you've probably ever had), buying an existing business, or investing in someone else's small business.

Launching your own enterprise

When you have self-discipline and a product or service you can sell, starting your own business can be both profitable and fulfilling. Consider first what skills and expertise you possess that you can use in your business. You don't need a "eureka-type" idea or invention to start a small business. Millions of people operate successful businesses that are hardly unique, such as dry cleaners, restaurants, tax preparation firms, and so on.

Begin exploring your idea by first developing a written business plan. Such a plan should detail what your product or service is going to be, how you're going to market it, who your customers and competitors are, and what the economics of the business are, including the start-up costs.

Of all the small-business investment options, starting your own business involves the greatest amount of work. Although you can do this work on a part-time basis in the beginning, most people end up running their business full-time — it's your new job, career, or whatever you want to call it.

I've been running my own business for most of my working years, and I wouldn't trade that experience for the corporate life. That's not to say that running my own business doesn't have its drawbacks and down moments. But in my experience counseling small-business owners, I've seen many people of varied backgrounds, interests, and skills succeed and be happy with running their own businesses.

In the eyes of most people, starting a new business is the riskiest of all small-business investment options. But if you're going into a business that utilizes your skills and expertise, the risk is not nearly as great as you may think. Many businesses can be started with little cash by leveraging your existing skills and expertise. You can build a valuable company and job if you have the time to devote. As long as you check out the competition and offer a valued service at a reasonable cost, the principal risk with your business comes from not doing a good job marketing what you have to offer. If you can market your skills, you're home free.

As long as you're thinking about the risks of starting a business, consider the risks of staying in a job you don't enjoy or that doesn't challenge or fulfill you. If you never take the plunge, you may regret that you didn't pursue your dreams.

Buying an existing business

If you don't have a specific product or service you want to sell, but you're skilled at managing and improving the operations of a company, buying a small business may be for you. Finding and buying a good small business takes much time and patience, so be willing to devote at least several months to the search. You may also need to enlist financial and legal advisors to help inspect the company, look over its financial statements, and hammer out a contract.

Although you don't have to go through the riskier start-up period if you buy a small business, you'll likely need more capital to buy an established enterprise. You'll also need to be able to deal with stickier personnel and management issues. The history of the organization and the way things work will predate your ownership of the business. If you don't like making hard decisions, firing people who don't fit with your plans, and coercing people into changing the way they do things, buying an existing business likely isn't for you.

Some people perceive buying an existing business as being safer than starting a new one. Buying someone else's business can actually be riskier. You're likely to shell out far more money upfront, in the form of a down payment, to buy an existing business. If you don't have the ability to run the business and it does poorly, you have more to lose financially. In addition, the business may be for sale for a reason — it may not be very profitable, it may be in decline, or it may generally be a pain in the neck to operate.

Good businesses don't come cheaply. If the business is a success, the current owner has already removed the start-up risk from the business, so the price of the business should be at a premium to reflect this lack of risk. When you have the capital to buy an established business and you have the skills to run it, consider going this route.

Investing in someone else's small business

Are you someone who likes the idea of profiting from successful small businesses but doesn't want the day-to-day headaches of being responsible for managing the enterprise? Then investing in someone else's small business may be for you. Although this route may seem easier, few people are actually cut out to be investors in other people's businesses. The reason: Finding and analyzing opportunities isn't easy.

Are you astute at evaluating corporate financial statements and business strategies? Investing in a small, privately held company has much in common with investing in a publicly traded firm (as is the case when you buy stock), but it also has a few differences. One difference is that private firms aren't required to produce comprehensive, audited financial statements that adhere to certain accounting principles. Thus, you have a greater risk of not having sufficient or accurate information when evaluating a small private firm.

Another difference is that unearthing private small-business investing opportunities is harder. The best private companies who are seeking investors generally don't advertise. Instead, they find prospective investors through networking with people such as business advisors. You can increase your chances of finding private companies to invest in by speaking with tax, legal, and financial advisors who work with small businesses. You can also find interesting opportunities through your own contacts or experience within a given industry.

You shouldn't consider investing in someone else's business unless you can afford to lose all of what you're investing. Also, you should have sufficient assets so that what you're investing in small, privately held companies represents only a small portion (20 percent or less) of your total financial assets.

Off the Beaten Path: Investment Odds and Ends

The investments that I discuss in this section sometimes belong on their own planet (because they're not an ownership or lending vehicle). Here are the basics on these other common, but odd, investments.

Precious metals

Gold and silver have been used by many civilizations as currency or a medium of exchange. One advantage of precious metals as a currency is that they can't be debased by the government. With paper currency, such as U.S. dollars, the government can simply print more. This process can lead to the devaluation of a currency and inflation. It takes a whole lot more work to make more gold. Just ask Rumpelstiltskin.

Holdings of gold and silver can provide a so-called *hedge* against inflation. In the late 1970s and early 1980s, inflation rose dramatically in the United States. This largely unexpected rise in inflation depressed stocks and bonds. Gold and silver, however, rose tremendously in value — in fact, more than 500 percent (even after adjusting for inflation) from 1972 to 1980 (see Chapter 7). Such periods are unusual. Over many decades, precious metals tend to be lousy investments. Their rate of return tends to keep up with the rate of inflation but not surpass it.

When you want to invest in precious metals as an inflation hedge, your best option is to do so through mutual funds (see Chapter 9). Don't purchase precious metals futures. They're not investments; they're short-term gambles on which way gold or silver prices may head over a short period of time. You should also stay away from firms and shops that sell coins and *bullion* (not the soup, but bars of gold or silver). Even if you can find a legitimate firm (not an easy task), the cost of storing and insuring gold and silver is quite costly. You won't get good value for your money. I hate to tell you this, but the Gold Rush is over.

Annuities

Annuities are a peculiar type of insurance and investment product. They're a sort of savings-type account with slightly higher yields that are backed by insurance companies.

As with other types of retirement accounts, money placed in an annuity compounds without taxation until it is withdrawn. However, unlike most other types of retirement accounts, such as 401(k)s, SEP-IRAs, and Keoghs, you don't receive upfront tax breaks on contributions you make to an annuity. Annuities also tend to have much higher ongoing investment expenses than retirement plan accounts. Therefore, consider an annuity only after you fully fund tax-deductible retirement accounts. (For more help on deciding whether to invest in an annuity, read Chapter 11.)

Collectibles

The collectibles category is a catchall for antiques, art, autographs, baseball cards, clocks, coins, comic books, diamonds, dolls, gems, photographs, rare books, rugs, stamps, vintage wine, and writing utensils — in other words, any material object that, through some kind of human manipulation, has become more valuable to certain humans.

Notwithstanding the few people who discover on *The Antiques Road Show* that they own an antique of significant value, collectibles are generally lousy investment vehicles. Dealer markups are enormous, maintenance and protection costs are draining, research is time-consuming, and people's tastes are quite fickle. All this for returns that, after you factor in the huge markups, rarely keep up with inflation.

Buy collectibles for your love of the object, not for financial gain. Treat collecting as a hobby, not as an investment. When buying a collectible, try to avoid the big markups by cutting out the middlemen. Buy directly from the artist or producer if you can.

Life insurance with a cash value

Life insurance shouldn't be used as an investment, especially if you haven't exhausted your contributions to retirement accounts. Life insurance that combines insurance protection with an account that has a cash value is often referred to as universal, whole, or variable life. Agents love to sell it for the high commissions.

The only time you may want to consider buying cash value life insurance is if the proceeds paid to your beneficiaries are free of estate taxes. You need to have a fairly substantial estate at your death to benefit from this feature. (See Chapter 15 for more on life insurance and why term life insurance is best for the vast majority of people.)

Chapter 9

Investing in Mutual Funds

In This Chapter

▶ Why funds?

▶ Checking out the different types of funds

▶ Choosing the best funds

▶ Evaluating your fund's performance

▶ Monitoring and selling your funds

*W*hen you invest in a mutual fund, an investment company pools your money with the money of many other like-minded individuals and invests it in stocks, bonds, and other securities. Think of it as a big investment club without the meetings! When you invest through a typical mutual fund, several hundred million to a billion dollars or more may be invested along with your money.

Understanding the Benefits of Mutual Funds

Mutual funds rank right up there with microwave ovens, videocassette recorders, sticky notes, and plastic wrap as one of the best modern inventions. To understand their success is to grasp how and why funds can work for you. Read on to discover the benefits you receive when you invest in mutual funds:

✔ **Professional management.** Mutual funds are managed by a portfolio manager and research team whose full-time jobs are to screen the universe of investments for those that best meet the stated objectives of the fund. These professionals call and visit companies, analyze companies' financial statements, and speak with companies' suppliers and customers. In short, the team does more work and research than you could ever hope to do in your free time.

Fund managers are typically graduates of the top business and finance schools in the country, where they learn the principles of portfolio management and securities valuation and selection. (Despite their time in the groves of academe, most of them do a good job of investing money.) The best fund managers typically have five or more years of experience in analyzing and selecting investments, and many measure their experience in decades rather than years.

✔ **Low cost.** The most efficiently managed stock mutual funds cost less than 1 percent per year in fees (bonds and money market funds cost much less). Because mutual funds typically buy or sell tens of thousands of shares of a security at a time, the percentage commissions these funds pay are generally far less than what you pay to buy or sell a few hundred shares on your own. In addition, when you buy a *no-load fund,* you avoid paying sales commissions (known as *loads*) on your transactions. I discuss these types of funds throughout this chapter.

✔ **Diversification.** Mutual fund investing enables you to achieve a level of diversification that is difficult to reach without tens of thousands of dollars and a lot of time to invest. If you go it alone, you should invest money in at least 8 to 12 different securities in different industries to ensure that your portfolio can withstand a downturn in one or more of the investments. Proper diversification allows a mutual fund to receive the highest possible return at the lowest possible risk given its objectives. However, the most unfortunate investors during major stock market downswings have been individuals who had all of their money riding on only a few stocks that plunged in price by 90 percent or more.

✔ **Low cost of entry.** Most mutual funds have low minimum-investment requirements, especially for retirement account investors. Even if you have a lot of money to invest, you should also consider mutual funds. Join the increasing numbers of companies and institutions (who have the biggest bucks of all) that are turning to the low-cost, high-quality money-management services that mutual funds provide.

✔ **Audited performance records and expenses.** In their prospectuses, all mutual funds are required to disclose historical data on returns, operating expenses, and other fees. The Securities and Exchange Commission (SEC) and accounting firms check these disclosures for accuracy. Also, several firms (such as Morningstar, Inc.) provide monthly reporting on hundreds of fund statistics, allowing comparisons of performance, risk, and many other factors.

✔ **Flexibility in risk level.** Among the different mutual funds, you can choose a level of risk that you're comfortable with and that meets your personal and financial goals. If you want your money to grow over a long period of time, you may want to select funds that invest more heavily in stocks. If you need current income and don't want investments that fluctuate in value as widely as stocks, you may choose more conservative bond funds. If you want to be sure that your invested principal doesn't drop in value (perhaps because you may need your money in the short term), you can select a money market fund.

The rise of the mutual fund industry

Just as computers have replaced typewriters because they allow for more efficient word processing, mutual funds are replacing less-efficient institutions that manage money. That's not to say that banks and commission-based brokerage firms are going to disappear — but you'll probably see fewer of them in the coming years.

As for safety, mutual funds have a virtually zero risk of bankruptcy. Unlike banks and insurance companies (which have failed and will continue to fail), mutual funds have never failed — and probably won't fail in the future. The situation where the demand for money back *(liabilities)* exceeds the value of a fund's investments *(assets)* can't occur with a mutual fund.

The value of a fund fluctuates with the value of the securities in which it is invested. But this variation doesn't lead to the failure or bankruptcy of a mutual fund company. In fact, because the Investment Company Act of 1940 was passed to regulate the mutual fund industry, no fund has ever gone under.

In contrast, hundreds of banks and dozens of insurance companies have failed in recent decades. Banks and insurers can fail because their liabilities can exceed their assets. When a bank makes too many loans that go sour at the same time that depositors want their money back, the bank fails. Likewise, if an insurance company makes several poor investments or underestimates the number of claims that will be made by insurance policy holders, it, too, can fail.

And you don't have to worry about fund companies stealing your money. The specific securities in which a mutual fund is invested are held at a *custodian* — a separate organization independent of the mutual fund company. The employment of a custodian ensures that the fund management company can't embezzle your funds and use assets from a better-performing fund to subsidize a poor performer.

Exploring Various Fund Types

One of the major misconceptions about mutual funds is that they're all invested in stocks. They're not. Figure 9-1 shows how the money currently invested in mutual funds breaks down.

As you can see, the majority of mutual fund money is *not* invested in stocks. When you hear folks talk about the "riskiness" of mutual funds, even in the media, you know that they're overlooking this fact: All mutual funds are not created equal. Some funds, such as money market funds, carry virtually *no* risk that your investment will decline in value.

When mutual fund companies package and market funds, the names they give their funds aren't always completely accurate or comprehensive. For example, a stock fund may not be *totally* invested in stocks. Twenty percent of it may be invested in bonds. Don't assume that a fund invests exclusively in U.S. companies, either — it may invest in international firms, as well.

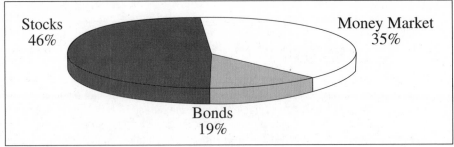

Figure 9-1:
How
mutual fund
assets are
invested.

Stocks
46%

Money Market
35%

Bonds
19%

Note: If you haven't yet read Chapters 7 and 8, which provide an overview of investment concepts and vehicles, doing so will enhance your understanding of the rest of this chapter.

Money market funds

Money market funds are the safest type of mutual funds for those concerned about losing their invested dollars. Money market funds are like bank savings accounts in that the value of your original investment does not fluctuate. (For more background on money funds, see Chapter 8.)

Money market funds have several advantages over bank savings accounts:

- ✔ The best money market funds have higher yields.

- ✔ If you're in a higher tax bracket, you have the option of using tax-free money market funds. No savings account pays tax-free interest.

- ✔ Most money market funds come with free check-writing privileges. (The only stipulation is that each check must be written for a minimum amount — $250 is common.)

As with money you put into bank savings accounts, money market funds are suitable for money that you can't afford to see dwindle in value.

Bond funds

Bonds are IOUs. When you buy a newly issued bond, you lend your money typically to a corporation or government agency. A *bond mutual fund* is nothing more than a large group (pack, herd, gaggle, whatever) of bonds.

Bond funds typically invest in bonds of similar *maturity* (the number of years that elapse before the borrower must pay back the money you lend). The names of most bond funds include a word or two that provides clues about the average length of maturity of their bonds. For example, a *short-term bond fund* typically concentrates its investments in bonds maturing in the next 2 to 3 years. An *intermediate-term fund* generally holds bonds that come due within 3 to 10 years. The bonds in a *long-term fund* usually mature in more than 10 years.

In contrast to an individual bond that you buy and hold until it matures, a bond fund is always replacing bonds in its portfolio to maintain its average maturity objective. Therefore, if you know that you absolutely, positively must have a certain principal amount back on a particular date, individual bonds may be more appropriate than a bond fund.

Like money market funds, bond funds can invest in tax-free bonds, which are appropriate for investing money you hold outside retirement accounts if you're in a reasonably high tax bracket.

Bond funds are useful when you want to live off dividend income or you don't want to put all your money in riskier investments such as stocks and real estate (perhaps because you plan to use the money soon).

Stock funds

Stock mutual funds, as their name implies, invest in stocks. These funds are often referred to as *equity funds. Equity* — not to be confused with equity in real estate — is another word for stocks. Stock mutual funds are often categorized by the type of stocks they primarily invest in.

Stock types are first defined by size of company (small, medium, or large). The total market value *(capitalization)* of a company's outstanding stock determines its size. Small-company stocks, for example, are usually defined as companies with total market capitalization of less than $1 billion.

Stocks are further categorized as growth or value. *Growth stocks* are companies that are experiencing rapidly expanding revenues and profits, and typically have high stock prices relative to their current earnings or asset (book) values. These companies tend to reinvest most of their earnings back into their infrastructure to fuel future expansion. Thus, growth stocks pay low dividends.

Value stocks are at the other end of the spectrum. Value stock investors look for good buys. They want to invest in stocks that are cheaply priced in relation to the assets and profits of the company.

These categories are combined in various ways to describe how a mutual fund invests its money. One fund may focus on large-company growth stocks, while another fund may limit itself to small-company value stocks. Funds are further classified by the geographical focus of their investments: U.S., international, worldwide, and so on (see the following section).

Balancing bonds and stocks: Hybrid funds

Hybrid funds invest in a mixture of different types of securities. Most commonly, they invest in bonds and stocks. These funds are usually less risky and volatile than funds that invest exclusively in stocks. In an economic downturn, bonds usually hold up in value better than stocks do. However, during good economic times when the stock market is booming, the bond portions of these funds tend to drag down their performance a bit.

Hybrid mutual funds are typically known as balanced funds or asset allocation funds. *Balanced funds* generally try to maintain a fairly constant percentage of investments in stocks and bonds. *Asset allocation funds* tend to adjust the mix of different investments according to the portfolio manager's expectations of the market. Of course, exceptions do exist — some balanced funds make major shifts in their allocations, whereas some asset allocation funds maintain a relatively fixed mix. You should note that most funds that shift money around instead of staying put in good investments rarely beat the market averages over a number of years.

Hybrid funds are a way to make fund investing simple. They give you instant diversification across a variety of investing options. They also make it easier for stock-skittish investors to invest in stocks while avoiding the high volatility of pure stock funds.

U.S., international, and global funds

Unless they have words like *international, global, worldwide,* or *world* in their names, most funds focus their investments in the United States. But even funds without one of these terms attached may invest money internationally.

The only way to know for sure where a fund is currently invested (or where the fund may invest in the future) is to ask. You can start by calling the toll-free number of the mutual fund company you're interested in. A fund's annual report (which often can be found on the fund company's Web site) also details where the fund is investing.

When a fund has the term *international* in its name, it typically means that the fund can invest anywhere in the world except the United States. The term *worldwide* or *global* generally implies that a fund invests anywhere in the world, including the United States. I generally recommend avoiding worldwide or global funds for two reasons. First, thoroughly following the financial markets and companies in so many parts of the world is difficult for a fund manager. Following financial markets and companies is hard enough to do solely in the United States or a specific international market. Second, most of these funds charge high operating expenses — often well in excess of 1 percent per year — which puts a drag on returns.

Funds of funds

An increasing number of fund providers are responding to overwhelmed investors by offering a simplified way to construct a portfolio: a mutual fund that diversifies across numerous other mutual funds — or a *fund of funds*. When a fund of funds is done right, it helps focus fund investors on the important big-picture issue of asset allocation — how much of your investment money you put into bonds versus stocks.

Although the best funds of funds appear to deliver a high-quality, diversified portfolio of funds in one fell swoop, funds of funds are not all created equal and are not all worthy of your investment dollars.

The funds of funds concept is not new. In fact, the concept has been around many years. High fees gave the earlier funds of funds, run in the 1950s by the late Bernie Cornfeld, a bad name. He established a fund of funds outside the United States and tacked on many layers of fees. While the funds were profitable for his enterprise, duped investors suffered a continual drain of high fees. The Cornfeld episode is an important reason why the Securities and Exchange Commission has been careful in approving new funds of funds.

The newer funds of funds developed by the larger fund companies are investor-friendly. Vanguard's LifeStrategy and T. Rowe Price's Spectrum funds of funds add no extra fees for packaging together the individual funds. Annual operating fees on the underlying funds at Vanguard are less than 0.3 percent.

Other funds of funds layer on high fees and merit a much more skeptical look. Some funds of funds charge annual operating expenses of 2 percent on top of the fees of the underlying mutual funds they invest in. When you add it all up, investing in mutual funds through these funds can siphon off a whopping 3+ percent of your investment balances annually.

Remember that stocks' historic annual returns average just 10 percent. So paying 2 to 3 percent in fees gives away about 20 to 30 percent of your expected returns. Not surprisingly, in terms of performance, the high-fee funds of funds have lagged far behind the market indexes.

Exceptions to this rule of shunning worldwide funds are the funds of funds — T. Rowe Price's Spectrum funds and Vanguard's Life Strategy funds — that I discuss in the sidebar, "Funds of funds." With these funds, multiple managers are at work.

Index funds

Index funds are funds that can be (and are, for the most part) managed by a computer. An index fund's assets are invested to replicate an existing market index such as Standard & Poor's 500, an index of 500 large U.S. company stocks. (**Important note:** In Chapters 10 and 11, I recommend and prefer, for its better diversification, a total U.S. stock market index fund over the S&P 500 index fund.)

Over long periods (ten years or more), index funds outperform about three-quarters of their peers! How is that possible? How can a computer making mindless, predictable decisions beat an intelligent, creative, MBA-endowed portfolio manager with a crack team of research analysts scouring the market for the best securities? The answer is largely cost. The computer does not demand a high salary or need a big corner office. And index funds don't need a team of research analysts.

Most active fund managers can't overcome the handicap of high operating expenses that pull down their funds' rates of return. As I discuss later in this chapter, operating expenses include all the fees and profit that a mutual fund extracts from a fund's returns before the returns are paid to you. For example, the average U.S. stock fund has an operating expense ratio of 1.3 percent per year. So a U.S. stock index fund with an expense ratio of just 0.2 percent per year has an advantage of 1.1 percent per year.

Another not-so-inconsequential advantage of index funds is that you can't underperform the market. Some funds do just that because of the burden of high fees and/or poor management. If you were unfortunate enough to have been involved in the following loser mutual funds (see Table 9-1) in the past ten years, you fared about 25 to 35 percent worse per year in return than you would have if you had invested in a boring old index fund. (Vanguard's Total Stock Market Index fund provided an average annual rate of return of +7.8 percent over the same time period.)

Table 9-1	Mutual Funds (Diversified) That Will Fetch a Stick
Fund	*Average Annual Rate of Return (10 Years)*
Frontier Equity	−26.3%
American Heritage	−24.1%
Apex Mid Cap Growth	−16.7%

For money invested outside retirement accounts, index funds have an added advantage: Lower taxable distributions are made to shareholders because less trading of securities is conducted and a more stable portfolio is maintained.

Yes, index funds may seem downright boring. When you invest in them, you give up the opportunity to brag to others about your shrewd investments that beat the market averages. On the other hand, with a low-cost index fund, you have no chance of doing much worse than the market (which more than a few mutual fund managers do).

Index funds make sense for a portion of your investments, because beating the market is difficult for portfolio managers. The Vanguard Group (800-662-7447, www.vanguard.com), headquartered in Valley Forge, Pennsylvania, is the largest and lowest-cost mutual-fund provider of index funds.

Specialty (sector) funds

Specialty funds don't fit neatly into the previous categories. These funds are often known as *sector funds,* because they tend to invest in securities in specific industries.

In most cases, you should avoid investing in specialty funds. Investing in stocks of a single industry defeats one of the major purposes of investing in mutual funds — diversification. Another good reason to avoid specialty funds is that they tend to carry much higher expenses than other mutual funds. For example, Fidelity, the nation's largest mutual fund company, offers many sector funds. The Fidelity Select funds are the result of slicing and dicing the universe of companies into various portfolios such as Banking, Biotechnology, Computers, Electronics, Retailing, Technology, Transportation, and so on. These funds carry high costs — in addition to a 3 percent sales load, the Select funds often carry hefty operating expense ratios well in excess of 1 percent.

Socially responsible funds

Select mutual funds label themselves *socially responsible.* This term means different things to different people. In most cases, though, it implies that the fund avoids investing in companies whose products or services harm people or the world at large — tobacco manufacturers, for example. Because cigarettes and other tobacco products kill hundreds of thousands of people and add billions of dollars to health-care costs, most socially responsible funds shun tobacco companies.

Socially responsible investing presents a couple of problems. For example, your definition of social responsibility may not match the definition offered by the investment manager who's running a fund. Another problem is that even if you can agree on what's socially irresponsible (such as selling tobacco products), funds aren't always as clean as you would think or hope. Even though a fund avoids tobacco manufacturers, it may well invest in retailers that sell tobacco products.

If you want to consider a socially responsible fund, review the fund's recent annual report that lists the specific investments the fund owns. Also consider giving directly to charities, and get a tax deduction, as well.

Specialty funds that invest in real estate or precious metals may make sense for a small portion (10 percent or less) of your investment portfolio. These types of funds can help diversify your portfolio, because they can do better during times of higher inflation. When the previous edition of this book was published in early 2000, here's what I had to say about technology stock funds:

> "Be careful with technology funds, which were hot during the late 1990s. Many of these stocks are selling at premium valuations. When you invest in diversified stock funds, you get plenty of exposure to the technology sector."

Technology stocks plunged 80 percent in value by 2003.

Selecting the Best Mutual Funds

When you go camping in the wilderness, you can do a number of things to maximize your chances for happiness and success. You can take maps to keep you on course, food for nourishment, proper clothing to stay dry and warm, and some first-aid gear to treat minor injuries. But regardless of how much advance preparation you do, you may have a problematic experience. You may take the wrong trail, trip on a rock and break your ankle, or lose your food to a tenacious bear that comes romping through camp one night.

And so it is with mutual funds. Although most mutual fund investors are rewarded for their efforts, you get no guarantees. You can, however, follow some simple, common-sense guidelines to help keep you on the trail and increase your odds of investment success and happiness. The issues in the following sections are the main ones you should consider.

Reading prospectuses and annual reports

Mutual fund companies produce information that can help you make decisions about mutual fund investments. Every fund is required to issue a *prospectus*. This legal document is reviewed and audited by the U.S. Securities and Exchange Commission. Most of what's written isn't worth the time it takes to slog through it.

The most valuable information — the fund's investment objectives, costs, and performance history — is summarized in the first few pages of the prospectus. Make sure that you read this part. Skip the rest, which is comprised mostly of tedious legal details.

Funds also produce *annual reports* that discuss how the fund has been doing and provide details on the specific investments a fund holds. If, for example, you want to know which countries an international fund invests in, you can find this information in the fund's annual report.

Keeping costs low

The charges you pay to buy or sell a fund, as well as the ongoing fund operating expenses, can have a big impact on the rate of return you earn on your investments. Many novice investors pay too much attention to a mutual fund's prior performance (in the case of stock funds) or to the fund's current yield (in the case of bond funds). Doing so is dangerous because a fund can inflate its return or yield in many (risky) ways. And what worked yesterday may flop tomorrow.

A study conducted by the Investment Company Institute confirms what I've long observed among fund buyers: Only 43 percent of fund buyers who were surveyed bothered to examine the fees and expenses of the fund they ended up buying. The majority of fund buyers — 57 percent, to be exact — didn't know what the funds were charging them to manage their money!

Fund costs are an important factor in the return you earn from a mutual fund. Fees are deducted from your investment. All other things being equal, high fees and other charges depress your returns. What are a fund's fees, you ask? Good question — read on to find the answers.

Eliminating loads

Loads are upfront commissions paid to brokers who sell mutual funds. Loads typically range from 3 percent to as high as 8.5 percent of your investment. (An astonishing 73 percent of fund buyers surveyed by the Investment Company Institute didn't know whether the fund they bought charged a sales load!) Sales loads have two problems:

> ✔ **Sales loads are a needless cost that drags down your investment returns.**
>
> Because commissions are paid to the salesperson and not to the fund manager, the manager of a load fund doesn't work any harder and isn't any more qualified than a manager of a no-load fund. Common sense suggests, and studies confirm, that load funds perform *worse,* on average, than no-loads when factoring in the load, because the load charge is subtracted from your payment before being invested.
>
> And don't think that spotting a load fund is easy. Just as some jewelers flog fake diamonds on late-night TV commercials, increasing numbers of brokers and financial planners are selling bogus funds that they *call* no-loads, but these funds are *not* no-loads — they just hide the sales commission.

"Stay in this fund for five to seven years," the broker tells you, "and you don't have to pay the back-end sales charge that would normally apply upon sale of the investment." Although this claim may be true, the fund is probably also charging you high ongoing operating expenses (usually 1 percent more per year than true no-load funds) that the fund uses to pay the salesperson a hefty commission. So one way or another, the broker gets his pound of flesh (that is, his commission) from your investment dollars.

✔ **The power of self-interest can bias your broker's advice.**

Although this issue is rarely discussed, it's even more problematic than the issue of extra sales costs. Brokers who work for a commission are interested in selling you commission-based investment products; therefore, their best interests often conflict with your best interests.

Although you may be mired in high-interest debt or underfunding your retirement plan, salespeople almost never advise you to pay off your credit cards or put more money into your 401(k). To get you to buy, they tend to exaggerate the potential benefits and obscure the risks and drawbacks of what they sell. They don't take the time to educate investors. I've seen too many people purchase investment products through brokers without understanding what they're buying, how much risk they're taking, and how these investments will affect their overall financial lives.

Invest in no-load (commission-free) funds. The only way to be sure that a fund is truly no-load is to look at the prospectus for the fund. Only there, in black and white and without marketing hype, must the truth be told about sales charges and other fund fees. When you want investing advice, hire a financial advisor on a fee-for-service basis (see Chapter 17), which can cost you less and minimize potential conflicts of interest.

Minimizing operating expenses

All mutual funds charge ongoing fees. The fees pay for the operational costs of running the fund — employees' salaries, marketing, servicing the toll-free phone lines, printing and mailing published materials, computers for tracking investments and account balances, accounting fees, and so on. Despite being labeled "expenses," the profit a fund company extracts for running the fund is added to the tab, as well.

The fund's operating expenses are quoted as an annual percentage of your investment and are essentially invisible to you, because they're deducted before you're paid any return. The expenses are charged on a daily basis, so you don't need to worry about trying to get out of a fund before these fees are deducted.

You can find a fund's operating expenses in the fund's prospectus. Look in the expenses section and find a line that says something like "Total Fund Operating Expenses." You can also call the fund's toll-free number and ask a representative.

Within a given sector of mutual funds (for example, money market, short-term bonds, or international stock), funds with low annual operating fees can more easily produce higher total returns for you. Although expenses matter on all funds, some types of funds are more sensitive to high expenses than others. Expenses are critical on money market mutual funds and very important on bond funds. Fund managers already have a hard time beating the averages in these markets; with higher expenses added on, beating the averages is nearly impossible.

With stock funds, expenses are a less important (but still significant) factor in a fund's performance. Don't forget that, over time, stocks average returns of about 10 percent per year. So if one stock fund charges 1 percent more in operating expenses than another fund, you're already giving up an extra 10 percent of your expected returns.

Some people argue that stock funds that charge high expenses may be justified in doing so if they generate higher rates of return. Evidence doesn't show that these stock funds actually generate higher returns. In fact, funds with higher operating expenses tend to produce *lower* rates of return. This trend makes sense, because operating expenses are deducted from the returns a fund generates.

Stick with funds that maintain low total operating expenses and don't charge loads (commissions). Both types of fees come out of your pocket and reduce your rate of return.

You have no reason to pay a lot for the best funds, as Table 9-2 shows. (In Chapters 10 and 11, I provide some specific fund recommendations as well as sample portfolios for investors in different situations.)

Table 9-2	Mutual Fund Operating Expense Ratios	
Fund Type	*Expense Ratio Range*	*Who Offers Good Ones*
Money market funds	0.2% to 0.5%	Vanguard, Fidelity (Spartan), USAA
Bond funds	0.2% to 0.5%	Vanguard, Fidelity (Spartan), Dodge & Cox, Harbor, USAA
Hybrid	0.2% to 0.8%	Vanguard, Dodge & Cox, Fidelity, T. Rowe Price
U.S. stock	0.2% to 1%	Fidelity, Vanguard, T. Rowe Price, Dodge & Cox, others
International stock	0.4% to 1.3%	Vanguard, T. Rowe Price, Masters' Select, others
Index	0.1% to 0.4%	Vanguard

Evaluating historic performance

A fund's *performance,* or historic rate of return, is another factor to weigh when selecting a mutual fund. As all mutual funds are supposed to tell you, past performance is no guarantee of future results. An analysis of historic mutual fund performance proves that some of yesterday's stars turn into tomorrow's skid-row bums.

Many former high-return funds achieved their results by taking on high risk. Funds that assume higher risk should produce higher rates of return. But high-risk funds usually decline in price faster during major market declines. Thus, in order for a fund to be considered a *best* fund, it must consistently deliver a favorable rate of return given the degree of risk it takes.

When assessing an individual fund, compare its performance and volatility over an extended period of time (five or ten years will do) to a relevant market index. For example, compare funds that focus on investing in large U.S. companies to the Standard & Poor's 500 Index. Compare funds that invest in U.S. stocks of all sizes to the Wilshire 5000 Index. Indexes also exist for bonds, foreign stock markets, and almost any other type of security you can imagine.

Assessing fund manager and fund family reputations

Much is made of who manages a specific mutual fund. As Peter Lynch, the retired and famous former manager of the Fidelity Magellan fund, said, "The financial press made us Wall Street types into celebrities, a notoriety that was largely undeserved. Stock stars were treated as rock stars. . . ."

Although the individual fund manager is important, no fund manager is an island. The resources and capabilities of the parent company are equally important. Different companies have different capabilities and levels of expertise in relation to the different types of funds. When you're considering a particular fund — for example, the Barnum & Barney High-Flying Foreign Stock fund — examine the performance history and fees not only of that fund but also of similar foreign stock funds at the Barnum & Barney company. If Barnum's other foreign stock funds have done poorly, or Barnum & Barney offers no other such funds because it's focused on its circus business, those are strikes against its High-Flying fund. Also be aware that "star" fund managers tend to be associated with higher-expense funds to help pay their rock-star salaries.

Rating tax-friendliness

Investors often overlook tax implications when selecting mutual funds for nonretirement accounts. Numerous mutual funds effectively reduce their shareholders' returns because of their tendency to produce more taxable distributions — that is, capital gains (especially short-term gains which are taxed at the highest federal income tax rate) and dividends. (See the sections, "Dividends" and "Capital gains," later in this chapter.)

Mutual fund capital gains distributions have a significant impact on an investor's after-tax rate of return. All mutual fund managers buy and sell stocks during the course of a year. Whenever a mutual fund manager sells securities, any gain or loss from those securities must be distributed to fund shareholders. Securities sold at a loss can offset securities sold at a profit.

When a fund manager has a tendency to cash in more winners than losers, investors in the fund receive a high amount of taxable gains. So, even though some funds can lay claim to producing higher total returns, *after* you factor in taxes, they actually may not produce higher total returns.

Choosing mutual funds that minimize capital gains distributions helps you defer taxes on your profits. By allowing your capital to continue compounding as it would in a retirement account, you receive a higher total return. When you're a long-term investor, you benefit most from choosing mutual funds that minimize capital gains distributions. The more years that appreciation can compound without being taxed, the greater the value to you as the investor.

Investors who purchase mutual funds outside tax-sheltered retirement accounts should also consider the time of year they purchase shares in funds. December is the most common month in which mutual funds make capital gains distributions. When making purchases late in the year, ask if and when the fund may make a significant capital gains distribution. Consider delaying purchases in such funds until after the distribution date.

Determining your needs and goals

Selecting the best funds for you requires an understanding of your investment goals and risk tolerance. What may be a good fund for your next-door neighbor may not necessarily be a good fund for you. You have a unique financial profile.

Considering fund directories: Morningstar and Value Line

Value Line and Morningstar both put out behemoth mutual fund directories (which can be found in most public libraries) that track thousands of mutual funds. These directories are reference publications, not newsletters or magazines. Given their substantial subscription costs (their three-month trials being an exception), you won't find buying your own copies worthwhile unless you have a significant amount to invest.

The services provided by each directory are more similar than they are different. Value Line is the newer kid on the block. Both use a similar format, devoting a single page to all sorts of details and numbers, and a bit of commentary about each fund.

Focusing too much on the ranking of specific funds is the most common mistake investors make when using these publications. Both publications' lengthy guidebooks (which most people don't read) warn against focusing too much on the ranking of specific funds, although they don't say it strongly enough for my taste.

Their ratings are somewhat useful in that they look at *risk-adjusted performance* — the performance of a fund in relation to the risk (or volatility) it took to achieve it. The rankings have a number of limitations, however. One flaw with both services is that they lump funds into broad categories, when in fact, funds within the category invest in different types of securities.

For example, in the various stock fund categories, you find some funds that invest exclusively in stocks, and others that invest some of their money in bonds or other high-dividend-paying securities, such as preferred stocks. These types of securities tend to reduce the volatility of a portfolio and perform well in times of declining interest rates, whereas they underperform when stocks are beating bonds.

The rankings also ignore fund operating expenses. Because the past is at best a weak predictor of things to come, you're more likely to succeed with funds that keep expenses down. As I explain earlier in this chapter, high expenses are a handicap to generating good future returns.

Also, the star rankings don't help much in differentiating funds investing in the same market category. For example, if small company value stocks have been hot lately, most will have 4 or 5 stars.

If you've already determined your needs and goals — terrific! If you haven't, refer to Chapter 2. Understanding yourself is a good part of the battle. But don't shortchange yourself by not being educated about the investment you're considering. If you don't understand what you're investing in and how much risk you're taking, you should stay out of the game.

Deciphering Your Fund's Performance

When you look at a statement for your mutual fund holdings, odds are that you're not going to understand it. Getting a handle on how you're doing is the hardest part. Most people want to know (and have a hard time figuring out) how much they made or lost on their investment.

You can't simply calculate your return by comparing the share price of the fund today to the share price you originally paid. Why not? Because mutual funds make distributions (of dividends and capital gains), which lead to your getting more shares of the fund.

Distributions create an accounting problem, because they reduce the share price of a fund. (Otherwise you could make a profit from the distribution by buying into it just before a distribution is made.) Therefore, over time, following just the share price of your fund doesn't tell you how much money you made or lost.

Imagine that the share price of your mutual fund is like a balloon with a small rock tied to the end of its string. The balloon (representing fund share price) struggles to rise, but the rock (representing fund distributions) keeps pulling down on it.

The only way to figure out exactly how much you made or lost on your investment is to compare the total value of your holdings in the fund today with the total dollar amount you originally invested. If you invested chunks of money at various points in time, and you want to factor in the timing of your various investments, this exercise becomes more complicated. (Check out my investment software recommendations in Chapter 18 if you want your computer to help you crunch the numbers.)

The *total return* of a fund is the percentage change of your investment over a specified period. For example, a fund may tell you that, in 2003, its total return was 15 percent. Therefore, if you invested $10,000 in the fund on the last day of 2002, your investment would be worth $11,500 at the end of 2003. To find out a fund's total return, you can call the fund company's toll-free number, visit the company's Web site, or read the fund's annual report.

The following three components make up your total return on a fund:

- ✔ Dividends (includes interest paid by money market or bond funds)
- ✔ Capital gains distributions
- ✔ Share price changes

Dividends

Dividends are income paid by investments. Both bonds and stocks can pay dividends. Bond fund dividends tend to be higher (as a percentage of the amount you have invested in a fund). When a dividend distribution is made, you can receive it as cash (which is good if you need money to live on) or as more shares in the fund. In either case, the share price of the fund drops to offset the payout. So if you're hoping to strike it rich by buying into a bunch of funds just before their dividends are paid, don't bother. You'll just end up paying more in income taxes.

If you hold your mutual fund outside a retirement account, the dividend distributions are taxable income (unless they come from a tax-free municipal bond fund). Dividends are taxable whether or not you reinvest them as additional shares in the fund. Thanks to the 2003 tax law changes, stock dividends are taxed at a low rate — 5 percent for those in the federal 10 and 15 percent tax brackets, and 15 percent for everyone in the higher federal tax brackets.

Capital gains

When a mutual fund manager sells a security in the fund, net gains realized from that sale (the difference from the purchase price) must be distributed to you as a *capital gain*. Typically, funds make one annual capital gains distribution in December, but distributions can be paid multiple times per year.

As with a dividend distribution, you can receive your capital gains distribution as cash or as more shares in the fund. In either case, the share price of the fund drops to offset the distribution.

For funds held outside retirement accounts, your capital gains distribution is taxable. As with dividends, capital gains are taxable whether or not you reinvest them in additional shares in the fund. Capital gains distributions can be partly comprised of short-term and long-term gains. As I discuss in Chapter 6, profits realized on securities sold after more than a one-year holding period are taxed at the lower long-term capital gains rate. Short-term gains are taxed at the ordinary income tax rate.

If you want to avoid making an investment in a fund that is about to make a capital gains distribution, check with the fund to determine when capital gains are distributed. Capital gains distributions increase your current-year tax liability for investments made outside of retirement accounts. (I discuss this concept in more detail in Chapter 11.)

Share price changes

You also make money with a mutual fund when the share price increases. This occurrence is just like investing in a stock or piece of real estate. If the mutual fund is worth more today than it was when you bought it, you made a profit (on paper, at least). In order to realize or lock in this profit, you need to sell your shares in the fund.

There you have it. Here are the components of a mutual fund's total return:

```
Dividends + Capital Gains + Share Price
           Distributions    Changes      = Total Return
```

Following and Selling Your Funds

How closely you follow your funds is up to you, depending on what makes you happy and comfortable. I don't recommend tracking the share prices of your funds (or other investments, for that matter) on a daily basis; it's time-consuming and nerve-racking, and it can make you lose sight of the long-term picture. When you track your investments too closely, you're more likely to panic when times get tough. And with investments held outside of retirement accounts, every time you sell an investment at a profit, you get hit with taxes.

A monthly or quarterly check-in is more than frequent enough for following your funds. Many publications carry total return numbers over varying periods so that you can determine the exact rate of return you're earning.

Trying to time and trade the markets so that you buy at lows and sell at highs rarely works. Yet an entire industry of investment newsletters, hotlines, online services, and the like purport to be able to tell you when to buy and sell. Don't waste your time and money on such nonsense. (See Chapter 7 for more info about gurus and newsletters.)

You should consider selling a fund when it no longer meets the criteria mentioned in the section, "Selecting the Best Mutual Funds," earlier in this chapter. If a fund underperforms its peers for at least a two-year period, or if a fund jacks up its management fees, it may be a good time to sell. But if you do your homework and buy good funds from good fund companies, you shouldn't have to do much trading.

Finding and investing in good funds isn't rocket science. Chapters 10 and 11 recommend some specific mutual funds using the criteria discussed earlier in this chapter. If you're still not satiated, pick up a copy of the latest edition of my book *Mutual Funds For Dummies* (Wiley Publishing, Inc.).

Chapter 10

Investing in Retirement Accounts

. . . .

In This Chapter

▶ Checking out the different types of retirement accounts

▶ Determining how to allocate money in retirement accounts

▶ Moving your retirement account to a new firm

. . . .

T his chapter helps you decide how to invest money you currently hold inside retirement accounts, or money you plan to contribute to a retirement account.

When compared to the often-overwhelming world of investing outside retirement accounts, investing inside tax-sheltered retirement accounts — IRAs, 401(k)s, SEP-IRAs, and Keoghs — is less complicated for two reasons:

✔ **The range of possible retirement account investments is more limited.** Direct investments, such as real estate and investments in small, privately owned companies, are not generally available or accessible in most retirement accounts.

✔ **When you invest in a retirement account, your returns aren't taxed as you earn them.** Money inside retirement accounts compounds and grows without taxation. You generally only pay taxes on these funds when you withdraw money from the account. (Direct transfers to another investment firm are not withdrawals, so they're not taxed.) So when you choose an investment for your retirement account, don't rack your brain over dividends and capital gains; save all that worry for the money you invest in nonretirement accounts.

Looking at Types of Retirement Accounts

Retirement accounts offer numerous benefits. In most cases, your contributions to retirement accounts are tax-deductible. Thanks to recent tax law changes, the contribution limits have been significantly increased and will rise even further in the years ahead. And when you place your money inside the retirement account, it compounds without taxation until you withdraw it.

(Some accounts, such as the newer Roth IRA, even allow for tax-free withdrawal of investment earnings.) If your adjusted gross income is below $50,000 per year ($25,000 for single taxpayers), you may be eligible for a new, special tax credit for making retirement account contributions — please refer to Table 6-2 in Chapter 6. The following sections describe the major types of retirement accounts and tell you how to determine whether you're eligible for them.

Employer-sponsored plans

Your employer sets up this type of retirement plan and usually provides a limited selection of investment options. All you have to do is contribute away and choose how to spread your money among the menu of investment choices.

401(k) plans

For-profit companies offer *401(k) plans.* The silly name comes from the section of the tax code that establishes and regulates these plans. A 401(k) generally allows you to save up to $12,000 per year (for 2003), usually through payroll deductions. If you're age 50 or older, you can stash away even more — $14,000 for 2003. (See Table 10-1 to find out how these contribution limits are going to increase in the years ahead.) Your employer's plan may have lower limits, though. Your contributions to a 401(k) are excluded from your reported income and thus are generally free from federal and state income taxes (although they are subject to Social Security and Medicare taxes).

Table 10-1	401(k), 403 (b), and 457 Retirement Plan Contribution Limits	
Year	*Contribution Limit for Those Under Age 50*	*Contribution Limit for Those Age 50 and Older*
2003	$12,000	$14,000
2004	$13,000	$16,000
2005	$14,000	$18,000
2006	$15,000	$20,000

Some employers don't allow you to contribute to a 401(k) plan until you work for them for a full year. Others allow you to start contributing right away. Some employers also match a portion of your contributions. They may, for example, match half of your first 6 percent of contributions; so in addition to saving a lot of taxes, you get a bonus from the company.

Can your employer steal your retirement plan money?

The short answer, unfortunately, is yes. However, the vast majority of employees, particularly those who work for larger and more established companies, need not worry.

Some companies that administer 401(k) plans have been cited by the U.S. Labor Department for being too slow in putting money that employees had deferred from their paychecks into employee 401(k) investment accounts. In the worst cases, companies diverted employees' 401(k) money to pay for corporate bills. Many business owners who engaged in such practices used 401(k) money as a short-term emergency fund.

In cases where companies failed and funds were diverted from employee 401(k) accounts, the funds were lost. In situations where the employer delayed placing the money into the

employees' 401(k) accounts, employees simply lost out on earning return on their investments during the period. When your contributions are in your 401(k) account, they're financially and legally separate from your employer. Thus, your funds are still protected even if your employer goes bankrupt.

After conducting hundreds of investigations, the Labor Department issued rulings requiring employers to contribute employee retirement contributions to their proper accounts within 90 days. In addition to keeping tabs on your employer to ensure that money withheld from your paycheck is contributed into your account within this time frame, you should also periodically check your 401(k) statement to make sure that your contributions are being invested as you instructed.

If you're a high-income earner, and you contribute such a significant percentage of each paycheck that you hit the plan maximum before the end of year, you may lose out on some matching money. You may be better off spreading your contributions over the full calendar year. Check with your company's benefits department for your plan's specifics.

Thanks to technological innovations and the growth of the mutual fund industry, smaller companies (those with fewer than 100 employees) can consider offering 401(k) plans, too. In the past, it was prohibitively expensive for smaller companies to administer 401(k)s. If your company is interested in this option, contact some of the leading mutual fund organizations and discount brokerage firms that I discuss in Chapter 11 and in the section, "Allocating money in plans you design," later in this chapter.

403 (b) plans

Nonprofit organizations offer *403 (b) plans* to their employees. As with 401(k)s, your contributions to these plans are excluded from federal and state income taxes. The 403 (b) plans are more often known as *tax-sheltered annuities,* the name for insurance company investments that satisfy the requirements for 403(b) plans. For the benefit of 403(b) retirement plan participants, *no-load* (commission-free) mutual funds can be used in 403(b) plans. (See Chapter 9 for more on mutual funds.)

Nonprofit employees are allowed to annually contribute up to 20 percent or $12,000 of their salary ($14,000 if age 50 or older), whichever is less. Refer to Table 10-1 to see how this contribution limit is going to increase in the years ahead. Employees who have 15 or more years of service may be allowed to contribute beyond the standard limits. Ask your employee benefits department or the investment provider for the 403(b) plan about eligibility requirements and the details of your personal contribution limit.

If you work for a nonprofit or public-sector organization that doesn't offer this benefit, make a fuss and insist on it. Nonprofit organizations have no excuse not to offer a 403(b) plan to their employees. Unlike a 401(k), this type of plan requires virtually no out-of-pocket expenses from the employer. The only requirement is that the organization must deduct the appropriate contribution from employees' paychecks and send the money to the investment company handling the 403(b) plan.

Some nonprofits don't offer 403(b)s. Or, in addition to 403(b)s, some nonprofits may offer insurance company tax-sheltered annuities. When compared to insurance company annuities, no-load (no sales charges) mutual funds are superior investment vehicles on several fronts:

- ✔ Mutual fund companies have a longer and more successful investment track record than do insurance companies, many of which have only recently entered the mutual fund arena.

- ✔ Insurance annuities charge higher annual operating expenses, often two to three times those of efficiently managed no-load mutual funds. These high expenses reduce your returns.

- ✔ Insurance company *insolvency* (bankruptcy) can risk the safety of your investment in an annuity, whereas the value of a mutual fund depends only on the value of the securities in the fund.

- ✔ Insurance annuities come with significant charges for early surrender; 403(b) plans with mutual funds do not include these charges.

With some 403(b) plans, you may borrow against your fund balance without penalty. If this capability is important to you, check with your employer to see whether the company plan allows you to borrow without penalty. Although many insurance annuities advertise borrowing as an advantage, it can also be a drawback, because it may encourage you to raid your retirement savings.

As long as your employer allows it, you may want to open a 403(b) account at the investment companies I suggest in the section, "Allocating money in plans you design," later in this chapter.

457 plans

Some nonprofit organizations offer *457 plans*. Like 403(b) or 401(k) plans, 457 plans offer participants the ability to contribute money from their paychecks on a pre-tax basis and thus save on federal and state taxes.

457 plans, however, differ in the following important ways:

✔ Money that you contribute to a 457 plan is not separate from the organization's finances. Thus, if the nonprofit goes belly up — a rare but not impossible occurrence in the nonprofit world — your retirement funds could be in jeopardy.

✔ The contributions made to a 457 plan are limited to $8,000 per year.

Don't consider contributing to a 457 plan until you exhaust contributions to your 403(b). Refer to Table 10-1 for 457 plan contribution limits.

Self-employment plans

When you work for yourself, you don't have an employer to do the legwork necessary for setting up a retirement plan. You need to take the initiative. Although setting up a retirement account on your own requires more work, the good news is that you can select and design a plan that meets your needs. Self-employment retirement savings plans often allow you to put *more* money away on a tax-deductible basis than do employers' plans.

When you have employees, you're required to provide coverage for them under these plans with contributions comparable to the company owners' (as a percentage of salary). Some part-time (fewer than 1,000 hours per year) and newer employees (less than a few years of service) may be excluded. Many small-business owners either don't know about this requirement or choose to ignore it; they set up plans for themselves but fail to cover their employees. The danger is that the IRS and state tax authorities may discover small-business owners' negligence, sock them with big penalties, and disqualify their prior contributions. Don't muck up this area, because self-employed people and small businesses get their tax returns audited at a relatively high rate.

Don't avoid setting up a retirement savings plan for your business just because you don't want to make contributions on your employees' behalf. Making retirement contributions doesn't have to increase your personnel costs. In the long run, you build the contributions you make for your employees into their total compensation package — which includes salary and other benefits such as health insurance.

To get the most from contributions as an employer, consider the following advice:

- ✔ Educate your employees about the value of retirement savings plans. You want them to understand, but more importantly, you want them to appreciate your investment.

- ✔ Select a Keogh plan (see "Keoghs," later in this chapter) that requires employees to stay a certain number of years before they vest fully in their contributions. Reward long-term contributors to your company's success.

- ✔ Consider offering a 401(k) or SIMPLE plan if you have more than ten employees.

SEP-IRAs

SEP-IRA (Simplified Employee Pension Individual Retirement Account) plans require little paperwork to set up. SEP-IRAs allow you to sock away 20 percent of your self-employment income (business revenue minus deductions), up to a maximum of $40,000. Thanks to recent tax law changes, this represents an enormous increase in the contribution limits. Future contribution limits will rise with inflation in $1,000 increments.

Each year, you decide the amount you want to contribute — with no minimums. Your contributions to a SEP-IRA are deducted from your taxable income, saving you big-time on federal and state taxes. As with other retirement plans, your money compounds without taxation until you withdraw it.

Don't be hoodwinked into a "private pension plan"

Employers who don't want to make retirement plan contributions on behalf of their employees are bait for insurance salespeople selling so-called "private pension plans." Basically, these plans are cash value life insurance policies that combine life insurance protection with a savings-type account. (See Chapter 15 for more details.)

The selling hook of these plans is that you can save money for yourself, but you don't need to contribute money on your employees' behalf. And your contributions compound without taxation over the years.

Sound good? Well, life insurance salespeople who earn hefty commissions from selling cash value life policies won't tell you about the big negatives of these plans. Unlike contributions to true retirement savings plans such as SEP-IRAs and Keoghs, you derive *no* upfront tax deduction.

Also, if you don't need life insurance protection, the cost of such coverage is wasted when you save through these plans.

Keoghs

Setting up and administering Keogh plans requires a bit more paperwork than SEP-IRAs. The historic appeal of certain types of Keoghs was that they allow you to put away a greater amount of your self-employment income (revenue less your deductions). However, Keogh plans now have the same contribution limits (20 percent of net self-employment income up to $40,000 per year) that SEP-IRA plans have.

Keogh plans still hold some unique appeal for business owners who seek to maximize their own personal retirement plan contributions relative to those made for employees. All types of Keogh plans allow *vesting schedules,* which require employees to remain with the company a number of years before they earn the right to their full retirement account balances.

Keogh plans also allow for Social Security integration. Without going into all the gory tax details, *integration* effectively allows those in the company who are high-income earners (usually the owners) to receive larger-percentage contributions for their accounts than the less-highly compensated employees. The logic behind this idea is that Social Security benefits top out when you earn more than $84,900 (for 2002). Social Security integration allows you to make up for this ceiling.

Keoghs come in several flavors:

- ✔ **Profit-sharing plans.** These plans have the same contribution limits as SEP-IRAs. So why would you want the headaches of a more complicated plan when you can't contribute more to it? These plans appeal to owners of small companies who want to minimize the contributions to which their employees are entitled, which is done through the use of vesting schedules and Social Security integration.

- ✔ **Money-purchase pension plans.** These plans now have the same contribution limits as SEP-IRA plans. Flexibility is *not* allowed on the percentage contribution you make each year — it's fixed. Thus, these plans make the most sense for employers who are comfortable enough financially to continue making contributions that are a high percentage of their salary.

- ✔ **Defined-benefit plans.** These plans are for people who are willing and able to put away more than $40,000 per year — which, as you can imagine, few people can do. If you're a consistently high-income earner who's older than 45, and you want to save more than $40,000 per year in a retirement account, you may want to consider these plans. If you're interested in defined-benefit plans, hire an actuary to crunch the numbers and calculate how much you can contribute to such a plan.

Individual retirement accounts (IRAs)

Anyone with employment income can contribute to IRA accounts. You may contribute up to $3,000 each year — $3,500 if you're age 50 or older. Table 10-2 details how the IRA contribution limits are going to rise significantly in the years ahead. If you earn less than $3,000 a year, you can contribute up to the amount you earn. The above rule has an exception if you're a non-working spouse: As long as the working spouse earned at least $6,000 in income, the non-working spouse can put up to $3,000 per year into a so-called *spousal IRA*, and the working spouse up to $3,000 into his or her own IRA.

Another exception to earning employment income makes you eligible to contribute to an IRA: Receiving alimony also qualifies you for an IRA contribution.

Table 10-2	IRA (Regular and Roth) Contribution Limits	
Year	*Contribution Limit for Those Under Age 50*	*Contribution Limit for Those Age 50 and Older*
2002–2004	$3,000	$3,500
2005	$4,000	$4,500
2006–2007	$4,000	$5,000
2008	$5,000	$6,000

Your contributions to an IRA may or may not be tax-deductible. For tax year 2003, if you're single and your adjusted gross income is $40,000 or less for the year, you can deduct your full IRA contribution. If you're married and file your taxes jointly, you're entitled to a full IRA deduction if your AGI (adjusted gross income) is $60,000 per year or less. (For 2004, these thresholds bump up to $45,000 and $65,000, respectively.) If you make more than these amounts, you can take a full IRA deduction if and only if you're *not* an active participant in any retirement plan. The only way to know for certain whether you're an active participant is to look at your W-2 Form — that smallish (4-by-8½-inch) document your employer sends you early in the year to file with your tax returns. An *X* mark in a little box in section 13 on that form indicates whether you're an active participant in an employer retirement plan.

If your adjusted gross income is higher than the previously mentioned amounts by less than $10,000, you're eligible for a partial IRA deduction, even if you're an active participant in another plan. The IRS 1040 instruction booklet comes with a worksheet that allows you to do the calculations for your situation.

If you can't deduct your contribution to a standard IRA account, consider making a contribution to a newer type of IRA account called the *Roth IRA*. Single taxpayers with an AGI less than $95,000, and joint filers with an AGI less than $150,000 can contribute up to $3,000 per year to a Roth IRA ($3,500 for those age 50 and older), provided that they have at least that amount in earned income. (Please refer to Table 10-2 for the contribution limits for future years.) Although the contribution is not deductible, earnings inside the account are shielded from tax; and unlike a standard IRA, qualified withdrawals from the account, including investment earnings, are free from income tax.

To make a qualified withdrawal, you must be at least 59½ and have held the account for at least 5 years. An exception to the age rule is made for first-time home buyers, who are allowed to withdraw up to $10,000 toward the down payment on a principal residence.

Annuities: An odd investment

Annuities are peculiar investment products. They are contracts that are backed by an insurance company. If you, the annuity holder (investor), die during the so-called *accumulation phase* (that is, prior to receiving payments from the annuity), your designated beneficiary is guaranteed to receive the amount of your contribution. In this sense, annuities look a bit like life insurance.

Annuities, like IRAs, allow your capital to grow and compound without taxation. You defer taxes until withdrawal. Annuities carry the same penalties for withdrawal prior to age 59½ as do other retirement accounts.

Unlike an IRA that has an annual contribution limit, you can deposit as much as you want into an annuity in any year — even a million dollars or more if you have it! As with a so-called nondeductible IRA, you get no upfront tax deduction for your contributions.

Because contributions to an annuity aren't tax-deductible, contributing to an annuity makes sense if:

- ✔ **You have exhausted contributions to employer-sponsored and self-employed plans.** Your contributions to these plans are tax-deductible, while annuity contributions are not.

- ✔ **You have made the maximum contribution possible to an IRA account, even if it's not tax-deductible.** Annuities carry higher fees (which reduce your investment returns) because of the insurance that comes with them; IRA investments offer you better returns. Roth IRAs also allow for tax-free withdrawal of investment earnings.

✔ **You expect to leave the money compounding in the annuity for at least 15 years.** It typically takes this long for the benefits of tax-deferred compounding to outweigh the higher annuity fees and treatment of all withdrawn annuity earnings at the higher ordinary income tax rates. If you're close to or are actually in retirement, tax-friendly investments made outside of retirement accounts (discussed in Chapter 11) are preferable.

Inappropriate retirement account investments

Some investments for retirement accounts are simply inappropriate. The basic problem stems from otherwise intelligent folks forgetting, ignoring, or simply not knowing that retirement accounts are sheltered from taxation; you want to maximize this benefit by selecting investment vehicles that would otherwise be taxed.

Investments that produce income that is tax-free either at the federal or state level don't make much sense inside retirement accounts. Tax-free securities always yield less than their taxable counterparts, so you're essentially giving away free yield when you invest in such securities inside retirement accounts.

Investing in municipal bonds inside a retirement account is a big no-no. Municipals are free from federal taxation (and state tax, too, if you buy such a bond issued in your state). As such, they yield significantly less than an equivalent bond that pays fully taxable dividends. Municipal bonds definitely don't belong in a retirement account. The better investment firms don't let you make this mistake.

Lots of people make the mistake (albeit a smaller one) of investing in Treasuries — that is, U.S. Treasury bills, notes, or bonds — inside retirement accounts. When you buy Treasuries, you get the safety net of a government guarantee, but you also get a bond that produces interest free of state tax. Fully taxable bonds yield more than state-tax-free Treasuries. And, the safety of Treasuries can be replicated in other bonds.

Although annuities are retirement vehicles, as noted earlier in this chapter, they have no place inside retirement accounts. Annuities allow your investment dollars to compound without taxation. In comparison to other investments that don't allow such tax deferral, annuities carry much higher annual operating expenses, which depress your returns.

Purchasing an annuity inside an IRA, 401(k), or other type of retirement account is like wearing a belt and suspenders together. Either you have a peculiar sense of style, or you're spending too much time worrying about your pants falling down. In my experience, many people who mistakenly invest in annuities inside retirement accounts have been misled by investment salespeople.

Limited partnerships are treacherous, high-commission, high-cost (and hence low-return) investments sold through investment salespeople. Part of their supposed allure, however, are the tax benefits they generate. But when you buy and hold a limited partnership in a retirement account, you lose the ability to take advantage of many of the tax deductions. The illiquidity of LPs may also mean that you can't make required retirement account withdrawals when needed. These are just some of the many reasons to avoid investing in limited partnerships. (For more reasons, see Chapter 8.)

For more details about other investment options and the best places to purchase annuities, see Chapter 11, where I discuss investing money outside of retirement accounts.

Allocating Your Money in Retirement Plans

With good reason, people are concerned about placing their retirement account money in investments that can decline in value. You may feel that you're gambling with dollars intended for the security of your golden years.

Most working folks need to make their money work hard in order for it to grow fast enough to provide this security. This involves taking some risk; you have no way around it. Luckily, if you have 15 to 20 years or more before you need to draw on the bulk of your retirement account assets, time is on your side. As long as the value of your investments has time to recover, what's the big deal if some of your investments drop a bit over a year or two? The more years you have before you're going to retire, the greater your ability to take risk.

The section on asset allocation in Chapter 7 can help you decide how to divide your money among different investment options based on your time frame and risk tolerance.

Prioritizing retirement contributions

When you have access to various retirement accounts, prioritize which account you're going to use first by determining how much each gives you in return. Your first contributions should be to employer-based plans that match your contributions. After that, contribute to any other employer or self-employed plans that allow tax-deductible contributions. After you contribute as much as possible to tax-deductible plans, or if you don't have access to such plans, contribute to an IRA. If you max out on contributions to an IRA, or you don't have this choice because you lack employment income, consider an annuity (see "Annuities: An odd investment," earlier in this chapter).

Setting up a retirement account

Investments and account types are different issues. People sometimes get confused when discussing the investments they make in retirement accounts — especially people who have a retirement account, such as an IRA, at a bank.

They don't realize that you can have your IRA at a variety of financial institutions (for example, a mutual fund company or brokerage firm). At each financial institution, you can choose among the firm's investment options for putting your IRA money to work.

No-load, or commission-free, mutual fund and discount brokerage firms are your best bet for establishing a retirement account. For more specifics, see my recommendations throughout the remainder of this chapter.

Allocating money when your employer selects the investment options

In some company-sponsored plans, such as 401(k)s, you're limited to the predetermined investment options your employer offers. In the following sections, I discuss typical investment options for 401(k) plans in order of increasing risk and, hence, likely return. Then I follow with examples for how to allocate your money across the different types of common employer retirement plan options.

Money-market/savings accounts

For regular contributions that come out of your paycheck, the money market or savings account option makes little sense. Some people who are skittish about the stock and bond markets are attracted to money market and savings accounts because they can't drop in value. However, the returns are low . . . so low that you have a great risk that your investment will not stay ahead of, or even keep up with, inflation and taxes (which are due upon withdrawal of your money from the retirement account).

Don't be tempted to use a money market fund as a parking place until the time that you think stocks and bonds are cheap. In the long run, you won't be doing yourself any favors. As I discuss in Chapter 7, timing your investments to attempt to catch the lows and avoid the peaks is impossible. If you can figure out how to do that, you're wasting your time in your current occupation: You can make a fortune as a professional money manager.

You may need to keep money in the money market investment option if you utilize the borrowing feature that some retirement plans allow. Check with your employee benefits department for more details. After you retire, you may also want to use a money market to hold money you expect to withdraw and spend within a year or so.

Bond mutual funds

Bond mutual funds (which I describe in Chapter 9) invest in a mixture of typically high-quality bonds. Bonds pay a higher rate of interest or dividends than money funds. Depending on whether your plan's option is a short-term, intermediate-term, or long-term fund (maybe you have more than one type), the bond fund's current yield is probably a percent or two higher than the money market fund's yield.

Bond funds carry higher yields than money market funds, but they also carry greater risk, because their value can fall if interest rates increase. However, bonds tend to be more stable in value than stocks.

Aggressive, younger investors should keep a minimum amount of money in bond funds. Older folks who want to invest conservatively can place more money in bonds (see the asset allocation discussion in Chapter 7).

Guaranteed-investment contracts (GICs)

GICs are backed by an insurance company, and they typically quote you a rate of return projected one or a few years forward. The positive return is certain — so you don't have the uncertainty that you normally face with bond or stock investments (unless, of course, the insurance company fails).

The attraction of these investments is that your account value does not fluctuate (at least, not that you can see). Insurers normally invest your money mostly in bonds and maybe a bit in stocks. The difference between what these investments generate for the insurer and what they pay in interest is profit to the insurer. A GIC's yield is usually comparable to that of a bond fund.

For people who hit the eject button the moment that a bond fund slides a bit in value, GICs are soothing to the nerves. And they're certainly higher yielding than a money market or savings account.

Like bonds, however, GICs don't give you the opportunity for long-term growth. Over the long haul, you should earn a better return in a mixture of bond and stock investments. In GICs, you pay for the peace of mind of a guaranteed return with lower long-term returns.

GICs also have another minor drawback: Insurance companies, unlike mutual funds, can and do fail, putting GIC investment dollars at risk. Some employers' retirement plans have been burned by insurance company failures.

Balanced mutual funds

Balanced mutual funds invest primarily in a mixture of stocks and bonds. This one-stop-shopping concept makes investing easier and smoothes out fluctuations in the value of your investments — funds investing exclusively in stocks or in bonds make for a rougher ride. These funds are solid options and, in fact, can be used for a significant portion of your retirement plan contributions. Refer to Chapter 9 to find out more about balanced funds.

Stock mutual funds

Stock mutual funds invest in stocks, which often provide greater long-term growth potential but also wider fluctuations in value from year to year. Some companies offer a number of different stock funds, including funds that invest overseas. Unless you plan to borrow against your funds to purchase a home (if your plan allows), you should have a healthy helping of stock funds. See Chapter 9 for an explanation of the different types of stock funds as well as for details on how to evaluate a stock fund.

Stock in the company you work for

Some companies offer employees the option of investing in the company's stock. I generally advocate avoiding this option for the simple reason that your future income and other employee benefits are already riding on the success of the company. If the company hits the skids, you may lose your job and your benefits. You certainly don't want the value of your retirement account to depend on the same factors.

In the early 2000s, you may have heard all the hubbub about companies such as Enron going under and the employees losing piles of money in their retirement savings plans. Enron's bankruptcy in and of itself shouldn't have caused direct problems in Enron's 401(k) plan. The problem was that Enron required employees to hold substantial amounts of Enron company stock. Thus, when the company tanked, employees lost their jobs *and* their retirement savings balances.

Congress is (belatedly) weighing bills that would greatly limit companies from being able to force employees to hold retirement plan money in company stock. In the mean time, many companies with Enron-like retirement savings plans are redesigning their plans and not requiring employees to hold such large portions in company stock for so many years.

Complain if your employer forces you to keep a large portion of your account balance in company stock or doesn't offer you other retirement account investing options. Start with your benefits department. Benefits folks should know that 401(k) plans are supposed to offer several diversified investment options — offering your employer's stock as the one and only option doesn't pass muster.

If you think that your company has its act together and the stock is a good buy, investing a portion of your retirement account is fine — but no more than 25 percent. Now, if your company is on the verge of hitting it big, and the stock is soon to soar, you'll of course be kicking yourself for not putting more of your money into the company's stock. But when you place a big bet on your company's stock, be prepared to suffer the consequences if the stock tanks. Don't forget that lots of smart investors track companies' prospects, so odds are that the current value of your company's stock is fair.

Some employers offer employees the option to buy company stock at a discount, sometimes as much as 15 percent, when compared to its current market value. If your company offers a discount on its stock, take advantage of it. When you sell the stock as your employer's plan allows (usually after a certain holding period), you should be able to lock in a decent profit.

Some asset allocation examples

Using the methodology that I outline in Chapter 7 for allocating money, Table 10-3 shows a couple of examples of how people in different employer plans may choose to allocate their 401(k) investments among the plan's investment options.

Please note that making allocation decisions is not a science. Use the formulas in Chapter 7 as a guideline.

Table 10-3	Allocating 401(k) Investments		
	25-Year-Old, Aggressive Risk	*45-Year-Old, Moderate Risk*	*60-Year-Old, Moderate Risk*
Bond Fund	0%	35%	50%
Balanced Fund (50% stock/50% bond)	10%	0%	0%
Blue Chip/Larger Company Stock Fund(s)	30–40%	20–25%	25%
Smaller Company Stock Fund(s)	25%	20%	10%
International Stock Fund(s)	25–35%	20–25%	15%

Allocating money in plans you design

With self-employed plans (SEP-IRAs and Keoghs), certain 403(b) plans for nonprofit employees, and IRAs, you get to select the investment options as well as the allocation of money among them. In the sections that follow, I give some specific recipes that you may find useful for investing at some of the premier investment companies.

To establish your retirement account at one of these firms, simply pick up your telephone, dial the company's toll-free number, and ask the representative to mail you an account application for the type of account (for example,

SEP-IRA, 403(b), and so on) you want to set up. You can also have the company mail you background information on specific mutual funds. (If you're less patient, and you're enamored with the Internet, many investment firms provide downloadable account applications. However, downloading an application can be a tedious process, especially if you also need other information such as investment prospectuses and annual reports.)

Note: I recommend a conservative portfolio and an aggressive portfolio for each firm. I use the terms *conservative* and *aggressive* in a relative sense. Because some of the funds I recommend do not maintain fixed percentages of their different types of investments, the actual percentage of stocks and bonds that you end up with may vary slightly from the targeted percentages. Don't sweat it.

Where you have more than one fund choice, you can pick one or split the suggested percentage among them. If you don't have enough money today to divide your portfolio up as I suggest, you can achieve the desired split over time as you add more money to your retirement accounts.

Vanguard

Vanguard (800-662-7447; www.vanguard.com) is a mutual fund powerhouse. It's the largest no-load fund company around, and it consistently has the lowest operating expenses in the business. Historically, Vanguard's funds have excellent performance when compared to those of its peers, especially among conservatively managed bond and stock funds.

A conservative portfolio with 50 percent stocks, 50 percent bonds

If you don't want to risk too much, try this:

- ✔ Vanguard Total Bond Market Index — 25 percent

- ✔ Vanguard Star (fund of funds) — 55 percent

- ✔ Vanguard International Value *and/or* Vanguard Total International Stock Index — 20 percent

An aggressive portfolio with 80 percent stocks, 20 percent bonds

If you can afford to be aggressive, try this:

- ✔ Vanguard Star (fund of funds) — 50 percent

- ✔ Vanguard Total Stock Market Index — 20 percent

- ✔ Vanguard Total International Stock Index — 30 percent

Or you can place 100 percent in Vanguard LifeStrategy Growth (fund of funds). Note that this portfolio places less money overseas than the previous example.

Should I use one investment firm, or more than one?

The firms I recommend in this chapter offer a large-enough variety of investment options, managed by different fund managers, that you can feel comfortable concentrating your money at one firm. Discovering the nuances and choices of just one firm rather than several and having fewer administrative hassles are the advantages of a focused approach.

If you like the idea of spreading your money around, you may want to invest through a number of different firms. With a discount brokerage account (see Chapter 7), you can have your cake and eat it too. You can diversify across different mutual fund companies through one brokerage firm. However, you'll pay small transaction fees on some of your purchases and sales of funds.

Fidelity

Fidelity Investments (800-544-8888; www.fidelity.com) is the largest provider of mutual funds in terms of total assets. However, a number of Fidelity's funds assess sales charges (no such funds are recommended in the sections that follow), so Vanguard is still the largest pure no-load fund company. Fidelity's strength has historically been with investing in domestic stocks. The company's bond funds have slightly high management fees, and its foreign funds have traditionally lagged, although they have perked up versus their peers in recent years.

A conservative portfolio with 50 percent stocks, 50 percent bonds

If you want to maintain a conservative portfolio, try this:

- ✔ Fidelity Asset Manager — 33⅓ percent
- ✔ Fidelity Puritan — 33⅓ percent
- ✔ Dodge & Cox Balanced — 33⅓ percent

An aggressive portfolio with 80 percent stocks, 20 percent bonds

If you want to maintain an aggressive portfolio, try this:

- ✔ Fidelity Puritan — 35 percent
- ✔ Fidelity Equity-Income — 25 percent
- ✔ Fidelity Low Priced Stock — 20 percent
- ✔ Vanguard Total International Stock Index *and/or* Masters' Select International — 20 percent

Discount brokers

As I discuss in Chapter 7, a discount brokerage account can allow you centralized, one-stop shopping and the ability to hold mutual funds from a variety of leading fund companies. Some funds are available without transaction fees, although most of the better funds require you to pay a small transaction fee when you buy funds through a discount broker. The reason: The discounter is a middleman between you and the fund companies. You have to weigh the convenience of being able to buy and hold funds from multiple fund companies in a single account versus the lower cost of buying funds directly from their providers. A $25 to $30 transaction fee can gobble a sizeable chunk of what you have to invest, especially if you're investing smaller amounts.

Among brokerage firms or brokerage divisions of mutual fund companies, for breadth of fund offerings and competitive pricing, I like TD Waterhouse (800-934-4448; www.tdwaterhouse.com), T. Rowe Price (800-225-5132; www.troweprice.com), and Vanguard (800-992-8327; www.vanguard.com).

A conservative portfolio with 50 percent stocks, 50 percent bonds

If you want to set up a conservative portfolio, try this:

- ✔ Vanguard Short-Term Corporate — 20 percent

- ✔ Harbor Bond or Dodge & Cox Income — 20 percent

- ✔ Dodge & Cox Balanced — 20 percent

- ✔ T. Rowe Price Spectrum Growth (fund of funds) — 30 percent

- ✔ Master's Select International *and/or* Tweedy Browne Global Value — 10 percent

An aggressive portfolio with 80 percent stocks, 20 percent bonds

If you want to set up an aggressive portfolio, try this:

- ✔ Harbor Bond *and/or* Vanguard Total Bond Market Index — 20 percent

- ✔ Vanguard Total Stock Market Index *and/or* Dodge & Cox Stock *and/or* Masters' Select Equity — 50 percent

- ✔ Masters' Select International *and/or* Vanguard International Growth — 30 percent

Transferring Retirement Accounts

With the exception of plans maintained by your employer that limit your investment options, such as most 401(k)s, you can move your money held in SEP-IRAs, Keoghs, IRAs, and many 403(b) plans (also known as *tax-sheltered annuities*) to almost any major investment firm. Moving the money is pretty simple; if you can fill out a couple of short forms and send them back in a postage-paid envelope, you can transfer an account. The investment firm to which you are transferring your account does the rest.

Transferring accounts you control

Here's a step-by-step list of what you need to do to transfer a retirement account to another investment firm. Even if you're working with a financial advisor, you should be aware of this process (called a *direct trustee to trustee transfer*) to ensure that no hanky-panky takes place on the advisor's part.

1. **Decide where you want to move the account.**

   I recommend several investment companies in this chapter, along with some sample portfolios within those firms. You may also want to consult the latest editions of some of my other books, including *Mutual Funds For Dummies* and *Investing For Dummies* (both published by Wiley Publishing, Inc.).

2. **Obtain an account application and asset transfer form.**

   Call the toll-free number of the firm you're transferring the money to and ask for an *account application and asset transfer form* for the type of account you're transferring — for example, SEP-IRA, Keogh, IRA, or 403(b). You can also visit the firm's Web site, but for this type of request, I think most people find it easier to speak directly to someone.

   Important note: Ask for the form for the *same* type of account you currently have at the company from which you are transferring the money. You can determine the account type by looking at a recent account statement — the account type should appear near the top of the form or in the section with your name and address. If you can't figure out the account type on a cryptic statement, call the firm where the account is currently held and ask a representative to tell you what kind of account you have.

   Never, ever sign over assets such as checks and security certificates to a financial advisor, no matter how trustworthy and honest he or she may seem. The advisor could bolt with them quicker than you can say "Bonnie and Clyde." Transfers should not be completed this way. Besides, you'll find it easier to handle the transfer by following the information I provide in this section.

3. **Complete and mail the account application and asset transfer form.**

   Completing these for your new investment firm opens your new account and authorizes the transfer.

You shouldn't take possession of the money in your retirement account when moving it over to the new firm. The tax authorities impose huge penalties if you perform a transfer incorrectly. Let the company to which you're transferring the money do the transfer for you. If you have questions or problems, the firm(s) to which you're transferring your account has armies of capable employees waiting to help you. Remember, these firms know that you're transferring your money to them, so they should roll out the red carpet.

4. **Figure out which securities you want to transfer and which need to be liquidated.**

   Transferring existing investments in your account to a new investment firm can sometimes be a little sticky. Transferring such assets as cash (money market funds) or securities that trade on any of the major stock exchanges is not a problem.

   If you own publicly traded securities, transferring them as is (also known as transferring them *in kind*) to your new investment firm is better, especially if the firm offers discount brokerage services. You can then sell your securities through that firm more cheaply.

   If you own mutual funds unique to the institution you're leaving, check with your new firm to see if it can accept them. If not, you need to contact the firm that currently holds them to sell them.

   CDs are tricky to transfer. Ideally, you should send in the transfer forms several weeks or so before the CDs mature — few people do this. If the CD matures soon, call the bank and tell it that, when the CD matures, you would like the funds to be invested in a savings or money market account that you can access without penalty when your transfer request lands in the bank's mailbox.

5. **Let the firm from which you're transferring the money know that you are doing so. (This step is optional.)**

   If the place you're transferring the money from doesn't assign a specific person to your account, you can definitely skip this step. When you're moving your investments from a brokerage firm where you dealt with a particular broker, deciding whether or not to follow this step can be more difficult.

   Most people feel obligated to let their representative know that they're moving their money. In my experience, calling the person with the "bad news" is usually a mistake. Brokers or others who have a direct financial stake in your decision to move your money will try to sell you on staying. Some may try to make you feel guilty for leaving, and some may even try to bully you.

Writing a letter may seem like the coward's way out, but writing usually makes leaving your broker easier for both of you. You can polish what you have to say, and you don't put the broker on the defensive. Although I don't want to encourage lying, not telling the *whole* truth may be an even better idea. Excuses, such as you have a family member in the investment business who will manage your money for free, may help you avoid an uncomfortable confrontation.

Then again, telling an investment firm that its charges are too high or that it misrepresented and sold you a bunch of lousy investments may help the firm improve in the future. Don't fret too much — do what's best for you and what you're comfortable with. Brokers are not your friends. Even though the broker may know your kids' names, your favorite hobbies, and your birthday, you have a *business* relationship with him.

Transferring your existing assets typically takes a month to complete. If the transfer is not completed within one month, get in touch with your new investment firm to determine the problem. If your old company isn't cooperating, call a manager there to help get the ball rolling.

The unfortunate reality is that an investment firm will cheerfully set up a new account to *accept* your money on a moment's notice, but it will drag its feet, sometimes for months, when the time comes to relinquish your money. To light a fire under the behinds of the folks at the investment firm, tell a manager at the old firm that you're going to send letters to the National Association of Securities Dealers (NASD) and the Securities and Exchange Commission (SEC) if it doesn't complete your transfer within the next week.

Moving money from an employer's plan

When you leave a job, particularly if you're retiring or being laid off after many years of service, money-hungry brokers and financial planners probably will be on you like a pack of bears on a tree leaking sweet honey. If you seek financial help, tread carefully — Chapter 17 helps you avoid the pitfalls of hiring such assistance.

When you leave a job, you're confronted with a slightly different transfer challenge: moving money from an employer plan into one of your own retirement accounts. (As long as your employer allows it, you may be able to leave your money in your old employer's plan. Evaluate the quality of the investment choices using the information I provide in this part of the book.) Typically, employer retirement plan money can be rolled over into your own IRA. Check with your employer's benefits department or a tax advisor for details.

Federal tax law requires employers to withhold, as a tax, 20 percent of any retirement account disbursements to plan participants. So if you're personally taking possession of your retirement account money in order to transfer it to an IRA, you must wait to be reimbursed by the government for this 20 percent withholding until you file your annual tax return. This withholding creates a problem, because if you don't replace the 20 percent withholding into the rollover IRA, the IRS treats the shortfall as an early distribution subject to income tax as well as penalties.

Never take personal possession of money from your employer's retirement plan. To avoid the 20 percent tax withholding and a lot of other hassles, simply inform your employer of where you want your money to be sent. Prior to doing so, you should establish an appropriate account (an IRA, for example) at the investment firm you intend to use. Then tell your employer's benefits department where you would like your retirement money transferred. You can send your employer a copy of your account statement, which contains the investment firm's mailing address and your account number.

Chapter 11

Investing Outside Retirement Accounts

. . . .

In This Chapter

▶ Taking advantage of frequently overlooked investment options

▶ Factoring taxes into your investment decisions

▶ Bolstering your emergency reserves

▶ Recommended long-term investments

. . . .

*I*n this chapter, I discuss investment options for money held *outside* retirement accounts, and I include some sample portfolio recommendations. Chapter 10 reviews investments for money *inside* retirement accounts. This distinction may seem somewhat odd — it's not one that is made in most financial books and articles. Thinking of these two types of investments differently can be useful.

✔ **Investments held outside retirement accounts are subject to taxation.** You have a whole range of different investment options to consider when taxes come into play.

✔ **Money held outside retirement accounts is more likely to be used sooner than funds held inside retirement accounts.** Why? Because you'll generally have to pay far more in income taxes to access money inside rather than outside retirement accounts.

✔ **Funds inside retirement accounts have their own nuances.** For example, when you invest through your employer's retirement plan, your investment options are usually limited to a handful of choices. And special rules govern transfer of your retirement account balances.

Getting Started

Suppose that you have some money sitting around in a bank savings account or money market mutual fund. Your money is earning a small amount of interest, but you want to invest it more profitably. You need to remember two things about investing this type of money:

- ✔ **Earning a little is better than losing 20 to 50 percent or more.** Just talk to anyone who bought a lousy investment. Be patient. Educate yourself *before* you invest.

- ✔ **To earn a higher rate of return, you must be willing to take more risk.** In order to earn a better rate of return, you need to consider investments that fluctuate in value — of course, the value can drop as well as rise.

You approach the vast sea of investment options and start stringing up your rod to go fishing. You hear stories of people catching big ones — cashing in big on stocks or real estate that they bought years ago. Even if you don't have delusions of grandeur, you'd at least like your money to grow faster than the cost of living.

But before you cast your investment line, consider the following frequently overlooked ways to put your money to work and earn higher returns without as much risk. These options may not be as exciting as hunting the big fish out there, but they should easily improve your financial health.

Paying off high-interest debt

Many folks have credit card or other consumer debt that costs more than 10 percent per year in interest. Paying off this debt with savings is like putting your money in an investment with a guaranteed return that's equal to the rate you're paying on the debt.

For example, if you have credit card debt outstanding at 14 percent interest, paying off that loan is the same as putting your money to work in an investment with a sure 14 percent annual return. Remember that the interest on consumer debt is not tax-deductible, so you actually need to earn *more* than 14 percent investing your money elsewhere in order to net 14 percent after paying taxes. (Refer to Chapter 4 for more details if you're still not convinced.)

Paying off some or all of your mortgage may make sense, too. This financial move isn't as clear, because the interest rate is lower than it is on consumer debt and is usually tax-deductible. (See Chapter 13 for more details on this strategy.)

Taking advantage of tax breaks

Make sure that you take advantage of the *terrific* tax benefits offered by a retirement account. If you work for a company that offers a retirement savings plan such as a 401(k), try to fund it at the highest level you can manage. If you earn self-employment income, look into SEP-IRAs and Keoghs. (Retirement-plan options are discussed in Chapter 10.)

If you need to save money outside retirement accounts for shorter-term goals (for example, to buy a car or a home), then, by all means, save money outside retirement accounts. But remember that investing money outside retirement accounts doesn't provide you tax deductions. It also requires greater thought and consideration, because your investments can produce taxable distributions.

Understanding Taxes on Your Investments

When you invest money outside of a retirement account, *investment distributions* — such as interest, dividends, and capital gains — are all exposed to taxation. Too many folks (and too many of their financial advisors) ignore the tax impact of their investment strategies. You need to pay attention to the tax implications of your investment decisions *before* you invest your money.

Consider a person in a combined 40 percent tax bracket (federal plus state taxes) who keeps extra cash in a taxable bond paying 3 percent interest. If she pays 40 percent of her interest earnings in taxes, she ends up keeping just 1.8 percent. With a similar but tax-free bond, she could easily earn more than this amount, completely free of federal and/or state taxes.

Another mistake some people make is investing in securities that produce tax-free income when they're not in a high enough tax bracket to benefit. Now consider a person in a combined 20 percent tax bracket who is investing in securities that produce tax-free income. Suppose that he invests in a tax-free investment that yields 4.5 percent. A comparable taxable investment is yielding 7 percent. If he had instead invested in the taxable investment at a 7 percent yield, the after-tax yield would be 5.6 percent. Thus, he is losing out on yield by being in the tax-free investment, even though he may feel happy in it because the yield isn't taxed.

To decide between comparable taxable and tax-free investments, you need to know your marginal tax bracket (tax rate you pay on an extra dollar of taxable income) and the rates of interest or yield on each investment. Here are some general guidelines based upon your federal income tax bracket. (Check out Table 6-1 in Chapter 6 to see what tax bracket you're in.)

In the sections that follow, I give specific advice about investing your money while keeping an eye on taxes.

Fortifying Your Emergency Reserves

In Chapter 2, I explain the importance of keeping sufficient money in an emergency reserve account. From such an account, you need two things:

- ✔ **Accessibility.** When you need to get your hands on the money for an emergency, you want to be able to do so quickly and without penalty.

- ✔ **Highest possible return.** You want to get the highest rate of return possible without risking your principal. This doesn't mean that you should simply pick the money market or savings option with the highest yield, because other issues such as taxes are a consideration. What good is earning a slightly higher yield if you pay a lot more in taxes?

Bank and credit union accounts

When you have a few thousand dollars or less, your best and easiest path is to keep this excess savings in a local bank or credit union. Look first to the institution where you keep your checking account.

Keeping this stash of money in your checking account, rather than in a separate savings account, makes financial sense if the extra money helps you avoid monthly service charges when your balance occasionally dips below the minimum. Compare the service charges on your checking account with the interest earnings from a savings account.

For example, suppose that you're keeping $2,000 in a savings account to earn 1 percent interest versus earning no interest on your checking account money. Over the course of a year, you earn $20 interest on that savings account. If you incur a $9 per month service charge on your checking account, you pay $108 per year. So, keeping your extra $2,000 in a checking account may be better if it keeps you above a minimum balance and erases that monthly service charge.

(However, if you're more likely to spend the extra money in your checking account, keeping it in a separate savings account where you won't be tempted to spend it may be better.)

Money market mutual funds

Money market funds, a type of mutual fund (see Chapter 10), are just like bank savings accounts — but better, in most cases. The best money market funds pay higher yields than bank savings accounts and offer you check-writing privileges. And if you're in a high tax bracket, you can select a tax-free money market fund, which pays interest that is free from federal and/or state tax — a feature you can't get with a bank savings account.

The yield on a money market is an important consideration. The operating expenses deducted before payment of dividends is the single biggest determinant of yield. All other things being equal (which they usually are with different money market funds), lower operating expenses translate into higher yields for you. With interest rates as low as they are these days, seeking out money funds with the lowest operating expenses is now more vital than ever.

The other types of fund investing you can do at the fund company where you establish a money market fund is another factor that may be important when choosing a money market fund. Doing most or all of your fund shopping (money-market and otherwise) at one good fund company can reduce the clutter in your investing life; chasing after a slightly higher yield offered by another company is sometimes not worth the extra paperwork and administrative hassle. On the other hand, there's no reason why you can't invest in funds at multiple firms (as long as you don't mind the extra paperwork), using each for its relative strengths.

Most mutual fund companies don't have many local branch offices, so you may have to open and maintain your money market mutual fund through the fund's toll-free phone line and the mail. Distance has its advantages. Because you can conduct business by mail, the Internet, and the phone, you don't need to go schlepping into a local branch office to make deposits and withdrawals. I'm *happy* to report that I haven't visited a bank office in years.

Despite the distance between you and your mutual fund company, your money is still accessible via check-writing, and you can also have money wired to your local bank on any business day. Don't fret about a deposit being lost in the mail; it rarely happens, and no one can legally cash a check made payable to you anyway. Just be sure to endorse the check with the notation "for deposit only" under your signature.

For that matter, driving or walking to your local bank isn't 100 percent safe. Imagine all the things that could happen to you or your money en route to the bank. You could slip on a banana peel, drop your deposit down a sewer grate, get mugged or kidnapped, walk into a bank holdup and get taken hostage, or get run over by a bakery truck.

Watch out for "sales"

Beware of money market mutual funds that have a "sale" by temporarily waiving (sometimes called *absorbing*) operating expenses, which results in a fund being able to boost its yield. These sales never last long; the operating expenses come back and deflate that too-good-to-be-true yield like a nail in a bike tire. Some fund companies run sales because they know that a major portion of the fund buyers that are lured in won't bother leaving when they jack up operating expenses.

You're better off sticking with funds that maintain "everyday low operating expenses" to get the highest long-term yield. I recommend such funds in the next section. However, if you want to move your money to companies having specials and then move it back out when the special is over, be my guest. If you have lots of money and don't mind paperwork, it may be worth the bother.

Recommended money market mutual funds

In the sections that follow, I recommend good money market mutual funds. As you peruse these lists, remember that the money market fund that works best for you depends on your tax situation. Throughout the list, I try to guide you to funds that generally make sense for people in particular tax brackets.

Money market funds that pay taxable dividends are appropriate when you're not in a high tax bracket (less than or equal to 30 percent federal). Some of my favorites include:

- ✔ Fidelity Cash Reserves and Spartan Money Market (800-544-8888; www.fidelity.com)
- ✔ USAA Money Market (800-382-8722; www.usaa.com)
- ✔ Vanguard Prime Money Market (800-662-7447; www.vanguard.com)

U.S. Treasury money market funds are appropriate if you prefer a money fund that invests in U.S. Treasuries, which have the safety of government backing, or if you're not in a high federal tax bracket (less than or equal to 30 percent) but are in a high state tax bracket (5 percent or higher). Vanguard (800-662-7447; www.vanguard.com) offers a couple of good options:

- ✔ Vanguard Treasury Money Market
- ✔ Vanguard Admiral Treasury Money Market

The following tax-free money market funds are appropriate when you're in a high federal (35+ percent) and state tax bracket (5+ percent):

- ✔ Fidelity Spartan AZ Muni Money Market (800-544-8888; www.fidelity.com)
- ✔ USAA CA Money Market (800-382-8722; www.usaa.com)
- ✔ Vanguard CA Tax-Exempt Money Market (800-662-7447; www.vanguard.com)
- ✔ Fidelity Spartan FL Muni Money Market (800-544-8888; www.fidelity.com)
- ✔ USAA FL Money Market (800-382-8722; www.usaa.com)
- ✔ Fidelity Spartan MA Muni Money Market (800-544-8888; www.fidelity.com)
- ✔ Vanguard NJ Tax-Exempt Money Market (800-662-7447; www.vanguard.com)
- ✔ USAA NY Money Market (800-382-8722; www.usaa.com)
- ✔ Vanguard NY Tax-Exempt Money Market (800-662-7447; www.vanguard.com)
- ✔ Vanguard OH Tax-Exempt Money Market (800-662-7447; www.vanguard.com)
- ✔ Vanguard PA Tax-Exempt Money Market (800-662-7447; www.vanguard.com)
- ✔ USAA TX Money Market (800-382-8722; www.usaa.com)
- ✔ USAA VA Money Market (800-382-8722; www.usaa.com)

A number of states do not offer the money market fund options listed in the previous list (and those that do may have minimums that are too high). In some cases, no options exist. In other cases, the funds available (and not on the recommended list) for that particular state have such high annual operating expenses, and therefore such low yields, that you're better off in one of the more competitively run federal-tax-free-only funds in the following list.

The following federal-tax-free-only money market funds (the dividends on these are state taxable) are appropriate when you're in a high federal (35+ percent) but not state (less than 5 percent) bracket, or if you live in a state that doesn't have competitive state- and federal-tax-free funds available.

> ✔ Vanguard Tax-Exempt Money Market (800-662-7447; www.vanguard.com)
>
> ✔ Fidelity Spartan Municipal Money Market (800-544-8888; www.fidelity.com)
>
> ✔ USAA Tax-Exempt Money Market (800-382-8722; www.usaa.com)

Investing Money for the Longer Term

Important note: This section (together with its recommended investments) assumes that you have a sufficient emergency reserve stashed away and are taking advantage of tax-deductible retirement account contributions. (Please see Chapter 3 for more on these goals.)

Which investments you should consider depends on how comfortable you are with risk. But your choice of investments should also be suited to how much *time* you have until you plan to use the money. I'm not talking about investments you won't be able to sell on short notice if necessary (most of them you can). Investing money in a more volatile investment is riskier if you need to liquidate it in the short term.

For example, suppose that you're saving money for a down payment on a house and are about one to two years away from having enough to make your foray into the real estate market. If you had put this "home" money into the U.S. stock market near the beginning of one of the stock market's 20 to 50 percent corrections, you'd have been a mighty unhappy camper. You would have seen a substantial portion of your money *vanish* in short order and your home dreams put on hold.

Defining your time horizons

The different investment options in the remainder of this chapter are organized by time frame. All the recommended investment funds that follow assume that you have *at least* a several-year time frame and are *no-load* (commission-free) mutual funds. Mutual funds can be sold on any business day, usually with a simple phone call. Funds come with all different levels of risk, so you can choose funds that match your time frame and desire to take risk. (Chapter 9 discusses all the basics of mutual funds.)

The recommended investments are also organized by your tax situation. (If you don't know your current tax bracket, be sure to review Chapter 6.) Following are summaries of the different time frames associated with each type of fund:

✔ **Short-term investments.** These investments are suitable for a period of a few years — perhaps you're saving money for a home or some other major purchase in the near future. When investing for the short-term, look for liquidity and stability — features that rule out real estate on one hand and stocks on the other. Recommended investments include shorter-term bond funds, which are higher-yielding alternatives to money market funds. If interest rates increase, these funds drop slightly in value — a couple of percent or so (unless rates rise tremendously). I also discuss treasury bonds and certificates of deposit (CDs) later in this chapter.

✔ **Intermediate-term investments.** These investments are appropriate for more than a few years but less than ten years. Investments that fit the bill are intermediate-term bonds and well-diversified hybrid funds (which include some stocks as well as bonds).

✔ **Long-term investments.** If you have a decade or more for investing your money, you can consider potentially higher-return (and therefore riskier) investments. Stocks, real estate, and other growth-oriented investments can earn the most money if you're comfortable with the risk involved.

Allocating assets for the long haul

Asset allocation refers to the process of figuring out what portion of your wealth you should invest in different types of investments. You often (and most appropriately) practice asset allocation with retirement accounts, because this money is earmarked for the long-term. Ideally, more of your saving and investing should be conducted through tax-sheltered retirement accounts. These accounts generally offer the best way to lower your long-term tax burden (see Chapter 10 for details).

If you have sufficient assets that you plan to invest outside retirement accounts, see Chapter 7 for information on investing the portion that you intend to hold for the long term (ten or more years).

Bond funds

Bond funds that pay taxable dividends are generally appropriate when you're not in a high tax bracket (less than or equal to 28 percent federal). Here are some of my favorites:

✔ **Short-term:** Vanguard Short-Term Corporate (800-662-7447; www. vanguard.com)

> ✔ **Intermediate-term:** Dodge & Cox Income (800-621-3979; www. dodgeandcox.com); Harbor Bond (800-422-1050; www.harborfunds. com); Vanguard Total Bond Market Index (800-662-7447; www. vanguard.com)
>
> ✔ **Long-term:** Vanguard Long-Term Corporate (800-662-7447; www. vanguard.com)

U.S. Treasury bond funds

U.S. Treasury bond funds are appropriate if you prefer a bond fund that invests in U.S. Treasuries (which have the safety of government backing), or when you're in a high state tax bracket (5 percent or higher) but not a high federal tax bracket (less than or equal to 28 percent). For good Treasury bond funds, look no further than the Vanguard Group, which offers short-, intermediate-, and long-term U.S. Treasury funds with a low 0.3 percent operating expense ratio. With a $50,000 minimum, Vanguard's Admiral series of U.S. Treasury funds offers even higher yields thanks to an even lower expense ratio of 0.15 percent.

Buying Treasuries direct

If you want an even cheaper method of investing in Treasury bonds than you can get through the thrifty Vanguard Treasury funds, try this: Purchase Treasuries directly from the Federal Reserve Bank. To open an account through the Treasury Direct program, call 800-722-2678, or visit their Web site at www.treasurydirect.gov.

The Federal Reserve Bank charges $25 annually for accounts with more than $100,000 in Treasury bonds. Smaller accounts are free of any fees. The operating expenses of even the leanest mutual funds can't compete with these rates!

You do sacrifice a bit of liquidity, however, when purchasing Treasury bonds directly from the government. You can sell your bonds through the Treasury, but it takes some time and hassle. If you want daily access to your money, buy a recommended Vanguard fund and pay the company's low management fee.

State- and federal-tax-free bond funds

State- and federal-tax-free bond funds are appropriate when you're in high federal (28+ percent) *and* state (5 percent or higher) tax brackets. Vanguard (800-662-7447; www.vanguard.com) has the best selection of state-specific tax-free bond funds. USAA (800-382-8722; www.usaa.com) and, to a lesser extent, Fidelity Spartan (800-544-8888; www.fidelity.com), for higher balance — $10,000 — customers, offer some of the better state-specific bond funds.

Federal-tax-free-only bond funds

Federal-tax-free-only bond funds (the dividends on them are state-taxable) are appropriate when you're in a high federal bracket (28+ percent) but a low state bracket (less than 5 percent), or when you live in a state that doesn't have state- and federal-tax-free funds available. Vanguard (800-662-7447; www.vanguard.com) offers the best selection of federal-tax-free bond funds.

Inflation-indexed Treasury bonds

Like a handful of other nations, the U.S. Treasury now offers *inflation-indexed* government bonds. Because a portion of these Treasury bonds' return is pegged to the rate of inflation, the bonds offer investors a safer type of Treasury bond investment option.

To understand the relative advantages of an inflation-indexed bond, take a brief look at the relationship between inflation and a normal bond. When an investor purchases a normal bond, he's committing himself to a fixed yield over a set period of time — for example, a bond that matures in 10 years and pays 6 percent interest. However, changes in the cost of living (inflation) are not fixed, so they're difficult to predict.

Suppose that an investor put $10,000 into a regular bond in the 1970s. During the life of his bond, he would've unhappily watched escalating inflation. During the time he held the bond, and by the time his bond matured, he would've witnessed the erosion of the purchasing power of his $600 of annual interest and $10,000 of returned principal.

Enter the inflation-indexed Treasury bond. Say that you have $10,000 to invest, and you buy a 10-year, inflation-indexed bond that pays you a real rate of return (this is the return above and beyond the rate of inflation) of, say, 2 percent.

This portion of your return is paid out in interest. The other portion of your return is from the inflation adjustment to the principal you invested. The inflation portion of the return gets put back into principal. So if inflation were running at about 2 percent, as it has in recent years, your $10,000 of principal would be indexed upwards after one year to $10,200. In the second year of holding this bond, the 2 percent real return of interest would be paid on the increased ($10,200) principal base.

If inflation skyrocketed and was running at, say, 8 percent rather than 2 percent per year, your principal balance would grow 8 percent per year, and you'd still get your 2 percent real rate of return on top of that. Thus, an inflation-indexed Treasury bond investor would not see the purchasing power of his invested principal or annual interest earnings eroded by unexpected inflation.

The inflation-indexed Treasuries can be a good investment for conservative, inflation-worried bond investors, as well as taxpayers who want to hold the government accountable for increases in inflation. The downside: Inflation-indexed bonds can yield slightly lower returns, because they're less risky compared to regular Treasury bonds.

Certificates of deposit (CDs)

For many decades, bank CDs have been a popular investment for folks with some extra cash that isn't needed in the near future. With a CD, you get a higher rate of return than you get on a bank savings account. And unlike bond funds, your principal does not fluctuate in value.

Compared to bonds, however, CDs have a couple of drawbacks:

- ✔ In a CD, your money is not accessible unless you cough up a fairly big penalty — typically six months' interest. With a no-load (commission-free) bond fund, you can access your money without penalty — whether you need some or all of your money next week, next month, or next year.

- ✔ CDs come in only one tax flavor — taxable. Bonds, on the other hand, come in tax-free (federal and/or state) and taxable flavors. So if you're a higher-tax-bracket investor, bonds offer you a tax-friendly option that CDs can't.

In the long run, you should earn more — perhaps 1 to 2 percent more per year — and have better access to your money in bond funds than in CDs. Bond funds make particular sense when you're in a higher tax bracket and you'd benefit from tax-free income on your investments. If you're not in a high tax bracket (25 percent federal or below), and you have a bad day whenever your bond fund takes a dip in value, consider CDs. Just make sure that you shop around to get the best interest rate.

One final piece of advice: Don't buy CDs simply for the FDIC (Federal Deposit Insurance Corporation) insurance. Much is made, particularly by bankers, of the FDIC government insurance that comes with bank CDs. The lack of this insurance on high-quality bonds shouldn't be a big concern for you. High-quality bonds rarely default; even if a fund held a bond that defaulted, it would probably only represent a tiny fraction (less than 1 percent) of the value of the fund, having little overall impact.

Besides, the FDIC itself is no Rock of Gibraltar. Banks have failed and will continue to fail. Yes, you are insured if you have less than $100,000 in a bank. However, if the bank crashes, you may have to wait a long time and settle for less interest than you thought you were getting. You're not immune from harm, FDIC or no FDIC.

If the government-backing you receive through FDIC insurance allows you to sleep better, you can invest in Treasuries (see "Bond funds," earlier in this chapter), which are government-backed bonds.

Stock funds

Selected tax-friendly stock funds are appropriate if you don't want current income or you're in a high federal tax bracket (28 percent and up). Vanguard (800-662-7447; www.vanguard.com) offers the best menu of tax-managed stock funds. Alternatively, you can invest in a wider variety of diversified stock funds inside an annuity (see the following section).

If you're not in a high tax bracket, you can also consider some of the stock funds I recommend in Chapter 10.

Annuities

As I discuss in Chapter 10, *annuities* are accounts that are partly insurance but mostly investment. You should only consider contributing to an annuity after you exhaust contributions to all your available retirement accounts. Because annuities carry higher annual operating expenses than comparable mutual funds, you should only consider them if you plan to leave your money invested, preferably, for 15 or more years. Even if you leave your money invested for that long, the tax-friendly funds discussed in the previous sections of this chapter can allow your money to grow without excessive annual taxation.

The best annuities can be purchased from no-load (commission-free) mutual fund companies — specifically Vanguard (800-662-7447; www.vanguard.com) and T. Rowe Price (800-638-5660; www.troweprice.com).

Real estate

Real estate can be a financially and psychologically rewarding investment. It can also be a money pit and a real headache if you buy the wrong property or get a "tenant from hell." (I discuss the investment particulars of real estate in Chapter 8, and the nuts and bolts of buying real estate in Chapter 13.)

Small-business investments

Investing in your own business or someone else's established small business can be a high-risk but potentially high-return investment. The best options are those you understand well. See Chapter 8 for more information about small-business investments.

Chapter 12

Investing for Educational Expenses

In This Chapter

▶ Understanding the financial aid system

▶ Looking at the right and wrong ways to save for college

▶ Exploring educational investment options

▶ Calculating how much you need to save

▶ Finding ways to pay for college when the time comes

*I*f you're like most parents (or potential future parents), just turning to this chapter makes you anxious. Such trepidation is understandable. According to much of what you read about educational expenses (particularly college expenses), if costs keep rising at the current rate, you'll have to spend upwards of a million dollars to give your youngster a quality (college and graduate school) education.

Whether you're about to begin a regular college investment plan or you've already started saving, your emotions may lead you astray. The hype about educational costs may scare you into taking a path that is less financially beneficial than others that are available. Quality education for your child doesn't have to — and probably won't — cost you as much as those gargantuan projections suggest.

Figuring Out How the Financial Aid System Works

Just as your child shouldn't choose a college based solely on whether she thinks she can get in, she shouldn't choose a college on the basis of whether you think you can afford it. Except for the affluent who have plenty of cash available to pay for the full cost of college, everyone else should apply for financial aid. More than a few parents who don't think that they qualify for financial aid are pleasantly surprised to find that they have access to loans as well as grants. (Grants, unlike loans, don't have to be repaid.)

Mary paid for the full cost of her daughter's first year at an expensive private college. In her 50s, Mary had little put away for retirement. "I didn't bother applying for financial aid," she says. "With the value of my home and savings, I thought I was too rich to qualify."

Mary was wrong. In fact, for her daughter's junior year, Mary, who most would consider middle-class, was delighted and shocked to learn that her daughter would receive nearly $9,000 in grants, as well as access to moderate-interest loans. Two things did the trick. First, Mary applied for aid. And second, before she applied, she invested a hefty chunk of savings into an *annuity,* which is a type of retirement account. In a moment, I tell you why the annuity helped.

Completing the Free Application for Federal Student Aid (FAFSA), which is available from any high school or college, is the first step in the financial aid process. (Internet users can fill out the form online at www.fafsa.ed.gov.) As its name makes clear, you pay nothing for submitting this application other than the time you take to complete the paperwork. (Completing the application takes more time than watching a TV sitcom but less time than getting a driver's license.) Some private colleges also require that you complete the Financial Aid Form (FAF), which asks for more information than the FAFSA.

States have their own financial aid programs, so apply to these programs, as well, if you're planning on attending an in-state college. You can check with your local high school or college financial aid office to get the necessary forms. Some colleges also require submission of supplementary forms directly to them.

The data you supply through student aid forms is run through a *financial needs analysis,* a standard methodology approved by the U.S. Congress. The needs analysis considers a number of factors, such as parents' income and assets, age and need for retirement income, number of dependents, number of family members in college, and unusual financial circumstances, which you explain on the application.

The financial needs analysis calculates how much money you, as the parent(s), and your child, as the student, are expected to contribute toward educational expenses. Even if the needs analysis determines that you don't qualify for needs-based financial aid, you may still have access to loans that are *not* based on need if you go through the financial aid application process. So make sure that you apply for financial aid!

Treatment of retirement accounts

Under the current financial needs analysis, the value of your retirement plans is *not* considered an asset. By contrast, money that you save *outside* retirement accounts, including money in the child's name, is counted as an asset and reduces your eligibility for financial aid.

Therefore, forgoing contributions to your retirement savings plans in order to save money in a taxable account for Junior's college fund doesn't make sense. When you do, you pay higher taxes both on your current income and on the interest and growth of the college fund money. In addition to paying higher taxes, you're expected to contribute more to your child's educational expenses.

So while your children are years away from applying to college, make sure that you fully fund your retirement accounts, such as 401(k)s, SEP-IRAs, and Keoghs. In addition to getting an immediate tax deduction in the year you contribute money, future growth on your earnings will grow without taxation while you're maximizing your child's chances of qualifying for aid.

Let me stress the need to get an early start on saving. If you read the example about Mary earlier in the chapter, you notice that she waited until the last minute — with her daughter already in college, you could say that she waited even beyond the last minute. She then had to resort to an annuity (explained in Chapter 10), because it was the only avenue available to her where she could put tens of thousands of dollars away at once in a retirement account. Her procrastination cost her thousands of dollars in tax-deductions she could have had over the years, as well as the financial aid she missed out on during her daughter's earlier years in college.

Some schools use *Profile forms* to supplement the FAFSA (which I describe earlier in the chapter). This form is mainly used by costly private schools to differentiate need among financial aid applicants. Individual schools may attach their own questions, which may require you to list information about retirement accounts. The information on this form is used to help determine how much money you'll receive from the school's privately endowed funds. You shouldn't ignore your retirement accounts. The vast majority of schools don't consider retirement account funds when making financial aid determinations. And even if your child ends up going to one of the schools that does examine such accounts, the reduction in your financial aid offer may not outweigh the tax benefits gained from the accounts.

Financial aid reform needed ASAP!

To some, structuring your finances to maximize financial aid seems, well, a bit underhanded. Let me discourage you from this type of thinking. The government has set up both a financial aid and tax system that encourage you to save for retirement. Therefore, saving for retirement is not selfish — it's financially responsible for you and your children (and the government that doesn't want to get stuck caring for you if you don't save for retirement). Because so many parents don't understand this idea, they're not receiving the financial aid that they deserve.

Perhaps you can criticize the government for not publicizing its intentions more effectively. But compare financial aid to the tax system. The tax system also rewards certain types of behavior, but if you ask the IRS for help, they won't tell you *how* to reduce your taxes. The same is true

of financial aid: *You* are responsible for understanding the system in order to receive the financial aid that your child deserves.

Of course, the financial aid system is far from perfect, but working for changes is our responsibility. For example, one inequity in the current financial aid determination process is that it makes no allowance for differences in the cost of living across the country. If you live in a high-cost urban area, such as New York, Los Angeles, or San Francisco, the financial aid system typically makes the erroneous assumption that you're able to contribute the same amount for college costs as someone with equivalent income who lives in a low-cost rural area. Adjustments for differences in cost of living should be considered in the system.

Treatment of money in the kids' names

If you plan to apply for financial aid, save money in your name rather than in your children's names (such as via custodial accounts). Colleges expect a much greater percentage of the money in your children's names (35 percent) to be used annually for college costs than the money in your name (about 6 percent).

If you're affluent enough to pay for your kid's entire educational costs, investing through custodial accounts can save you on taxes. Prior to your child reaching age 14, the first $750 of interest and dividend income is tax free; the next $750 is taxed at 10 percent. Any income above that is taxed at the parent's marginal tax rate. After age 14, all income generated by investments in your child's name is taxed at your child's rate, presumably a lower tax rate.

The newer Education Savings Account (ESA) is another option that, like a traditional custodial account, generally makes the most sense for affluent parents who don't expect to apply for or need any type of financial aid. As with regular custodial accounts, parents who have their kids apply for financial aid will be penalized by college financial aid offices for having ESA balances. Subject to eligibility requirements, you can put up to $2,000 per child per year into an ESA. Single taxpayers with adjusted gross incomes (AGIs) of $110,000 or more, and couples with AGIs of $220,000 or more may not contribute to an ESA (although another individual, such as a grandparent, may make the contribution to the child's account). While the contribution is not tax-deductible, the future investment earnings compound without taxation. Upon withdrawal, the investment earnings are not taxed (unlike with a traditional retirement account) as long as the money is used for qualified education expenses and, in the year of withdrawal, the HOPE or Lifetime Learning tax credit is not claimed for the student. See the latest edition of *Taxes For Dummies*, co-written by David J. Silverman and me (Wiley Publishing), for more details.

Treatment of home equity and other assets

Your family's assets may also include equity in real estate and businesses that you own. Although the federal financial aid analysis no longer counts equity in your primary residence as an asset, many private (independent) schools continue to ask parents for this information when making their own financial aid determinations. Therefore, paying down your home mortgage more quickly instead of funding retirement accounts can harm you financially: You may end up with less financial aid and a higher tax bill.

Strategizing to Pay for Educational Expenses

Now I'm going to get more specific about what college may cost your kids and how you're going to pay for it. I don't have just one solution, because how you help pay for your child's college costs depends on your own unique situation. However, in most cases you may have to borrow *some* money, even if you have some available cash that can be directed to pay the college bills as you receive them.

State-sponsored college savings plans: The new kid on the block

Section 529 plans (named after Internal Revenue Code Section 529, and also known as *qualified state tuition plans*) are among the newest educational savings plans. A parent or grandparent can generally put more than $200,000 per beneficiary into one of these plans. Up to $55,000 may be placed in a child's college savings account immediately, and this amount counts for the next five years' worth of $11,000 annual tax-free gifts allowed under current gifting laws. (Money contributed to the account is not considered part of the donor's taxable estate. However, if the donor gifts $55,000 and then dies before five years are up, a pro-rata amount of that gift will be charged back to the donor's estate.)

The biggest attraction of the Section 529 plans is that money inside the plans compounds without tax, and if it is used to pay for college tuition, room and board, and other related higher education expenses, the investment earnings and appreciation can be withdrawn tax-free. You can generally invest in any state plan to pay college expenses in any state, regardless of where you live.

In addition to paying college costs, the money in Section 529 plans may also be used for graduate school expenses. Some states provide additional tax benefits on contributions to their state-sanctioned plan.

Unlike the money in a custodial account, with which a child may do with as he pleases when he reaches either the age of 18 or 21 (the age varies by state), these state tuition plans must be used for higher education expenses. Most state plans even allow you to change the beneficiary. You can also take the money back out of the plan if you change your mind. (You will,

however, owe tax on the withdrawn earnings plus a penalty — typically 10 percent).

A big potential drawback of the Section 529 plans — especially for families hoping for some financial aid — is that college financial aid offices may treat assets in these plans as belonging to the child, which can greatly diminish financial aid eligibility.

Another potential drawback with some plans is that you can't control how the money is invested. Instead, the investment provider(s) may decide how to invest the money. In most plans, the farther your child is from college age, the more aggressive the investment mix. As your child approaches college age, the investment mix is tilted more to conservative investments. Most state plans have fairly high investment management fees, and some plans don't allow transfers to other plans.

Please also be aware that a future Congress could change the tax laws affecting these plans, diminishing the tax breaks or increasing the penalties for non-qualified withdrawals.

Clearly, these plans have both pros and cons. They generally make the most sense for affluent parents (or grandparents) to establish for children who don't expect to qualify for financial aid. Do a lot of research and homework before investing in any plan. Check out the investment track record, allocations, and fees in each plan, as well as restrictions on transferring to other plans or changing beneficiaries. These plans are relatively new, and the market for them is evolving, so take your time before committing to one of them.

Estimating college costs

College can cost a lot. The total costs — including tuition, fees, books, supplies, room, board, and transportation — vary substantially from school to school. The total average annual cost is running around $26,000 per year at private colleges, and around $12,000 at public colleges and universities. The more expensive schools can cost up to one-third more. Ouch!

Is all this expense worth it? Although many critics of higher education claim that the cost of a college education shouldn't be rising faster than inflation and that costs can, and should, be contained, denying the value of going to college is hard. Whether you're considering a local community college, your friendly state university, or a selective Ivy League institution, investing in education is usually worth the effort and the cost.

An *investment* is an outlay of money for an expected profit. Unlike a car that depreciates in value each year that you drive it, an investment in education yields monetary, social, and intellectual profit. A car is more tangible in the short term, but an investment in education (even if it means borrowing money) gives you more bang for your buck in the long run.

Colleges are now finding themselves subject to the same types of competition that companies confront. As a result, some colleges are clamping down on rising costs. As with any other product or service purchase, it pays to shop around. You can find good values — colleges that offer competitive pricing *and* provide a quality education.

Setting realistic savings goals

If you have money left over *after* taking advantage of retirement accounts, by all means try to save for your children's college costs. You should save in your name unless you know that you aren't going to apply for financial aid, including those loans that are available regardless of your economic situation.

Be realistic about what you can afford for college expenses given your other financial goals, especially saving for retirement (refer to Chapter 2). Being able to personally pay 100 percent of the cost of a college education, especially at a four-year private college, is a luxury of the affluent. If you're not a high-income earner, consider trying to save enough to pay a third or, at most, half of the cost. You can make up the balance through loans, your child's employment before and during college, and the like.

Use Table 12-1 to help get a handle on how much you should be saving for college.

Table 12-1	How Much to Save for College*	
Figure Out This	*Write It Here*	
1. **Cost of the school you think your child will attend.	$_____	
2. Percent of costs you'd like to pay (for example, 20% or 40%).	– _____	%
3. Line 1 times line 2 is amount you'll pay (in today's dollars).	= $ _____	
4. Number of months until your child reaches college age.	÷ _____	months
5. *** Line 3 answer divided by line 4 answer is amount to save per month (today's dollars).	= $ _____	/ month

Don't worry about correcting the overall analysis for inflation. This worksheet takes care of that through the assumptions made on the returns of your investments as well as the amount that you save over time. This way of doing the calculations works because you assume that the money you're saving will grow at the rate of college inflation. (In the happy event that your investment return exceeds the rate of college inflation, you end up with a little more than you expected.)

** *The average cost of a four-year private college education today is about $104,000; the average cost of a four-year public college education is about $48,000. If your child has an expensive taste in schools, you may want to tack 20 to 30 percent onto the average figures.*

*** *The amount you need to save (calculated in line 5) needs to be increased once per year to reflect the increase in college inflation — 5 or 6 percent should do.*

Tips for getting loans, grants, and scholarships

If you're a homeowner, you may be able to borrow against the *equity* (market value less the outstanding mortgage loan) in your property. This option is useful because you can borrow against your home at a reasonable interest rate, and the interest is generally tax-deductible. Some company retirement plans — for example, 401(k)s — allow borrowing, as well.

Parents are allowed to make penalty-free withdrawals from Individual Retirement Accounts if the funds are used for college expenses. Although you won't be charged an early-withdrawal penalty, the amount withdrawn will be treated by the IRS as income, and your income taxes will increase accordingly. On top of that, the financial aid office will look at your beefed-up income and assume that you don't need as much financial aid.

A host of financial aid programs, including a number of loan programs, allow you to borrow at fair interest rates. Federal government educational loans have *variable interest rates* — which means that the interest rate you're charged floats, or varies, with the overall level of interest rates. Most programs add 3.1 percent to the current interest rates on three-month to one-year Treasury bills. Thus, current rates on educational loans are in the vicinity of 5 percent. The rates are also capped so that the interest rate on your loan can never exceed a few percent more than the initial rate on the loan.

A number of loan programs, such as *Unsubsidized Stafford Loans* and *Parent Loans for Undergraduate Students* (PLUS), are available even when your family is not deemed financially needy. Only Subsidized Stafford Loans, on which the federal government pays the interest that accumulates while the student is still in school, are limited to students deemed financially needy.

Most loan programs limit the amount that you can borrow per year, as well as the overall total you can borrow for a student's educational career. If you need more money than your limits allow, PLUS loans can fill the gap: Parents can borrow the full amount needed after other financial aid is factored in. The only obstacle is that you must go through a credit qualification process. Unlike privately funded college loans, you can't qualify for a federal loan if you have negative credit (recent bankruptcy, more than three debts over three months past due, and so on). For more information from the federal government about these student loan programs, call the Federal Student Aid Information Center at 800-433-3243 or visit their Web site at `www.ed.gov/offices/OSFAP/Students/`.

In addition to loans, a number of grant programs are available through schools, the government, and independent sources. You can apply for federal government grants via the FAFSA (see "How the Financial Add System Works," earlier in this chapter). Grants available through state government programs may require a separate application. Specific colleges and other private organizations (including employers, banks, credit unions, and community groups) also offer grants and scholarships.

Many scholarships and grants don't require any extra work on your part — simply apply for financial aid through colleges. Other aid programs need seeking out — check directories and databases at your local library, your child's school counseling department, and college financial aid offices. You can also contact local organizations, churches, employers, and so on. You have a better chance of getting scholarship money through these avenues.

College scholarship search services are generally a waste of money; in some cases, they're actually scams. Some of these services charge up to $100 just to tell you about scholarships that you're either already being considered for or you're not even eligible for. The legitimate services may tell you about scholarships for, say, $500 that require you to complete an application and write essays. Most people who lack the initiative to use the free references that I describe earlier in this chapter probably won't take the time to apply for these small-potato scholarships.

Your child can work and save money during high school and college. In fact, if your child qualifies for financial aid, he or she is expected to contribute a certain amount to education costs from savings and employment during the school year or summer breaks. Besides giving Junior a stake in his or her own future, this training encourages sound personal financial management.

Investing Educational Funds

Financial companies pour millions of dollars into advertising for investment and insurance products that they claim are best for making your money grow for your little gremlins — I mean, children. Don't get sucked in by these ads.

What makes for good and bad investments in general, applies to investments for educational expenses, too. Stick with basic, proven, lower-cost investments. (Chapter 8 explains what you generally need to look for and beware of.) The following sections focus on considerations specific to college funding.

Good investments: No-load mutual funds

As I discuss in Chapter 9, the professional management and efficiency of the best no-load mutual funds makes them a tough investment to beat. Chapters 10 and 11 provide recommendations for investing money in funds both inside and outside tax-sheltered retirement accounts.

Gearing the investments to the time frame involved until your children will need to use the money is the most important issue with no-load mutual funds. The closer your child gets to attending college and using the money saved, the more conservatively the money should be invested.

Bad investments

Life insurance policies that have cash values are some of the most oversold investments for funding college costs. Here's the usual pitch: "Because you need life insurance to protect your family, why not buy a policy that you can borrow against to pay for college?"

The reason you shouldn't invest in this type of policy to fund college costs is that you're better off contributing to retirement accounts that give you an immediate tax deduction that saving through life insurance doesn't offer. Because life insurance that comes with a cash value is more expensive, parents are more likely to make a second mistake — not buying enough coverage. If you need and want life insurance, you're better off buying lower-cost term life insurance (see Chapter 15).

Another poor investment for college expenses is one that fails to keep you ahead of inflation, such as savings or money market accounts. You need your money to grow so that you can afford educational costs down the road.

Prepaid tuition plans should generally be avoided. A few states have developed plans that allow you to pay college costs at a specific school (calculated for the age of your child). The allure of these plans is that, by paying today, you eliminate the worry of not being able to afford rising costs in the future.

This logic doesn't work for several reasons. First, odds are quite high that you don't have the money today to pay in advance. Second, putting money into such plans reduces your eligibility for financial aid dollar for dollar. If you have that kind of extra dough around, you're better off using it for other purposes (and you're not likely to worry about rising costs anyway). You can invest your own money — that's what the school's going to do with it anyway.

Besides, how do you know which college your child will want to attend and how long it may take him or her to finish? Coercing your child into the school you've already paid for is a sure ticket to long-term problems in your relationship.

Overlooked investments

Too often, I see parents knocking themselves out to make more money so that they can afford to buy a bigger home, purchase more expensive cars, take better vacations, and send their kids to more expensive (and therefore supposedly better) private high schools and colleges. Sometimes families want to send younger children to costly elementary schools, too. Families stretch themselves with outrageous mortgages or complicated living arrangements so that they can get into neighborhoods with top-rated public schools or send their kids to expensive private elementary schools.

The best school in the world for your child is you and your home. The reason many people I know (including me and my siblings) were able to attend some of the top educational institutions in this country is that concerned parents worked hard, not just at their jobs, but at spending time with the kids when they were growing up. Rather than working to make more money (with the best of intentions of buying educational games or trips, or sending the kids to better schools), try focusing more attention on your kids. In my humble opinion, you can do more for your kids by spending more time with them.

I see parents scratching their heads about their child's lack of academic interest and achievement — they blame the school, TV, or society at large. These factors may contribute to the problem, but education begins in the home. Schools can't do it alone.

Living within your means not only allows you to save more of your income but it also frees up more of your time for raising and educating your children. Don't underestimate the value of spending more time with your kids and giving them your attention.

Chapter 13

Investing in Real Estate

• •

In This Chapter

▶ Choosing between buying and renting

▶ Determining how to finance your real estate purchase

▶ Finding a great property

▶ Working successfully with a real estate agent

▶ Making a solid offer

▶ Handling issues after you buy

• •

*B*uying a home or investing in real estate can be rewarding. On the other hand, owning real estate can be a real pain in the posterior, because purchasing and maintaining property can be time-consuming, emotionally draining, and financially painful.

Perhaps you're looking to escape your rented apartment and buy your first home. Or maybe you're interested in cornering the local real estate market and making millions in investment property. In either case, you can learn many lessons from real estate buyers who have traveled before you.

Note: Although this chapter focuses primarily on real estate in which you're going to live — otherwise known by those in the trade as *owner-occupied property* — much of what this chapter covers is relevant to real estate investors. For additional information on buying *investment real estate* — property that you rent out to others — see Chapter 8.

Deciding Whether to Buy or Continue Renting

You may be tired of moving from rental to rental. Perhaps your landlord doesn't adequately keep up the place, or you have to ask permission to hang a picture on the wall. You may desire the financial security and rewards that seem to come with home ownership. Or maybe you just want a place to call your own.

Any one of these reasons is a good enough reason to *want* to buy a home. But you should take stock of your life and your financial health *before* you decide to buy, so that you can decide whether you still want to buy a home and how much you can really afford to spend. You need to ask yourself some bigger questions.

Assessing your timeline

From a financial standpoint, you really shouldn't buy a place unless you can anticipate being there for at least three years (preferably five or more). Buying and selling a property entails a lot of expenses, including the cost of getting a mortgage (points, application, and appraisal fees), inspection expenses, moving costs, real estate agents' commissions, and title insurance. To cover these transaction costs plus the additional costs of ownership, a property needs to appreciate about 15 percent.

If you need or want to move in a couple of years, counting on 15 percent appreciation is risky. If you're fortunate, and you happen to buy before a sharp upturn in housing prices, you may get it. If you're not fortunate, you'll probably lose money on the deal.

Some people are willing to invest in real estate even when they don't expect to live in it for long and would consider turning their home into a rental. Doing so can work well financially in the long haul, but don't underestimate the responsibilities that come with being a landlord. Also, most people need to sell their first home in order to tap all the cash that they have in it so that they can buy the next one.

Determining what you can afford to buy

Although buying and owning your own home can be a wise financial move in the long run, it's a major purchase that can send shock waves through the rest of your personal finances. You'll probably have to take out a 15- to 30-year mortgage to finance your purchase. The home you buy will need maintenance over the years. Owning a home is a bit like running a marathon: Just as you have to be in good physical shape to successfully run a marathon, you have to be in good financial health when you buy a home. For as long as you own the home, you'll be paying for something or other all the time.

I have seen too many people fall in love with a home and make a rash decision without taking a hard look at the financial ramifications. Take stock of your overall financial health (especially where you stand in terms of retirement planning), *before* you buy property or agree to a particular mortgage. Don't let the financial burdens of a home control your financial future.

To determine how much a potential home buyer can borrow, lenders look primarily at annual income; they pay no attention to a borrower's overall financial situation. Even if you don't have money tucked away into retirement savings, or you have several children to clothe, feed, and help put through college, you still qualify for the same size loan as other people with the same income (assuming equal outstanding debts).

So don't trust a lender when he tells you what you can afford according to some formulas the bank uses to determine what kind of a credit risk you are. Only you can figure out how much you can afford, because only you know what your other financial goals are and how important they are to you.

Here are some important financial questions that no lender will ask or care about but that you should ask yourself before buying a home:

- ✔ Are you saving enough money monthly to reach your retirement goals?

- ✔ How much do you spend (and want to continue spending) on fun things such as travel and entertainment?

- ✔ How willing are you to budget your expenses in order to meet your monthly mortgage payments and other housing expenses?

- ✔ How much of your children's expected college educational expenses do you want to be able to pay for?

The other chapters in this book can help you answer these important questions. Chapter 2 in particular will help you think through saving for important financial goals.

Many new homeowners run into financial trouble because they don't know their spending needs and priorities, and they don't know how to budget for them. Some of these owners have trouble curtailing their spending despite the large amount of debt they just incurred; in fact, some spend even more for all sorts of home furniture and remodeling expenditures. Many people prop up their spending habits with credit. For this reason, a surprisingly large percentage — some studies say about half — of people who borrow additional money against their home equity use the funds to pay consumer debts.

Calculating how much lenders will allow you to borrow

Mortgage lenders want to know your ability to repay the money you borrow, as well as the likelihood that you're going to repay it. So you have to pass a few tests that calculate the maximum amount the lender is willing to lend you. For a home in which you will reside, lenders total up your monthly housing expenses. They define your housing costs as

```
Mortgage Payment + Property Taxes + Insurance
```

Lenders typically loan you up to about 33 percent of your monthly gross (before taxes) income for the housing expense. If you're self-employed, take your net income from the bottom line of your federal tax form Schedule C and divide by 12 to get your monthly gross income.

Lenders also consider your other debts when deciding how much to lend you. These other debts diminish the funds available to pay your housing expenses. Lenders add the amount you need to pay down your other consumer debts (auto loans, credit cards) to your monthly housing expense. The monthly total costs of these debt payments plus your housing costs typically cannot exceed 38 percent.

One general rule says that you can borrow up to three times (or two and one-half times) your annual income when buying a home. But this rule is a really rough estimate. The maximum that a mortgage lender will loan you depends on interest rates. If rates fall (as they have during much of the past decade), the monthly payment on a mortgage of a given size also drops. Thus, lower interest rates make buying real estate more affordable.

Table 13-1 gives you a ballpark idea of the maximum amount you may be eligible to borrow. Multiply your gross annual income by the number in the second column to determine the approximate maximum you may be able to borrow. For example, if you're getting a mortgage with a rate around 7 percent, and your annual income is $50,000, multiply 3.5 by $50,000 to get $175,000 — the approximate maximum mortgage allowed.

Table 13-1	What's the Approximate Maximum You Can Borrow?
When Mortgage Rates Are	*Multiply Your Gross Annual Income* by This Figure to Estimate the Maximum You May Be Able to Borrow*
4%	4.6
5%	4.2
6%	3.8
7%	3.5
8%	3.2
9%	2.9

When Mortgage Rates Are	Multiply Your Gross Annual Income* by This Figure to Estimate the Maximum You May Be Able to Borrow
10%	2.7
11%	2.5

If you're self-employed, this is your net income (after expenses, but before taxes).

Comparing the cost of owning versus renting

The cost of owning a home is an important financial consideration for many renters. Some people assume that owning costs more. In fact, owning a home doesn't have to cost a truckload of money; it may even cost less than renting.

On the surface, buying a place seems a lot more expensive than renting. You're probably comparing your monthly rent (measured in hundreds of dollars to more than $1,000, depending on where you live) to the purchase price of a property, which is usually a much larger number — perhaps $150,000 to $500,000 or more. When you consider a home purchase, you're forced to think about your housing expenses in one huge chunk rather than in small monthly installments (like a rent check).

Tallying up the costs of owning a place can be a useful and not-too-complicated exercise. To make a fair comparison between ownership and rental costs, you need to figure what it will cost on a *monthly basis* to buy a place you desire versus what it will cost to rent a *comparable* place. The worksheet in Table 13-2 enables you to do such a comparison. ***Note:*** In the interest of reducing the number of variables, all this "figuring" assumes a fixed-rate mortgage, *not* an adjustable-rate mortgage. (For more info on mortgages, see "Financing Your Home," later in this chapter.)

Also, I ignore what economists call the *opportunity cost of owning.* In other words, when you buy, the money you put into your home can't be invested elsewhere, and the foregone investment return on that money, say some economists, should be considered a cost of owning a home. I choose to ignore this concept for two reasons. First, and most importantly, I don't agree with this line of thinking. When you buy a home, you're investing your money in real estate, which historically has offered solid long-term returns (see Chapter 8). And secondly, I have you ignore opportunity cost because it greatly complicates the analysis.

Table 13-2	Monthly Expenses: Renting Versus Owning
Figure Out This	*Write It Here ($ per Month)*
1. Monthly mortgage payment (see "Mortgage")	$
2. Plus monthly property taxes (see "Property taxes")	+ $
3. Equals total monthly mortgage plus property taxes	= $
4. Your income tax rate (refer to Table 6-1 in Chapter 6)	%
5. Minus tax benefits (line 3 multiplied by line 4)	– $
6. Equals after-tax cost of mortgage and property taxes (subtract line 5 from line 3)	= $
7. Plus insurance ($30 to $150/mo., depending on property value)	+ $
8. Plus maintenance (1% of property cost divided by 12 months)	+ $
9. Equals total costs of owning (add lines 6, 7, and 8)	= $

Now compare Line 9 in Table 13-2 with the monthly rent on a comparable place to see which costs more — owning or renting.

Mortgage

To determine the monthly payment on your mortgage, simply multiply the relevant number (or multiplier) from Table 13-3 by the size of your mortgage expressed in (divided by 1,000) thousands of dollars. For example, if you're taking out a $100,000, 30-year mortgage at 6.5 percent, you multiply 100 by 6.32 for a $632 monthly payment.

Table 13-3	Your Monthly Mortgage Payment Multiplier	
Interest Rate	*15-Year Mortgage Multipliers*	*30-Year Mortgage Multipliers*
4.0%	7.40	4.77
4.5%	7.65	5.07
5.0%	7.91	5.37
5.5%	8.17	5.68

Interest Rate	15-Year Mortgage Multipliers	30-Year Mortgage Multipliers
6.0%	8.44	6.00
6.5%	8.71	6.32
7.0%	8.99	6.65
7.5%	9.27	6.99
8.0%	9.56	7.34
8.5%	9.85	7.69
9.0%	10.14	8.05
9.5%	10.44	8.41
10.0%	10.75	8.78

Property taxes

You can ask a real estate person, mortgage lender, or your local assessor's office what your annual property tax bill would be for a house of similar value to the one you are considering buying (the average is 1.5 percent of your property's value). Divide this amount by 12 to arrive at your monthly property tax bill.

Tax savings in home ownership

Generally speaking, mortgage interest and property tax payments for your home are tax-deductible on Schedule A of IRS Form 1040 (see Chapter 6). Here's a shortcut that works quite well in determining your tax savings in home ownership: Multiply your federal tax rate (refer to Table 6-1 in Chapter 6) by the total amount of your property taxes and mortgage payment. Technically speaking, not all of your mortgage payment is tax-deductible — only the portion of the mortgage payment that goes toward interest is tax-deductible. In the early years of your mortgage, nearly all of your payment goes toward interest. On the other hand, your property taxes will probably rise over time. You may earn state tax benefits from your deductible mortgage interest and property taxes, as well.

If you want to more accurately determine how home ownership may affect your tax situation, get out your tax return and try plugging in some reasonable numbers to estimate how your taxes will change. You can also speak with a tax advisor or pick up a copy of the latest edition of *Taxes For Dummies*, co-written by David J. Silverman and me (Wiley Publishing).

Recognizing advantages to renting

Renting has its advantages. Some of the financially successful renters I've seen include people who pay low rent, either because they made housing sacrifices or they live in a rent-controlled building. If you're consistently able to save 10 percent or more of your earnings, you're probably well on your way to achieving your future financial goals.

As a renter, you can avoid worrying about or being responsible for fixing up the property — that's your landlord's responsibility. You also

have more financial and psychological flexibility as a renter. If you want to move, you can generally do so a lot easier as a renter than you can as a homeowner.

Having a lot of your money tied up in your home is another problem that you don't face when renting over the long haul. Some people enter their retirement years with a substantial portion of their wealth in their homes. As a renter, you can have all your money in financial assets that you can tap into more easily.

Considering the long-term costs of renting

When you crunch the numbers to find out what owning rather than renting a comparable place may cost you on a monthly basis, you may discover that owning isn't as expensive as you thought. Or you may find that owning costs a bit more than renting. This discovery may tempt you to think that, financially speaking, renting is cheaper than owning.

Be careful not to jump to conclusions. Remember that you're looking at the cost of owning versus renting *today.* What about 5, 10, or 30 years from now? As an owner, your biggest monthly expense — the mortgage payment — does not increase (assuming that you buy your home with a fixed-rate mortgage). Your property taxes, homeowner's insurance, and maintenance expenses — which are generally far less than your mortgage payment — are the items that increase with the cost of living.

When you rent, however, your entire monthly rent is subject to the vagaries of inflation. Living in a rent-controlled unit, where the annual increase allowed in your rent is capped, is the exception to this rule. Rent control does not eliminate price hikes, it just limits them.

Suppose that you're comparing the costs of owning a home that costs $160,000 to renting that same home for $800 a month. Table 13-4 compares the cost per month of owning the home (after factoring in tax benefits) to your rental costs over 30 years. This comparison assumes that you take out a mortgage loan equal to 80 percent of the cost of the property at a fixed rate of 7 percent, and that the rate of inflation of your homeowner's insurance, property taxes, maintenance, and rent is 4 percent per year. I further assume that you're in a moderate combined 35 percent federal and state tax bracket.

Table 13-4	Cost of Owning versus Renting over 30 Years	
Year	*Ownership Cost per Month*	*Rental Cost per Month*
1	$920	$800
5	$980	$940
10	$1,080	$1,140
20	$1,360	$1,690
30	$1,800	$2,500

As you can see in Table 13-4, in the first few years, owning a home costs a little more than renting it. In the long run, however, owning becomes less expensive, because more of your rental expenses increase with inflation. And don't forget that you're building equity in your property as a home-owner; that equity will be quite substantial by the time that you have your mortgage paid off.

You may be thinking that if inflation doesn't rise 4 percent per year, renting could end up being cheaper. This is not necessarily so. Suppose that infla-tion didn't exist. Your rent wouldn't escalate, but home ownership expenses wouldn't either. And, with no inflation, you could probably refinance your mortgage at a rate lower than 7 percent. If you do the math, owning would still cost less in the long run with lower inflation, but the advantage of own-ing is less than during periods of higher inflation. Also, in case you're wonder-ing what happens in this analysis if you're in a different tax bracket, owning would still cost less in the long run — the cost savings widen a bit for people in higher tax brackets and lessen a bit for those in lower tax brackets.

Financing Your Home

After you look at your financial health, figure out your timeline, and compare renting costs to owning costs, you need to confront the tough task of obtain-ing a hunk of debt to buy a home (unless you're independently wealthy). A mortgage loan from a bank or other source makes up the difference between the cash you intend to put into the purchase and the agreed-upon selling price of the real estate.

Understanding the two types of mortgages

Like many other financial products, you have zillions of different mortgages to choose from. The differences can be important or trivial, and expensive or cost-free. Two major types of mortgages exist — those with a *fixed interest rate* and those with a *variable* or *adjustable rate.*

Fixed-rate mortgages, which are usually issued for a 15- or 30-year period, have interest rates that never, ever change. The interest rate you pay the first month is the same rate you pay the last month (and every month in between). Because the interest rate stays the same, your monthly mortgage payment amount does not change. With a fixed-rate mortgage, you have no uncertainty or interest rate worries.

Fixed-rate loans are not risk-free, however. If interest rates fall significantly after you obtain your mortgage, you face the danger of being stuck with your higher-cost mortgage if you're unable to refinance (see "Refinancing your mortgage," later in this chapter). You can be turned down for a refinance because of deterioration in your financial situation or a decline in the value of your property. Even if you're eligible to refinance, you may have to spend significant time and money to complete the process.

In contrast to a fixed-rate mortgage, an *adjustable-rate mortgage* (ARM) carries an interest rate that varies over time. With an adjustable-rate mortgage, you can start with one interest rate and then have different rates for every year (or possibly every month) during a 30-year mortgage. Thus, the size of your monthly payment fluctuates. Because a mortgage payment makes an unusually large dent in most homeowners' checkbooks anyway, signing up for an ARM without understanding its risks is dangerous.

The attraction of ARMs is the potential interest savings. For the first few years of an adjustable loan, the interest rate is typically lower than it is on a comparable fixed-rate loan. After that, the cost depends on the overall trends in interest rates. When interest rates drop, stay level, or rise just a little, you continue to pay less for your adjustable. On the other hand, when rates rise more than a percent or two and then stay elevated, the adjustable can cost you more than a fixed-rate loan.

Choosing between fixed- and adjustable-rate mortgages

You should weigh the pros and cons of each mortgage type and decide what's best for your situation *before* you go out to purchase a piece of real estate or refinance a loan. In the real world, most people ignore this advice. The excitement of purchasing a home tends to cloud one's judgment. My experience has been that few people look at their entire financial picture before making major real estate decisions. You may end up with a mortgage that could some-day seriously overshadow the delight you have for your little English herb garden out back.

Consider the issues I discuss in this section before you decide which kind of mortgage — fixed or adjustable — is right for you.

How willing and able are you to take on financial risk?

Take stock of how much risk you can take with the size of your monthly mort-gage payment. You can't afford much risk, for example, if your job and income are unstable and you need to borrow a lot. I define *a lot* as "close to the maxi-mum a bank is willing to lend you." *A lot* can also mean that you have no slack in your monthly budget — in other words, you're not regularly saving money. If you're in this situation, stick with a fixed-rate loan.

Don't take an adjustable simply because the initially lower interest rates allow you to afford the property you want to buy (unless you're absolutely certain that your income will rise to meet future payment increases). Try setting your sights on a property that you can afford — with a fixed-rate mortgage.

If interest rates rise, a mushrooming adjustable mortgage payment may test the lower limits of your checking account balance. When you don't have emergency savings you can tap to make the higher payments, how can you afford the monthly payments — much less all the other expenses of home ownership?

And don't forget to factor in reasonably predictable future expenses that may affect your ability to make payments. For example, are you planning to start a family soon? If so, your income may fall while your expenses rise (as they surely will).

If you can't afford the highest allowed payment on an adjustable-rate mortgage, don't take it. You shouldn't accept the chance that the interest rate may not rise that high — it might, and then you could lose your home! Ask your lender to calculate the highest possible *maximum monthly payment* on your loan. That's the payment you'd face if the interest rate on your loan went to the highest level allowed (the *lifetime cap*).

You need to also consider your stress level. If you have to start following interest rate movements, it's probably not worth gambling on rates. Life is too short!

On the other hand, maybe you're in a position to take the financial risks that come with an adjustable-rate mortgage. An adjustable places much of the risk of fluctuating rates on you (most adjustables, however, limit, or *cap,* the rise in the interest rate allowed on your loan). In return for your accepting some interest-rate risk, lenders cut you a deal — an adjustable's interest rate starts lower and stays lower if the overall level of interest rates doesn't rise substantially. Even if rates go up, they'll probably come back down over the life of your loan. So if you can stick with your adjustable for better and for worse, you may still come out ahead over the long term. Typical caps are 2 percent per year and 6 percent over the life of the loan.

You may feel financially secure in choosing an adjustable loan if you have a hefty financial cushion accessible in the event that rates go up, you take out a smaller loan than you're qualified for, or you're saving more than 10 percent of your income.

How long do you plan to keep the mortgage?

A mortgage lender takes extra risk when committing to a constant interest rate for 15 to 30 years. Lenders generally don't know any better than you or me what may happen in the intervening years, so they charge you a premium for their risk.

The savings on most adjustables is usually guaranteed in the first two or three years, because an adjustable-rate mortgage starts at a lower interest rate than a fixed one. If rates rise, you can end up giving back or losing the savings you achieve in the early years of the mortgage. In most cases, if you aren't going to keep your mortgage more than five to seven years, you're probably paying unnecessary interest costs to carry a fixed-rate mortgage.

Another mortgage option is a *hybrid loan,* which combines features of both the fixed- and adjustable-rate mortgages. For example, the initial rate may hold constant for a number of years — three to five years is common — and then adjust once a year or every six months thereafter. These hybrid loans may make sense for you if you foresee a high probability of keeping your loan seven to ten years or less but want some stability in your monthly payments. The longer the initial rate stays locked in, the higher the rate.

Shopping for fixed-rate mortgages

Of the two major types of mortgages I discuss earlier in this chapter, fixed-rate loans are generally easier to shop for and compare. The following sections cover what you need to know when shopping for fixed-rate mortgages.

Trading off interest rates and points

The *interest rate* is the rate of interest a lender charges you for borrowing its money. Just as a seesaw doesn't work with one rider missing, an interest-rate quote is completely meaningless on its own. The interest rate on a fixed-rate loan must always be quoted with the points on the loan.

Points are upfront fees paid to your lender when you close on your loan. Points are actually percentages: One point is equal to 1 percent of the loan amount. So when a lender tells you that 1.5 points are on a quoted loan, you pay 1.5 percent of the amount you borrow as points. On a $100,000 loan, for example, 1.5 points cost you $1,500.

If one lender offers 30-year mortgages at 6.75 percent, and another lender offers them at 7 percent, the 7 percent loan is not necessarily worse. You also need to take into account how many points each lender charges.

The seesaw analogy explains how the interest rate and points on a fixed-rate loan go together and move in opposite directions. If you're willing to pay more points on a given loan (one end of the seesaw goes up), the lender will often reduce the interest rate (the other end of the seesaw goes down). Paying more in upfront points can save you a lot of money in interest, because the interest rate on your loan determines your payments over a long, long time — 15 to 30 years. If you pay fewer points, your interest rate increases. Paying less in points may appeal to you if you don't have much cash for closing on your loan.

Suppose Lender X quotes you 6.75 percent on a 30-year fixed-rate loan and charges one point (1 percent). Lender Y, who quotes 7 percent, doesn't charge any points. Which is better? The answer depends mostly on how long you plan to keep the loan.

The 6.75 percent loan is 0.25 percent less than the 7 percent loan. Year in and year out, the 6.75 percent loan saves you 0.25 percent. But because you have to pay 1 percent (one point) upfront on the 6.75 percent loan, it takes about four years to earn back the savings to cover the cost of that point. So if you expect to keep the loan less than 4 years, go with the 7 percent option.

To perform an apples-to-apples comparison of mortgages from different lenders, get interest rate quotes at the same point level for each mortgage. For example, ask each lender for the interest rate on a loan for which you pay one point.

Be wary of lenders who advertise no-point loans as though they're offering something for nothing. Remember, if a loan has no points, it's *guaranteed* to have a higher interest rate. That's not to say that the loan is better or worse than comparable loans from other lenders. But don't get sucked in by a no-points sales pitch. Most lenders who spend big bucks advertising these types of loans rarely have the best deals.

Understanding other lender fees

In addition to charging you points and the ongoing interest rate, lenders tack on all sorts of other upfront fees when processing your loan. You need to know the total of all lender fees so that you can compare different mortgages and determine how much completing your home purchase is going to cost you.

Lenders can nickel and dime you with a number of different fees other than points. Actually, you pay more than nickels and dimes — $300 here and $50 there adds up in a hurry! Here are the main culprits:

- **Application and processing fees.** Most lenders charge several hundred dollars to complete your paperwork and process it through their *under-writing* (loan evaluation) department. The justification for this fee is that if your loan is rejected or you decide not to take it, the lender needs to cover the costs. Some lenders return this fee to you upon closing if you go with their loan (after you're approved).

- **Credit report.** Many lenders charge a modest fee to pay for the cost of obtaining a copy of your credit report. This report tells the lender whether you've been naughty or nice to other lenders in the past. If you have problems on your credit report, clean them up before you apply (see "Increasing your approval chances," later in this chapter).

- **Appraisal.** The property for which you're borrowing money needs to be valued. If you default on your mortgage, your lender doesn't want to get stuck with a property worth less than you owe. For most residential properties, the appraisal cost is typically several hundred dollars.

- **Title and escrow charges.** These not-so-inconsequential costs are discussed in the section, "Title insurance and escrow fees," later in this chapter.

Get a written itemization of charges from all lenders you are seriously considering so that you can more readily compare different lenders' mortgages, and so that you have no surprises when you close on your loan. And to minimize your chances of throwing money away on a loan for which you may not qualify, ask the lender if you may not be approved for some reason. Be sure to disclose any problems you're aware of on your credit report or with the property.

Some lenders offer loans without points or other lender charges. Remember: Lenders aren't charities. If they don't charge points or other fees, they have to make up the difference by charging a higher interest rate on your loan. Only consider such loans if you lack cash for closing or if you're planning to use the loan for just a few years.

Shunning balloon loans

Be wary of balloon loans. They look like fixed-rate loans but they really aren't. With a *balloon loan,* the large remaining loan balance becomes fully due at a predetermined time — typically within three to ten years. Balloon loans are dangerous because you may not be able to refinance into a new loan to pay off the balloon loan when it comes due. What if you lose your job or your income drops? What if the value of your property drops, and the appraisal comes in too low to qualify you for a new loan? What if interest rates rise and you can't qualify for the higher rate on a new loan? Taking a balloon loan is a high-risk maneuver that can backfire.

Beware of prepayment penalties

Avoid loans with prepayment penalties. You pay this charge, usually 2 to 3 percent of the loan amount, when you pay off your loan before you're supposed to.

Prepayment penalties don't typically apply when you pay off a loan, because you sell the property. But if you refinance such a loan in order to take advantage of lower interest rates, you almost always get hit by the prepayment penalties.

The only way to know whether a loan has a prepayment penalty is to ask. If the answer is yes, find yourself another mortgage.

You shouldn't take a balloon loan unless the following three conditions are true:

- ✔ You *really, really* want a certain property.
- ✔ The balloon loan is your *only* financing option.
- ✔ You're *positive* that you're going to be able to refinance when the balloon loan comes due.

If you take a balloon loan, get one that takes as much time as possible before it comes due.

Inspecting adjustable-rate mortgages (ARMs)

While sorting through the myriad of fixed-rate mortgage options is enough to give most people a headache, comparing the bells and whistles of ARMs can give you a mortgage migraine. Caps, indexes, margins, and adjustment periods — you can spend weeks figuring it all out. If you're clueless about personal finances — or just think that you are — shopping for adjustables scores a 9.9 degree of difficulty on the financial frustration scale.

Unfortunately, you have to wade through a number of details to understand and compare one adjustable to another. Bear with me. And remember throughout this discussion that calculating exactly which ARM is going to cost you the least is impossible, because the cost depends on so many variables. Selecting an ARM has a lot in common with selecting a home. You have to make trade-offs and compromises based on what's important to you.

Understanding the start rate

Just as the name implies, the *start rate* is the interest rate your ARM starts with. Don't judge a loan by this rate. You won't be paying this attractively low rate for long. The interest rate will rise as soon as the terms of the mortgage allow.

Start rates are probably one of the least important items to focus on when comparing adjustables. (You'd never know this from the way some lenders advertise adjustables — you see ads with the start rate in 3-inch bold type, and everything else in microscopic footnotes!)

The formula (which includes index and margin) and rate caps are far more important for determining what a mortgage is going to cost you in the long run. Some people have labeled the start rate a *teaser rate,* because the initial rate on your loan is set artificially low to entice you. In other words, even if the market level of interest rates doesn't change, your adjustable is destined to increase — 1 to 2 percent is not uncommon.

Determining the future interest rate

You'd never (I hope) agree to a loan if your lender's whim and fancy determined your future interest rate. You need to know exactly how a lender figures out how much your interest rate is going to increase. All adjustables are based on the following formula, which specifies how the future interest rate on your loan is set:

```
Index + Margin = Interest Rate
```

Indexes are often (but not always) widely quoted in the financial press, and the specific one used on a given adjustable loan is chosen by the lender. The six-month Treasury bill rate is an example of an index that is used on some mortgages.

The *margin* is the amount added to the index to determine the interest rate you pay on your mortgage. Most loans have margins of around 2.5 percent.

So, for example, the interest rate of a mortgage driven by the following formula

```
Six-month Treasury bill rate + 2.5 percent
```

is set at the going rate for six-month Treasuries plus 2.5 percent. For example, if six-month Treasuries are yielding 3 percent, the interest rate on your loan should be 5.5 percent. This figure is known as the *fully indexed rate.* If this loan starts at 4 percent and the rate on six-month Treasuries stays the same, your loan should eventually increase to 5.5 percent.

Avoid loans with negative amortization

As you make mortgage payments over time, the loan balance you still owe is gradually reduced — this process is known as *amortizing* the loan. The reverse of this process — increasing your loan balance — is called *negative amortization*.

Negative amortization is allowed by some ARMs. Your outstanding loan balance can grow even though you're continuing to make mortgage payments when your mortgage payment is less than it really should be.

Some loans cap the increase of your monthly payment but not of the interest rate. The size of your mortgage payment may not reflect all the interest you owe on your loan. So rather than paying off the interest and some of your loan balance (or principal) every month, you're paying off some but not all of the interest you

owe. Thus, the extra unpaid interest you still owe is added to your outstanding debt.

Taking on negative amortization is like paying only the minimum payment required on a credit card bill. You keep racking up greater interest charges on the balance as long as you make only the artificially low payment. Doing so defeats the whole purpose of borrowing an amount that fits your overall financial goals. And you may never get your mortgage paid off!

Avoid ARMs with negative amortization. The only way to know whether a loan includes negative amortization is to ask. Some lenders aren't forthcoming about telling you. You'll find it more frequently on loans that lenders consider risky. If you're having trouble finding lenders who are willing to deal with your financial situation, be especially careful.

The margin on a loan is enormously important. When you're comparing two loans that are tied to the same index and are otherwise equivalent, the loan with the lower margin is better. The margin determines the interest rate for every year you hold the mortgage.

Representatives at one large mortgage lender told me that their market research shows that most borrowers care more about the start rate than the margin on their mortgage. So they happily jacked up their loans' margins and lowered the start rates. Rather than educate their borrowers about the longer-term importance of the margin, they chose to pursue short-term profits.

Indexes differ mainly in how rapidly they respond to changes in interest rates. Following are the more common indexes:

- **Treasury bills (T-bills).** These indexes are based on government IOUs (Treasury bills), and there are a whole lot of them out there. Most adjustables are tied to the interest rate on 6-month or 12-month T-bills.

- **Certificates of deposit (CDs).** Certificates of deposit are interest-bearing bank investments that lock you in for a specific period of time. ARMs are usually tied to the average interest rate banks are paying on six-month CDs. Like T-bills, CDs tend to respond quickly to changes in the market level of interest rates. Unlike T-bills, CD rates tend to move up a bit more slowly when rates rise, and come down faster when rates decline.

✔ **11th district cost of funds.** This index tends to be among the slower-moving indexes. ARMs tied to 11th district cost of funds tend to start out at a higher interest rate. A slower-moving index has the advantage of moving up less quickly when rates are on the rise. On the other hand, you need to be patient to realize the benefit of falling interest rates.

Adjustment period or frequency

Every so many months, the mortgage-rate formula is applied to recalculate the interest rate on an adjustable-rate loan. Some loans adjust monthly. An adjustment every 6 or 12 months is more typical.

In advance of each adjustment, the lender should send you a notice telling you what your new rate is. All things being equal, the less frequently your loan adjusts, the less financial uncertainty you have in your life. Although less-frequent adjustments usually indicate that your loan starts at a higher interest rate.

Understanding rate caps

When the initial interest rate expires, the interest rate fluctuates based on the formula of the loan. Almost all adjustables come with *rate caps*. The *adjustment cap* limits the maximum rate change (up or down) allowed at each adjustment. On most loans that adjust every six months, the adjustment cap is 1 percent.

Loans that adjust more than once per year often limit the maximum rate change allowed over the entire year, as well. On most such loans, the annual rate cap is 2 percent.

Finally, almost all adjustables come with *lifetime caps,* which limit the highest rate allowed over the entire life of the loan. ARMs commonly have lifetime caps that are 5 to 6 percent higher than the initial start rate (although higher lifetime caps are increasingly common during the current low interest rate period). Before taking an adjustable, figure out the maximum possible payment at the lifetime cap to be sure that you can handle it.

Other ARM fees

Just as with fixed-rate mortgages, ARMs can carry all sorts of additional lender-levied charges. See the section "Understanding other lender fees," earlier in this chapter, for details.

Avoiding the down payment blues

When you buy a home, ideally you want to make a down payment of at least 20 percent of the purchase price of the property. Why? Because you can generally qualify for the most favorable terms on a mortgage with such a down payment, and you can avoid the added cost of private mortgage insurance (PMI). To protect against losing money in the event you default on your loan, lenders usually require PMI, which costs several hundred dollars per year on a typical mortgage.

Many people don't have the equivalent of 20 percent or more of the purchase price of a home so that they can avoid paying private mortgage insurance. Here are a number of solutions for coming up with that 20 percent faster or buying with less money down:

- **Go on a spending diet.** One sure way to come up with a down payment is to raise your savings rate by slashing your spending. Take a tour through Chapter 5 to find strategies for cutting back on your spending.

- **Consider lower-priced properties.** Some first-time home buyers have expectations that are too grand. Smaller properties and ones that need some work can help keep down the purchase price and, therefore, the required down payment.

- **Find partners.** You can often get more home for your money when you buy a building in partnership with one, two, or a few people. Make sure that you write up a legal contract to specify what is going to happen if a partner wants out.

- **Seek reduced-down-payment financing.** Some lenders will offer you a mortgage even though you may only be able to put down 3 to 10 percent of the purchase price. You must have solid credit to qualify for such loans, and you generally have to obtain and pay for the extra expense of private mortgage insurance (PMI), which financially protects the lender in the event that you default on the loan. When the property rises enough in value or you pay down the mortgage enough to have 20 percent equity in the property, you can drop the PMI.

  Some property owners or developers may be willing to finance your purchase with as little as 5 to 10 percent down. You can't be as picky about properties, because not as many are available under these terms — many need work or haven't been sold yet for other reasons.

- **Get assistance from family.** If your parents, grandparents, or other relatives have money dozing away in a savings or CD account, they may be willing to lend (or even give) you the down payment. You can pay them an interest rate that's higher than the rate they're currently earning but lower than what you'd pay to borrow from a bank — a win/win situation for both of you. Lenders generally ask if any portion of the down payment is borrowed and will reduce the maximum amount they are willing to loan you accordingly.

For more home-buying strategies, get a copy of the latest edition of *Home Buying For Dummies* (Wiley Publishing), which I co-authored with real estate guru Ray Brown.

Comparing 15-year and 30-year mortgages

Many people don't have a choice between 15- and 30-year mortgages. To afford the monthly payments on their desired home, they need to spread the loan payments over a longer period of time, and a 30-year mortgage is the only answer. A 15-year mortgage has higher monthly payments because you pay it off faster. With fixed-rate mortgages hovering around 6 percent, a 15-year mortgage comes with payments that are about 35 to 40 percent higher than those for a 30-year mortgage.

Even if you can afford these higher payments, taking the 15-year option is not necessarily better. The money for making extra payments doesn't come out of thin air. You may have better uses (which I discuss later in this section) for your excess funds.

And, if you opt for a 30-year mortgage, you maintain the flexibility to pay it off faster (except in those rare cases where you have to pay a prepayment penalty). By making additional payments on a 30-year mortgage, you can create your own 15-year mortgage. But if the need arises, you can fall back to making only the payments required on your 30-year schedule.

Locking yourself into higher monthly payments with a 15-year mortgage comes with a risk. If money gets too tight in the future, you can fall behind in your mortgage payments. You may be able to refinance your way out of the predicament, but you can't count on it. If your finances worsen or your property declines in value, you may have trouble qualifying for a refinance.

Considering faster mortgage payoffs

Suppose that you qualify for a 15-year mortgage and you're financially comfortable with the higher payments. The appeal of paying off your mortgage 15 years sooner is enticing. Besides, the interest rate is lower — generally up to ½ percent lower — on a 15-year mortgage. So if you can afford the higher payments on the 15-year mortgage, you'd be silly not to take it, right? Not so fast. You're really asking whether you should pay off your mortgage slowly or more quickly. And the answer isn't simple — it depends.

If you have the time and inclination (and a good financial calculator), you can calculate how much interest you can save or avoid through a faster payback. I have a friendly word of advice about spending hours crunching numbers: *don't.* You can make this decision by considering some qualitative issues.

Consider alternative uses for savings

First, think about *alternative uses* for the extra money you'd be throwing into paying down the mortgage. What's best for you depends on your overall financial situation and what else you can do with the extra money. If you would end up blowing the extra money at the racetrack or on an expensive car, pay down the mortgage. That's a no-brainer.

But suppose that you take the extra $100 or $200 per month that you were planning to add to your mortgage payment and contribute it to a retirement account instead. This step may make financial sense. Why? Because contributions to 401(k)s, SEP-IRAs, Keoghs, and other types of retirement accounts (discussed in Chapter 10) are tax-deductible.

When you add an extra $200 to your mortgage payment to pay off your mortgage faster, you receive *no* tax benefits. When you dump that $200 into a retirement account, you get to subtract that $200 from the income on which you pay taxes. If you're paying 35 percent in federal and state income taxes, you shave $70 (that's $200 multiplied by 35 percent) off your tax bill.

In most cases, you get to deduct your mortgage interest on your tax return. So if you're paying 6 percent interest, your mortgage may really only cost you around 4 percent after you factor in the tax benefits. If you think you can do better by investing elsewhere (stocks, investment real estate), go for it. Investments such as stocks and real estate have generated better returns over the long haul. These investments carry risk, though, and they're not guaranteed to produce any return.

If you're uncomfortable investing, and you'd otherwise leave the extra money sitting in a money market fund or savings account, you're better off paying down the mortgage. When you pay down the mortgage, you invest your money in a sure thing with a modest return.

If you have pre-college-age kids, you have an even better reason to fund your retirement accounts before you consider paying down your mortgage quickly. Retirement account balances are generally not counted as an asset when determining financial aid for college expenses. Equity in your home (the difference between its market value and your loan balance), by contrast, is still counted by many schools as an asset. Your reward for paying down your mortgage balance may be less financial aid! (See Chapter 12 for more details about financing educational expenses.)

Paying down your mortgage faster, especially when you have children, is rarely a good financial decision if you haven't exhausted contributions to your retirement accounts. Save in your retirement accounts first and get the tax benefits.

Finding the best lender

As with other financial purchases, you can save a lot of money by shopping around. It doesn't matter whether you shop around on your own or hire someone to help you. Just do it!

On a 30-year, $120,000 mortgage, for example, getting a mortgage that costs 0.5 percent less per year saves you about $13,500 in interest over the life of the loan (given current interest rate levels). That's enough to buy a decent car! On second thought, save it!

Shopping for a lender on your own

In most areas, you can find many mortgage lenders. Although having a large number of lenders to choose from is good for competition, it also makes shopping a chore.

Large banks whose names you recognize from their advertising usually don't offer the best rates. Make sure that you check out some of the smaller lending institutions in your area, as well. Also, check out mortgage bankers, who, unlike banks, only do mortgages. The better mortgage bankers offer some of the most competitive rates.

Real estate agents can also refer you to lenders with whom they've previously done business. These lenders may not necessarily offer the most competitive rates — the agent simply may have done business with them in the past.

You can also look in the real estate section of one of the larger Sunday newspapers in your area for charts of selected lender interest rates. These tables are by no means comprehensive or reflective of the best rates available. In fact, many of them are sent to newspapers for free by firms that distribute mortgage information to mortgage brokers. Use the tables as a starting point by calling the lenders who list the best rates.

HSH Associates (800-873-2837; www.hsh.com) publishes mortgage information for most metropolitan areas. For $20, the company will send you a list of dozens of lenders' rate quotes. You need to be a real data junkie to wade through these multipage reports full of numbers and abbreviations, though.

Hiring a mortgage broker

Insurance agents peddle insurance, real estate agents sell real estate, and mortgage brokers deal in mortgages. They buy mortgages at wholesale from lenders and then mark them up to retail before selling them to you. The mortgage brokers get their income from the difference, or *spread*. The terms of the loan obtained through a broker are generally the same as the terms you obtain from the lender directly.

Mortgage brokers get paid a percentage of the loan amount — typically 0.5 to 1 percent. This commission is negotiable, especially on larger loans that are more lucrative. Ask a mortgage broker what his cut is. Many people don't ask for this information, so some brokers may act taken aback when you inquire. Remember, it's your money!

The chief advantage of using a mortgage broker is that the broker can shop among lenders to get you a good deal. If you're too busy or disinterested to shop around for a good deal on a mortgage, a competent mortgage broker can probably save you money. A broker can also help you through the tedious process of filling out all those horrible documents lenders demand before giving you a loan. And if you have credit problems or an unusual property, a broker may be able to match you up with a hard-to-find lender who is willing to offer you a mortgage.

When evaluating a mortgage broker, be on guard for those who are lazy and don't continually shop the market looking for the best mortgage lenders. Some brokers place their business with the same lenders all the time, and those lenders don't necessarily offer the best rates. Also watch out for salespeople who earn big commissions pushing certain loan programs that are not in your best interests. These brokers aren't interested in taking the time to understand your needs and discuss your options. Thoroughly check a broker's references before you do business with him or her.

Even if you plan to shop on your own, talking to a mortgage broker may still be worthwhile. At the very least, you can compare what you find with what brokers say they can get for you. Just be careful. Some brokers tell you what you want to hear and then aren't able to deliver when the time comes.

When a loan broker quotes you a really good deal, make sure that you ask who the lender is. (Most brokers refuse to reveal this information until you pay the few hundred dollars to cover the appraisal and credit report.) You can check with the actual lender to verify the interest rate and points the broker quotes you and make sure that you're eligible for the loan.

Increasing your approval chances

A lender can take several weeks to complete your property appraisal and an evaluation of your loan package. When you're under contract to buy a property, having your loan denied after waiting several weeks can mean that you lose the property as well as the money you spent applying for the loan and having the property inspected. Some property sellers may be willing to give you an extension, but others won't.

Here's how to increase your chances of having your mortgage approved:

✔ **Get your finances in shape before you shop.** You're not going to have a good handle on what you can afford to spend on a home until you whip your personal finances into shape. Do so before you begin to make offers on properties. This book can help you. If you have consumer debt, get rid of it — the more credit card, auto loan, and other consumer debt you rack up, the less mortgage you qualify for. In addition to the high interest rate and the fact that it encourages you to live beyond your means, you now have a third reason to get rid of consumer debt. Hang on to the dream of owning a home and plug away at paying off consumer debts.

✔ **Clear up credit report problems.** Late payments, missed payments, or debts that you never bothered to pay can come back to haunt you. If you think that you have problems on your credit report, get a copy before you apply for a mortgage. The major credit bureaus are Equifax (800-685-1111; www.equifax.com), Experian (888-397-3742; www.experian.com), and Trans Union (800-888-4213; www.transunion.com). These credit bureaus generally charge less than $10 for a copy of your report. (You can obtain a free copy if you ask within 60 days of being denied credit, employment, or insurance based on the information in your credit report.)

Mistakes crop up on credit reports. The only way to fix them, unfortunately, is to get on the phone with the credit bureaus and start squawking. If specific creditors have reported erroneous information, call them too. If the customer service representatives you talk with are no help, dash off a nice letter to the president of each company. If you have bona fide problems documented on your credit report, try explaining them to your lender. If the lender is unsympathetic, try calling other lenders. Tell the lenders your credit problems upfront, and see if you can find one that is willing to give you a loan. Mortgage brokers (see the previous section) can also help you shop for lenders who are willing to offer you a loan despite credit problems.

✔ **Get preapproved or prequalified.** When you get *prequalified*, a lender speaks with you about your financial situation and then calculates the maximum amount they're willing to lend you based on what you tell them. *Preapproval* is much more in-depth and includes a lender's actual review of your financial statements. Although neither requires a lender to actually make you a mortgage loan, preapproval means more, especially in qualifying you financially in the eyes of a seller. Just be sure not to waste your time and money getting preapproved if you're not really ready to get serious about buying.

✔ **Be upfront about problems.** The best defense against loan rejection is to avoid it in the first place. You can sometimes head off potential rejection by disclosing to your lender anything that may cause a problem before you apply for the loan. That way, you have more time to correct problems and find alternate solutions.

✔ **Work around low/unstable income.** When you've been changing jobs or you're self-employed, your recent economic history may be as unstable as a communist country trying out capitalism. Making a larger down payment is one way around this problem. If you put down 30 percent or more, you may be able to get a no-income verification loan. You may try getting a co-signer, such as a relative or good friend. As long as they aren't borrowed up to their eyeballs, they can help you qualify for a larger loan than you can get on your own. Be sure that all parties understand the terms of the agreement, including who is responsible for monthly payments!

✔ **Consider a backup loan.** You certainly should shop among different lenders, and you may even want to apply to more than one for a mortgage. Although applying for a second loan means additional fees and work, it can increase your chances of getting a mortgage if you're attempting to buy a difficult-to-finance property, or if your financial situation makes some lenders leery. Also be sure to disclose to each lender what you're doing — the second lender to pull your credit report will see that another lender has been there already.

Finding the Right Property and Location

Shopping for a home can be fun. You get to peek inside other people's refrigerators and closets. But for most people, finding the right house at the right price can take a lot of time. When you're buying with partners or a spouse (or children, if you choose to share the decision-making with them), it can also entail a lot of compromise. A good agent (or several who specialize in different areas) can help with the legwork. The following sections cover the main things you need to consider when shopping for a home to call your own.

Condo, town house, co-op, or detached home?

Some people's image of a home is a single-family dwelling — a stand-alone house with a lawn and white picket fence. In some areas, however — particularly in higher-cost neighborhoods — you find *condominiums* (you own the unit and a share of everything else), *town homes* (attached or row houses), and *cooperatives* (you own a share of the entire building).

The allure of such higher-density housing is that it's generally less expensive. In some cases, you don't have to worry about some of the general maintenance, because the owner's association (which you pay for, directly or indirectly) takes care of it.

If you don't have the time, energy, or desire to keep up a property, shared housing may make sense for you. You generally get more living space for your dollar and it may also provide you with more security than a stand-alone home.

As investments, however, single-family homes generally do better in the long run. Shared housing is easier to build and hence easier to overbuild; on the other hand, single-family houses are harder to put up because more land is required. But most people, when they can afford it, still prefer a stand-alone home.

With that being said, you should remember that a rising tide raises all boats. In a good real estate market, all types of housing appreciate, although single-family homes tend to do better. Shared housing values tend to increase the most in densely populated urban areas with little available land for new building.

From an investment return perspective, if you can afford a smaller single-family home instead of a larger shared-housing unit, buy the single-family home. Be especially wary of buying shared housing in suburban areas with lots of developable land.

Casting a broad net

You may have an idea about the type of property and location you're interested in or think you can afford before you start your search. You may think, for example, that you can afford only a condominium in the neighborhood you're interested in. But if you take the time to check out other communities, you may be surprised to find one that meets most of your needs and also has affordable single-family homes. You'd never know about this community, though, if you narrowed your search too quickly.

Even if you've lived in an area for a while and you think that you know it well, look at different types of properties in a number of different areas before you start to narrow your search. Be open-minded, and figure out which of your many criteria for a home you *really* care about. You may have to be flexible on some of your preferences.

Finding out actual sale prices

Don't look at just a few of the homes listed at a particular price and then get depressed because they're all dogs or you can't afford what you really want. Before you decide to renew your apartment lease, remember that properties often sell for less than the price at which they are listed.

Find out what the places you look at eventually sell for. Doing so gives you a better sense of what you can really afford as well as what places are really worth. Ask the agent or owner who sold the property what the sales price was, or contact the town's assessors' office for information on how to obtain property sales price information.

Researching the neighborhood and area

Even (and especially) if you fall in love with a house at first sight, go back to the neighborhood at different times of the day and on different days of the week. Travel to and from your prospective new home during commute hours to see how long your commute will really take. Knock on a few doors and meet your potential neighbors. You may discover, for example, that a flock of chickens lives in the backyard next door, or that the street and basement flood every other winter.

What are the schools like? Go visit them. Don't rely on statistics about test scores. Talk to parents and teachers. What's really going on at the school? Even if you don't have kids, the quality of the local school has direct bearing on the value of your property. Is crime a problem? Call the local police department. Will future development be allowed? If so, what type? Talk to the planning department. What are your property taxes going to be? Is the property located in an area susceptible to major risks, such as floods, mud slides, fires, or earthquakes? Consider these issues even if they're not important to you, because they can affect the resale value of your property.

When you buy a home, you're stuck with it. Make sure that you know what you're getting yourself into *before* you buy.

Working with Real Estate Agents

When you buy (or sell) a home, you're probably going work with a real estate agent. Real estate agents earn their living on commission. As such, their incentives, which are different from yours, can be at odds with what's best for you.

Real estate agents usually do not hide the fact that they get a cut of the deal. Property buyers and sellers generally understand the real estate commission system. I credit the real estate profession for calling its practitioners "agents" instead of coming up with some silly obfuscating title such as "housing consultants."

A top-notch real estate agent can be a significant help when you purchase or sell a property. On the other hand, a mediocre, incompetent, or greedy agent can be a real liability. Real estate agents don't have as bad a reputation as used car salespeople, but they still don't have a very good reputation. The following sections help you sort the good from the bad.

Recognizing real estate agents' conflicts of interest

Real estate agents, because they work on commission, face numerous conflicts of interest. Some agents may not even recognize the conflicts in what they're doing. The following list presents the most common conflicts of interest that you need to watch out for.

- Because agents work on commission, it costs them when they spend time with you and you don't buy or sell. They want you to complete a deal, and they want that deal as soon as possible — otherwise, they don't get paid. Don't expect an agent to give you objective advice about what you should do given your overall financial situation. Examine your overall financial situation *before* you decide to begin working with an agent.

- Because real estate agents get a percentage of the sales price of a property, they have a built-in incentive to encourage you to spend more. Adjustable-rate mortgages (see "Financing Your Home," earlier in this chapter) allow you to spend more, because the interest rate starts at a lower level than that of a fixed-rate mortgage. Thus, real estate agents are far more likely to encourage you to take an adjustable. But adjustables are a lot riskier — you need to understand these drawbacks before signing up for one.

- Agents often receive a higher commission when they sell listings that belong to other agents in their office. Beware. Sometimes the same agent represents both the property seller and the property buyer in the transaction — a real problem. Agents who are holding open houses for sale may try to sell to an unrepresented buyer they meet at the open house. There's no way one person can represent the best interests of both sides.

- Because agents work on commission and get paid a percentage of the sales price of the property, many are not interested in working with you if you can't or simply don't want to spend a lot. Some agents may reluctantly take you on as a customer and then give you little attention and time. Before you hire an agent, check references to make sure that he works well with buyers like you.

- Real estate agents typically work a specific territory. As a result, they usually can't objectively tell you the pros and cons of the surrounding region. Most won't admit that you may be better able to meet your needs by looking in another town (or some other part of town) where they don't normally work. Before you settle on an agent (or an area), spend time figuring out the pros and cons of different territories on your own. If you want to seriously look in more than one area, find agents who specialize in each area.

✔ If you don't get approved for a mortgage loan, your entire real estate deal will unravel. So some agents may refer you to a more expensive lender who has the virtue of high approval rates. Be sure to shop around — you can probably get a loan more cheaply. Be especially wary of agents who refer you to mortgage lenders and mortgage brokers who pay agents referral fees. Such payments clearly bias a real estate agent's "advice."

✔ Home inspectors are supposed to be objective third parties who are hired by prospective buyers to evaluate the condition of a property. Some agents may encourage you to use a particular inspector with a reputation of being "easy" — meaning he may not "find" all the house's defects. Remember, it's in the agent's best interest to seal the deal, and the discovery of problems may sidetrack that accomplishment.

✔ Some agents, under pressure to get a house listed for sale, agree to be accomplices and avoid disclosing known defects or problems with the property. In most cover-up cases, it seems, the seller doesn't explicitly ask an agent to help cover up a problem, the agent just looks the other way or avoids telling the whole truth. Never buy a home without having a home inspector look it over from top to bottom.

Looking for the right qualities in real estate agents

When you hire a real estate agent, you want to find someone who is competent and with whom you can get along. Working with an agent costs a lot of money — so make sure that you get your money's worth.

Buyer's brokers

An increasing number of agents are marketing themselves as buyer's brokers. Supposedly, these brokers represent your interests as a property buyer exclusively.

Legally speaking, buyer's brokers may sign a contract saying that they represent your — and only your — interests. Before this enlightened era, all agents contractually worked for the property seller.

The title "buyer's broker" is one of those things that sounds better than it really is. Agents who represent you as buyer's brokers still get paid only when you buy. And they still get paid on commission as a percentage of the purchase price. So they still have an incentive to sell you a piece of real estate; and the more expensive it is, the more commission they make.

Interview several agents. Check references. Ask agents for the names and phone numbers of at least three clients they worked with in the past six months (in the geographical area in which you are looking). You should look for the following traits in any agent you work with:

- **Full-time employment.** Some agents work in real estate as a second or even third job. Information in this field changes constantly. The best agents work at it full-time so that they can stay on top of the market.

- **Experience.** Hiring someone with experience doesn't necessarily mean looking for an agent who's been kicking around for decades. Many of the best agents come into the field from other occupations, such as business or teaching. Some sales, marketing, negotiation, and communication skills can certainly be picked up in other fields, but experience in buying and selling real estate does count.

- **Honesty and integrity.** You're trusting your agent with a lot. If your agent doesn't level with you about what a neighborhood or particular property is really like, you suffer the consequences.

- **Interpersonal skills.** An agent has to be able to get along not only with you but also with a whole host of other people who are typically involved in a real estate deal: other agents, property sellers, inspectors, mortgage lenders, and so on. An agent doesn't have to be Mr. or Ms. Congeniality, but he or she should be able to put your interests first without upsetting others.

- **Negotiation skills.** Putting a real estate deal together involves negotiation. Is your agent going to exhaust all avenues to get you the best deal possible? Be sure to ask the agent's references how well the agent negotiated for them.

- **High quality standards.** Sloppy work can lead to big legal or logistical problems down the road. If an agent neglects to recommend an inspection, for example, you may be stuck with undiscovered problems after the deal is done.

Agents sometimes market themselves as *top producers,* which means that they sell a relatively large volume of real estate. This title doesn't count for much for you, the buyer. It may be a red flag for an agent that focuses on completing as many deals as possible. When you're buying a home, you need an agent who has the following additional traits:

- **Patience.** When you're buying a home, the last thing you want is an agent who tries to push you into making a deal. You need an agent who is patient and willing to allow you the necessary time it takes to get educated and make the best decision for yourself.

- **Local market and community knowledge.** When you're looking to buy a home in an area in which you're not currently living, an informed agent can have a big impact on your decision.

✔ **Financing knowledge.** As a buyer (especially a first-time buyer or someone with credit problems), you should look for an agent who knows which lenders can best handle your type of situation.

Buying real estate requires somewhat different skills than selling real estate. Few agents can do both equally well. No law or rule says that you must use the same agent when you sell a property as you do when you buy a property. Don't feel obliged to sell through the agent who worked with you as a buyer, just because he sends you holiday cards every year asking how your garden is growing. Remember, he works on commission.

Putting Your Deal Together

After you do your homework on your personal finances, discover how to choose a mortgage, and research neighborhoods and home prices, you'll hopefully be ready to close in on your goal. Eventually you'll find a home you want to buy. Before you make that first offer, though, you need to understand the importance of negotiations, inspections, and the other elements of a real estate deal.

Negotiating 101

When you work with an agent, the agent usually handles the negotiation process. But you need to have a plan and strategy in mind — otherwise, you may end up overpaying for your home. Here are some recommendations for getting a good deal:

✔ **Never fall in love with a property.** If you have money to burn, and you can't imagine life without the home you just discovered, then pay what you will. Otherwise, always remind yourself that other good properties are out there. Having an actual backup property in mind never hurts.

✔ **Find out about the property and owner before you make your offer.** How long has the property been on the market? What are its flaws? Why is the owner selling? For example, if the seller is moving because she got a job in another town where she's about to close on a home purchase, she may be eager to get her money out of the home and may be willing to reduce the price. The more you understand about the property that you want to buy and the seller's motivations, the better able you will be to draft an offer that meets both parties' needs.

Games real estate agents play to get a deal done

The thirst for commission brings out the worst in some agents. They tell you fibs to motivate you to buy on the seller's terms. Saying that other offers are coming in on the property you're interested in is one common fib. Or they say that the seller already turned down an offer for *X* dollars because he is holding out for a higher offer.

The car dealer trick — blaming the office manager for not allowing them to reduce their commission — is another tactic. Be sure to spend the time needed to find a good agent and to understand an agent's potential conflicts of interest (see the section on agents earlier in the chapter).

✔ **Get comparable sales data to support your price.** Too often, home buyers and their agents pick a number out of the air when making an offer. But if the offer has no substance behind it, the seller will hardly be persuaded to lower his asking price. Pointing to recent and comparable home sales to justify your offer price strengthens your case.

✔ **Remember that price is only one of several negotiable items.** Sometimes sellers get fixated on selling their homes for a certain amount. Perhaps they want to get at least what they paid for it several years ago. You may be able to get a seller to pay for certain repairs or improvements, or to offer you an attractive loan without all the extra loan fees that a bank would charge. Likewise, the real estate agent's commission is negotiable, too.

Inspecting before you buy

When you buy a home, you may be making one of the biggest (if not *the* biggest) purchases of your life. Unless you build homes and do contracting work, you probably have no idea what you're getting yourself into when it comes to furnaces and termites.

Spend the time and money to locate and hire good inspectors and other experts to evaluate the major systems and potential problem areas of the home. Areas that you want to check include

✔ Overall condition of the property

✔ Electrical, heating, and plumbing systems

✔ Foundation

✔ Roof

✔ Pest control and dry rot

✔ Seismic/slide/flood risk

Inspection fees often pay for themselves. When problems that you weren't aware of are uncovered, the inspection reports give you the information you need to go back and ask the property seller to fix the problems or reduce the purchase price of the property to compensate you for correcting the deficiencies yourself.

As with other professionals whose services you retain, you need to make sure that you interview at least a few inspection companies. Ask which systems they inspect and how detailed a report they are going to prepare for you (ask for a sample copy). Ask them for names and phone numbers of three people who used their service within the past six months.

Never accept a seller's inspection report as your only source of information. When a seller hires an inspector, he may hire someone who won't be as diligent and critical of the property. What if the inspector is buddies with the seller or the agent selling the property? By all means, review the seller's inspection reports if available, but get your own, as well.

And here's one more inspection for you to do: The day before you close on the purchase of your home, do a brief walk-through of the property to make sure that everything is still in good order and that all the fixtures, appliances, curtains, and other items that were to be left per the contract are still there. Sometimes sellers (and their movers) "forget" what they are supposed to leave or try to test your powers of observation.

Remembering title insurance and escrow fees

Mortgage lenders require *title insurance* to protect against someone else claiming legal title to your property. This claim can happen, for example, when a husband and wife split up and the one who remains in the home decides to sell and take off with the money. If both spouses are listed as owners on the title, the spouse who sells the property (possibly by forging the other's signature) has no legal right to do so.

Both you and the lender can get stuck holding the bag if you buy the home that the one spouse of this divided couple is selling. But title insurance acts as the salvation for you and your lender. Title insurance protects you against the risk that the other spouse (whose name was forged to sell the home) is going to come back and reclaim rights to the home after it is sold.

If you're in the enviable position of paying cash for a property, you should still buy title insurance, even though a mortgage lender won't prod you to do so. You need to protect your investment.

Escrow charges pay for neutral third-party services to ensure that the instructions of the purchase contract or refinance are fulfilled and that everyone gets paid.

Many people don't seem to understand that title insurance and escrow fees vary from company to company. As a result, they don't bother to shop around; they simply use the company that their real estate agent or mortgage lender suggests.

When you call around for title insurance and escrow fee quotes, make sure that you understand all the fees. Many companies tack on all sorts of charges for things such as courier fees and express mail. If you find a company with lower prices and want to use it, ask for an itemization in writing so that you don't have any surprises.

Real estate agents and mortgage lenders can be a good starting point for referrals, because they usually have a broader perspective on the cost and service quality of different companies. Call other companies, as well — agents and lenders may be biased toward certain companies simply because they're in the habit of using them or they referred clients to them before.

After You Buy

After you buy a home, you'll make a number of important decisions regarding your castle (or shoe box) over the months and years ahead. This section discusses the key issues you need to deal with as a homeowner and tells what you need to know to make the best decision for each of them.

Refinancing your mortgage

Three reasons motivate people to *refinance* –– obtaining a new mortgage to replace your old one. One is obvious — to save money because interest rates have dropped. Refinancing also can be a way to raise capital for some other purpose. You can also use refinancing to get out of one type of loan and into another. The following sections can help you to decide on the best option in each case.

Spending money to save money

If your current loan has a higher rate of interest than comparable new loans, you may be able to save money by refinancing. Because refinancing usually costs money, whether you can save enough to justify the cost is open to question. If you can recover the costs of the refinance within a few years, go for it. If recovering the costs is going to take longer, refinancing may still make sense if you anticipate keeping the property and mortgage that long.

Be wary of mortgage lenders or brokers who tout how soon your refinance will pay for itself; they usually oversimplify their calculations. For example, if the refinance costs you $2,000 to complete (accounting for appraisals, loan fees and points, title insurance, and so on) and reduces your monthly payment by $100, lenders or brokers typically say that it is going to take 20 months for you to recoup the refinance costs. This estimate isn't accurate, however, because you lose some tax write-offs if your mortgage interest rate and payment are reduced. You can't simply look at the reduced amount of your monthly payment. (Mortgage lenders like to look at it, however, because it makes refinancing more attractive.) And your new mortgage will be reset to a different term than the number of years remaining on your old one.

If you want a better estimate of your likely cost savings, but you don't want to spend hours crunching numbers, take your tax rate — for example, 27 percent — and reduce your monthly payment savings on the refinance by this amount (see Chapter 6). Continuing with the example in the preceding paragraph, if your monthly payment drops by $100, you're really only saving about $73 a month after factoring in the lost tax benefits. So it takes about 28 months ($2,000 divided by $73) — not 20 — to recoup the refinance costs.

Note that not all refinances cost tons of money. So-called no-cost refinances or no-point loans minimize your out-of-pocket expenses, but, as I discuss earlier in this chapter, they may not be your best long-term options. Such loans usually come with higher interest rates.

Using money for another purpose

Refinancing to pull out cash from your home for some other purpose can make good financial sense because, under most circumstances, mortgage interest is tax-deductible. Paying off other higher-interest consumer debt — such as on credit cards or on an auto loan — is a common reason for borrowing against a home. The interest on consumer debt is not tax-deductible and is generally at a much higher interest rate than what mortgages charge you.

If you're starting a business, consider borrowing against your home to finance the launch of your business. You can usually do so at a lower cost than on a business loan.

You need to find out whether a lender is willing to lend you more money against the equity in your home (which is the difference between the market value of your house and the loan balance). You can use Table 13-1 to estimate the maximum loan for which you may qualify.

Changing loans

You may want to refinance even though you aren't forced to raise cash or you're able to save money. Perhaps you're not comfortable with your current loan — holders of adjustable-rate mortgages often face this problem. You may find out that a fluctuating mortgage payment makes you a nervous wreck and wreaks havoc on your budget. The certainty of a fixed-rate mortgage may be your salvation.

Paying money to go from an adjustable to a fixed is a lot like buying insurance. The cost of the refinance is "insuring" you a level mortgage payment. Consider this option only if you want peace of mind and you plan to stay with the property for a number of years.

Sometimes jumping from one adjustable to another makes sense. Suppose that you can lower the maximum lifetime interest rate cap and the refinance won't cost much. Your new loan should have a lower initial interest rate than the one you're paying on your current loan. Even if you don't save megabucks, the peace of mind of a lower ceiling can make refinancing worth your while.

Mortgage life insurance

Shortly after you buy a home or close on a mortgage, you start getting mail from all kinds of organizations who keep track of publicly available information about mortgages. Most of these organizations want to sell you something, and they don't tend to beat around the bush.

"What will your dependents do if you meet with an untimely demise and they are left with a gargantuan mortgage?" they ask. In fact, this is a good financial-planning question. If your family is dependent on your income, can they survive financially if you and your income disappear from life as we know it?

 Don't waste your money on mortgage life insurance. You may need life insurance to provide for your family and help meet large obligations such as mortgage payments or educational expenses for your children. But mortgage life insurance is typically grossly overpriced. (Check out the life insurance section in Chapter 15 for advice about term life insurance.) You should consider mortgage life insurance only if you have a health problem and the mortgage life insurer does not require a physical examination. Be sure to compare it with term life options.

Is getting a reverse mortgage a good idea?

An increasing number of homeowners are finding, particularly in their later years of retirement, that they lack cash. The home in which they live is usually their largest asset. Unlike other investments, such as bank accounts, bonds, or stocks, a home does not provide any income to the owner unless he or she decides to rent out a room or two.

A *reverse mortgage* allows a homeowner who's low on cash to tap into home equity. For an elderly homeowner, tapping into home equity can be a difficult thing to do psychologically. Most people work hard to feed a mortgage month after month, year after year, until it is finally all paid off. What a feat and what a relief after all those years!

Taking out a reverse mortgage reverses this process. Each month, the reverse mortgage lender sends you a check that you can spend on food, clothing, travel, or whatever suits your fancy. The money you receive each month is really a loan from the bank against the value of your home, which makes the monthly check free from taxation. A reverse mortgage also allows you to stay in your home and use its equity to supplement your monthly income.

The main drawback of a reverse mortgage is that it can diminish the estate that you may want to pass on to your heirs or use for some other purpose. Also, some loans require repayment within a certain number of years. The fees and the effective interest rate you're charged to borrow the money can be quite high.

Because some loans require the lender to make monthly payments to you as long as you live in the home, lenders assume that you will live many years in your home so that they won't lose money when making these loans. If you end up keeping the loan for only a few years because you move, for example, the cost of the loan is extremely high.

You may be able to create a reverse mortgage within your own family network. This technique can work if you have family members who are financially able to provide you with monthly income in exchange for ownership of the home when you pass away.

You also have some other alternatives to tapping the equity in your home. Simply selling your home and buying a less expensive property (or renting) is one alternative. Under current tax laws, qualifying house sellers can exclude a sizable portion of their profits from capital gains tax: up to $250,000 for single taxpayers and $500,000 for married couples.

Selling your house

The day will someday come when you want to sell your house. If you're going to sell, make sure that you can afford to buy the next home you desire. Be especially careful if you're a trade-up buyer — that is, if you're going to buy an even more expensive home. All of the affordability issues discussed at the beginning of this chapter apply. You need to also consider the following issues.

Selling through an agent

When you're selling a property, you want an agent who can get the job done efficiently and for as high a price as possible. As a seller, you need to seek agents who have marketing and sales expertise, and are willing to put in the time and money necessary to sell your house. Don't necessarily be impressed by an agent who works for a large company. What matters more is what the agent is going to do to market your property.

When you list your house for sale, the contract you sign with the listing agent includes specification of the commission to be paid if the agent is successful in selling your house. In most areas of the country, agents usually ask for a 6 percent commission. In an area that has lower-cost housing, they may ask for 7 percent.

Regardless of what an agent says is "typical," "standard," or "what my manager requires," *always* remember that commissions are negotiable. Because the commission is a percentage, you have a much greater possibility of getting a lower commission on a higher-priced house. If an agent makes 6 percent selling both a $200,000 house and a $100,000 house, the agent makes twice as much on the $200,000 house. Yet selling the higher-priced house does not take twice as much work. (Selling a $400,000 house certainly doesn't take four times the effort of selling a $100,000 house.)

If you live in an area with higher-priced homes (above $250,000), you have no reason to pay more than a 5 percent commission. For expensive properties ($500,000 and up), a 4 percent commission may be reasonable. You may find, however, that your ability to negotiate a lower commission is greatest when an offer is on the table. Because you don't want to give other agents (working with buyers) a reason not to sell your house, have your listing agent cut his take rather than reduce the commission that you advertise you're willing to pay to an agent who brings you a buyer.

In terms of the length of the listing sales agreement you make with an agent, three months is reasonable. When you give an agent a listing that is too long (6 to 12 months), the agent may simply toss your listing into the multiple listing book and expend little effort to sell your property. Practically speaking, you can fire your agent whenever you want, regardless of the length of the listing agreement. But a shorter listing may be more motivating for your agent.

Selling without a real estate agent

You may be tempted to sell without an agent so that you can save the commission that's deducted from your house's sale price. If you have the time, energy, and marketing experience, you can sell your house without an agent and possibly save some money.

The major problem with attempting to sell your house on your own is that you generally can't list it in the *multiple listing service* (MLS), a listing service that only real estate agents can access. Some people say (and I concur) that the MLS functions as an effective near-monopoly over the selling of houses. And if you're not listed in the MLS, many potential buyers will never know that your house is for sale. Agents who are working with buyers don't generally look for or show their clients properties that are for sale by owner.

Besides saving you time, a good agent can help ensure that you're not sued for failing to disclose the known defects of your property. If you decide to sell your house on your own, make sure that you have access to a legal advisor who can review the contracts. Whether you sell through an agent or not, be sure to read *House Selling For Dummies*, which I co-wrote with real estate expert Ray Brown (published by Wiley).

Should you keep your home until prices go up?

Many homeowners are tempted to hold on to their properties (when they need to move) if the property is worth less than when they bought it or if the real estate market is soft. Renting out your property is probably not worth the hassle, and holding on to it is probably not worth the financial gamble. If you need to move, you're better off, in most cases, selling your house.

You may reason that, in a few years, the real estate storm clouds will clear and you'll be able to sell your property at a much higher price. Here are three risks associated with this line of thinking:

- ✔ You can't know what's going to happen to property prices in the next few years. They may rebound, but they can stay the same or drop even further. A property generally needs to appreciate at least a few percent per year just to make up for all the costs of holding and maintaining it.

- ✔ If you've never been a landlord, don't underestimate the hassle and headaches associated with this job.

- ✔ If you convert your home into a rental property, and it appreciates in value, you're going to have to pay capital gains tax on your profit when you sell it. This tax wipes out much of the advantage of having held on to the property until prices recovered. (If you want to be a long-term rental property owner, you can do a *tax-free exchange* into another rental property when you sell.)

If you would realize little cash from selling, *and* you lack other money to come up with the down payment to purchase your next property, you have good reason for holding on to a home that has plunged in value.

Should you keep your home as investment property if you move?

Converting your home into rental property is worth considering if you need or want to move. Don't consider doing so unless it really is a long-term proposition (ten or more years). As discussed in the preceding section, selling rental property has tax consequences.

If you want to convert your home into an investment property, you have an advantage over someone who is looking to buy an investment property, because you already own your home. Locating and buying investment property takes time and money. You also know what you have with your current home. If you go out and purchase a property to rent, you're starting from scratch.

If your property is in good condition, consider what damage renters may do it — few renters will take care of your home the way that you will. Also consider whether you're cut out to be a landlord. For more information, read the section on real estate as an investment in Chapter 8.

Part IV

Insurance: Protecting What You've Got

The 5th Wave   By Rich Tennant

©RICHTENNANT

"Frankly sir, issuing you reasonably priced auto insurance isn't going to be easy given the number of crashes you've been involved in."

In this part . . .

I show you how to obtain the right kind of insurance to shield you from the brunt of unexpected major expenses and protect your assets and future earnings. Just because insurance is boring, it doesn't mean that you can ignore it! I reveal which types of insurance you do and do not need, what to include and what not to include in your policies, and how much of which things you should insure. Plus, I help you face other creepy but important stuff such as wills, probate, and estate planning.

Chapter 14

Insurance: Getting What You Need at the Best Price

In This Chapter

▶ Understanding my three laws of buying insurance

▶ What to do if you're denied coverage

▶ Getting your claim money

*U*nless you work in the industry (by choice), you may find insurance to be a dreadfully boring topic. Most people associate insurance with disease, death, and disaster, and would rather do just about anything other than review or spend money on insurance. But because you don't want to deal with money hassles when you're coping with catastrophes — illness, disability, death, fires, floods, earthquakes, and so on — you must take care of insurance well before you need it.

Insurance is probably the least understood and least monitored area of personal finance. Studies show that more than nine in ten Americans purchase and carry the wrong types and amounts of insurance coverage. My own experience as a financial counselor confirms this statistic. Most people are overwhelmed by all the jargon in sales and policy statements. As a result, people get insurance from the wrong companies, pay more than is necessary for their policies, or get insured through companies with poor customer service reputations.

Discovering My Three Laws of Buying Insurance

I know your patience and interest in finding out about insurance may be limited, so I boil the subject down to three fairly simple but powerful concepts that can easily save you thousands of dollars over the rest of your insurance-buying years. And while you're saving money, you can still get the coverage you need in order to avoid a financial catastrophe.

Law 1: Insure for the big stuff, not the small stuff

Imagine, for a moment, that you're offered a chance to buy insurance that reimburses you for the cost of a magazine subscription in the event that the magazine folds and you don't get all the issues you paid for. Because a magazine subscription doesn't cost much, I don't think you'd buy that insurance.

What if you could buy insurance that pays for the cost of a restaurant meal if you get food poisoning? Even if you're splurging at a fancy restaurant, you don't have a lot of money at stake, so you'd probably decline that coverage, as well.

The point of insurance is to protect against losses that would be financially catastrophic to you, not to smooth out the bumps of everyday life. The previous examples are silly, but some people buy equally foolish policies without knowing it. In the following sections, I tell you how to get the most appropriate insurance coverage for your money. I start off with the "biggies" that are worth every penny you pay in premiums, and then I work down to some of insurance options that are less worthy of your dollars.

Buy insurance to cover financial catastrophes

You should insure against what could be a huge financial loss for you or your dependents. The price of insurance isn't cheap, but it is relatively small in comparison to the potential total loss from a financial catastrophe.

The beauty of insurance is that it spreads risks over millions of other people. Should your home burn to the ground, paying the rebuilding cost out of your own pocket probably would be a financial catastrophe. If you have insurance, the premiums paid by you and all the other homeowners collectively can easily pay the bills.

Think for a moment about what your most valuable assets are. (No, they're not your dry wit and your charming personality.) Also consider potential large expenses.

- ✔ During your working years, your most valuable asset is probably your future earnings. If you were disabled and unable to work, what would you live on? Long-term disability insurance exists to help you handle this type of situation. If you have a family that is financially dependent on your earnings, how would your family manage if you died? Life insurance can fill the monetary void left by your death.

- ✔ If you're a business owner, what would happen if you were sued for $1,000,000 for negligence in some work that you messed up? Liability insurance can bail you out.

✔ In this age of soaring medical costs, you can easily rack up a $100,000 hospital bill in short order. Major medical health insurance coverage helps you handle these expenses. And yet, a surprising number of people don't carry any health insurance — particularly those who work in small businesses. (See Chapter 15 for more on health insurance.)

Psychologically, buying insurance coverage for the little things that are more likely to occur is tempting. You don't want to feel like you're wasting your insurance dollars. You want to get some of your money back, darn it! You're more likely to get into a fender bender with your car or have a package lost in the mail than you are to lose your home to fire or suffer a long-term disability. But if the fender bender costs $500 (which you end up paying out of your pocket because you took my advice to take a high deductible), it isn't going to be a financial disaster.

On the other hand, if you lose your ability to earn an income because of a disability, or if you're sued for $1,000,000 and you're not insured against such catastrophes, you'll not only be extremely unhappy but you'll also face financial ruin. "Yes, but what are the odds," I hear people rationalize, "that I'll suffer a long-term disability or that I'll be sued for $1,000,000?" I agree that the odds are quite low, but the risk is there. The problem is that you just don't know what, or when, bad luck may befall you.

And don't make the mistake of thinking that you can figure the odds any better than the insurance companies can. The insurance companies predict the probability of your making a claim, large or small, with a great deal of accuracy. They employ armies of number-crunching actuaries to calculate the odds of bad things happening and the frequency of current policyholders making particular types of claims. The companies then price their policies accordingly.

So buying (or not buying) insurance based on your perception of the likelihood of needing the coverage is foolish. Insurance companies aren't stupid; in fact, they're ruthlessly smart! When insurance companies price policies, they look at a number of factors to determine the likelihood of your filing a claim. Take the example of auto insurance. Who do you think will pay more: a single male, age 20, living the fast life in a high-crime city, driving a macho, turbo sports car, and who has received two speeding tickets in the past year; or a couple in their 40s, living in a low-crime area, driving a four-door sedan, and having a clean driving record?

Take the highest deductible you can afford

Most insurance policies have *deductibles* — the maximum amount you must pay, in the event of a loss, before your insurance coverage kicks in. On many policies, such as auto and homeowner's/renter's coverage, most folks opt for a $100 to $250 deductible.

Here are two benefits to taking a higher deductible:

- ✔ **You save premium dollars.** Year in and year out, you can enjoy the lower cost of an insurance policy with a high deductible. You may be able to shave 15 to 20 percent off the cost of your policy. Suppose, for example, that you can reduce the cost of your policy by $150 per year by raising your deductible from $250 to $1,000. That $750 worth of coverage is costing you $150 per year. Thus, you'd need to have a claim of $1,000 or more every five years — highly unlikely — to come out ahead. If you are that accident-prone — guess what — the insurance company will crank up your premiums.

- ✔ **You don't have the hassles of filing small claims.** If you have a $300 loss on a policy with a $100 deductible, you need to file a claim to get your $200 (the amount you're covered for after your deductible). Filing an insurance claim can be an aggravating experience that takes hours of time. In some cases, you may even have your claim denied after jumping through all the necessary hoops.

When you have low deductibles, you may file more claims (although this doesn't necessarily mean that you'll get more money). After filing more claims, you may be rewarded with higher premiums — in addition to the headache you get from preparing all those blasted forms! Filing too many claims may even cause cancellation of your coverage!

Avoid small-potato policies

A good insurance policy can seem expensive. A policy that doesn't cost much, on the other hand, can fool you into thinking that you're getting something for next to nothing. Policies that cost little also cover little — they're priced low because they aren't covering large potential losses.

Following are examples of common, "small-potato" insurance policies that are generally a waste of your hard-earned dollars. As you read through this list, you may find examples of policies that you bought and that you feel paid for themselves. I can hear you saying, "But I collected on that policy you're telling me not to buy!" Sure, getting "reimbursed" for the hassle of something being lost or going wrong is comforting. But consider all such policies that you bought or may buy over the course of your life. You're not going to come out ahead in the aggregate — if you did, insurance companies would lose money! These policies aren't worth the cost relative to the small potential benefit. On average, insurance companies pay out just 60¢ in benefits on every dollar collected. Many of the following policies pay you back even less — around 20¢ in benefits (claims) for every insurance premium dollar spent:

- ✔ **Extended warranty and repair plans:** Isn't it ironic that right after the salesperson persuades you to buy a television, computer, or car — in part by saying how reliable the goods are — he tries to convince you to spend more money to insure against the failure of the item? If the product is so good, why do you need such insurance?

Extended warranty and repair plans are expensive and unnecessary insurance policies. Product manufacturers' warranties typically cover any problems that occur in the first three months to a year. After that, paying for a repair out of your own pocket won't be a financial catastrophe. Reputable manufacturers often fix problems or replace the product without charge after a warranty has expired (within a reasonable time period).

✔ **Home warranty plans:** If your real estate agent or the seller of a home wants to pay the cost of a home warranty plan for you, turning down the offer would be ungracious. (As grandma would say, you shouldn't look a gift horse in the mouth.) But don't buy this type of plan for yourself. In addition to requiring some sort of fee (around $50) if you need a contractor to come out and look at a problem, home warranty plans limit how much they'll pay for problems.

Your money is much better spent on hiring a competent inspector to uncover problems and fix them *before* you buy the home. If you're buying a house, you should expect to spend money on repairs and maintenance. Buying insurance for the smaller repairs and maintenance is a waste of money.

✔ **Dental insurance:** If your employer pays for dental insurance, take advantage of it. But you shouldn't pay for this coverage on your own. Dental insurance generally covers a couple of teeth cleanings each year and limits payments for more expensive work.

✔ **Credit life and credit disability policies:** *Credit life policies* pay a small benefit if you die with an outstanding loan. *Credit disability policies* pay a small monthly income in the event of a disability. Banks and their credit card divisions usually sell these policies. Some companies sell insurance to pay off your credit card bill in the event of your death or disability.

The cost of such insurance seems low, but that's because the potential benefits are relatively small. In fact, given what little insurance you're buying, these policies are usually extraordinarily expensive. If you need life or disability insurance, purchase it. But get enough coverage, and buy it in a separate, cost-effective policy (see Chapter 15 for more details).

If you're in poor health, and you can buy these insurance policies without a medical evaluation, you represent an exception to the "don't buy it" rule. In this case, these policies may be the only ones to which you have access — another reason why these policies are expensive. If you're in good health, you're paying for the people with poor health who can enroll without a medical examination and who undoubtedly file more claims.

✔ **Daily hospitalization insurance:** Hospitalization insurance policies that pay a certain amount per day, such as $100, prey on people's fears of running up big hospital bills. Health care is expensive — there's no doubt about that.

But what you really need is a comprehensive (major medical) health insurance policy. One day in the hospital can lead to several thousand dollars in charges, so that $100-per-day policy might pay for less than an hour of your 24-hour day! Daily hospitalization policies don't offer coverage for the big-ticket expenses. If you don't have a comprehensive health insurance policy, make sure you get one (see Chapter 15)!

✔ **Insuring packages in the mail:** You buy a $40 gift for a friend, and when you go to the post office to ship it, the friendly postal clerk asks if you want to insure it. For a few bucks, you think, "Why not?" The U.S. Postal Service may have a bad reputation for many reasons, but it rarely loses or damages things. Go spend your money on something else — or better yet, invest it.

✔ **Contact lens insurance:** The things that people in this country come up with to waste money on just astound me. Contact lens insurance really does exist! The money goes to replace your contacts if you lose or tear them. Lenses are cheap. Don't waste your money on this kind of insurance.

✔ **Little stuff riders:** Many policies that are worth buying, such as auto and disability insurance, have all sorts of riders added on. These *riders* are extra bells and whistles that insurance agents and companies like to sell because of the high profit margin they provide (for *them*). On auto insurance policies, for example, you can buy a rider for a few bucks per year that pays you $25 each time your car needs to be towed. Having your vehicle towed isn't going to bankrupt you, so it isn't worth insuring against.

Likewise, small insurance policies that are sold as add-ons to bigger insurance policies are usually unnecessary and overpriced. For example, you can buy some disability insurance policies with a small amount of life insurance added on. If you need life insurance, purchasing a sufficient amount in a separate policy is less costly.

Law 11: Buy broad coverage

Purchasing coverage that is too narrow is another major mistake people make when buying insurance. Such policies often seem like cheap ways to put your fears to rest. For example, instead of buying life insurance, some folks buy flight insurance at an airport self-service kiosk. They seem to worry more about their mortality when getting on an airplane than they do when getting into a car. If they die on the flight, their beneficiaries collect. But should they die the next day in an auto accident or get some dreaded disease — which is statistically far more likely than going down in a jumbo jet — the beneficiaries don't collect anything from flight insurance. Buy life insurance (broad coverage to protect your loved ones financially in the event of your death no matter how you die), not flight insurance (narrow coverage).

Examining our misperceptions of risks

How high do you think your risks are for expiring prematurely if you're exposed to toxic wastes or pesticides, or if you live in a dangerous area that has a high murder rate? Well, actually, these risks are quite small when compared to the risks you're subjecting yourself to when you get behind the wheel of a car or light up yet another cigarette.

ABC reporter John Stossel was kind enough to share with me the results of a study done for him by physicist Bernard Cohen. In the study, Cohen compared different risks. Cohen's study showed that our riskiest behaviors are smoking and driving. Smoking whacks an average of seven years off a person's life, whereas driving a car results in a bit more than half a year of life lost, on average. Toxic waste shaves an average of one week off an American's life span.

Knowing what's risky and what isn't is part of what you need to know to buy the proper insurance. Unfortunately, you can't buy a formal insurance policy to protect yourself against all of life's great dangers and risks. But that does not mean that you must face these dangers as a helpless victim. Simple changes in behavior can help you improve your security.

Personal health habits are a good example of the types of behavior you can change. If you're overweight, and you eat fatty, high-cholesterol foods, drink excessively, and don't exercise,

you're asking for trouble, especially during post-middle age. Engage in these habits, and you dramatically increase your risk of heart disease and cancer.

So does this mean that we should all eat bean sprouts, stay out of cars, and cease being concerned about toxic waste? No. But you should understand the consequences of your behaviors before you engage in them, and minimize your risks accordingly.

You can buy all the types of traditional insurance that I recommend in this book and still not be well-protected, for the simple reason that you're overlooking uninsurable risks. But just because you can't buy formal insurance to protect against some dangers, it doesn't mean that you can't drastically reduce your exposure to such risks by modifying your behavior. For example, you can't buy an auto insurance policy that protects your personal safety against drunk drivers, who are responsible for about 17,400 American deaths annually — more than five times the death toll of the horrific September 11th terrorist attacks. However, you can choose to drive a safe car, practice safe driving habits, and minimize driving on the roads during the late evening hours and on major holidays when drinking is prevalent (such as New Year's, July 4th, and so on).

The medical equivalent of flight insurance is cancer insurance. Older people, who are fearful of having their life savings depleted by a long battle with this dreaded disease, are easy prey for unscrupulous insurance salespeople pitching this narrow insurance. If you get cancer, cancer insurance pays the bills. But what if you get heart disease, diabetes, AIDS, or some other disease? Cancer insurance won't pay these costs. Purchase major medical coverage, not cancer insurance.

Our fears in life are natural and inescapable; they're also often arbitrary and irrational. Although we may not have control over the emotions that our fears invoke, we must often ignore those emotions in order to make rational insurance decisions. In other words, getting shaky in the knees and sweaty in the palms when boarding an airplane is okay, but letting your fear of flying cause you to make poor insurance decisions is not okay, especially when those decisions affect the lives of your loved ones.

You can't possibly predict what's going to happen to you. Buy the broadest possible coverage.

Law 111: Shop around and buy direct

Whether you're looking at auto, home, life, disability, or other types of coverage, some companies may charge double or triple the rates that other companies charge for the same coverage. The companies that charge the higher rates may not be better about paying claims, however. You may even end up with the worst of both possible worlds — high prices *and* lousy service.

Most insurance is sold through agents and brokers who earn commissions based on what they sell. The commissions, of course, tend to bias what they recommend you buy. A study done by Cummins and Weisbart, cited in Andrew Tobias's book *Invisible Bankers,* confirms this bias: ". . . 48% of the time, an agent's decision on where to place a customer's business was based on which insurer paid the highest commission."

Not surprisingly, policies that pay agents the biggest commissions also tend to be more costly. In fact, insurance companies compete for the attention of agents by offering bigger commissions. When I browse through magazines and other publications targeted to insurance agents, I often see ads in which the largest text is the commission percentage offered to agents who sell the advertiser's products.

Besides the attraction of policies that pay higher commissions, agents also get hooked, financially speaking, to companies whose policies sell frequently. After an agent sells a certain amount of a company's insurance policies, he or she is rewarded with higher commission percentages on any future sales. Just as airlines bribe frequent fliers with mileage bonuses, insurers bribe agents with fatter commissions.

Shopping around is a challenge not only because most insurance is sold by agents working on commission but also because insurers set their rates in mysterious ways. Every company has a different way of analyzing how much of a risk you are; one company may offer low rates to me but not to you, and vice versa.

Choosing your insurers carefully

In addition to the price of the policy and the insurer's reputation and track record for paying claims, an insurer's financial health is important to consider when choosing a company. If you faithfully pay your premium dollars year after year, you're going to be upset if the insurer goes bankrupt right before you have a major claim.

Insurance companies can fail just like any other company, and dozens do in a typical year. A number of organizations evaluate and rate, with some sort of letter grade, the financial viability and stability of insurance companies. The major rating agencies include A. M. Best, Moody's, Standard & Poor's, Duff & Phelps, and Weiss.

The rating agencies' letter-grade system works just the way it does in high school: A is better than B or C. Each company uses a different scale. Some companies have AAA as their highest rating, and then AA, A, BBB, BB, and so on. Others use A, A–, B+, B, B–, and so on. Just as some teachers grade more easily, some firms, such as A. M. Best, have a reputation for giving out a greater number of high grades. Other firms, such as Weiss, are tough graders. Unlike in school, however, you want the tough critics when researching where to put your money and future security.

Just as getting more than one medical opinion is a good idea, getting two or three financial ratings can give you a better sense of the safety of an insurance company. Stick with companies that are in the top two — or, at worst, three — levels on the different rating scales.

You can obtain current rating information about insurance companies, free of charge, by asking your agent for a listing of the current ratings. If you're interested in a policy sold without the involvement of an agent, you can request the current ratings from the insurer itself.

Although the financial health of an insurance company is important, it's not as big a deal as some insurers (usually those with the highest ratings) and agents make it out to be. Just as financially unhealthy banks are taken over and merged into viable ones, sickly insurers usually follow a similar path under the direction of state insurance regulators.

With most insurance company failures, claims still get paid. The people who had money invested in life insurance or annuities with the failed insurer are the ones who usually lose out. Even then, you typically get back 80¢ to 90¢ on the dollar of your account value with the insurer, but you may have to wait years to get it.

Despite the obstacles, several strategies exist for obtaining low-cost, high-quality policies. The following tips offer smart ways to shop for insurance. (Chapters 15 and 16 recommend how and where to get the best deals on specific types of policies.)

Employer and other group plans

When you buy insurance as part of a larger group, you generally get a lower price because of the purchasing power of the group. Most of the health and disability policies that you can access through your employer are less costly than equivalent policies that you can buy on your own.

Likewise, many occupations have professional associations through which you may be able to obtain lower-cost policies. Not all associations offer better deals on insurance — compare their policy features and costs with other options.

Life insurance is the one exception to the rule that states that group policies offer better value than individual policies. Group life insurance plans usually aren't cheaper than the best life insurance policies that you can buy individually. However, group policies may have the attraction of convenience (ease of enrollment and avoidance of lengthy sales pitches from life insurance salespeople). Group life insurance policies that allow you to enroll without a medical evaluation are probably going to be more expensive, because such plans attract more people with health problems who can't get coverage on their own. If you're in good health, you should definitely shop around for life insurance (see Chapter 15 to find out how).

Insurance agents who want to sell you an individual policy can come up with 101 reasons why buying from them is preferable to buying through your employer or some other group. In most cases, agents' arguments for buying an individual policy from them include a lot of self-serving marketing hype. In some cases, agents tell outright lies (which are hard to detect if you're not insurance-savvy).

One valid issue that agents will raise is that, if you leave your job, you'll lose your group coverage. Sometimes that may be true. For example, if you know that you're going to be leaving your job to become self-employed, securing an individual disability policy before you leave your job makes sense. However, your employer's health insurer may allow you to buy an individual policy when you leave.

In the chapters that follow, I explain what you need in the policies you're looking for so that you can determine whether a group plan meets your needs. In most cases, group plans, especially through an employer, offer good benefits. So as long as the group policy is cheaper than a comparable individual policy, you'll save money buying through the group plan.

Insurance without sales commissions

Buying policies from the increasing number of companies that are selling their policies directly to the public without the insurance agent and the agent's commission is your best bet for getting a good insurance value. Just as you can purchase no-load mutual funds directly from an investment company without paying any sales commission (see Chapter 9), you also can buy no-load insurance. Be sure to read Chapters 15 and 16 for more specifics on how to buy insurance directly from insurance companies.

Annuities, investment/insurance products traditionally sold through insurance agents, are also now available directly to the customer, without sales commission. Simply contact some of the leading no-load mutual fund companies such as Vanguard or T. Rowe Price (see Chapter 10).

The straight scoop on commissions and how insurance is sold

The commission paid to an insurance agent is never disclosed through any of the documents or materials that you receive when buying insurance. This information ought to be disclosed by insurers and agents, just as sales charges on mutual funds are disclosed through a prospectus.

The only way you can know what the commission is on a policy and how it compares with other policies is to ask the agent. Nothing is wrong or impolite about asking. After all, your money pays the commission. You need to know whether a particular policy is being pitched harder because of its higher commission.

Commissions are typically paid as a percentage of the first year's premium on the insurance policy. (Many policies pay smaller commissions on subsequent years' premiums.) With life and disability insurance policies, for example, a 50 percent commission on the first year's premium is not unusual. With life insurance policies that have a cash value, commissions of 80 to 100 percent of your first year's premium are possible. Commissions on health insurance are lower, but generally not as low as commissions on auto and homeowner's insurance.

In the late 1990s, legislation before Congress was aimed at repealing the insurance industry's federal antitrust exemption and allowing agents in all 50 states to compete on the pricing of the policies they sell and rebate commissions to consumers. Few people knew about the legislation or how it could benefit them, and the insurance companies and agents maneuvered stealthily to defeat it. If you'd like to see the insurance industry opened up to the same competitive forces as other industries (which would save us all big bucks), write a letter to your state insurance commissioner or congressperson today.

Dealing with Insurance Problems

When you seek out insurance or have insurance policies, sooner or later you're bound to hit a roadblock. Although insurance problems can be among the more frustrating in life, in the following sections, I explain how to successfully deal with the more common obstacles.

Knowing what to do if you're denied coverage

Just as you can be turned down when you apply for a loan, you can also be turned down when applying for insurance. With medical, life, or disability insurance, a company may reject you if you have an existing medical problem (a preexisting condition) and are therefore more likely to file a claim. When it comes to insuring assets such as a home, you may have difficulty getting coverage if the property is deemed to be in a high-risk area.

Here are some strategies to employ if you're denied coverage:

- **Ask the insurer why you were denied.** Perhaps the company made a mistake or misinterpreted some information that you provided in your application. If you're denied coverage because of a medical condition, find out what information the company has on you and determine whether it's accurate.

- **Request a copy of your medical information file.** Many people don't know that, just as you have a credit report file that details your use (and misuse) of credit, you also have a medical information report. You can request a current copy of your medical information file (which typically highlights only the more significant problems over the past seven years; not your entire medical file or history) for $9 by writing to the Medical Information Bureau at P.O. Box 105, Essex Station, Boston, MA 02112, or visiting its Web site at www.mib.com. If you find a mistake on your report, you have the right to request that it be fixed. However, the burden is on you to prove that the information in your file is incorrect. Proving that your file is incorrect can be a major hassle — you may even need to contact physicians you saw in the past, because their medical records may be the source of the incorrect information.

- **Shop other companies.** Just because one company denies you coverage, it doesn't mean that all insurance companies will deny you coverage. Some insurers better understand certain medical conditions and are more comfortable accepting applicants with those conditions. Most insurers, however, charge higher rates to people with blemished medical histories than they do to people with perfect health records, but some companies penalize you less than others. An agent who sells policies from multiple insurers, called an *independent agent,* can be helpful, because he or she can shop among a number of different companies.

- **Find out about state high-risk pools.** If you're turned down for health or property insurance, check with your state department of insurance (see the "Government" section of your local white pages phone directory). A number of states act as the insurer of last resort and provide insurance for those who can't get it from insurance companies. State high-risk pool coverage is usually bare bones, but it beats going without any coverage.

- **Check for coverage availability before you buy.** If you're considering buying a home, for example, and you can't get coverage, the insurance companies are trying to tell you something. What they are effectively saying is, "We think that property is so high-risk, we're not willing to insure it even if you pay a high premium."

Getting your due on claims

In the event that you suffer a loss and file an insurance claim, you may hope that your insurance company is going to cheerfully and expeditiously pay your claims. Given all the money that you shelled out for coverage, and all the hoops you jumped through to get approved for coverage in the first place, that's a reasonable expectation.

Insurance companies may refuse to pay you what you think they owe you for many reasons, however. In some cases, your claim may not be covered under the terms of the policy. At a minimum, the insurer wants documentation and proof of your loss. Other people who have come before you have been known to cheat, so insurers won't simply take your word, no matter how honest and ethical you are.

In other cases, the insurance company may jerk you around. Some companies view paying claims as an adversarial situation and take a "negotiate tough" stance. Thinking that all insurance companies are going to pay you a fair and reasonable amount unless you make your voice heard is a mistake.

The tips that I discuss in this section help you ensure that you get paid what your policy entitles you to.

Documenting your assets and case

When you're insuring assets, such as your home and its contents, having a record of what you own can be helpful if you need to file a claim. The best offense is a good defense. If you keep records of valuables and can document their cost, you should be in good shape.

A videotape is the most efficient record for documenting your assets, but a handwritten list detailing your possessions works, too. Just remember to keep this record someplace away from your home — if your home burns to the ground, you'll lose your documentation, too!

If you're robbed or are the victim of an accident, get the names, addresses, and phone numbers of witnesses. Take pictures of property damage and solicit estimates for the cost of repairing or replacing whatever has been lost or damaged. File police reports when appropriate, if for no other reason than to bolster your documentation for the insurance claim.

Preparing your case

Filing a claim should be viewed the same way as preparing for a court trial or an IRS audit. Any information you provide verbally or in writing can and will be used against you to deny your claim. First, you should understand whether your policy covers your claim (this is why getting the broadest coverage possible helps). Unfortunately, the only way to find out whether the policy covers your claim is to read it. Policies are hard to read because they use legal language in non-user-friendly ways.

A possible alternative to reading your policy is to call the claims department and, *without* providing your name, ask a representative whether a particular loss (such as the one that you just suffered) is covered under its policy. You have no need to lie to the company, but you have no need to tell the representative who you are and that you're about to file a claim, either. Your call is informational so that you can understand what your policy covers. Some companies are not willing to provide detailed information, however, unless a specific case is cited.

After you initiate the claims process, keep records of all conversations and all copies of the documents you gave to the insurer's claims department. If you have problems down the road, this "evidence" may bail you out.

For property damage, you should get at least a couple of reputable contractors' estimates. Demonstrate to the insurance company that you're trying to shop for a low price, but don't agree to use a low-cost contractor without knowing that he or she can do quality work.

Approaching your claim as a negotiation

To get what you're owed on an insurance claim, you must approach most claims' filings for what they are — a negotiation that is often not cooperative. And the bigger the claim, the more your insurer will play the part of adversary.

A number of years ago, when I filed a homeowner's insurance claim after a major rain and wind storm significantly damaged my backyard fence, I was greeted on a weekday by a perky, smiley adjuster. When the adjuster entered my yard and started to peruse the damage, her demeanor changed dramatically. She had a combative, hard-bargainer type attitude that I last witnessed when I worked on some labor-management negotiations during my days as a consultant.

The adjuster stood on my back porch, a good distance away from the fences that had been blown over by wind and crushed by two large trees, and said that my insurer preferred to repair damaged fences rather than replace them. "With your deductible of $1,000, I doubt this will be worth filing a claim for," she said.

The fence that had blown over, she reasoned, could have new posts set in concrete. Because we had already begun to clean up some of the damage for safety reasons, I presented to her some pictures of what the yard looked like right after the storm; she refused to take them. She took some measurements and said that she'd have her settlement check to us in a couple of days. The settlement she faxed was for $1,119 — nowhere near what it would cost me to fix the damage that was done.

Practicing persistency

When you take an insurance company's first offer and don't fight for what you're due, you may be leaving a lot of money on the table. To make my long fence-repair story somewhat shorter, after *five* rounds of haggling with the adjusters, supervisors, and finally managers, I was awarded payment to replace the fences and clean up most of the damage. Even though all the contractors I contacted recommended that the work be done this way, the insurance adjuster discredited their recommendations by saying, "Contractors try to jack up the price and recommended work once they know an insurer is involved."

My final total settlement came to $4,888, more than $3,700 higher than the insurer's first offer. Interestingly, my insurer backed off its preference for repairing the fence when the contractor's estimates for doing that work exceeded the cost of a new fence.

I was disappointed with the behavior of that insurance company. I know from conversations with others that my homeowner's insurance company is not unusual in its adversarial strategy, especially with larger claims. And to think that this insurer at the time had one of the better track records for paying claims!

Enlisting support

If you're doing your homework, and you're not making progress with the insurer's adjuster, ask to speak with supervisors and managers. This is the strategy I had to use to get the additional $3,700 that was needed to get things back to where they were before the storm.

The agent who sold you the policy may be helpful in preparing and filing the claim. A good agent can help increase your chances of getting paid — and getting paid sooner. If you're having difficulty with a claim for a policy obtained through your employer or other group, speak with the benefits department or a person responsible for interacting with the insurer. These folks have a lot of clout, because the agent and/or insurer doesn't want to lose the entire account.

If you're having problems getting a fair settlement from the insurer of a policy you bought on your own, try contacting the state department of insurance. You can find the phone number in the "Government" section of the white pages of your phone book or possibly in your insurance policy, or you can peruse the list at the National Association of Insurance Commissioners Web site at www.naic.org/state_contacts/index.htm.

Hiring a public adjuster who, for a percentage of the payment (typically 5 to 10 percent), can negotiate with insurers on your behalf is another option.

When all else fails, and you have a major claim at stake, try contacting an attorney who specializes in insurance matters. You can find these specialists in the yellow pages of your phone directory under "Attorneys — Insurance Law." Expect to pay around $100 or more per hour. Look for a lawyer who is willing to negotiate on your behalf, help draft letters, and perform other necessary tasks on an hourly basis without filing a lawsuit. Your state department of insurance, the local bar association, or other legal, accounting, or financial practitioners also may be able to refer you to someone.

The possible headache of filing a claim is another reason to take the highest insurance deductibles you're comfortable with. Remember that you buy insurance to protect against large losses, not small ones. With a high deductible and a small loss, you'll save yourself some haggling.

Chapter 15

Insurance on You: Life, Disability, and Health

In This Chapter

▶ Checking out life insurance

▶ Looking into disability insurance

▶ Selecting the best health insurance

▶ Considering an overlooked form of personal insurance

*M*ultiply your typical annual income by the number of years you plan to continue working — you come up with a pretty big number, don't you (unless you're in or near retirement)? That dollar amount equals what is probably your most valuable asset — your ability to earn an income. You need to protect this asset by purchasing some insurance on you.

This chapter explains the ins and outs of buying insurance to protect your income: life insurance in case of death, and disability insurance in case of an accident or severe medical condition that prevents you from working. I tell you what coverage you should have, where to look for it, and what to avoid.

In addition to protecting your income, you also need to insure against financially catastrophic expenses. I'm not talking about December's credit card bill; you're on your own with that one. I'm talking about the type of bills that are racked up from a major surgery and a multi-week stay in the hospital. Medical expenses today can make even the most indulgent shopping sprees look dirt-cheap. To protect yourself from potentially astronomical medical bills, you also need to have comprehensive health insurance.

Providing for Your Loved Ones: Life Insurance

You generally only need life insurance when other people depend on your income.

The following types of people don't need life insurance to protect their incomes:

- ✔ Single people
- ✔ Working couples who could maintain an acceptable lifestyle if one of the incomes disappeared
- ✔ Independently wealthy people who don't need to work
- ✔ Retired people who are living off their retirement nest egg
- ✔ Minor children (Are you financially dependent upon your children?)

If others are either fully or partly dependent on your paycheck (usually a spouse and/or children), you should buy life insurance, especially if you have major financial commitments such as a mortgage or years of child rearing ahead. You may also want to consider life insurance if an extended family member is currently or likely to be dependent on your future income.

Determining how much life insurance to buy

Determining how much life insurance to buy is as much a subjective decision as it is a quantitative decision. I've seen some worksheets that are incredibly long and tedious (some are worse than your tax returns). There's no need to get fancy. If you're like me, your eyes start to glaze over if you have to complete 20-plus lines of calculations. Figuring out how much life insurance you need doesn't have to be that complicated.

The main purpose of life insurance is to provide a lump sum payment to replace the deceased person's income. You need to ask yourself how many years of income you want to replace. Table 15-1 provides a simple way to figure how much life insurance you need to consider purchasing. To replace a certain number of years of income, simply multiply the appropriate number in the table by your annual after-tax income.

Table 15-1	Life Insurance Calculation
Years of Income to Replace	*Multiply Annual After-Tax Income* By*
5	4.5
10	8.5
20	15
30	20

*You can roughly determine your annual after-tax income in one of two ways: You can calculate it by getting out last year's tax return (and Form W-2) and subtracting the federal, state, and Social Security taxes you paid from your gross employment income; or you can estimate it by multiplying your gross income by 80 percent if you're a low-income earner, 70 percent if you're a moderate-income earner, or 60 percent if you're a high-income earner. (You need to replace only after-tax income, and not pre-tax income, because life insurance policy payouts are not taxed.)

Another way to determine the amount of life insurance to buy is to think about how much you will need to pay for major debts or expenditures, such as your mortgage, other loans, and college for your children. For example, suppose that you want your spouse to have enough of a life insurance death benefit to be able to pay off your mortgage and half of your children's college education. Simply add your mortgage amount to half of your children's estimated college costs (refer to Chapter 12 for approximate numbers) and then buy that amount of life insurance.

Social Security, if you're covered, can provide *survivors' benefits* to your spouse and children. However, if your surviving spouse is working and earning even a modest amount of money, he or she is going to get little if any survivor's benefits. Prior to reaching "full retirement age," which is between the ages of 65 and 67 depending on when you were born (see Chapter 2), your survivor's benefits get reduced by $1 for every $2 you earn above $11,520 (in 2003).

If either you or your spouse anticipates earning such a low income, however, you may want to factor your Social Security survivor's benefits into how much life insurance to buy. Contact the Social Security Administration by phone at 800-772-1213, or visit its Web site at www.ssa.gov, and request Form 7004, which gives you an estimate of your Social Security benefits.

The Social Security Administration can tell you how much your survivors will receive per month in the event of your death. You should factor this benefit into the amount of life insurance that you calculate in Table 15-1. For example, suppose that your annual after-tax income is $15,000, and Social Security provides a survivor's benefit of $8,000 annually. Therefore, for the purposes of Table 15-1, you should determine the amount of life insurance needed to replace $7,000 annually ($15,000 – $8,000), not $15,000.

"Other" life insurance

Contemplating the possibility of your untimely demise is surely depressing. You'll likely feel some peace of mind when purchasing a life insurance policy to provide for your dependents.

However, let's take things a step further. Suppose that you (or your spouse) pass away. Do you think that simply buying a life insurance policy will be sufficient "help" for the loved ones you leave behind? Probably not. Surely your contribution to your household involves far more than being a breadwinner.

For starters, you should make sure that all of your important financial documents — investment account statements, insurance policies, emloyee benefits materials, small-business accounting records, and so on — are kept in one place (such as a file drawer) that your loved ones know about.

Do you have a will? See Chapter 16 for more details on wills and other estate-planning documents.

You may also want to consider providing a list of key contacts — such as who you recommend calling (or what you recommend reading) in the event of legal, financial, or tax quandaries.

So, in addition to trying to provide financially for your dependents, you also need to take some time to reflect on what else you can do to help point them in the right direction on matters you normally handle. With most couples, it's natural for one spouse to take more responsibility, say, for money management. That's fine; just make sure to talk about what's being done so that in the event that the responsible spouse dies, the surviving person knows how to jump into the driver's seat.

If you have kids (and even if you don't), you may want to give some thought to philosophical leave-behinds for your loved ones. These leave-behinds can be something like a short note telling them how much they meant to you and what you'd like them to remember about you.

Comparing term life insurance to cash value life insurance

I'm going to tell you how you can save hours of time and thousands of dollars. Ready? *Buy term life insurance.* (The only exception is if you have a high net worth — several million bucks or more — in which case you may want to consider other options. See the estate-planning section in Chapter 16.) If you already figured out how much life insurance to purchase, and this is all the advice you need to go ahead, you can skip the rest of this section and jump to the "Buying term insurance" section that follows.

If you want the details behind my recommendation for term insurance, the following information is for you. Or maybe you heard (and have already fallen prey to) the sales pitches from life insurance agents, most of whom love selling cash value life insurance because of its huge commissions.

I'm going to start with some background. Despite the variety of names that life insurance marketing departments have cooked up for policies, life insurance comes in two basic flavors:

- ✔ **Term insurance.** This insurance is pure life insurance. You pay an annual premium for which you receive a predetermined amount of life insurance protection. If the insured person passes away, the beneficiaries collect; otherwise, the premium is gone.

- ✔ **Cash value insurance.** All other life insurance policies (whole, universal, variable, and so on) combine life insurance with a supposed savings feature. Your premiums not only pay for life insurance, but some of your dollars are also credited to an account that grows in value over time, assuming you keep paying your premiums. On the surface, this sounds potentially attractive. People don't like to feel that all their premium dollars are getting tossed away.

  But cash value insurance has a big catch. For the same amount of coverage (for example, for $100,000 of life insurance benefits), cash value policies cost you about eight times (800 percent) more than comparable term policies.

Insurance salespeople know the buttons to push to get you interested in buying the wrong kind of life insurance. In the following sections I give you some of the typical arguments they make for purchasing cash value polices, followed by my perspective on each one.

"Cash value policies are all paid up after x years. You don't want to be paying life insurance premiums for the rest of your life, do you?"

Agents who pitch cash value life insurance present projections that imply that after the first ten or so years of paying your premiums, you don't need to pay more premiums to keep the life insurance in force. The only reason you may be able to stop paying premiums is if you pour so much extra money into the policy in the early years of payment. Remember that cash value life insurance costs about eight times as much as term insurance.

Imagine that you're currently paying $500 a year for auto insurance, and an insurance company comes along and offers you a policy for $4,000 per year. The representative tells you that after 10 years, you can stop paying and still keep your same coverage. I'm sure that you wouldn't fall for this sales tactic, but many people do when they buy cash value life insurance.

You also need to be wary of the projections, because they often include unrealistic and lofty assumptions about the investment return that your cash balance can earn. When you stop paying into a cash value policy, the cost of each year's life insurance is deducted from the remaining cash value. If the rate of return on the cash balance is not sufficient to pay the insurance cost, the cash balance declines, and eventually you receive notices saying that your policy needs more funding to keep the life insurance in force.

"You won't be able to afford term insurance when you're older."

As you get older, the cost of term insurance increases because the risk of dying rises. But life insurance is not something you need all your life! It's typically bought in a person's younger years when financial commitments and obligations outweigh financial assets. Twenty or thirty years later, the reverse should be true.

When you retire years from now, you won't need life insurance to protect your employment income, because there won't be any to protect! You may need life insurance when you're raising a family and/or you have a substantial mortgage to pay off, but by the time you retire, the kids should be out on their own (you hope!), and the mortgage should be paid down.

In the meantime, term insurance saves you a tremendous amount of money. For most people, it takes 20 to 30 years for the premium they're paying on a term insurance policy to finally catch up to (equal) the premium they've been paying all along on a comparable amount of cash value life insurance.

"You can borrow against the cash value at a low rate of interest."

Such a deal! It's your money in the policy, remember? If you deposited money in a savings or money market account, how would you like to pay for the privilege of borrowing your own money back? Borrowing on your cash value policy is potentially dangerous: You increase the chances of the policy exploding on you — leaving you with nothing to show for your premiums.

"Your cash value grows tax-deferred."

Ah, a glimmer of truth at last. The cash value portion of your policy grows without taxation until you withdraw it, but if you want tax-deferral of your investment balances, you should first take advantage of such savings plans as 401(k)s, 403(b)s, SEP-IRAs, and Keoghs. Such accounts give you an immediate tax deduction for your current contributions in addition to growth without taxation until withdrawal.

The money you pay into a cash value life policy gives you no upfront tax deductions. If you exhaust the tax-deductible plans, variable annuities or a nondeductible individual retirement account (IRA) can provide access to better investment options and tax-deferred compounding of your investment dollars. (See Chapter 10 for details on retirement accounts.)

Life insurance tends to be a mediocre investment. The insurance company quotes you an interest rate for the first year only; after that, the company pays you what it wants. If you don't like the future interest rates, you can be penalized for quitting the policy. Would you ever invest your money in a bank account that quoted an interest rate for the first year only and then penalized you for moving your money within the next seven to ten years?

"Cash value policies are forced savings."

Many agents argue that a cash value plan is better than nothing — at least it's forcing you to save. This line of thinking is silly because so many people drop cash value life insurance policies after just a few years of paying into them.

You can accomplish "forced savings" without using life insurance. Any of the retirement savings accounts mentioned in Chapter 10 can be set up for automatic monthly transfers. Employers offering such a plan can deduct contributions from your paycheck — and it doesn't take a commission! You can also set up monthly electronic transfers from your bank checking account to contribute to mutual funds (see Chapter 9).

"Life insurance is not part of your taxable estate."

If the ownership of a life insurance policy is properly structured, the death benefit is free of estate taxes. This part of the sales pitch is about the only sound reasoning that exists for buying cash value life insurance. Under current federal laws, you can pass on $1,000,000 free of federal estate taxes for tax year 2003 ($1,500,000 beginning in 2004). But even if you're expecting such an estate, you have numerous other ways to reduce your taxable estate (see Chapter 16).

Making your decision

Insurance salespeople aggressively push cash value policies because of the high commissions that insurance companies pay them. Commissions on cash value life insurance range from 50 to 100 percent of your first year's premium. An insurance salesperson, therefore, can make *eight to ten times more money* (yes, you read that right) selling you a cash value policy than he can selling you term insurance.

Ultimately, when you purchase cash value life insurance, you pay the high commissions that are built into these policies. As you can see in the policy's cash value table, you don't get back any of the money that you dump into the policy if you quit the policy in the first two to three years. The insurance company can't afford to give you any of your money back in those first few years because so much of it has been paid to the selling agent as commission. That's why these policies explicitly penalize you for withdrawing your cash balance within the first seven to ten years.

Because of the high cost of cash value policies relative to the cost of term, you're more likely to buy less life insurance coverage than you need — that's the sad part of the insurance industry's pushing of this stuff. *The vast majority of life insurance buyers need more protection than they can afford to buy with cash value coverage.*

Cash value life insurance is the most oversold insurance and financial product in the history of the financial services industry. Cash value life insurance makes sense for a small percentage of people, such as small-business owners who own a business worth more than several million dollars and don't want their heirs to be forced to sell their business to pay estate taxes in the event of their death. (See "Considering the purchase of cash value life insurance," later in this chapter.)

Purchase low-cost term insurance and do your investing separately. Life insurance is rarely a permanent need; over time, you can reduce the amount of term insurance you carry as your financial obligations lessen and you accumulate more assets.

Buying term insurance

Term insurance policies have several features to choose from. I cover the important elements of term insurance in this section so that you can make an informed decision about purchasing it.

Choosing how often your premium adjusts

As you get older, the risk of dying increases, so the cost of your insurance goes up. Term insurance can be purchased so that your premium adjusts (increases) annually or every 5, 10, 15, or 20 years. The less frequently your premium adjusts, the higher the initial premium and its incremental increases will be.

The advantage of a premium that locks in for, say, 15 years is that you have the security of knowing how much you'll be paying each year for the next 15 years. You also don't need to go through medical evaluations as frequently to qualify for the lowest rate possible.

The disadvantage of a policy with a long-term rate lock is that you pay more in the early years than you do on a policy that adjusts more frequently. In addition, you may want to change the amount of insurance you carry as your circumstances change. You throw money away when you dump a policy with a long-term premium guarantee before its rate is set to change.

Policies that adjust the premium every five to ten years offer a happy medium between price and predictability.

Ensuring guaranteed renewability

Guaranteed renewability, which is standard practice on the better policies, guarantees that the policy can't be canceled because of poor health. Don't buy a life insurance policy without this feature unless you expect that your life insurance needs will disappear when the policy is up for renewal.

Deciding where to buy term insurance

A number of sound ways to obtain high-quality, low-cost term insurance are available. You may choose to buy through a local agent — because you know her, or because you prefer to buy from someone close to home. However, you should invest a few minutes of your time getting quotes from one or two of the following sources to get a sense of what's available in the insurance market. Gaining familiarity with the market can prevent an agent from selling you an overpriced, high-commission policy.

Here are some sources for high-quality, low-cost term insurance:

- ✔ **USAA** sells low-cost term insurance directly to the public. You can contact USAA by phone at 800-531-8000.

- ✔ **Insurance agency quotation services** provide proposals from the highest-rated, lowest-cost companies available. Like other agencies, the services receive a commission if you buy a policy from them, which you're under no obligation to do. They ask your date of birth, whether you smoke, and how much coverage you want. My favorite quotation service in terms of customer service, pricing, and presentation of information is **TD Waterhouse Insurance Services.** You can contact TD Waterhouse Insurance Services by calling 800-622-3699. (See Chapter 18 for information on how to use your computer when making life insurance decisions.)

Getting rid of cash value life insurance

If you were snookered into buying a cash value life insurance policy, and you want to part ways with it, go ahead and do so. *But don't cancel the coverage until you first secure new term coverage.* When you need life insurance, you don't want to leave open a period when you're not covered (Murphy's Law says *that's* when disaster will strike).

Ending a cash value life insurance policy has tax consequences. For most of these policies, you must pay tax on the amount you receive in excess of the premiums you paid over the life of the policy. Because some life insurance policies feature tax-deferred retirement savings, you may incur a 10 percent penalty on earnings withdrawn before age 59½, just as you would with an IRA.

If you want to withdraw the cash balance in your life insurance policy, consider checking with the insurer or a tax advisor to clarify what the tax consequences may be.

You can avoid early withdrawal penalties and taxation on accumulated interest in a life insurance policy by doing a tax-free exchange into a no-load (commission-free) variable annuity. The no-load mutual fund company through which you buy the annuity takes care of transferring your existing balance. (Refer to Chapter 11 for more information about annuities.)

Considering the purchase of cash value life insurance

Don't expect to get objective information from anyone who sells cash value life insurance. Beware of insurance salespeople masquerading under the guise of self-anointed titles, such as estate-planning specialists or financial planners.

As I discuss earlier in the chapter, purchasing cash value life insurance may make sense if you expect to have an estate-tax problem. However, cash value life insurance is just one of numerous ways to reduce your estate taxes (see the section on estate planning in Chapter 16).

Among the best places to shop for cash value life insurance policies are

- **USAA** (800-531-8000)
- **Ameritas** (800-552-3553)
- **TD Waterhouse** (800-622-3699)

If you want to obtain some cash value life insurance, make sure that you avoid local insurance agents, especially while you're in the learning stage. Agents aren't as interested in educating as they are in selling (big surprise). Besides, the best cash value policies can be obtained free of most (or all) sales commissions when you buy them from the sources I provide in the previous list. The money saved on commissions is reflected in a much higher cash value for you — up to several thousand dollars worth.

Preparing for the Unpredictable: Disability Insurance

As with life insurance, the purpose of disability insurance is to protect your income. The only difference is that, with disability insurance, you're protecting the income for yourself (and perhaps also your dependents). If you're completely disabled, you still have living expenses, but you probably can't earn employment income.

I'm referring to long-term disabilities. If you throw out your back while reliving your athletic glory days, and you wind up in bed for a couple of weeks, it won't be as much of a disaster to your finances as it is to your ego! What would be a financial disaster, however, is if you were disabled in such a way that you couldn't work for several years.

Most large employers offer disability insurance to their employees. Many small-company employees and all self-employed people are left to fend for themselves without disability coverage. Being without disability insurance is a risky proposition, especially if, like most working people, you need your employment income to live on.

If you're married, and your spouse earns a large enough income that you can make do without yours, you may want to consider skipping disability coverage. The same is true if you already accumulated enough money for your future years (in other words, you're financially independent). Keep in mind, though, that your expenses may go up if you become disabled and require specialized care.

For most people, dismissing the need for disability coverage is easy. The odds of suffering a long-term disability seem so remote — and they are. But if you meet up with bad luck, disability coverage can relieve you (and possibly your family) of a major financial burden.

Most disabilities are caused by medical problems, such as arthritis, heart conditions, hypertension, and back/spine or hip/leg impairments. Some of these ailments occur with advancing age, but more than one-third of all disabilities are suffered by people under the age of 45. The vast majority of these medical problems cannot be predicted in advance, particularly those caused by random accidents.

If you think that you have good disability coverage through government programs, you'd better think again:

✔ **Social Security disability.** Social Security pays long-term benefits only if you're not able to perform any substantial, gainful activity for more than a year, or if your disability is expected to result in death. In fact, 70 percent of all applicants for Social Security disability benefits coverage are turned down. Furthermore, Social Security disability payments are quite low because they're intended to provide only for basic, subsistence-level living expenses.

✔ **Worker's compensation.** Worker's compensation (if you have such coverage through your employer) pays you benefits if you're injured on the job, but it doesn't pay any benefits if you get disabled away from your job. You need coverage that pays regardless of where and how you are disabled.

✔ **State disability programs.** A few states have disability insurance programs, but the coverage is typically not extensive enough, because benefits are paid over too short a period of time (rarely more than a year). State programs are also generally not a good value because of the cost for the small amount of coverage they provide.

Determining how much disability insurance you need

You need enough disability coverage to provide you with sufficient income to live on until other financial resources become available. If you don't have much saved in the way of financial assets, and you want to continue with the lifestyle supported by your current income if you suffer a disability, get enough disability coverage to replace your entire monthly take-home (after-tax) pay.

The benefits you purchase on a disability policy are quoted as the dollars per month you receive if disabled. So if your job provides you with a $2,000-per-month income after payment of taxes, seek a policy that provides a $2,000-per-month benefit.

If you pay for your disability insurance, the benefits are tax-free (but hopefully you won't ever have to collect them). If your employer picks up the tab, your benefits are taxable, so you need a higher amount of benefits.

In addition to the monthly coverage amount, you also need to select the duration of time you want a policy to pay you benefits. You need a policy that pays benefits until you reach an age where you become financially self-sufficient. For most people, that's around age 65, when their Social Security benefits kick in. If you anticipate needing your employment income past your mid-60s, you may want to obtain disability coverage that pays you until a later age.

On the other hand, if you crunched some numbers (see Chapter 3), and you expect to be financially independent by age 55, you can get a policy that pays benefits up to that age — it'll cost you less than one that pays benefits to you until age 65. If you're within five years of being financially independent or able to retire, five-year disability policies are available, too. You may also consider such short-term policies when you're sure that someone (for example, a family member) can support you financially over the long-term.

Identifying other features you need in disability insurance

Disability insurance policies have many confusing features. Here's what to look for — and look out for — when purchasing disability insurance:

- **Definition of disability.** An *own-occupation* disability policy provides benefit payments if you can't perform the work you normally do. Some policies pay you only if you're unable to perform a job for which you are *reasonably trained.* Other policies revert to this definition after a few years of being own-occupation.

  Own-occupation policies are the most expensive, because there's a greater chance that the insurer will have to pay you. The extra cost may not be worth it unless you're in a high-income or specialized occupation, and you'd have to take a significant pay cut to do something else (and you wouldn't be happy about a reduced income and the required lifestyle changes).

- **Noncancelable and guaranteed renewable.** These features guarantee that your policy can't be canceled because of poor health conditions. With policies that require periodic physical exams, you can lose your coverage just when you're most likely to need it.

- **Waiting period.** This is the "deductible" on disability insurance — the lag time between the onset of your disability and the time you begin collecting benefits. As with other types of insurance, you should take the highest deductible (longest waiting period) that your financial circumstances allow. The waiting period significantly reduces the cost of the insurance and eliminates the hassle of filing a claim for a short-term disability. The minimum waiting period on most policies is 30 days. The maximum waiting period can be up to one to two years. Try a waiting period of three to six months if you have sufficient emergency reserves.

- **Residual benefits.** This option pays you a partial benefit if you have a disability that prevents you from working full-time.

- **Cost-of-living adjustments (COLAs).** This feature automatically increases your benefit payment by a set percentage or in accordance with changes in inflation. The advantage of a COLA is that it retains the purchasing power of your benefits. A modest COLA, such as 4 percent, is worth having.

- **Future insurability.** A clause that many agents encourage you to buy, future insurability allows you, regardless of health, to buy additional coverage. For most people, paying for the privilege of buying more coverage later is not worth it if the income you earn today fairly reflects your likely long-term earnings (except for cost-of-living increases).

Disability insurance is sold only as a proportion of your income. You may benefit from the future insurability option if your income is artificially low now and you're confident that it will rise significantly in the future. (For example, you just got out of medical school, and you're earning a low salary while being enslaved as a resident.)

✔ **Insurer's financial stability.** As I discuss in Chapter 14, you should choose insurers that will be here tomorrow to pay your claim. But don't get too hung up on the stability of the company; benefits are paid even if the insurer fails, because the state or another insurer will almost always bail the unstable insurer out.

Deciding where to buy disability insurance

The best place to buy disability insurance is through your employer or professional association. Unless these groups have done a lousy job shopping for coverage, group plans offer a better value than disability insurance you can purchase on your own. Just make sure that the group plan meets the specifications discussed in the preceding section.

Don't trust an insurance agent to be enthusiastic (or even honest) about the quality of a disability policy your employer or other group is offering. Agents have a huge conflict of interest when they criticize these options, because your group insurance cuts them out of the picture.

If you don't have access to a group policy, check with your agent or a company you already do business with. You can also contact USAA, which offers competitively priced disability policies, by calling 800-531-8000.

Other types of "insurance" for protecting your income

Life insurance and disability insurance replace your income if you die or suffer a disability. But you may also see your income reduced or completely eliminated if you lose your job. Although no formal insurance exists to protect you against the forces that can cause you to lose your job, you can do some things to reduce your exposure to such risk:

✔ Make sure that you have an emergency reserve of money that you can tap into if you lose your job. (Chapter 2 offers specific guidelines for deciding how much money is right for you.)

✔ Attend to your skills and professional development on a continual basis. Not only does upgrading your education and skills ensure that you'll be employable if you have to look for a new job, but it may also help you keep your old job and earn a higher income.

Tread carefully when purchasing disability insurance through an agent. Some agents try to load down your policy with all sorts of extra bells and whistles to pump up the premium along with their commission.

If you buy disability insurance through an agent, use a process called *list billing*. With list billing, you sign up with several other people for coverage at the same time and are invoiced together for your coverage. It can knock up to 15 percent off an insurer's standard prices. Ask your insurance agent how list billing works.

Getting the Care You Need: Health Insurance

Almost everyone (except the super-wealthy) needs health insurance, but not everyone has it. Some people who can afford health insurance choose not to buy it because they believe that they're healthy and they're not going to need it. Others who opt not to buy health insurance figure that if they ever really need health care, they'll get it even if they can't pay. To a large extent, they're right. People without health insurance generally put off getting routine care, which can lead to small problems turning into big ones (and which cost more due to advanced illness, emergency room visits, and so on).

Choosing the best health plan

Before Medicare (the government-run insurance program for the elderly) kicks in at age 65, odds are that you'll obtain your health insurance through your employer. Be thankful if you do. Employer-provided coverage eliminates the headache of having to shop for coverage, and it's usually cheaper than coverage you buy on your own.

Whether you have options through your employer or you have to hunt for a plan on your own, the following sections cover the major issues to consider when selecting among the health insurance offerings in the marketplace.

Major medical coverage

You need a plan that covers the *big* potential expenses: hospitalization, physician, and ancillary charges such as X-rays and laboratory work. If you're a woman, and you think that you may want to have children, make sure that your plan has maternity benefits.

Choice of health care providers

Plans that allow you to use any health care provider you want are becoming less common and more expensive in most areas. Health maintenance organizations (HMOs) and preferred provider organizations (PPOs) are the main plans that restrict your choices. They keep costs down because they negotiate lower rates with selected providers.

HMOs and PPOs are more similar than they are different. The main difference is that PPOs still pay the majority of your expenses if you use a provider outside their approved list. If you use a provider outside the approved list with an HMO, you typically aren't covered at all.

If you have your heart set on particular physicians or hospitals, find out which health insurance plans they accept as payment. Ask yourself whether the extra cost of the open-choice plan is worth being able to use their services if they're not part of a restricted-choice plan. Also be aware that some plans allow you to go outside their network of providers as long as you pay a portion of the incurred medical costs. If you're interested in being able to use alternative types of providers, such as acupuncturists, find out whether the plans you're considering cover these services.

Don't let stories of how hard it is to get an appointment with a doctor or other logistical hassles deter you from going with an HMO or PPO plan. These things can happen in plans with open choice, too — some doctors are always running late or are overbooked. The idea that doctors who can't get patients on their own are the only ones who sign up with restricted-choice plans is a myth. Although HMO and PPO plans do offer less choices when it comes to providers, objective surveys show that customer satisfaction with these plans is as high as it is for plans that offer more choices.

Lifetime maximum benefits

Health insurance plans specify the maximum total benefits they'll pay over the course of time you're insured by their plan. Although a million dollars may be more money than you could ever imagine being spent on your health care, it's the minimum acceptable level of total benefits. With the cost of healthcare today, you can blow through that in short order if you develop major health problems. Ideally, choose a plan that has no maximum or that has a maximum of at least several million dollars.

Deductibles and co-payments

To reduce your health insurance premiums, choose a plan with the highest deductible and co-payment you can afford. As with other insurance policies, the more you're willing to share in the payment of your claims, the less you'll have to pay in premiums. Most policies have annual deductible options (such as $250, $500, $1,000, and so on), as well as co-payment options, which are typically 20 percent or so.

When choosing a co-payment percentage, don't let your imagination run wild and unnecessarily scare you. A 20 percent co-payment does not mean that you have to come up with $20,000 for a $100,000 claim. Insurance plans generally set a maximum out-of-pocket limit on your annual co-payments (such as $1,000, $2,000, and so on); the insurer covers 100 percent of any medical expenses that go over that cap.

For insurance provided by your employer, consider plans with low out-of-pocket expenses if you know that you have health problems. Because you're part of a group, the insurer won't increase your individual rates just because you're filing more claims.

Most HMO plans don't have deductible and co-payment options. Most just charge a set amount — such as $25 — for a physician's office visit.

Saving on your taxes when spending on health care

If you expect to have out-of-pocket medical expenses, find out whether your employer offers a flexible spending or health care reimbursement account. These accounts enable you to pay for uncovered medical expenses with pre-tax dollars. If, for example, you're in a combined 35 percent federal and state income tax bracket, these accounts allow you to pay for necessary health care at a 35 percent discount. These accounts can also be used to pay for vision and dental care.

Be forewarned of the major stumbling blocks you face when saving through medical reimbursement accounts. First, you need to elect to save money from your paycheck prior to the beginning of each plan year. The only exception is at the time of a "life change," such as a family member's death, marriage, spouse's job change, divorce, or the birth of a child. You also need to use the money within the year you save it, because these accounts contain a "use or lose it" feature.

Under a test program, the federal government authorized a *Medical Savings Account (MSA)* for the self-employed and people who work for

small firms. To qualify, you must have a high-deductible individual health insurance policy; then you can put money earmarked for medical expenses into an investment account that offers the tax benefits — deductible contributions and tax-deferred compounding — of a retirement account (see Chapter 2). And, unlike a flexible spending account, you don't have to deplete the MSA by the end of the year: Money can compound tax-deferred inside the MSA for years.

Because MSAs are still in their infancy, the best investment companies that I mention in this book are holding back from offering them. Stay tuned for future developments.

You may also be able to save on taxes if you have a substantial amount of health care expenditures in a year. You can deduct medical and dental expenses as an itemized deduction on Schedule A to the extent that they exceed 7.5 percent of your adjusted gross income (refer to Chapter 6). Unless you're a low income earner, you need to have substantial expenses, usually caused by an accident or major illness, to take advantage of this tax break.

Guaranteed renewable

You want a health insurance plan that keeps renewing your coverage without your having to prove continued good health.

Buying health insurance

You can buy many health plans through agents, and you can also buy some directly from the insurer. When health insurance is sold both ways, buying through an agent usually doesn't cost more.

If you're self-employed or you work for a small employer that doesn't offer health insurance as a benefit, get proposals from the larger and older health insurers in your area. Larger plans can negotiate better rates from providers, and older plans are more likely to be here tomorrow.

Many insurers operate in a bunch of different insurance businesses. You want those that are the biggest in the health insurance arena and are committed to that business. If your coverage is canceled, you might have to search for coverage that allows an existing medical problem. Other health insurers won't want to insure you. (Find out whether your state department of insurance offers a plan for people unable to get coverage.)

Nationally, Blue Cross, Blue Shield, Kaiser Permanente, Aetna, United Healthcare, Cigna, Fortis, Golden Rule, and Anthem are among the older and bigger health insurers.

Also check with professional or other associations that you belong to as such plans sometimes offer decent benefits at a competitive price due to the purchasing power clout that they possess. A competent independent insurance agent who specializes in health insurance can help you find insurers who are willing to offer you coverage.

Health insurance agents have a conflict of interest that is common to all financial salespeople working on commission: The higher the premium plan they sell you, the bigger the commission they earn. So an agent may try to steer you into higher-cost plans and avoid suggesting some of the strategies I discuss in the previous section for reducing your cost of coverage.

Dealing with insurance denial

When you try to enroll in a particular health insurance plan, you may be turned down because of current or previous health problems. Your *medical information file* (the medical equivalent of a credit report) may contain information explaining why you were turned down. (See Chapter 14 for more about medical information files.)

If you have a so-called *preexisting condition* (current or prior medical problems), you have several options to pursue when trying to secure health insurance:

✔ **Try health insurance plans that don't discriminate.** A few plans — typically Blue Cross, Blue Shield, and some HMO plans, such as Kaiser Permanente — will sometimes take you regardless of your condition.

✔ **Find a job with an employer whose health insurer doesn't require a medical exam.** Of course, this shouldn't be your only reason for seeking new employment, but it can be an important factor. If you're married, you may also be able to get into an employer group plan if your spouse takes a new job.

✔ **Find out whether your state offers a plan.** A number of states maintain pools that insure people who have preexisting conditions and are unable to find coverage elsewhere. Contact your state's insurance department (see the state government section of your phone book) to see if your state offers such plans. The Web site www.healthinsuranceinfo.net lists all such state plans. If your state doesn't offer one of these plans, I suppose that, in a drastic situation, you could move to a nearby state that does.

Dealing with medical claims headaches

If you sign up for a health plan that has deductibles and co-payments, make sure that you review the benefits statements your insurer sends you. Errors often pop up on these statements and during the claims filing process. Not surprisingly, the errors are rarely in your favor; they're usually at your expense.

Make sure that your insurer has kept accurate track of your contributions toward meeting your plan's annual deductible and maximum out-of-pocket charges. Also, don't pay any health care providers who send you bills until you receive proper notification from the insurance company detailing what you are obligated to pay those providers according to the terms of your plan. Because most insurance companies have negotiated discounted fee schedules with health care providers, the amount that a provider bills you is often higher than the amount they are legally due as per the terms of their contract with your insurer. Your insurer's benefit statement should detail the approved and negotiated rate.

And don't let providers try to bully you into paying them the difference between what they billed you for and what the insurer says they are due. Providers are only due the discounted fees they agreed to with your insurer.

Haggling with your health insurer is a real pain, and it usually happens after you rack up significant medical expenses and may still not be feeling well. But if you don't stay on top of your insurer, you can end up paying thousands of dollars in overpayments.

If you're overwhelmed with an avalanche of claims and benefits statements, you may want to consider using a health insurance claims processing service. You can get a referral to firms that engage in this line of work by visiting the Alliance of Claims Assistance Professionals Web site at www.claims.org.

Looking at retiree medical care insurance

Medicare, the government-run health insurance plan for the elderly, is a two-part major medical plan. Enrollment in Part A (hospital expenses) is automatic. Part B, which covers physician expenses and other charges, including home health care coverage, is optional. Supplemental insurance policies may be of interest to you if you want help paying for the costs that Medicare doesn't pay.

Medigap insurance

Medigap coverage generally pays the deductibles and co-payments that Medicare charges. For the first 60 days of hospitalization, you pay $840 out of your own pocket. If you have an unusually long hospital stay, you pay $210 per day for the 61st through 90th day, $420 per day for the 91st through 150th day, and all costs beyond 150 days. Clearly, if you stay in a hospital for many months, your out-of-pocket expenses can escalate; however, the longest hospitalizations tend not to last for many months. Also note that Medicare's hospitalization benefits refresh when you're out of the hospital for 60 consecutive days.

If the costs from a long hospital stay would be a financial catastrophe for you, and if you're unable to pay for the deductibles and co-payments because your income is low, *Medicaid* (the state-run medical insurance program for low-income people) may help pay your bills. Alternatively, Medigap insurance can help close the gap.

Check with your physician(s) to see that he or she does not charge a fee higher than the one listed on Medicare's fee schedule. If your physician does charge a higher fee, you may want to consider going to another physician if you can't afford the fee or if you want to save some money. Medicare often pays only 80 percent of the physician charges the program allows on its fee schedule. Some physicians charge higher fees than those allowed by Medicare.

The biggest reason that elderly people consider extra health insurance is that Medicare only pays for the first 100 days in a skilled nursing facility. Anything over that is your responsibility. Unfortunately, Medigap policies don't address this issue either.

Long-term care insurance

Insurance agents who are eager to earn a hefty commission will often tell you that *long-term care insurance* (LTC) is the solution to your concerns about an extended stay in a nursing home. Don't get your hopes up. Policies are complicated and filled with all sorts of exclusions and limitations. On top of all that, they're expensive, too.

The decision to purchase LTC insurance is a trade-off. Do you want to pay thousands of dollars annually, beginning at age 60, to guard against the possibility of a long-term stay in a nursing home? If you live into or past your mid-80s, you can end up paying more than $50,000 to $100,000 or more on a LTC policy (not to mention the lost investment earnings on these insurance premiums).

People who end up in a nursing home for years on end may come out ahead financially when buying LTC insurance. The majority of people who stay in a nursing home are there for less than a year, though, because they either pass away or move out.

Medicare pays for the bulk of the cost of the first 100 days in a nursing home as long as certain conditions are satisfied. Medicare pays for all basic services (telephone, television, and private room charges excluded) for the first 20 days and then requires a co-payment of $105 per day for the next 80 days. First, the nursing-home stay must follow hospitalization by 30 days, and the nursing-home stay must be for the same medical condition that caused the hospitalization. When you're discharged from the nursing home, you can qualify for an additional 100-day benefit period so long as you haven't been hospitalized or in a nursing home in the 60 days prior to your readmission.

If you have relatives or a spouse who will likely care for you in the event of a major illness, you should definitely *not* waste your money on nursing-home insurance. You can also bypass this coverage if you have and don't mind using retirement assets to help pay nursing-home costs.

Even if you do deplete your assets, remember that you have a backup: Medicaid (state-provided medical insurance) can pick up the cost if you can't. However, be aware of a number of potential drawbacks to getting coverage for nursing-home stays under Medicaid:

- ✔ **Medicaid patients are at the bottom of the priority list.** Most nursing homes are interested in the bottom line, so the patients who bring in the least revenue — namely Medicaid patients — get the lowest priority on nursing-home waiting lists.

- ✔ **Some nursing homes don't take Medicaid patients.** Check with your preferred nursing homes in your area to see if they accept Medicaid.

- ✔ **The states may squeeze Medicaid further.** Deciding what medical conditions warrant coverage is up to your state. With the budget noose tightening, some states are disallowing certain types of coverage (for example, mental problems for elderly people who are otherwise in good physical health.) Also, the federal government finances part of Medicaid, and the federal trend these days is to give states blocks of money and then let them decide what they want to do with it. In such an environment, more states may restrict Medicaid access.

If you're concerned about having your stash of money wiped out by an extended nursing-home stay, and you have a strong desire to pass money to your family or a favorite charity, you can start giving your money away while you're still healthy. (If you're already in poor health, legal experts can do *Medicaid planning* — strategizing to preserve your assets and keep them from being used to pay nursing-home costs.)

Consider buying nursing-home insurance if you want to retain and protect your assets, and it gives you peace of mind to know that a long-term nursing-home stay is covered. But do your homework. Do some comparison shopping, and make sure that you buy a policy that pays benefits for the long-term. A year's worth (or even a few years' worth) of benefits won't protect your assets if your stay lasts longer. Also be sure to get a policy that adjusts the daily benefit amount for increases in the cost of living. Watch out for policies that restrict benefits to limited types of facilities and settings. Get a policy that covers care in your home or other settings if you don't need to be in a high-cost nursing home, and make sure that it does not require prior hospitalization for benefits to kick in. Also consider a longer exclusion or waiting period — 3–6 months, or a year, before coverage starts to keep premiums down.

You may also want to consider retirement communities if you're willing to live as a younger retiree in such a setting. After paying an entrance fee, you pay a monthly fee, which usually covers your rent, care, and meals. Make sure that any such facility you're considering guarantees care for life and accepts Medicaid in case you deplete your assets.

Discovering the Most Overlooked Form of Insurance

You buy health insurance to cover large medical expenses, disability insurance to replace your income in the event of a long-term disability, and perhaps life insurance to provide money to those dependent on your income in the event of your death. Many people buy all the right kinds of personal insurance, spending a small fortune over the course of their lives. Yet they overlook the obvious, virtually free protection: taking care of themselves.

If you work at a desk all day and use many of life's modern conveniences, you may end up being the Great American Couch Potato. Odds are that you've heard of most of these methods of enhancing longevity and quality of life, but if you're still on the couch, the advice apparently didn't sink in.

So, for you sofa spuds, here are seven healthful tips:

- ✔ Don't smoke.

- ✔ Drink alcohol in moderation, if you drink at all.

- ✔ Get plenty of rest.

- ✔ Exercise regularly.

- ✔ Eat a healthy diet (see Chapter 5 for diet tips that can save you money and improve your health).

- ✔ Get regular health care checkups to detect medical, dental, and vision problems.

- ✔ Take time to smell the roses.

Chapter 16

Covering Your Assets

· ·

In This Chapter

▶ Checking out homeowner's/renter's insurance

▶ Considering automobile insurance

▶ Looking at umbrella insurance

▶ Planning your estate

· ·

*I*n Chapter 15, I discuss the importance of protecting your future income from the possibilities of disability, death, or large, unexpected medical expenses. But you also need to insure major assets that you acquired in the past: your home, your car, and your personal property.

You need to protect these assets for two reasons:

✔ **Your assets are valuable.** If you were to suffer a loss, replacing the assets with money out of your own pocket could be a financial catastrophe.

✔ **A lawsuit could drain your finances.** This reason is less well-known. If someone were injured or killed in your home or because of your car, a lawsuit could be even more financially devastating than an outright loss of the asset.

Protecting Where You Live

When you buy a home, most lenders require you to purchase homeowner's insurance. But even if they don't, you're wise to do so, because your home and the personal property within it are worth a great deal and would cost a bundle to replace.

As a renter, damage to the building in which you live is not your immediate financial concern, but you still have personal property you may want to insure. You also have the possibility (albeit remote) that you can be sued by someone who is injured in your rental.

When shopping for a homeowner's or renter's policy, you need to consider the important features that I cover in the following sections.

Dwelling coverage: The cost to rebuild

How much would you have to spend to *rebuild* your home if it were completely destroyed in a fire, an attack of locusts, or whatever? The cost to rebuild should be based on the size (square footage) of your home. Neither the purchase price nor the size of your mortgage should determine how much *dwelling coverage* you need.

If you're a renter, rejoice that you don't need dwelling coverage. If you're a condominium owner, find out whether the coverage the condo association bought for the entire building is sufficient.

Be sure that your homeowner's policy includes a *guaranteed replacement cost* provision. This useful feature ensures that the insurance company will rebuild the home even if the cost of construction is more than the policy coverage. If the insurance company underestimates your dwelling coverage, it has to make up the difference.

Unfortunately, insurers define guaranteed replacement cost differently. Some companies pay for the full replacement cost of the home, no matter how much it ends up costing. Other insurers set limits. For example, some insurers may only pay up to 25 percent more than the dwelling coverage on your policy. Ask your insurer how it defines guaranteed replacement cost.

If you have an older property that doesn't meet current building standards, consider buying a rider (supplemental coverage to your main insurance policy that you costs extra money) that pays for code upgrades. This rider covers the cost of rebuilding your home to comply with current building codes that may be more stringent than when your home was built. Ask your insurance company what your basic policy does and does not cover. Some companies include a certain amount (for example, 10 percent of your dwelling coverage) for code upgrades in the base policy.

Personal property coverage: For your things

On your homeowner's policy, the amount of personal property coverage is typically derived from the amount of dwelling coverage you carry. Generally, you get personal property coverage that is equal to 50 to 75 percent of the dwelling coverage. This amount is usually more than enough.

I'm not a fan of buying riders to cover jewelry, computers, furs, and other somewhat costly items that may not be fully covered by typical homeowner's policies. Ask yourself if the out-of-pocket expense from the loss of such items would constitute a financial catastrophe. Unless you have tens of thousands of dollars worth of jewelry or computer equipment, skip such riders.

Some policies come with _replacement cost guarantees_ that pay you the cost to replace an item. This payment can be considerably more than what the used item was worth before it was damaged or stolen. When this feature is not part of the standard policy sold by your insurer, you may want to purchase it as a rider, if available.

As a renter or condominium owner, you need to choose a dollar amount for the personal property you want covered. Tally it up instead of guessing — the total cost of replacing all your personal property may surprise you.

Make a list of your belongings — or even better, take pictures or make a video — with an estimate of what they're worth. Keep this list updated; you'll need it if you have to file a claim. Keeping receipts for major purchases may also help your case. No matter how you document your belongings, don't forget to keep the documentation somewhere besides your home — otherwise, it could be destroyed along with the rest of your house in a fire or other disaster.

Liability insurance: Coverage for hurting others

Liability insurance protects you financially against lawsuits that may arise if someone gets injured on your property, including wounds inflicted by the family pit bull or terrible tabby. (Of course, you should keep Bruno restrained when guests visit — even your in-laws.) At a minimum, get enough liability insurance to cover your financial assets — covering two times your assets is better. Buying extra coverage is inexpensive and well worth the cost.

The probability of being sued is low, but if you _are_ sued, and you lose, you could end up owing big bucks. If you have substantial assets to protect, you may want to consider an umbrella, or excess liability, policy. (See "Protecting Against Mega-Liability: Umbrella Insurance," later in this chapter.)

Liability protection is one of the side benefits of purchasing a renter's policy — you protect your personal property as well as insure against lawsuits. (But don't be reckless with your banana peels if you get liability insurance!)

Flood and earthquake insurance:
Protection from Mother Nature

You want to purchase the broadest possible coverage when buying any type of insurance (see Chapter 14). The problem with homeowner's insurance is that it's not comprehensive enough — it doesn't typically cover losses due to earthquakes and floods. You must buy such disaster coverage piecemeal.

If an earthquake or flood struck your area and destroyed your home, you'd be out tens (if not hundreds) of thousands of dollars without proper coverage. Yet many people don't carry these important coverages, often as a result of some common misconceptions:

- ✔ **"Not in my neighborhood."** Many people mistakenly believe that earthquakes occur only in California. I wish this were true for those of you who live in the other 49 states, but it's not. In fact, one of the strongest earthquakes in the 20th century occurred in the Midwest, and known (though not very active) fault lines lie along the East Coast. The cost of earthquake coverage is based on insurance companies' assessment of the risk of your area and property type, so you shouldn't decide whether to buy insurance based on how small you think the risk is. The risk is already built into the price.

    An estimated 20,000 communities around the country face potential flood damage. Like earthquakes, floods are not a covered risk in standard homeowner's policies, so you need to purchase a flood insurance rider. Check with your current homeowner's insurer or with the insurers recommended in this chapter. The federal government flood insurance program (phone 800-638-6620; Web site `www.fema.gov/nfip`) provides background information on flood insurance policies.

- ✔ **"The government will bail me out."** The vast majority of government financial assistance is obtained through low-interest loans. Loans, unfortunately, need to be repaid, and the money comes out of your pocket.

- ✔ **"In a major disaster, insurers would go bankrupt anyway."** This is highly unlikely given the reserves insurers are required to keep and the fact that the insurance companies *reinsure* — that is, they buy insurance to back up the policies they write.

People who have little equity in their property and are willing to walk away from the property and the mortgage in the event of a major quake or flood may consider not buying earthquake or flood coverage. Keep in mind that doing so damages your credit report, because you're essentially defaulting on your loan.

You may be able to pay for much of the cost of earthquake or flood insurance by raising the deductibles (discussed in the next section) on the main part of your homeowner's/renter's insurance and other insurance policies (such as auto insurance). You can more easily afford the smaller claims, not the big ones. If you think flood or earthquake insurance is too costly, compare those costs with the costs you may have to incur to completely replace your home and personal property. Buy this insurance if you live in an area that has a chance of being affected by these catastrophes. To help keep the cost of earthquake insurance down, consider taking a 10 percent deductible. Most insurers offer deductibles of 5 or 10 percent of the cost to rebuild your home. Ten percent of the rebuilding cost is a good chunk of money. But losing the other 90 percent is what you want to insure against.

Deductibles: Your cost with a claim

As I discuss in Chapter 14, the point of insurance is to protect against catastrophic losses, not the little losses. By taking the highest deductibles you're comfortable with, you save on insurance premiums year after year, and you don't have to go through the hassle of filing small claims.

Special discounts

You may qualify for special discounts. Companies and agents that sell homeowner's and renter's insurance don't always check to see if you're eligible for discounts. After all, the more you spend on policy premiums, the more money they make! If your property has a security system, you're older, or you have other policies with the same insurer, you may qualify for a lower rate. Don't forget to ask.

Buying homeowner's or renter's insurance

Each insurance company prices its homeowner's and renter's policies based on its own criteria. So the lowest-cost company for your friend's property may not be the lowest-cost company for you. You have to shop around at several companies to find the best rates. The following list features companies that historically offer lower-cost policies for most people and have decent track records regarding customer satisfaction and the payment of claims:

- **Amica.** Although Amica does have good customer satisfaction, in some areas, its prices are high. You can contact the company by calling 800-242-6422.

- **Erie Insurance.** This company does business primarily in the Midwest and Mid-Atlantic. Check your local phone directory for agents, or call 800-458-0811 for a referral to a local agent.

✓ **GEICO.** You can contact the company by calling 800-841-3000.

✓ **Liberty Mutual.** Check your local phone directory for agents.

✓ **Nationwide Mutual.** Check your local phone directory for agents.

✓ **State Farm.** Check your local phone directory for agents.

✓ **USAA.** This company provides insurance for military officers and their family members. Call the company at 800-531-8080 to see if you qualify.

Don't worry that some of these companies require you to call a toll-free number for a price quote. This process saves you money, because these insurers don't have to pay commissions to local agents hawking their policies. These companies have local claims representatives to help you if and when you have a claim.

A number of the companies mentioned in the previous list sell other types of insurance (for example, life insurance) that aren't as competitively priced. Be sure to check out the relevant sections in this part of the book for the best places to buy these other types of coverage if you need them.

Some state insurance departments conduct surveys to determine the insurers' prices and tabulate complaints received. Look up your state's department of insurance phone number in the government section of your local phone directory or visit the National Association of Insurance Commissioner's Web site at `www.naic.org/state_contacts/sid_websites.htm` to find links to each state's department of insurance site.

Auto Insurance 101

Over the course of your life, you'll probably spend tens of thousands of dollars on auto insurance. Much of the money people spend on auto insurance is not spent where it's needed most. In other cases, the money is simply wasted. Look for the following important features when searching for an auto insurance policy.

Bodily injury/property damage liability

As with homeowner's liability insurance, auto liability insurance provides insurance against lawsuits. Accidents happen, especially with a car. Make sure that you have enough bodily injury liability insurance, which pays for harm done to others, to cover your assets. (Coverage of double your assets is preferable.)

Coping with teen drivers

If you have a teenage driver in your household, you're going to be spending a lot more on auto insurance (in addition to worrying a lot more). Try to keep your teenager out of your car as long as possible — this is the best advice I can offer.

If you allow your teenager to drive, you can take a number of steps to avoid spending all of your take-home pay on auto insurance bills:

✔ Make sure that your teen does well in school. Some insurers offer discounts if your child is a strong academic achiever and has successfully completed a driver's education class (which is not required).

✔ Get price quotes from several insurers to see how adding your teen driver to your policy affects the cost.

✔ Have your teenager share in the costs of using the car. If you pay all the insurance, gas, and maintenance bills, your teenager won't value the privilege of using your "free" car.

Of course, letting your teen drive shouldn't just be about keeping your insurance bills to a minimum. Auto accidents are the number one cause of death for teens. So, before you let your teen drive, be sure to educate him or her about the big risks of driving and the importance of not riding in a car driven by someone who's intoxicated or sleep deprived. Also be sure that your teen drives safe cars.

If you're just beginning to accumulate assets, don't mistakenly assume that you don't need liability protection. Many states require a minimum amount — insurers should be able to fill you in on the details for your state. Also, don't forget that your future earnings, which are an asset, can be garnished in a lawsuit.

Property damage liability insurance covers damage done by your car to other people's cars or property. The amount of property damage liability coverage in an auto insurance policy is usually determined as a consequence of the bodily injury liability amount selected. Coverage of $50,000 is a good minimum to start with.

Uninsured or underinsured motorist liability

When you're in an accident with another motorist, and he doesn't carry his own liability protection (or doesn't carry enough), *uninsured or underinsured motorist liability coverage* allows you to collect for lost wages, medical expenses, and pain and suffering incurred in the accident.

If you already have comprehensive health and long-term disability insurance, uninsured or underinsured motorist liability coverage is largely redundant. Although, if you drop this coverage, you do give up the ability to sue for general pain and suffering and to insure passengers in your car who may lack adequate medical and disability coverage.

To provide a death benefit to those financially dependent on you in the event of a fatal auto accident, buy term life insurance (see Chapter 15).

Deductibles

To keep your auto insurance premiums down and eliminate the need to file small claims, take the highest deductibles you're comfortable with. (Most people should consider a $500 to $1,000 deductible.) On an auto policy, two deductibles exist: *collision* and *comprehensive.* Collision applies to claims arising from collisions (Note that if you have collision coverage on your own policy, you can generally bypass collision coverage when you rent a car.) Comprehensive applies to other claims for damages not caused by collision (for example, a window broken by vandals).

As your car ages and loses its value, you can eventually eliminate your comprehensive and collision coverages altogether. The point at which you do this is up to you. Insurers won't pay more than the book value of your car, regardless of what it costs to repair or replace it. Remember that the purpose of insurance is to compensate you for losses that are financially catastrophic to you. For some people, this amount may be as high as $5,000 or more — others may choose $1,000 as their threshold point.

Special discounts

You may be eligible for special discounts on auto insurance. Don't forget to tell your agent or insurer if your car has a security alarm, air bags, or anti-lock brakes. If you're older, or you have other policies or cars insured with the same insurer, you may also qualify for discounts. And make sure that you're given appropriate "good driver" discounts if you've been accident- and ticket-free in recent years.

And here's another idea: *Before* you buy your next car, call insurers and ask for insurance quotes for the different models you're considering. The cost of insuring a car should factor into your decision of which car you buy, because the insurance costs represent a major portion of your car's ongoing operating expenses.

Little-stuff coverage to skip

Auto insurers have dreamed up all sorts of riders, such as towing and rental car reimbursement. On the surface, these riders appear to be inexpensive. But they're expensive given the little amount you'd collect from a claim and the hassle of filing.

Riders that waive the deductible under certain circumstances make no sense, either. The point of the deductible is to reduce your policy cost and eliminate the hassle of filing small claims.

Medical payments coverage typically pays a few thousand dollars for medical expenses. If you and your passengers carry major medical insurance coverage, this rider isn't really necessary. Besides, a few thousand dollars of medical coverage doesn't protect you against catastrophic expenses.

Roadside assistance, towing, and rental car reimbursement coverage only pay small dollar amounts, and they aren't worth buying. In fact, if you belong to an automobile club, you may already have some of these coverages.

Driving safely: Overlooked auto insurance

A pipe bomb explodes in a crowded park and kills a person. An airplane crashes and several dozen people die.

Such tragic events are well-covered by our media, but the number of deaths that make the front pages of our newspapers pales in comparison to the approximately 40,000 people who die on America's roads every year.

I'm not suggesting that our national media should start reporting every automobile fatality. Even 24 hours of daily CNN coverage probably couldn't keep up with all the accidents on our roads. But the real story with auto fatalities lies not in the who, what, and where of specific accidents but in the why. When we ask the why question, we see how many of them are preventable.

No matter what kind of car you drive, you can and should drive safely. Stay within the speed limits and don't drive while intoxicated or tired, or in adverse weather conditions. Wear your seat belt — a U.S. Department of Transportation study found that 60 percent of auto passengers killed were not wearing their seat belts. And don't try to talk on your cell phone and write notes on a pad of paper attached to your dashboard while balancing your coffee cup between your legs!

You can also greatly reduce your risk of dying in an accident by driving a safe car. You don't need to spend buckets of money to get a car with desirable safety features. The *Consumer Reports* annual auto-buying guide has lots of good information on individual car model safety.

Buying auto insurance

You can use the homeowner's insurers list I present earlier in this chapter to obtain quotes for auto insurance. In addition, you can contact Progressive by calling 800-288-6776 or visiting their Web site at www.progressive.com. You can also contact Mercury Insurance (which currently sells in CA, FL, GA, IL, NY, OK, TX, and VA) through its Web site at www.mercuryinsurance.com, or by checking your local phone directory for agents.

Protecting Against Mega-Liability: Umbrella Insurance

Umbrella insurance (which is also referred to as *excess liability insurance*) is additional liability insurance that is added on top of the liability protection on your home and car(s). If, for example, you have $700,000 in assets, you can buy a one-million-dollar umbrella liability policy for around $200 per year to add to the $300,000 liability insurance that you have on your home and car. This is a small cost for big protection. Each year, thousands of people suffer lawsuits of more than one million dollars related to their cars and homes.

Umbrella insurance is generally sold in increments of one million dollars. So how do you decide how much you need if you have a lot of assets? As with other insurance coverages, you should have at least enough liability insurance to protect your assets, and preferably enough to cover twice the value of those assets.

Purchasing umbrella insurance through your existing homeowner's or auto insurance company is usually necessary.

Insuring your assets: Investment insurance

Insurance companies don't sell policies that protect the value of your investments, but you can shield your portfolio from many of the dangers of a fickle market through diversification.

If all of your money is invested in bank accounts or bonds, you're exposed to the risks of inflation, which can erode your money's purchasing power. Conversely, if the bulk of your money is invested in one high-risk stock, your financial future could go up in smoke if that stock explodes.

Chapter 8 discusses the benefits of diversification and tells you how to choose investments that do well under different conditions. Chapter 9 discusses why mutual funds are powerful investment vehicles that make diversification easy and cost-effective.

You Can't Take It with You: Planning Your Estate

Estate planning is the process of determining what will happen to your assets after you die. Thinking about your mortality in the context of insurance may seem a bit odd. But the time and cost of various estate-planning maneuvers is really nothing more than buying insurance: You're ensuring that, after you die, everything will be taken care of as you wish and taxes will be minimized. Thinking about estate planning in this way can help you better evaluate whether certain options make sense at particular points in your life.

Depending upon your circumstances, you may eventually want to contact an attorney who specializes in estate-planning matters. However, educating yourself first about the different options is worth your time. More than a few attorneys have their own agendas (increased fees) about what you should do, so be careful. And most of the estate-planning strategies that you're likely to benefit from don't require hiring an attorney.

Wills, living wills, and medical powers of attorney

When you have children who are minors (dependent), a *will* is a necessity. The will names the guardian to whom you entrust your children if both you and your spouse die. Should you and your spouse both die without a will (called *intestate*), the state (courts and social-service agencies) decides who will raise your children. Therefore, even if you can't decide at this time who you want to raise your children, you should *at least* appoint a trusted guardian who can decide for you.

Having a will makes good sense even if you don't have kids, because it gives instructions on how to handle and distribute all your worldly possessions. When you die without a will, your state decides how to distribute your money and other property, according to state law. Therefore, your friends, distant relatives, and favorite charities will probably receive nothing. Without any living relatives, your money may go to the state government!

Without a will, your heirs are legally powerless, and the state may appoint an administrator to supervise the distribution of your assets at a fee of around 5 percent of your estate. A bond typically must also be posted at a cost of several hundred dollars.

A living will and a medical power of attorney are useful additions to a standard will. A *living will* tells your doctor what, if any, life-support measures you prefer. A *medical (or health care) power of attorney* grants authority to someone you trust to make decisions regarding your medical care options.

The simplest and least costly way to prepare a will, a living will, and a medical power of attorney is to use the high-quality, user-friendly software packages that I recommend in Chapter 18. Be sure to give copies of these documents to the guardians and executors named in the documents.

You don't need an attorney to make a legal will. Most attorneys, in fact, prepare wills and living trusts using software packages! What makes a will valid is that three people witness your signing it.

If preparing the will all by yourself seems overwhelming, you can (besides hiring an attorney) use a paralegal typing service to help you prepare the documents. These services generally charge 50 percent or less of what an attorney charges.

Avoiding probate through living trusts

Because of our quirky legal system, even if you have a will, some or all of your assets must go through a court process known as probate. *Probate* is the legal process for administering and implementing the directions in a will. Property and assets that are owned in joint tenancy or inside retirement accounts, such as IRAs or 401(k)s, generally pass to heirs without having to go through probate. Most other assets pass through probate.

A *living trust* effectively transfers assets into a trust. You control those assets, and you can revoke the trust whenever you desire. The advantage of a living trust is that, upon your death, assets can pass directly to your beneficiaries without going through probate. Probate can be a lengthy, expensive hassle for your heirs — with legal fees tallying around 5 to 7 percent of the value of the estate. In addition, your assets become a matter of public record as a result of probate.

Living trusts are likely to be of greatest value to people who meet the following criteria:

- Age 60 or older
- Single
- Assets worth more than $100,000 that must pass through probate (including real estate, non-retirement accounts, and small businesses)

As with a will, you do *not* need an attorney to establish a legal and valid living trust. (See my software recommendations in Chapter 18 and consider the paralegal services that I mention in the previous section on wills.) Attorney fees for establishing a living trust can range from $700 to $2,000. Hiring an attorney is of greatest value to people with large estates (see the next section) who do not have the time, desire, and expertise to maximize the value derived from estate planning.

Note: Living trusts keep assets out of probate but have nothing to do with minimizing estate or inheritance taxes.

Reducing estate taxes

For tax year 2003, an individual can pass $1,000,000 to beneficiaries without having to pay federal estate taxes. (This exclusion increases to $1,500,000 in 2004, $2,000,000 in 2006, and $3,500,000 in 2008.) Thanks to the tax law changes passed in the early 2000s, fewer and fewer people will have an estate tax "problem" in the years ahead.

Whether you should be concerned about possible estate taxes depends on several issues. How much of your assets you're going to use up during your life is the first and most important issue you need to consider. This amount depends on how much your assets grow over time, as well as how rapidly you spend money. During retirement, you'll (hopefully) be utilizing at least some of your money.

I've seen too many affluent individuals worry about estate taxes on their money throughout their retirements. If your intention is to leave your money to your children, grandchildren, or a charity, why not start giving while you're still alive so that you can enjoy the act? You can give $11,000 annually to each of your beneficiaries, *tax-free.* By giving away money, you reduce your estate and, therefore, the estate taxes owed on it. Any appreciation on the value of the gift between the date of the gift and your date of death is also out of your estate and not subject to estate taxes.

In addition to gifting, a number of trusts allow you to minimize estate taxes. For example, if you're married, both you and your spouse can each pass up to $1,000,000 to your heirs (for a total of $2,000,000), free of federal estate taxes. You can accomplish this by establishing a *bypass trust.* Upon the death of the first spouse, assets held in his or her name go into the bypass trust, effectively removing those assets from the remaining spouse's taxable estate. As the amount that can be passed free of estate taxes escalates to $3,500,000 by 2008, a bypass trust will allow for the estate-tax-free passage of up to $7,000,000.

Cash value life insurance is another estate planning tool. Unfortunately, it's a tool that is overused. People who sell cash value insurance — that is, insurance salespeople and others masquerading as financial planners — too often advocate life insurance as the one and only way to reduce estate taxes. Other methods for reducing estate taxes are usually superior, because they don't require wasting money on life insurance.

Small-business owners whose businesses are worth several million dollars or more may want to consider cash value life insurance under specialized circumstances. If you lack the necessary additional assets to pay expected estate taxes, and you don't want your beneficiaries to be forced to sell the business, you can buy cash value life insurance to pay expected estate taxes.

To find out more about how to reduce your estate (and other) taxes, pick up a copy of the latest edition of *Taxes For Dummies,* co-written by David J. Silverman and me (Wiley Publishing).

Part V

Where to Go for More Help

The 5th Wave   By Rich Tennant

"IT HASN'T HELPED ME SELL MORE HOT DOGS, BUT I'VE HAD SEVERAL INQUIRIES FOR INVESTMENT ADVICE."

In this part . . .

I help you sift through the morass of financial resources competing for your attention and dollars. Many people who call themselves financial planners claim to be able to make you rich, but I show you how you may end up poorer if you don't choose an advisor wisely. I also cover software and Internet resources and name the best of the bunch. Finally, I discuss how to benefit from the financial coverage in print and on the air, as well as how to sidestep the problematic advice in these media.

Chapter 17

Working with Financial Planners

In This Chapter

▶ Taking a journey through financial-planner land

▶ Checking out your financial management options

▶ Determining whether you need help from a financial planner

▶ Understanding why it's hard to find good financial help

▶ Looking for a good financial planner

▶ Interviewing financial planners before you hire them

The financial planning business has two problems. One is credibility, and the other is conflict of interest.

— *Fortune* magazine

Financial planners often end up being wolves in sheep's clothing with hidden agendas to sell mutual funds, for example, or life insurance.

— *Consumer Reports*

Hiring a competent, ethical, and unbiased financial planner or advisor to help you make and implement financial decisions *can* be money well spent. But if you pick a poor advisor or someone who really isn't a financial planner but a salesperson in disguise, your financial situation can get worse instead of better. So before I talk about the different types of help to hire, I'm going to take a little journey with Alice to give you an idea of what you're up against in the land of financial planners.

Alice in Financial-Planner Land

Alice is a client who once landed on my doorstep. She struck out the first four times she sought financial help. Her story illustrates many of the pitfalls you may face when trying to find a good financial planner.

Alice's (mis)adventures

First, on the recommendation of her accountant, Alice called a financial consultant who was a certified financial planner (CFP) at a well-known investment (brokerage) firm. Alice explained that she wanted a conservative investment, but the broker sold her a mutual fund that, unbeknownst to Alice, primarily held *aggressive growth* (volatile) stocks.

After buying the fund and getting her first account statement a few days later, Alice noticed that the fund contained several thousand dollars less than she had invested. The broker told her that he earns a 4 percent commission and assured her that she need not concern herself with it because the fund paid him and it wouldn't affect her investment.

After a little investigation, Alice discovered that the fund had, in fact, paid the broker out of her investment — a hefty 6.5 percent commission. Thus, the broker not only lied about where the commission dollars came from (all such commissions come from the investors' money), but he also understated the size of his commission.

Alice, who was understandably steamed, called the Securities and Exchange Commission (SEC); after she jumped through many hoops, the brokerage firm coughed up nearly $2,000 for the broker's fib about the commission amount.

Thinking that perhaps men and women simply don't communicate well, Alice then turned to a female financial planner on the recommendation of a friend. The planner told Alice, "Women need to stick together." Then she promptly tried to sell Alice a limited partnership that, according to the planner, was *sure* to return upward of 20 to 40 percent per year.

Alice took a gander at the *prospectus* — a delightfully long document, written by attorneys, that contains detailed information about an investment and the firm offering it. She saw in black and white on page 2 that the partnership paid the selling broker a 10 percent sales commission (which, she now knew, would be deducted from her investment).

Because Alice is a conscientious investor, she did more research in financial books and magazines and found out that limited partnerships are also handicapped by high, ongoing management fees. Alice did not return the dozen or so follow-up calls ("to see how you are doing") from her "sister" financial planner. Fortunately, she passed on the partnership.

Alice wanted to find out more about investing before her next attempt to get help, so she enrolled in an "adult education class" at a local college. Alice, a student eager to learn, attended all the classes but soon felt only more confused. Her teacher said that the world of finance and investments is *very, very complicated.* Unless, of course, you're a financial expert.

The "teacher" told the class that he was just such an expert. He offered a free, one-hour consultation to all his students at the end of his "course." During her free session, Alice was told that she should invest in an annuity. Investigation, however, revealed (you guessed it) high sales commissions and management fees.

Alice was also uncomfortable because planner number three didn't inquire about other aspects of her situation, and he seemed intent only on selling her an annuity. She later found out that an annuity didn't make sense for her because she was in a low tax bracket and nearly retired.

At this point, most people would probably buy a good financial book or put their money in a mattress or the next best place — their local bank — but Alice really wanted to talk to someone about her money issues and ideas.

After listening to a financial planner on a radio call-in program, Alice had the planner mail his background materials to her. In addition to a certified financial-planning credential, *this* planner had a seemingly endless list of other, lofty-sounding credentials, such as RIA, BSCE, LLB, and MBA.

Alice, who was quite wary of sales commissions by now, also liked the sound of the planner's fee: $350 for his time to help with her investment decisions and to discuss her financial questions. Partway through their two-hour, $350 consultation, however, planner number four tried to persuade Alice to hire him as an ongoing manager of her money. For just $2,000 per year (commissions and management fees were extra), he would trade her in and out of investments based on his economic analyses and expert prognostications.

That seemed like a lot of money to Alice (who had $150,000 to invest), and she did not like the thought of turning over her money to someone who could move it around among various investments without her approval. Besides, she was interested in finding out more about finance, and this "planner" kept telling her how complicated it is to make investing and other financial decisions. Alice declined planner number four's sales pitch for managing her investments, whereupon the moody planner stormed out of her house, complaining that she had wasted his time (for which he had a $350 check in hand for a mere two hours of his time!).

Learning from Alice's journey

Alice's case highlights four major problems that people often encounter when hiring financial help:

✔ First, you absolutely, positively *must* do your homework before hiring any financial advisor. Despite enthusiastic recommendations from her accountant and a friend, Alice ended up with bad advice from biased advisors.

✔ Second, the financial planning and brokerage fields are minefields for consumers. The fundamental problem is the enormous conflict of interest that is created when "advisors" sell products that earn them sales commissions. Selling ongoing money management services, as Alice found out from the last "advisor," creates a conflict of interest as well.

As an analogy, imagine that you have flu symptoms. Would you be comfortable seeing a physician who didn't charge for office visits but instead made money only by selling you drugs? Maybe you don't *need* the drugs — or at least not so many expensive ones. Maybe what you really need is Mom's chicken soup and ten hours of sleep.

What's truly amazing about Alice's situation is that none of the so-called financial planners ever bothered to ask about her insurance and debt situation. As it turns out, I learned that Alice not only lacked adequate homeowner's insurance but she also amazingly had no health insurance! Alice also had some relatively high-interest consumer debt that none of the "planners" ever asked about — probably because paying off her debt would've diminished the funds that Alice would have available for investment.

✔ Third, financial advisors often like to make things far more complicated than they need to be, and they're generally not interested in educating you. As others have observed, financial planning is hardly the only occupation guilty of this. As author George Bernard Shaw put it, "All professions are conspiracies against the laity."

The more you know, and the more you understand that investing and other financial decisions needn't be complicated, the more you realize that you don't need to spend gobs of money (or any money at all) on financial planners and advisors. When you look in the mirror, you see the person who has your best interests at heart and is your best financial advisor.

✔ Fourth, don't place a whole lot of faith in credentials, especially the Certified Financial Planning (CFP) moniker. *Forbes* magazine called *CFP* a "meaningless label," adding, "When picking a financial planner, pay a lot of attention to how the planner is compensated. Pay no attention to CFPs. . . ."

Finally, in case you're wondering, Alice did happily invest her money in a nice portfolio of commission-free mutual funds (see Chapter 10), which have been performing just swimmingly for her over the years.

What credentials qualify a financial advisor?

It seems that everywhere I turn today, more and more people carry credentials after their names. We have certified lactation consultants, certified foot reflexologists, and registered dietitians.

Among salespeople, especially in the financial services industry, the use of dubious credentials and self-anointed and misleading titles is on the rise. Stockbrokers are no longer called stockbrokers — they're "financial consultants" and "financial advisors." Some life insurance agents now call themselves "estate planning specialists." Next thing I know, when I visit an auto dealer, I'll speak with a certified transportation consultant, and when I buy my next home, it will be through a certified housing consultant rather than a real estate agent. It seems that everything today is certified — even used cars are now referred to as "certified pre-owned" by some dealers!

Speaking of *certified,* tens of thousands of people have earned the Certified Financial Planning credential. This credential is basically a home-study course that — unlike gaining entrance into medical, law, or business school — virtually anyone can take. Unbelievably, the College for Financial Planning allows students to take exams online (with a self-selected proctor who needs to simply supply a name, mailing address, and e-mail address to register)! The test itself isn't difficult to pass — an astounding 77 percent of people recently enrolled in the College for Financial Planning passed the CFP test. Gaining admission to a top professional school and becoming an architect, attorney, or doctor is extraordinarily more difficult and demanding.

The CFP Board of Standards, which licenses the CFP credential, claims that the combination of passing a test and meeting continuing education requirements ensures that their profession is doing the best it can. To that, I and others who regularly observe CFP incompetence and conflicts of interest politely say, "Bunk!"

✔ The CFP doesn't test the planner's business ethics or how the planner earns income.

✔ The CFP exam covers arcane financial details, which can easily be addressed in a handy reference book and are rarely encountered by consumer-oriented planners.

✔ The few individuals who don't pass the CFP exam on their first try are told which answers they got wrong so that they can focus their time memorizing the trivial details and pass the exam on the second try.

Boston Globe columnist Charles Jaffe took the CFP exam and concluded that ". . . financial planning is a long way from qualifying as a profession."

Unfortunately, the vast majority of people with CFPs work on commission and are employed by securities and insurance brokerage firms, so they're not really financial planners so much as salespeople with a credential. Most of the rest sell ongoing money management services.

Meeting the CFP continuing education requirements is a sham. CFPs can earn continuing education credit hours simply by attending what amount to sales presentations by companies pitching financial products. CFPs can also meet the requirements by reading financial planning journals that have multiple-choice and true-false questions in the back. The planner can take the test on his or her own time and even refer to the relevant articles to find the answers!

If you're interested in hiring financial help, be sure to read the "Interviewing Financial Advisors: Asking the Right Questions" section, later in this chapter, where I detail questions you should ask financial advisors before hiring them and tell you how to make sense of all the credential gobbledygook.

Surveying Your Financial Management Options

Everyone has three basic choices when it comes to managing money: You can do nothing, you can do it yourself, or you can hire someone to help you.

Doing nothing

The *do-nothing* approach has a large following (and you thought that you were the only one!). People who fall into this category may be leading terribly exciting, interesting lives and are therefore too busy to attend to something as mundane as dealing with their personal finances. Or they may be leading terribly mundane lives but are too busy fantasizing about more-appealing ways to spend their time. For both types, everything from a major UFO sighting to taking out the garbage captures their imagination more than thinking about financial management.

But the dangers of doing nothing are many. Problem areas, when left to themselves, get worse. Putting off saving for retirement or ignoring your buildup of debt eventually comes back to haunt you. If you don't carry adequate insurance, accidents can be devastating. Fires and earthquakes in California, flooding in the Midwest, and hurricanes in the South and East show how precarious living in paradise actually is.

If you've been following the do-nothing approach all your life, you're now officially promoted out of it! You bought this book to find out more about personal finance and make changes in your money matters, right? So take control and keep reading!

Doing it yourself

The do-it-yourselfers learn enough about financial topics to make informed decisions on their own. Doing anything yourself, of course, requires you to invest some time in learning the basic concepts and keeping up with changes. For some, personal financial management becomes a challenging and absorbing interest. Others focus on what they need to do to get the job done efficiently.

The idea that you're going to spend endless hours on your finances if you direct them yourself and make your own decisions is a myth. The hardest part of managing money for most people is catching up to where they should be and correcting past mistakes. After you get things in order, which you can easily do with this book as your companion, you shouldn't have to spend more than an hour or two working on your personal finances every few months (unless a major issue, like a real estate purchase, comes up).

Some people in the financial advisory business like to make what they do seem so complicated, comparing it to brain surgery! Their argument goes, "You wouldn't perform brain surgery on yourself, so why would you manage your money yourself?" Well, to this I say, "Personal financial management ain't brain surgery — not even close." You can manage on your own. In fact, you can do a better job than most advisors. Why? Because you're not subject to their conflicts of interest, and you care the most about your money.

Hiring financial help

Realizing that you need to hire someone to help you make and implement financial decisions can be a valuable insight. Spending a few hours and several hundred dollars to hire a competent professional can be money well spent, even if you have a modest income or assets. But you need to know what your money is buying.

Financial planners or advisors make money in one of three ways:

- ✔ They earn commissions based on the sales of financial products.
- ✔ They can charge a percentage of the assets they're investing.
- ✔ They can charge by the hour.

As you can see from Alice's journey into this area at the beginning of this chapter, hiring financial assistance can be anything but a tea party. The following sections help you differentiate among the three main types of financial planners.

Commission-based planners

Commission-based planners aren't really planners, advisors, or counselors at all — they're salespeople. Many *stockbrokers* and *insurance brokers* are now called *financial consultants* or *financial service representatives* in order to glamorize the profession and obscure how they're compensated. Ditto for insurance salespeople calling themselves *estate planning specialists*.

A stockbroker referring to himself as a financial consultant is like a Honda dealer calling himself a transportation consultant. A Honda dealer is a salesperson who makes a living selling Hondas — period. He's definitely not going to tell you nice things about Ford, Chrysler, or Toyota cars — unless, of course, he happens to sell those, too. He also has no interest in educating you about money-saving public-transit possibilities!

As I discuss earlier in this chapter, salespeople and brokers masquerading as planners can have an enormous self-interest when they push certain products, particularly those products that pay generous commissions. Getting paid on commission tends to skew their recommendations toward certain strategies (such as buying investment or life-insurance products) and cause them to ignore or downplay other aspects of your finances. For example, they'll gladly sell you an investment rather than persuade you to pay off your high-interest debts or save and invest through your employer's retirement plan, thereby reducing your taxes.

Table 17-1 gives you an idea of the commissions that a financial planner/salesperson can earn by selling particular financial products.

Table 17-1	Financial Product Commissions
Product	**Commission**
Life Insurance ($250,000, age 45):	
Term Life	$125 to $500
Universal/Whole Life	$1,000 to $2,500
Disability Insurance:	
$4,000/month benefit, age 35	$400 to $1,500
Investments ($20,000):	
Mutual Funds	$800 to $1,700
Limited Partnerships	$1,400 to $2,000
Annuities	$1,000 to $1,800

Percentage-of-assets-under-management advisors

A financial advisor who charges a percentage of the assets that are being managed or invested is generally a better choice than a commission-based planner. This compensation system removes the incentive to sell you products with high commissions and initiate lots of transactions (to generate more of those commissions).

The fee-based system is an improvement over product-pushers working on commission, but it has flaws, too. First off, suppose that you're trying to decide whether to invest in stocks, bonds, or real estate. A planner who earns her living managing your money likely won't recommend real estate, because that will deplete your investment capital. The planner also won't recommend paying down your mortgage for the same reason — she'll claim that you can earn more investing your money (with her help, of course) than it will cost you to borrow.

Fee-based planners are also only interested in managing the money of those who have already accumulated a fair amount of it — which rules out most people. According to the Boston Company, an economics research firm, the median household (*median* means half have more, half have less) headed by a person age 35 to 49 has just $6,000 in financial assets — far below the six-figure minimums of most fee-based advisors.

Hourly-based advisors

Your best bet for professional help with your personal finances is an advisor who charges for his time. Because he doesn't sell any financial products, his objectivity is maintained. He doesn't perform money management, so he can help you make comprehensive financial decisions with loans, retirement planning, and the selection of good investments, including real estate, mutual funds, and small business.

Hiring someone who is incompetent is the primary risk you face when selecting an hourly-based planner. So be sure to check references and find out enough about finances on your own to discern between good and bad financial advice. Another risk comes from not clearly defining the work to be done and the approximate total cost of the planner's service before you begin. You should also review some of the other key questions that I outline in the "Interviewing Financial Advisors: Asking the Right Questions" section, later in this chapter.

A drawback of an entirely different kind occurs when you don't follow through on the recommendations of your advisor. You paid for her work, but you didn't act on it, so you didn't capture its value. If part of the reason that you hired the planner in the first place was that you're too busy or not interested enough to make changes to your financial situation, then you should look for this type of support in the services you buy from the planner.

If you just need someone to act as a sounding board for ideas or to recommend a specific strategy or product, you can hire an hourly-based planner for one or two sessions of advice. You save money doing the legwork and implementation on your own. Just make sure that the planner is willing to give you specific advice so that you can properly implement the strategy.

Deciding Whether to Hire a Financial Planner

If you're like most people, you don't need to hire a financial planner, but you may benefit from hiring help.

The good reasons you have for hiring a financial planner can be similar to the reasons you have for hiring someone to clean your home or do your taxes. If you're too busy, you don't enjoy doing it, or you're terribly uncomfortable making decisions on your own, using a planner for a second opinion makes good sense. And if you shy away from numbers and bristle at the thought of long division, a good planner can help you.

How a good financial planner can help

The following list gives you a rundown of some of the important things a competent financial planner can assist you with.

- **Identifying problems and goals.** Many otherwise intelligent people have a hard time being objective about their financial problems. They may ignore their debts or have unrealistic goals and expectations given their financial situations and behaviors. And many are so busy with other aspects of their lives that they never take the time to think about what their financial goals are. A good financial planner can give you the objective perspective you need.

  Surprisingly, some people are in a better financial position than they thought they were in relation to their goals. Good counselors really enjoy this aspect of their jobs — good news is easier and much more fun to deliver.

- **Identifying strategies for reaching your financial goals.** Your mind may be a jumble of various plans, ideas, and concerns, along with a cobweb or two. A good counselor can help you sort out your thoughts and propose alternative strategies for you to consider as you work to accomplish your financial goals.

- **Setting priorities.** You may be doing dozens of things to improve your financial situation, but making just a few key changes will likely have the greatest value. Identifying the changes that fit your overall situation and that won't keep you awake at night is equally important. Good planners help you prioritize.

- **Saving research time and hassle.** Even if you know what major financial decisions are most important to you, doing the research can be time-consuming and frustrating if you don't know where to turn for good information and advice. A good planner does research to match your needs to the best available strategies and products. So much lousy information on various financial topics is out there that you can easily get lost, discouraged, sidetracked, or swindled. A good advisor can prevent you from making a bad decision based on poor or insufficient information.

- **Purchasing commission-free financial products.** When you hire a planner who charges for her time, you can easily save hundreds or thousands of dollars by avoiding the cost of commissions in the financial products you buy. Purchasing commission-free is especially valuable when it comes to purchasing investments and insurance.

✔ **Providing an objective voice for major decisions.** When you're trying to figure out when to retire, how much to spend on a home purchase, and where to invest your money, you're faced with some big decisions. Getting swept up in the emotions of these issues can cloud your perspective and objectivity. A competent and sensitive advisor can help you cut through the cloud and provide you with sound counsel.

✔ **Helping you to just do it.** Deciding what you need to do is not enough — you have to actually do it, too. And although you can use a planner for advice and then make all the changes on your own, a good counselor can help you follow through with your plan, as well. After all, part of the reason you hired the advisor in the first place may be that you're too busy or uninterested to manage your finances.

✔ **Mediating.** If you have a spouse or partner, financial decisions can produce real fireworks — particularly financial decisions involving the extended family. Although a counselor can't be a therapist, a good one can be sensitive to the different needs and concerns of each party and can try to find middle ground on the financial issues you're grappling with.

✔ **Making you money and allowing you peace of mind.** The whole point of professional financial planning is to help you make the most of your money and plan for and attain your financial and personal goals. In the process, the financial planner should show you how to enhance your investment returns; reduce your spending, taxes, and insurance costs; increase your savings; improve your catastrophic-insurance coverage; and achieve your financial-independence goals. Putting your financial house in order should take some weight off your mind — like that clean, lightheaded feeling after a haircut.

Why financial planners aren't for everyone

Finding a good financial planner isn't easy, so make sure that you want to hire an advisor before you venture out in search of a competent one.

You should also consider your personality type before you decide to hire help. My experience has been that some people (believe it or not) enjoy the research and number-crunching. If this sounds like you, or if you're not really comfortable taking advice, you may be better off doing your own homework and creating your own plan.

Likewise, if you have a specific tax or legal matter, you may be better off hiring a good professional who specializes in that specific field rather than a financial planner.

The Frustrations of Finding Good Financial Planners

Overwhelmed consumers like Alice (see "Alice in Financial-Planner Land," earlier in this chapter, for Alice's story), especially those in low- and middle-income brackets, have few attractive options when hiring financial help. The vast majority of the people who call themselves *financial planners* and *financial consultants* sell products and work on commission, which, as Alice found out, creates enormous conflicts of interest. The conflicts of interest stem from the fact that the broker has an incentive to recommend strategies and sell products that pay generous commissions and to ignore strategies and products that pay no or low commissions.

The few financial advisors who are fee-only make most of their fees from money-management services. (*Fee-only* or *fee-based* means that the advisors' fees are paid by their clients, not by companies whose products they recommend.) Thus, fee-based advisors tend to focus on clients who have already accumulated significant wealth. Fee-based advisors may also have conflicts of interest in that they gravitate toward strategies and recommendations that involve their ongoing management of your money, and they may ignore or dismiss tactics that diminish the pool of investment money that they can manage for you for an ongoing fee.

The following sections describe some of the problems associated with finding a good planner.

Regulatory problems

The financial-planning field has a problem when it comes to oversight. Oversight is minimal *at best*. In many states, anyone can hang out a shingle and call him- or herself a financial planner. The U.S. Securities and Exchange Commission (SEC) polices only those financial planners who provide investment advice; these advisors must register with the SEC as registered investment advisors (RIAs). The SEC provides no oversight of planners who do not provide investment advice.

States police the hundreds of thousands of people who call themselves financial planners. But most states have done little to monitor planners and protect consumers. Thus, as the nonprofit Consumer Federation of America said in its assessment of the industry, "Today's investors go up against a deadly combination of abusive securities industry practices and regulatory inattentiveness when investing their money."

Prior to working with a client, financial planners *should* be required to disclose, in writing, how they're compensated. This disclosure would make it easier for people to know how the planner earns a living. And it would eliminate much of the need for more formal government regulation. Several bills that had this sort of common-sense provision were squashed when introduced to state and federal governments. Financial planners, insurance brokers, and others selling products with commissions that are hidden from the public have lobbied successfully (by spending and contributing money to politicians' campaigns) to stop such bills.

Recognizing financial planners' conflicts of interest

All professions have conflicts of interest. Some fields have more than others, and the financial-planning field is one of those fields. Knowing where some of the land mines are located can certainly help. Here, then, are the most-common reasons why planners may not have 20/20 vision when giving financial directions.

Selling and pushing products that pay commissions

If a financial planner isn't charging you a fee for his time, you can rest assured that he's earning commissions on the products he tries to sell you. In order to sell financial products, this planner must have a broker's license. A person who sells financial products and then earns commissions from those products is a salesperson, *not* a financial planner. Financial planning involves taking an objective, holistic look at your financial puzzle to determine which pieces fit it well — something that brokers are neither trained nor financially motivated to do.

To make it even harder for you to discern a planner's agenda, you can't assume that planners who charge fees for their time don't also earn commissions selling products. This compensation *double dipping* is common.

Selling products that provide a commission tends to skew a planner's recommendations. Products that carry commissions result in fewer of your dollars going to the investments and insurance you buy. Because a commission is earned only when a product is sold, such a product or service is inevitably more attractive in the planner's eyes than other options. For example, consider the case of a planner who sells disability insurance that you can obtain at a lower cost through your employer or a group trade association (see Chapter 15). He may overlook or criticize your most attractive option (buying through your employer) and focus on *his* most attractive option — selling you a higher-cost disability policy on which he derives a commission.

"Financial planning" in banks

Over recent decades, banks have witnessed an erosion of the money in their coffers and vaults because increasing numbers of investors realized that banks are generally lousy places to build wealth. The highest-yielding bank savings accounts and certificates of deposit barely keep an investor ahead of inflation. If you factor in both inflation and taxes, these bank "investments" provide no real growth on your investment dollars.

Increasingly, banks have "financial representatives" and "investment specialists" sitting in their branches, waiting to pounce on bank customers with big balances. In many banks, these "financial planners" are simply brokers who are out to sell investments that pay them (and the bank) hefty sales commissions.

Although you may expect your bank account balances to be confidential and off-limits to the eager eyes of investment salespeople in banks, numerous studies have demonstrated that banks are betraying customer trust.

Customers often have no idea that these bank reps are earning commissions, and that those commissions are being siphoned out of customers' investment dollars. Many customers are mistaken (partly due to the banks' and salespeople's poor disclosure) in believing that these investments, like bank savings accounts, are FDIC-insured and cannot lose value.

Another danger of trusting the recommendation of a commission-based planner is that she may steer you toward the products that have the biggest payback for her. These products are among the *worst* for you because they siphon off even more of your money upfront to pay the commission. They also tend to be among the costliest and riskiest financial products available.

Planners who are commission-greedy may also try to *churn* your investments. They encourage you to buy and sell at the drop of a hat, attributing the need to changes in the economy or the companies you invested in. More trading means more commissions for the broker.

Taking a narrow view

Because of the way they earn their money, many planners are biased in favor of certain strategies and products. As a result, they typically don't keep your overall financial needs in mind. For example, if you have a problem with accumulated consumer debts, some planners may never know (or care) because they're focused on selling you an investment product. Likewise, a planner who sells a lot of life insurance tends to develop recommendations that require you to purchase it.

Not recommending saving through your employer's retirement plan

Taking advantage of saving through your employer's retirement savings plan(s) is one of your best financial options. Although this method of saving may not be as exciting as risking your money in cattle futures, it's not as dull as watching paint dry — and, most importantly, it's tax-deductible. Some planners are reluctant to recommend taking full advantage of this option: It doesn't leave much money for the purchase of their commission-laden investment products.

Ignoring debts

Sometimes paying off outstanding loans — such as credit card, auto, or even mortgage debts — is your best investment option. But most financial planners don't recommend this strategy, because paying down debts depletes the capital with which you could otherwise buy investments — the investments that the broker may be trying to sell you to earn a commission, or that the advisor would like to manage for an ongoing fee.

Not recommending real estate and small-business investments

Investing in real estate and small business, like paying off debts, takes away from your interest and ability to invest elsewhere. Most planners won't help with these choices. They may even tell you tales of real-estate and small-business-investing disasters to try to give you cold feet.

The value of real estate can go down just like any other investment. But over the long haul, owning real estate makes good financial sense for most people. With small business, the risks are higher, but so are the potential returns. Don't let a financial planner convince you that these options are foolish — in fact, if you do your homework and know what you're doing, you can make higher rates of return investing in real estate and small business than you can in traditional securities such as stocks and bonds. See Part III to read more about your investing options.

Selling ongoing money-management services

The vast majority of financial planners who don't work on commission make their money by managing your money for an ongoing fee percentage (typically 1 to 2 percent of your investment annually). Although this fee removes the incentive to *churn* your account (frequently trade your investments) to run up more commissions, the service is something that you're unlikely to need. (As I explain in Part III, you can hire *professional money managers* for 1 percent per year or less.)

An ongoing fee percentage still creates a conflict of interest; the financial planner will tend to steer you away from beneficial financial strategies that reduce the asset pool from which he derives his percentage. Financial strategies such as maximizing contributions to your employer's retirement savings plan, paying off debts like your mortgage, investing in real estate or small business, and so on may make the most sense for you. Advisors who work on a percentage-of-assets-under-management basis may be biased against such beneficial strategies.

Selling legal services

Some planners are in the business of drawing up *trusts* and providing other estate-planning services for their clients. Although these and other legal documents may be right for you, legal matters are complex enough that the competence of someone who isn't a full-time legal specialist should be carefully scrutinized. And lower-cost options may be available if your situation is not complicated.

If you need help determining whether you need these legal documents, do a little investigating: Do some additional reading or consult an advisor who won't actually perform the work. If you do ultimately hire someone to perform estate-planning services for you, make sure that you hire someone who specializes and works at it full-time. See Chapter 16 to find out more about estate planning.

Scaring you unnecessarily

Some planners put together nifty computer-generated projections that show you that you're going to need millions of dollars by the time you retire to maintain your standard of living, or that show that tuition will cost hundreds of thousands of dollars by the time your two-year-old is ready for college.

Waking up a client to the realities of his or her financial situation is an important and difficult job for good financial planners. But some unscrupulous planners take this task to an extreme, deliberately scaring you into buying what they're selling. They paint a bleak picture and imply that you can fix your problems only if you do what they say. Don't let them scare you — read this book and get your financial life in order.

Creating dependency

Many financial planners create dependency by making things seem so complicated, that their clients feel as though they could never manage their finances on their own. If your advisor is reluctant to tell you how you can educate yourself about personal money management, or if she tells you that your time would be better spent learning yoga, you probably have a self-perpetuating consultant.

Finding a Good Financial Planner

Locating a good financial planner who is willing to work with the not-yet-rich-and-famous and who doesn't have conflicts of interest can be like trying to find a needle in a haystack. Personal referrals and associations are two methods that can serve as good starting points.

Soliciting personal referrals

Getting a personal referral from a satisfied customer you trust is one of the best ways to find a good financial planner. Finding a referral from an accountant or attorney whose judgment you tested can help as well.

The best financial planners continue to build their practices through word of mouth. Satisfied customers are a professional's best and least costly marketers.

Watching for possible warning signs in planners' cultivation techniques

The channel through which you hear of a planner may provide clues to the planner's integrity and way of doing business. Beware of planners you find (or that find you) through these avenues:

✓ **Cold calling.** You've just come home after a hard day. No sooner has your posterior hit the recliner to settle in for the night when the phone rings. It's Joe the financial planner, and he wants to help you achieve all your financial dreams. *Cold calling* (the salesperson calls you, without an appointment) is the most inefficient way for a planner to get new clients. Cold calling is intrusive, and it's typically used by aggressive salespeople who work on commission.

Keep a log beside your telephone. Record the date, time, name of the organization, and name of the caller every time you receive a cold call. Politely but firmly tell cold callers to never call you again. Then, if they do call you again, you can sue them for $500 in small claims court!

✓ **Adult education classes.** Here's what often happens at the adult education classes that are offered at local universities: You pay a reasonable fee for the course. You go to class giddy at the prospect of learning how to manage your finances. And then the instructor ends up being a broker or financial planner hungry for clients. He confuses more than he conveys. He's short on specifics. But he's more than happy to show you the way if you contact (and hire) him outside of class.

The instructors for these courses are paid to teach. They don't need to solicit clients in

(continued)

(continued)

class, and, in fact, it's unethical for them to do so. I should note, however, that part of the problem is that some universities take advantage of the fact that such "teachers" want to solicit business, setting the pay at a low level. So *never* assume that someone who is teaching a financial-planning course at a local college is ethical, competent, or looking out for your best interests. Although I may sound cynical in saying so, assume that these people are none of the above until they clearly prove otherwise.

Ethical instructors who are there to teach do *not* solicit clients. In fact, they may actively discourage students from hiring them. Smart universities pay their instructors well and weed out the instructors who are more interested in building up their client base than they are in teaching.

✓ **"Free" seminars.** This is a case of "you get what you pay for." Because you don't pay a fee to attend "free seminars," and the "teachers" don't get paid either, these events tend to be clear-cut sales pitches. The "instructor" may share some

information, but smart seminar leaders know that the goal of a successful seminar is to establish himself or herself as an expert and to whet the prospects' appetites.

Note: Be *especially* wary of seminars targeted at select groups, such as special seminars for people who have received retirement-plan distributions or seminars touting "Financial Planning for Women." Financial planning is not specific to gender, ethnicity, or marital status.

Don't assume that the financial planner giving a presentation at your employer's office is the right planner for you either. You may be surprised at how little some corporate benefits departments investigate the people they let in. In most cases, planners are accepted simply because they don't charge. One organization I'm familiar with gave preference to planners who, in addition to doing free presentations, also brought in a catered lunch! Guess what — this preference attracted a lot of brokers who sell high-commission products.

However, you should *never* take a recommendation from anyone as gospel. I don't care *who* is making the referral — even if it's your mother or the Pope. You must do your homework: Ask the planner the interview questions I list in the "Interviewing Financial Advisors: Asking the Right Questions" section, later in this chapter. I've seen people get into real trouble because of blindly accepting someone else's recommendation. Remember that the person making the recommendation is (probably) not a financial expert. He or she may be just as bewildered as you are.

You may get referred to a planner or broker who returns the favor by sending business to the tax, legal, or real estate person who referred you. On more than a few occasions, professionals in other fields have made it clear that they would refer business to me if I referred business to them. I refused, of course. Good professionals don't do tit for tat. Hire professionals who make referrals to others based on their competence and ethics.

Seeking advisors through associations

Associations of financial planners are more than happy to refer you to planners in your area. But as I discuss earlier in this chapter, the major trade associations are composed of planners who sell products and work on commission.

Here are two of the best places to start searching for good financial planners:

- ✔ **The National Association of Personal Financial Advisors.** The NAPFA (800-366-2732; www.napfa.org) is made up of fee-only planners. Its members are not supposed to earn commissions from products they sell. However, most planners in this association earn their living by providing money-management services and charging a fee that is a percentage of assets under management.

- ✔ **The American Institute of Certified Public Accountants.** The AICPA (888-999-9256; www.cpapfs.org) is the professional association of CPAs that can provide names of members who have completed the Institute's Personal Financial Specialist (PFS) program. Many, but certainly not all, of the CPAs who have completed the PFS program provide financial advice on a fee basis. Competent CPAs have the advantage of understanding the tax consequences of different choices, which are important components of any financial plan. On the other hand, it can be hard for a professional to keep current in two broad fields.

Interviewing Financial Advisors: Asking the Right Questions

Don't consider hiring a financial advisor until you read the rest of this book. If you're not educated about personal finance, how can you possibly evaluate the competence of someone you may hire to help you make important financial decisions?

I firmly believe that you are your own best financial advisor. However, I know that some people don't want to make financial decisions without getting assistance. Perhaps you're busy, or you simply can't stand making money decisions.

You need to recognize that you have a lot at stake when you hire a financial advisor. Besides the cost of his services, which generally don't come cheap, you're placing a lot of trust in his recommendations. The more you know, the better the advisor you end up working with, and the fewer services you need to buy.

The following questions will help you get to the core of an advisor's competence and professional integrity. Get answers to these questions *before* you decide to hire a financial advisor.

What percentage of your income comes from clients' fees versus commissions from the products that you sell?

Asking this question first may save you the trouble and time of asking the next nine questions. The right answer is "100 percent of my income comes from fees paid by clients." Anything less than 100 percent means that the person you're speaking to is a salesperson with a vested interest in recommending certain strategies and products.

Sadly, more than a few financial advisors don't tell the truth. In an undercover investigation done by *Money* magazine, nearly one-third of advisors who claimed that they were fee-only turned out to be brokers who also sold investment and insurance products on a commission basis.

How can you ferret these people out? All advisors who provide investment advice must register with the U.S. Securities and Exchange Commission (SEC). They must file Form ADV, otherwise known as the Uniform Application for Investment Advisor Registration. This lengthy document asks for specific information from investment advisors, such as

- A breakdown of where their income comes from
- Relationships and affiliations with other companies
- Education and employment history
- The types of securities the advisory firm recommends
- The advisor's fee schedule

In short, Form ADV provides — in black and white — answers to all the previous questions. With a sales pitch over the phone or marketing materials sent in the mail, a planner is much more likely to gloss over or avoid certain issues. Although some advisors fib on Form ADV, most advisors are likely to be more truthful on this form than they are in their own marketing.

You can ask the advisor to send you a copy of Form ADV. You can also find out whether the advisor is registered and whether he or she has a track record of problems by calling the U.S. Securities and Exchange Commission (SEC) at 800-732-0330, or by visiting its Web site at www.sec.gov. You can also contact the department in your state that oversees investment advisors (nearly all states have one).

What percentage of fees paid by your clients is for ongoing money management versus hourly financial planning?

The answer to how the advisor is paid provides clues to whether he has an agenda to convince you to hire him to manage your money. If you want objective and specific financial planning recommendations, give preference to advisors who derive their income from hourly fees. Many counselors and advisors call themselves "fee-based," which usually means that they make their living managing money for a percentage.

If you want a money manager, you can hire the best quite inexpensively through a mutual fund. Or, if you have substantial assets, you can hire an established money manager (refer to Chapter 9).

What is your hourly fee?

The rates for financial advisors vary all over the map (as they do with legal and tax advisors). I've seen and heard of fees that range from as low as $50 per hour all the way up to several hundred dollars per hour. If you shop around, you can find terrific planners who charge around $100 to $150 per hour and work faster than a snail's pace.

Because good planners spend a reasonable portion of their time researching and running their business, don't assume that they're getting rich at your expense by charging you around $100 to $150 per hour. Running a business is costly, but you shouldn't pay hundreds of dollars per hour unless you're wealthy and you want an advisor who works only with people like you. You also need to be aware that a number of planners who manage money or sell products charge very high hourly rates because they don't really want to work with people on an hourly-fee basis.

Do you also perform tax or legal services?

Be wary of someone who claims to be an expert beyond one area. The tax, legal, and financial fields are vast in and of themselves, and they're difficult for even the best and brightest advisor to cover simultaneously.

One exception is the accountant who also performs some basic financial planning by the hour. Likewise, a good financial advisor should have a good grounding in the basic tax and legal issues that relate to your personal finances. Large firms may have specialists available in different areas.

What work and educational experience qualifies you to be a financial planner?

This question doesn't have one right answer. Ideally, a planner should have experience in the business or financial services field. Some say to look for planners with at least five or ten years of experience. I've always wondered how planners earn a living their first five or ten years if folks won't hire them until they reach these benchmarks! A good planner should also be good with numbers, speak in plain English, and have good interpersonal skills.

Education is sort of like food. Too little leaves you hungry. Too much can leave you feeling stuffed and uncomfortable. And a small amount of high quality is better than a lot of low quality.

As I discuss earlier in this chapter, don't place too much value in the CFP (certified financial planner) degree. Most advisors with this "credential," which can be earned by taking a home-study course, sell investments.

Because investment decisions are a critical part of financial planning, take note of the fact that the most-common designations of educational training among professional money managers are MBA (master of business administration) and CFA (chartered financial analyst). And some tax advisors who work on an hourly basis have the Personal Financial Specialist credential.

Have you ever sold limited partnerships? Options? Futures? Commodities?

The correct answers here are *no, no, no,* and *no.* If you don't know what these disasters are, refer to Chapter 8. You also need to be wary of any financial advisor who used to deal in these areas but now claims to have seen the light and reformed his ways.

Professionals with poor judgment may not repeat the same mistakes, but they're more likely to make some new ones at your expense. My experience is that even advisors who have been "reformed" are unlikely to be working by the hour. Most of them either work on commission or want to manage your money for a hefty fee.

Do you carry liability (errors and omissions) insurance?

Some counselors may be surprised by this question or think that you're a problem customer looking for a lawsuit. On the other hand, accidents happen; that's why insurance exists. So if the planner doesn't have liability insurance, she missed one of the fundamental concepts of planning: Insure against risk. Don't make the same mistake by hiring her.

You wouldn't (and shouldn't) let contractors into your home to do work without knowing that they have insurance to cover any mistakes they make. Likewise, you should insist on hiring a planner who carries protection in case she makes a major mistake for which she is liable. Make sure that she carries enough coverage given what she is helping you with.

Can you provide references from clients with needs similar to mine?

Take the time to talk to other people who have used the planner. Ask what the planner did for them, and find out what the advisor's greatest strengths and weaknesses are. You can learn a bit about the planner's track record and style. And because you want to have as productive a relationship as possible with your planner, the more you find out about him, the easier it will be for you to hit the ground running if you hire him.

Some financial advisors offer a "free" introductory consultation. If an advisor offers a free consultation to allow you to check him out, and it makes you feel more comfortable about hiring him, fair enough. But be careful: Most free consultations end up being a big sales pitch for certain products or services the advisor offers.

The fact that a planner doesn't offer a free consultation may be a good sign. Counselors who are busy and who work strictly by the hour can't afford to burn an hour of their time for an in-person free session. They also need to be careful of folks seeking free advice. Such advisors usually are willing to spend some time on the phone answering background questions. They should also be able to send background materials by mail and provide references.

Will you provide specific strategies and product recommendations that I can implement on my own if I choose?

This is an important question. Some advisors may indicate that you can hire them by the hour. But then they provide only generic advice without specifics. Some planners even *double dip* — they charge an hourly fee initially to make you feel like you're not working with a salesperson, and they try selling commission-based products. Also be aware of advisors who say that you can choose to implement their recommendations on your own and then recommend financial products that carry commissions.

How is implementation handled?

Ideally, you should find an advisor who lets you choose whether you want to hire him to help with implementation after the recommendations have been presented to you. If you know that you're going to follow through on the advice, and you can do so without further discussions and questions, don't hire the planner to help you implement his recommendations.

On the other hand, if you hire the counselor because you lack the time, desire, and/or expertise to manage your financial life in the first place, building implementation into the planning work makes good sense.

Chapter 18

Computer Money Management

• •

In This Chapter

▶ Evaluating the different types of software and Web sites

▶ Performing financial tasks with your computer

• •

*S*oon, everybody is going to own a computer, and every business is going to have a Web site. So shouldn't you just join up with everyone else in the cyberuniverse?

The short answer is *no*. I know plenty of people who either don't own a computer or use one sparingly and still do an excellent job managing their money.

Although a computer may be able to assist you with your personal finances, it simply represents one of many tools. Computers are best for performing routine tasks faster (such as processing lots of bills or performing many calculations) and to aid you with research.

Surveying Software and Web Sites

You can access two major repositories of personal finance information through your computer. Although the lines are sometimes a bit blurry between these two categories, they're roughly defined as software and the Internet:

> ✔ *Software* refers to computer programs that are either packaged in a box or CD-ROM case or available to be downloaded online. Most of the mass-marketed financial software packages sell for under $100. If you've ever used a word-processing program such as Word or WordPerfect, or a spreadsheet program such as Excel, then you've used software.

✔ *The Internet* is a vast ocean of information that you can generally access via a modem, cable modem, or DSL (Digital Subscriber Line). These devices allow your computer to talk with other computers. To access the Internet, you need a Web browser, which you can obtain through your Internet service provider (ISP). Most of the financial stuff on the Internet is supplied by companies marketing their wares and, hence, is available for free. Some sites sell their content for a fee.

Adding up financial software benefits

Although the number of personal-finance software packages and Web sites is large and growing, quality is having a hard time keeping up, especially among the free Internet sites. The best software can

✔ Guide you to better organization and management of your personal finances

✔ Help you complete mundane tasks or complex calculations more quickly and easily, and provide basic advice in unfamiliar territory

✔ Make you feel in control of your life

Mediocre and bad software, on the other hand, can make you feel stupid or, at the very least, make you want to tear your hair out. Lousy packages usually end up in the software graveyard.

Having reviewed many of the packages available, I can assure you that if you are having a hard time with some of the programs out there (and sometimes even with the more useful programs), you are not at fault. Too many packages assume that you already know things such as your tax rate, your mortgage options, and the difference between stock and bond mutual funds. Much of what's out there is too technically oriented and isn't user-friendly. Some of it is even flawed in its financial accuracy.

A good software package, like a good tax or financial advisor, should help you better manage your finances. It should simply and concisely explain financial terminology, and it should help you make decisions by offering choices and recommendations, allowing you to "play" with alternatives before following a particular course of action.

With increasing regularity, financial software packages are being designed to perform more than one task or to address more than one area of personal finances. But remember that no software package covers the whole range of issues in your financial life. Later in this chapter, I recommend some of my favorite financial software.

Treading carefully on the Web

"Go surfing!"

"Cool!"

No, you're not eavesdropping on a beach conversation in southern California. To hear promoters of companies with Web sites on the globe's largest computer network (the Internet) talk, you may think that the Internet is not only a hip place to be but *The Place to Be.*

Like the information you receive from any medium, you have to sift out the good from the bad. If you blindly navigate the Internet, and you naively think that everything out there is useful "information," "research," or "objective advice," you're going to be in for a rude awakening.

Most personal-finance sites on the Internet are free, which — guess what — means that these sites are basically advertising or are dominated and driven by advertising. If you're looking for written material by unbiased experts or writers — well — you can find some on the Web, but you'll find far more biased and uninformed stuff.

Consider the source

A report on the Internet published by a leading investment-banking firm provides a list of the "coolest finance" sites. On the list is the Web site of a major bank. Because it's been a long time since I was in junior high school, I'm not quite sure what "cool" means anymore. If cool can be used to describe a well-organized and graphically pleasing Web site, then I guess I can say that the bank's site is cool.

However, if you're looking for sound information and advice, then the bank's site is decidedly "uncool." It steers you in a financial direction that benefits (not surprisingly) the bank and not you. For example, in the real-estate section, users are asked to plug in their gross monthly income and down payment. The information is then used to spit out the supposed amount that users can "afford" to spend on a home. No mention is given to the other financial goals and concerns — such as saving for retirement — that affect one's ability to spend a particular amount of money on a home.

Consider this advice in the lending area of the site: "Maybe you *can* have it now. When you don't have the cash on hand for important purchases, we can help you borrow what you need. From a new car, to that vacation you've been longing for, to new kitchen appliances, you can make these dreams real now." Click on a button at the bottom of this screen — and presto, you're on your way to racking up credit-card and auto debt. Why bother practicing delayed gratification, living within your means, or buying something used if getting a loan is "easy" and comes with "special privileges"?

Watch out for "sponsored" content

"Sponsored" content, a euphemism for advertising under the guise of editorial content, is another problem to watch out for on Web sites. You may find a disclaimer or note, which is often buried in small print in an obscure part of the Web site, saying that an article is sponsored by (in other words, paid advertising by) the "author."

For example, one mutual-fund site states that its "primary purpose is to provide viewers with an independent guide that contains information and articles they can't get anywhere else." The "content" of the site suggests otherwise. In the "Expert's Corner" section of the site, material is reprinted from a newsletter that advocates frequent trading in and out of mutual funds to time market moves. Turns out that the article is "sponsored by the featured expert": In other words, it's a paid advertisement. (The track record of the newsletter's past recommendations, which isn't discussed on the site, is poor.)

Steer clear of biased financial-planning advice

I also suggest skipping the financial-planning advice offered by financial service companies with financial products to sell. Such companies can't take the necessary objective, holistic view required to render useful advice.

For example, on one major mutual-fund company's Web site, you find a good deal of material on the company's mutual funds. The site's college-planning advice is off the mark because it urges parents to put money in a custodial account in the child's name. Ignored is the fact that this will undermine your child's ability to qualify for financial aid (see Chapter 12), and that you're likely better off funding your employer's retirement plan. If you did that, though, you couldn't set up a college savings-plan account at the fund company, which this area of the site prods you to do.

Shun short-term thinking

Many financial Web sites provide real-time stock quotes as a hook to some site that is cluttered with advertising. My experience working with individual investors is that the more short term they think, the worse they do. And checking your portfolio during the trading day certainly promotes short-term thinking.

Also, beware of tips offered around the electronic water cooler — message boards. As in the real world, chatting with strangers and exchanging ideas is sometimes fine. However, if you don't know the identity and competence of message-board posters or chat-room participants, why would you follow their financial advice or stock tips? Getting ideas from various sources is okay, but educate yourself and do your homework before making personal financial decisions.

If you want to best manage your personal finances and find out more, remember that the old expression "You get what you pay for" contains a grain of truth. Free information on the Internet, especially information provided by companies in the financial-services industry, is largely self-serving. Stick with information providers who have proven themselves offline or who don't have anything to sell except objective information and advice.

Accomplishing Computer Money Tasks

In the remainder of this chapter, I detail important personal financial tasks that your computer can help you accomplish. I also provide my recommendations for the best software and Web sites to help you accomplish these chores.

Paying your bills and tracking your money

Checkbook software automates the process of paying your bills. When you have to make your monthly payment to the phone company, for example, your monthly check, already made payable to the phone company, pops up on-screen at your command. All you have to do is fill in the new amount that you have to pay and print your check on your computer's printer. (As I discuss later in this section, you also can pay your bills electronically, completely eliminating the process of writing and mailing in checks.)

Checkbook programs can track your check writing and prepare reports that detail your spending by category — so that you can get a handle on where the fat is in your budget. One drawback of using these programs to track your spending is that it only captures what is entered. So the amount and spending category of your individual credit-card and cash purchases, which for most people are substantial, are omitted unless you enter such data (or get a credit card from the software company, which allows you to download your credit-card transactions via your computer). For a complete discussion on how to track your spending, see Chapter 3.

Quicken and Microsoft's Money are good programs that I've reviewed in this category. In addition to offering the printed checks and electronic bill-payment features, both of these packages are financial organizers. The programs allow you to list your investments and other assets, along with your loans and other financial liabilities.

In addition to the significant investment of time necessary to figure out how to use the software program, another drawback is cost — computer checks are pricey. If you order checks directly from the software manufacturers (order forms come with your software), expect to pay about $75 for 500 checks. You can beat those prices by ordering from other companies. PC Checks and Supplies (www.pcchecks.com), for example, sells 500 checks for $43.

You can avoid dealing with paper checks — written or printed — by signing up for *online bill payment*. With such services, you save on stamps and envelopes, and the cost of the service may be comparable to what you're spending on those supplies. Such services are becoming available, to anyone with a checking account, through an increasing number of banks, credit unions, and brokerage firms, as well as through the checkbook programs. An intermediary company that receives your electronic instructions and pays the bill for you enacts the service. No more stamp licking and envelope stuffing. You can even set up regularly recurring bills to be paid automatically.

You don't need a checkbook program to pay your bills online. Simply sign up through a financial institution offering the service. CheckFree's Web site (www.checkfree.com) can direct you to firms that offer its bill-paying service. Because most online bill-payment services charge a minimum monthly fee, you can find cheaper ways to avoid check writing and stamp licking. For example, some businesses that you must pay monthly allow you to establish a monthly electronic payment service directly with them.

Online bill paying should not be confused with *online banking,* which is a direct, two-way electronic avenue between you and your particular bank. You can make transfers online, get up-to-date check-clearing information, and download your current balance and account statement. This service eliminates the need to enter such transactions as ATM withdrawals into your checkbook program, makes reconciling your account a snap, and is offered by some banks for free.

Planning for retirement

Good retirement-planning software and online tools can help you plan for retirement by crunching the numbers for you. But they can also teach you how particular changes — such as your investment returns, rate of inflation, or your savings rate — can affect when, and in what style, you can retire. The biggest time-savings aspect of retirement-planning software and Web sites is that they let you more quickly play with and see the consequences of changing the assumptions.

Tracking your investment returns often isn't worth the headache

Accurately tracking the return on your investments can be an extremely complicated, tedious, and time-consuming task — exactly the type of chore that computers were designed to relieve us of. You'd think that a number of excellent investment-tracking software packages would be on the market today, but I feel that the available packages are too often complicated, tedious, and time-consuming. Many programs aren't any more efficient than the old-fashioned method of pencil, paper, and a calculator.

My big gripe with the investment-tracking software programs is that most of them don't allow you to determine your investment's total return, and the programs that do allow you to calculate total return require a lot of time to get to that point. Your effective or *internal rate of return* (IRR), which compares your original amounts invested to the current market value, is the best way to measure the success of your investments over time.

Most of the other packages calculate your *cost basis,* which is your original investment plus reinvested dividends and capital gains, for which you would have already paid taxes in a nonretirement account. When you sell a nonretirement-account investment, you need to know the cost basis for tax purposes (see Chapter 6). Cost-basis reports make your returns look less generous because reinvested distributions increase your original investment and seemingly reduce your returns. I know from direct experience that investors often look at the cost-basis reports — which are sometimes misleadingly named "investment performance" or "investment analysis" — and assume that the reports tell

them their total investment returns. Using software for cost-basis calculations is generally not worthwhile, because most investment companies provide cost-basis information to you upon request or when you sell an investment.

If you want to analyze your historic returns, you need to gather all your old account statements (if you can find them) and enter every investment you made, as well as all reinvestments of dividends, interest, and capital-gains distributions.

For buy-and-hold mutual fund investors, investment-tracking software has limited benefit given the time required to enter your data. Mutual funds and many other published resources tell you what the funds' total return was for the past year, so you don't need to enter every dividend and capital-gain distribution for yourself.

As for calculating the return of your overall portfolio with the old-fashioned method of paper and pencil, simply weight the return of each investment by the portion of your portfolio invested in it. For example, with a simple portfolio equally divided between two investments that returned 10 percent and 0 percent, respectively, your overall portfolio return would be 5 percent.

Investment-tracking software may be more useful for stock traders. In my experience, stock traders don't usually track their overall returns. If they actually used one of these programs, they could at least see how all their trading depresses their returns. (I've never worked with a stock picker who went through this exercise with me and beat the market indexes over the long term.)

Some of the major investment companies I profile in Part III of this book are sources for some high-quality, low-cost retirement planning tools. Here are some good ones to consider:

✔ T. Rowe Price's Web site (www.troweprice.com) has several tools that can help you determine where you stand in terms of reaching a given retirement goal. T. Rowe Price (800-638-5660) also offers some excellent workbooklets for helping you plan for retirement. The company's Retirement Planning Guide is for those who are more than five years from retirement, and the Retirees Readiness Guide is intended for people who are already retired or are within five years of retirement. Expect some marketing of T. Rowe Price's mutual funds in these booklets and software.

✔ Vanguard's Web site (www.vanguard.com) can help with figuring savings goals to reach retirement goals as well as with managing your budget and assets in retirement.

Preparing your taxes

Good, properly used tax-preparation software can save you time and money. The best programs "interview" you to gather the necessary information and select the appropriate forms based on your responses. Of course, you're still the one responsible for locating all the information needed to complete your return. More-experienced taxpayers can bypass the interview and jump directly to the forms they know they need to complete. These programs also help flag overlooked deductions and identify other tax-reducing strategies.

TurboTax and Taxcut are among the better tax-preparation programs I've reviewed.

In addition to the federal tax packages, tax-preparation programs are available for state income taxes, too. Many state tax forms are fairly easy to complete because they're based on information from your federal form. If your state tax forms are based on your federal form, you may want to just skip buying the state income-tax preparation packages and prepare your state return by hand.

If you're mainly looking for tax forms, you can get them at no charge in tax-preparation books or through the IRS Web site (www.irs.gov).

Researching investments

Rather than schlepping off to the library and fighting over the favorite investing reference manuals, ponying up hundreds of dollars to buy print versions for your own use, or slogging through voice-mail hell when you call government agencies, you can access a variety of materials with your computer. You can also often pay for just what you need:

✔ **FreeEdgar.com.** This Web site supplies information from Securities and Exchange Commission filings and other sources on public companies. FreeEdgar is a useful place to start if you already have particular stocks in mind and want to find out more about the companies' businesses and financials. If you want to access more than the one free report per day allowed by this service, you must upgrade to Edgar Online Premium for $14.95 per month. To sidestep these charges, you can get unlimited free access to SEC documents directly via the SEC's Web site (www.sec.gov), but be aware that navigating this site takes patience. All public corporations, as well as mutual funds, file with the agency.

✔ **Morningstar.com.** This site provides access to Morningstar's individual stock and mutual fund reports. The reports are free, but they're watered-down versions of the company's comprehensive software and paper products. If you want to buy Morningstar's unabridged fund reports online, you can do so for a fee.

✔ **Vanguard.com.** Although I'm leery of financial service company "educational" materials because of bias and self-serving advice, some companies do a worthy job on these materials. The investor-friendly, penny-pinching Vanguard Group of mutual funds has an online university on its Web site, where investors can learn the basics of fund investing. Additionally, investors in Vanguard's funds can access up-to-date personal account information through the site.

Trading online

If you do your investing homework, trading securities online may save you money and perhaps some time. For years, discount brokers (which I discuss in Chapter 7) were heralded as the low-cost source for trading. Now, online brokers such as Brown & Company (800-822-2021; www.brownco.com) and TD Waterhouse (800-934-4448; www.tdwaterhouse.com) have set a new lower-cost standard. The major mutual fund companies, such as T. Rowe Price and Vanguard, also offer competitive online services.

A number of the newer discount brokers have built their securities brokerage business around online trading. By eliminating the overhead of branch offices, and by accepting and processing trades by computer, online brokers keep their costs and brokerage charges to a minimum. Cut-rate electronic brokerage firms are for people who want to direct their own financial affairs and don't want or need to work with a personal broker. However, some of these brokers have limited products and services. For example, some don't offer many of the best mutual funds. And, my own experience with reaching live people at some online brokers has been trying — I've had to wait on hold for more than ten minutes before a customer service representative answered the call.

While online trading may save you on transaction costs, it can also encourage you to trade more than you should, resulting in higher total trading costs, lower investment returns, and higher income tax bills. Following investments on a daily basis encourages you to think short term. Remember that the best investments are bought and held for the long haul (see Part III for more information).

Reading and searching periodicals

Many business and financial publications are going online to offer investors news and financial market data. *The Wall Street Journal* offers an online personalized edition of the paper (`http://update.wsj.com`). You can tailor the content to meet your specific needs. The cost is $79 per year ($39 if you're already a *Journal* subscriber).

Leading business publications such as *Forbes* (`www.forbes.com`) and *BusinessWeek* (`www.businessweek.com`) put their magazines' content on the Internet, allowing you to conduct searches for articles on specific topics that interest you. Be careful, though, to take what you read and hear in the mass media with many grains of salt (see Chapter 19). Much of the content revolves around tweaking people's anxieties and dwelling on the latest crises and fads.

Buying life insurance

If loved ones are financially dependent on you, you probably know that you need some life insurance. But, add together the dread of life-insurance salespeople and a fear of death and you have a recipe for procrastination. While your computer can't stave off the grim reaper, it can help you find a quality, low-cost policy that can be more than 80 percent less costly than the most expensive options, without having to deal with high-pressure sales tactics.

The best way to shop for term life insurance online is through one of the quotation services that I discuss in Chapter 15. At each of these sites, you fill in your date of birth, whether you smoke, how much coverage you'd like, and for how long you'd like to lock in the initial premium. When you're done filling in this information, a new Web page pops up with a list of low-cost quotes (based on assumed good health) from highly rated (for financial stability) insurance companies.

Invariably, the quotes are ranked by how cheap they are. While cost is certainly an important factor, many of these services don't do as good a job explaining the other important factors to consider when doing your comparison shopping. For example, the projected and maximum rates after the initial term has expired are sometimes not covered. Be sure to ask about these other future rates before you agree to a specific policy.

If you decide to buy a policy from one of the online agencies, you can fill out an online application form. The quotation agency will then mail you a detailed description of the policy and insurer, and your completed application. In addition to having to deal with snail mail, you're also going to have to deal with a *medical technician,* who will drop by your home to check on your health status . . . at least until some computer genius figures out a way for you to give a blood and urine sample online!

Preparing legal documents

Just as you can prepare a tax return with the advice of a software program, you can also prepare common legal documents. This type of software may save you from the often difficult task of finding a competent and affordable attorney.

Using legal software is generally preferable to using fill-in-the-blank documents. Software has the built-in virtues of directing and limiting your choices and preventing you from making common mistakes. Quality software also incorporates the knowledge and insights of the legal eagles who developed the software. And it can save you money.

If your situation isn't unusual, legal software may work well for you. As to the legality of documents that you create with legal software, remember that a will, for example, is made legal and valid by your witnesses; the fact that an attorney prepares the document is *not* what makes it legal.

An excellent package for preparing your own will is WillMaker, which is published by Nolo Press, a name synonymous with high quality and user-friendliness in the legal publishing world. In addition to allowing you to prepare wills, WillMaker can also help you prepare a *living will* and medical power of attorney document (see Chapter 16).

Nolo's Living Trust software allows you to create a living trust that serves to keep property out of probate in the event of your death (see Chapter 16). Like wills, living trusts are fairly standard legal documents that you can properly create with the guidance of a top-notch software package. The Living Trust package also advises you to seek professional guidance for your situation, if necessary.

Chapter 19

On Air and in Print

In This Chapter

▶ Recognizing the mass media's impact on investors

▶ Deciding whether to tune in or tune out radio and television investing coverage

▶ Surfing safely for investing information on the Internet

▶ Evaluating newspapers and magazines

▶ Finding the best investing books

*Y*ou aren't going to lack for options when it comes to finding radio and television news, Web sites, newspapers, magazines, and books that talk about money and purport to help you get rich. Tuning out poor resources and focusing on the best ones is the real challenge.

Because you probably don't consider yourself a financial expert, more often than not you aren't going to know who to believe and listen to. I help you solve that problem in this chapter.

Observing the Mass Media

For better and for worse, America's mass media has a profound influence on our culture. On the good side, news is widely disseminated these days. So if a product is recalled or a dangerous virus breaks out in your area, you'll probably hear about it, perhaps more than you want to, through the media — or perhaps from tuned-in family members!

The downsides of the mass media are plenty, though.

Alarming or informing us?

Imagine sitting down to watch the evening news and hearing the following stock market report:

> "On Wall Street today, stock prices dropped a bit less than one percent, extending the market's decline of the past week. The reason: There were more people wanting to sell than there were people wanting to buy. For the year, the U.S. market is still up 15 percent, which is well above the historic average annual return of 10 percent."

Now contrast that report with the following report for the same day:

> "Stocks plunged sharply today as the Dow Jones Industrial Average plummeted more than 100 points to close at its lowest level in the past 168 hours. Dell Computer saw its shares get creamed 10 percent, as the company issued a profit warning that third-quarter revenues would take a big hit due to the Taiwan earthquake. Banking stocks got hammered again, and the sector is now off more than 20 percent from its peak this past spring."

While the second news report goes into more detail, it is meant to be more provocative and anxiety-producing. Most of the daily stock market reports I hear in the media sound more like the second report than they do the mundane, calming first report. News producers, in their quest for ratings and advertising dollars, try to be alarming. The more you watch, the more unnerved you get over short-term, especially-negative events.

Teaching what kind of values?

Daily doses of American mass media, including all the advertising that comes with it, essentially communicate the following messages to us:

- ✔ Your worth as a person is directly related to your physical appearance (including the quality of clothing and jewelry you wear) and your material possessions — cars, homes, electronics, and other gadgets.
- ✔ The more money you make, the more "successful" you clearly are.
- ✔ The more famous you are (especially movie and sports stars), the more you're worth listening to and admiring.
- ✔ Don't bother concerning yourself with the consequences of your behavior before engaging in negative behavior.
- ✔ Delaying gratification and making sacrifices is for boring losers.

Some of the programming in the mass media is so bad that former U.S. Secretary of Education William J. Bennett teamed up with Senator Joseph Lieberman to create the "Silver Sewer Award." Each year, this honor is bestowed upon a deserving media organization in recognition of its outrageous contribution to the degradation and coarsening of our culture, and its unswerving dedication to the pursuit of profit above principle.

 Continually inundating yourself with poor messages can cause you to behave in a way that undermines your long-term happiness and financial success. Don't support (by watching, listening, or reading) forms of media that don't reflect your values and morals.

Worshipping prognosticating pundits

Quoting and interviewing experts is perhaps the only thing that the media loves more than hyping short-term news events. What's the economy going to do next quarter? What's stock XYZ going to do next month? What's the stock market going to do in the next hour? No, I'm not kidding about that last one — the stock market cable channel CNBC regularly interviews floor traders from the New York Stock Exchange late in the trading day to get their opinions about what the market will do in the last hour before closing!

 Prognosticating pundits keep many people tuned in because their advice is constantly changing (and therefore entertaining and anxiety producing), and they lead investors to believe that investments can be maneuvered in advance to outfox future financial market moves. Common sense suggests, though, that no one has a working crystal ball, and if they did, they certainly wouldn't share such insights with the mass media for free. (For more on experts who purport to predict the future, see Chapter 7.)

Rating Radio and Television Financial Programs

Over the years, money issues have received increased coverage through the major media of television and radio. Is managing your money much more complicated than it was a generation ago? Not really — while we do have more financial products and services to choose from these days, the best of these resources simplify rather than complicate your financial life. For example, while there are far more mutual funds to choose from today than in decades past, many of the better fund companies offer funds of funds (see Chapter 9) to simplify the process of building a portfolio of mutual funds.

Some topics gain more coverage in radio and television because they help draw more advertising dollars (which follow what people are watching). When you click on the radio or television, you don't pay a fee to tune in to a particular channel (with pay cable channels being an exception). Advertising doesn't necessarily prevent a medium from delivering coverage that is objective and in your best interest, but it sure doesn't help foster this type of coverage either.

For example, can you imagine a financial radio or television correspondent saying:

> "We've decided to stop providing financial market updates every five minutes because we've found it causes some investors to become addicted to tracking the short-term movements in the markets and to lose sight of the bigger picture. We don't want to encourage people to make knee-jerk reactions to short-term events."

Sound-bite-itis is another problem with both of these media. Producers and network executives believe that if you go into too much detail, viewers and listeners will change the channel.

Now, radio and television are hardly the only types of media that offer poor advice and cause investor myopia. The Internet can be even worse, for example. And I've read plenty of lousy money books over the years.

Learning to Surf the Internet

Yes, the Internet is changing the world, but certainly not always for the better and not always in such a big way. Consider the way we shop. Okay, you can buy things online that you couldn't in the past. Big deal — what's the difference between buying something by calling a toll-free number or doing mail order (which many of us did for years before the Internet got commercialized), and buying something by clicking your computer mouse? Purchasing things online simply broadens the avenues through which you can spend money. I see a big downside here: Overspending is easier to do when you surf the Internet a lot.

Some of the best Web sites allow you to more efficiently access information that may help you make important investing decisions. However, this doesn't mean that your computer allows you to compete at the same level as a professional money manager. No, the playing field isn't level. The best pros work at their craft full time and have far more expertise and experience than the rest of us. Some nonprofessionals have been fooled into believing that investing online makes them better investors. My experience has been that people who spend time online every day dealing with investments tend to trade and react more to short-term events and have a harder time keeping the bigger picture and their long-term goals and needs in focus.

If you know where to look, you can more easily access some types of information. However, you often find a lot of garbage online — just as you do on other advertiser-dominated media like television and radio. In Chapter 18, I explain how to safely navigate online to find the best of what's out there.

Navigating Newspapers and Magazines

Compared with radio and television, print publications generally offer lengthier discussions of topics. And, in the more financially focused publications, the editors who work on articles generally have more background in the topics they write about.

Even within the better publications, I find a wide variety of quality, so don't instantly believe what you read, even if you read a piece in a publication you like. Here's how to get the most from financial periodicals:

✔ **Read some back issues.** Go to your local library (or perhaps visit the publication's Web site) and read some issues that are at least one to two years old. While reading old issues may seem silly and pointless, it can actually be enlightening. By reviewing a number of past issues in one sitting, you can begin to get a flavor for a publication's style, priorities, and philosophies. You can also generally get old content for free.

✔ **Look for solid information and perspective.** Headlines reveal a lot about how a publication perceives its role. Publications with cover stories such as "10 hot stocks to buy now!" and "Funds that will double your money in the next three years!" are probably best avoided. Look for articles that seek to educate with accuracy, not predict.

✔ **Note bylines.** As you read a given publication over time, you should begin to make note of the different writers. After you get to know who the better writers are, you can skip over the ones you don't care for and spend your limited free time reading the best.

✔ **Don't react.** Here's a common example of how not to use information and advice you glean from publications. I had a client who had some cash he wanted to invest. He would read an article about investing in real estate investment trusts and then go out the next week and buy several of them. Then he'd see a mention of some technology stock funds and invest in some of those. Eventually his portfolio was a mess of investments that reflected the history of what he had read rather than an orchestrated, well-thought-out investment portfolio.

Betting on Books

Reading a good book is one of my favorite ways to get a crash course on a given financial topic. As with the other types of resources I discuss in this chapter, you definitely have to choose carefully — there's plenty of mediocrity and garbage out there (see the sidebar "Don't book publishers exercise due diligence?").

Good books can go into depth on a topic in a way that simply isn't possible with other resources. Books also aren't cluttered with advertising and the conflicts inherent therein.

Don't book publishers exercise due diligence?

Book publishers are businesses first. And, like most businesses, their business practices vary. Some have a reputation for care and quality; some just want to push a product out the door with maximum hype and minimum effort.

For instance, you may think that book publishers check out an author before they sign him or her to write an entire book. Well, you may be surprised to find out that some publishers don't do their homework.

What most publishers care about first is how marketable an author is. Some authors are marketable because of their well-earned reputation for sound advice. Others are marketable because of stellar promotional campaigns built on smoke and mirrors. Still others may have the potential for marketability if a publisher is willing to take a chance on them, but most publishers like a sure thing.

Even more troubling is that few publishers require advice guides to be technically reviewed for accuracy by an expert in the field other than the author, who sometimes is not an expert. You, the reader, are expected to be your own technical reviewer. But do you have the expertise to do that? (Don't worry; this book has been checked for accuracy.)

As an author and financial counselor, I know that financial ideas and strategies can differ considerably. Different is not necessarily wrong. When a technical reviewer looks at my text and tells me that a better way is out there, I take a second look. I may even see things in a new way. If I'm the only expert who sees my book before publication, I'm not going to get this second expert opinion. How do you know whether a book's been technically reviewed? Check the credits page or the author's acknowledgments.

Authors write books for many reasons other than to teach and educate. The most common reason financial book authors write books is to further their own business interests. Taking care of business interests may not always be a bad thing, but it's not the best thing for you when you're trying to educate yourself and better manage your own finances. For example, some investment books are written by investment newsletter sellers. Rather than teach you how to make good investments, the authors make the investment world sound complicated so that you feel the need to subscribe to their ongoing newsletters.

ERIC'S PICKS

Here's a list of some of my favorite financial titles:

- *Dematerializing: Taming the Power of Possessions* by Jane Hammerslough (Perseus)

- *The Ultimate Credit Handbook: How to Cut Your Debt and Have a Lifetime of Great Credit* by Gerri Detweiler (Plume)

- *A Random Walk Down Wall Street* by Burton Malkiel (Norton)

- *Built to Last: Successful Habits of Visionary Companies* by James Collins and Jerry Porras (HarperCollins)

- *Good to Great: Why Some Companies Make the Leap and Others Don't* by James Collins (HarperCollins)

- *Paying for College Without Going Broke* by Kalman A. Chany (Princeton Review)

- *Don't Miss Out: The Ambitious Student's Guide to Financial Aid* by Anna and Robert Leider (Octameron Associates)

- Nolo Press's legal titles

- And, not surprisingly, my *For Dummies* books on Investing, Mutual Funds, Taxes, Home Buying, House Selling, Mortgages, and Small Business, which are all published by Wiley Publishing, Inc.

Part VI
The Part of Tens

The 5th Wave • By Rich Tennant

"...and don't tell me I'm not being frugal enough. I hired a man last week to do nothing but clip coupons!"

In this part . . .

You find some fun and useful chapters that will help you with financial strategies for ten life changes and remind you of ten things more important than money. Why "tens"? Why not?

Chapter 20

Survival Guide for Ten Life Changes

● ●

In This Chapter

▶ Handling the financial challenges that arise during life changes

▶ Minimizing financial worries so you can focus on your life

● ●

Some of life's changes come unexpectedly, like earthquakes. Others you can see coming when they're still far off on the horizon, like a big storm moving in off the ocean. Whether a life change is predictable or not, your ability to navigate successfully through its challenges and adjust quickly to its new circumstances depends largely on your degree of preparedness.

Perhaps you find my comparison of life changes to earthquakes and storms to be a bit negative. After all, some of the changes I discuss in this chapter should be occasions for joy, and here I am comparing them to natural disasters. But understand that what one defines as a "disaster" has everything to do with his or her preparedness. To the person who has stored no emergency rations in his basement, the big snowstorm that traps him in his home can lead to problems. But to the prepared person with plenty of food and water, that same storm may mean a vacation from work and some relaxing days in the midst of a winter wonderland.

Before I discuss critical financial issues for you to deal with before and during major life changes, here are some general tips that apply to all types of life changes:

✔ **Stay in financial shape.** An athlete is best able to withstand physical adversities during competition by training and eating well in advance. Likewise, the sounder your finances are to begin with, the better you'll be able to deal with life changes.

✔ **Changes require change.** Even if your financial house is in order, a major life change — starting a family, buying a home, starting a business, divorcing, retiring — should prompt you to review your personal financial strategies. Why? Because life changes often affect your income, spending, insurance needs, and ability to take financial risk.

✔ **Don't procrastinate.** With a major life change on the horizon, procrastination can be costly. You (and your family) may overspend and accumulate high-cost debts, lack proper insurance coverage, or take other unnecessary risks. Early preparation can save you from these pitfalls.

✔ **Manage stress and your emotions.** Life changes often are accompanied by stress and other emotional upheavals. Don't make knee-jerk decisions during these changes. Take the time to become fully informed and recognize and acknowledge your feelings. Educating yourself is key. You may want to hire experts to help (see Chapter 17). Don't abdicate decisions and responsibilities to advisors — the advisors may not have your best interests at heart or fully appreciate your needs.

Here, then, are the major life changes that you may have to deal with at some point in your life. I wish you more of the good changes than the bad.

Starting Out: Your First Job

If you just graduated from college or some other program, or you're otherwise entering the workforce, your increased income and reduction in educational expenses are probably a welcome relief. You'd think, then, that more young adults would be able to avoid financial trouble and challenges. But they face these challenges largely because of poor financial habits picked up at home or from the world at large. Here's how to get on the path to financial success:

✔ **Don't use consumer credit.** The use and abuse of consumer credit can cause long-term financial pain and hardship. You want furniture, a new television, and lots of fun vacations, but all these things cost money. To get off on the right financial foot, young workers need to shun the habit of making purchases on credit cards that they can't pay for in full when the bill arrives in the mail. Here's the simple solution for overspending and running up outstanding credit card balances: Don't carry a credit card. Cash and checks worked fine for decades before credit cards arrived on the scene. If you need the convenience of making purchases with a piece of plastic instead of with cash or checks, get a debit card (see Chapter 4).

✔ **Get in the habit of saving and investing.** If you hope to someday own a home and cease working full-time, you'll need to save over many years. Ideally, your savings should be directed into retirement accounts that offer tax benefits unless you want to accumulate down-payment money for a home or small-business purchase (see Chapter 2). Thinking about a home purchase or retirement is usually not in the active thought patterns of first-time job seekers. I'm often asked, "At what age should a person start saving?" To me, that's similar to asking at what age you should start brushing your teeth. Well, when you have teeth to brush! So I say you should start saving and investing money from your first paycheck. Try saving 5 percent of every paycheck and then eventually increase your saving to 10 percent of every paycheck. If you're having trouble saving money, track your spending and make cutbacks as needed (refer to Chapters 3 and 5).

✔ **Get insured.** Many people who are starting out are able to rationalize not buying insurance. When you're young and healthy, imagining yourself feeling otherwise is hard. Many twentysomethings give little thought to the potential for health care expenses. But because accidents and unexpected illnesses can strike at any age, forgoing coverage can be financially devastating. Buying disability coverage, which replaces income lost to a long-term disability, in your first full-time job with more-limited benefits is also wise. And as you begin to build your assets, consider making out a will so that your assets go where you want in the event of your death.

✔ **Continue your education.** After you get out in the work force, you (like many other people) may realize how little you learned in formal schooling that can actually be used in the real world and, conversely, how much you need to learn (like personal financial management) that school never taught you. Read, learn, and continue to grow. Continuing education will help you advance in your career and enjoy the world around you.

Changing Jobs or Careers

During your adult life, you'll almost surely change jobs — perhaps as often as several times a decade. I hope that most of the time you'll be changing by your own choice. But let's face it: Job security is not what it used to be. Corporate downsizing has made victims of even the most talented workers.

Always be prepared for a job change. No matter how happy you are in your current job, knowing that your world won't fall apart if you're not working tomorrow will give you an added sense of security and encourage an openness to possibility. Whether you're changing your job by choice or necessity, the following financial maneuvers will help ease the transition:

✔ **Structure your finances to afford an income dip.** Spending less than you earn always makes good financial sense, but if you're coming up to a possible job change, spending less is even more important, particularly if you're entering a new field or starting your own company, and you expect a short-term income dip. Many people view a lifestyle of thriftiness as restrictive, but ultimately those thrifty habits can give you more freedom to do what you want to do. Be sure to keep an emergency reserve fund (refer to Chapter 7).

If you lose your job, batten down the hatches. You normally get little advance warning when you lose your job through no choice of your own. When you get little advance warning, it does not mean, however, that you can't do anything financially. Evaluating and slashing your current level of spending may be necessary. Everything should be fair game, from how much you spend on housing to how often you eat out to where you do your grocery shopping. Avoid at all costs the temptation to maintain your level of spending by accumulating consumer debt.

✔ **Evaluate the total financial picture when relocating.** At some point in your career, you may have the option of relocating. But don't call the moving company until you understand the financial consequences of such a move. You can't simply compare salaries and benefits between the two jobs. You also need to compare the cost of living between the two areas: That includes housing, commuting, state income and property taxes, food, utilities, and all the other major expenditure categories that I discuss in Chapter 3.

✔ **Track your job search expenses for tax purposes.** If you're seeking a new job in your current (or recently current) field of work, your job search expenses may be tax-deductible. Even if you don't get a specific job you desire, you can deduct the expenses related to your search and interviews. Remember, however, that if you're moving into a new career, your job search expenses are not tax-deductible. (See Chapter 6 for details.)

Getting Married

Ready to tie the knot with the one you love? Congratulations — I hope that you'll have a long, healthy, and happy life together. In addition to the emotional and moral commitments that you and your spouse are going to be making to one another, you're probably going to be merging many of your financial decisions and resources. Having identical money personalities may be highly unusual for you and your spouse; after all, opposites often attract. Even if you're largely in agreement about your financial goals and strategies, managing as two is different from managing as one.

✔ **Take a compatibility test.** Many couples never discuss their goals and plans before marriage; failing to do so breaks up way too many of these marriages. Finances are just one of the many issues you need to discuss. Others include expectations for having and raising children, dealing with in-laws, career goals, and so on. Ensuring that you know what you're getting yourself into is a good way to minimize your chances for heartache. Ministers, priests, and rabbis sometimes offer premarital counseling to help bring issues and differences to the surface. Don't let romance blind you to important issues that are vital to the long-term health of your marriage.

✔ **Consider taxes.** Some couples are depressed to find that their joint income tax bill is going to be higher, perhaps significantly higher, after they're married. More than a few couples actually allow their joint tax burdens to influence when and even if they marry. You're more likely to be hit with a higher combined tax bill when married if both you and your spouse each earn above-average incomes and/or are high-income earners. The only way to know what is going to happen to your tax bill is to get out a tax return, plug in the relevant numbers, and see what the IRS is going to do to you after you're married. If you're flexible in terms of the timing of your wedding, and a late-in-the-year wedding will cause you to pay much more in taxes, consider waiting until early the following year.

✔ **Discuss and set joint goals.** After you're married, you and your spouse should set aside time once a year, or every few years, to discuss personal and financial goals for the years ahead. When you talk about where you want to go, you help ensure that you're both rowing your financial boat in the same direction.

✔ **Decide whether to keep finances separate or jointly managed.** Some couples choose to keep separate financial accounts, and others decide to pool their resources. Philosophically, I like the idea of pooling better. After all, marriage is a partnership, and it shouldn't be a *his* versus *hers* affair. In some marriages, however, spouses may choose to keep some money separate, particularly for spending purposes, so that they don't feel the scrutiny of a spouse with different spending preferences. Spouses who have been through divorce may choose to keep the assets they bring into the new marriage separate in order to earmark and protect their money in the event of another divorce. As long as you're jointly accomplishing what you need to financially, some separation of money is okay. But for the health of your marriage, don't hide money from one another, and, if you're the higher-income spouse, don't assume power and control over your joint income.

✔ **Coordinate and maximize employer benefits.** If one or both of you have access to a package of employee benefits through an employer, understand how best to make use of those benefits. Coordinating and using the best that each package has to offer is like giving yourselves a pay raise. For example, if you both have access to health insurance, compare which of you has better benefits. Likewise, one of you may have a better retirement savings plan — one that matches and offers superior investment options. Unless you can afford to save the maximum through both your plans, saving more in the better plan will increase your combined assets. (*Note:* If you're concerned about what will happen if you save more in one of your retirement plans and then you divorce, in most states, the money is considered part of your joint assets to be divided equally.)

✔ **Discuss life and disability insurance needs.** If you and your spouse can make do without each other's income, you may not need any income-protecting insurance. However, if, like many husbands and wives, you both depend on each other's incomes, or if one of you depends fully or partly on the other's income, you may each need long-term disability and term life insurance policies (refer to Chapter 15).

✔ **Update your wills.** When you marry, you should update your wills. If you haven't gotten around to making a will, having a will is potentially more valuable when you're married, especially if you want to leave money to others in addition to your spouse, or if you have children for whom you need to name a guardian. See Chapter 15 for more on wills.

✔ **Reconsider beneficiaries on investment and life insurance.** With retirement accounts and life insurance policies, you name beneficiaries to whom the money or value in those accounts will go in the event of your passing. When you marry, you'll probably want to rethink your beneficiaries.

Buying a Home

Most Americans eventually buy a home. You don't need to own a home to be a financial success, but home ownership certainly offers financial rewards. Over the course of your adult life, the real estate that you own is likely going to appreciate in value. Additionally, you're going to pay off your mortgage someday, which will greatly reduce your housing costs. As a renter, on the other hand, your full housing costs are going to increase over time with inflation.

If you're thinking about buying a home:

✔ **Get your overall finances in order.** Before buying, you need to analyze your current budget, your ability to afford debt, and your future financial goals. Make sure that your expected housing expenses still allow you to save properly for retirement and other long- or short-term objectives. Don't buy a home based on what lenders are willing to lend. Read and digest the relevant portions of this book so that you can get your financial house in order before you buy.

✔ **Determine if now's the time.** Buying a house when you don't see yourself staying put three to five years rarely makes financial sense, especially if you're a first-time home buyer. Buying and selling a home gobbles up a good deal of money in transaction costs — you'll be lucky to recoup all those costs even within a five-year period. Also, if your income is likely to drop or you have other pressing goals, such as starting a business, you may want to wait to buy.

To find out more about buying a home, be sure to read Chapter 13.

Having Children

If you think that being a responsible adult, holding down a job, paying your bills on time, and preparing for your financial future are tough, wait 'til you add kids to the equation. Most parents find that, with kids in the family, the already precious commodities of free time and money become even more precious — sometimes even extinct. The more efficiently you discover how to manage your time and money, the better able you'll be to have a sane, happy, and financially successful life as a parent.

Budgeting for life changes

One thing is certain about life: It changes — marriage, buying a home, family expansion, starting a business, divorce, retirement, or the death of a spouse. Although some life events bring joy and others sorrow, all bring financial change. If you don't manage this change, it may end up managing and ruling you.

I've seen the best of savers turn into deficit financiers due to the financial upheaval and shock waves from a major life event — even events that were anticipated. You should budget ahead for life changes.

For example, if you want to take the entrepreneurial plunge and leave your full-time job, you need to determine whether you can afford to do that, and what impact the change in your expenses and income is going to have on your ability to save money. Wannabe parents, likewise, need to consider how increased expenses and a likely reduction in income are going to affect their monthly budget.

Going through this budgeting exercise is a great way to estimate what impact a child or other significant life change will have on your financial situation. I advised some nervous expectant parents to go through this exercise because they were wondering what financial impact having a baby would have on their household finances. Their findings: Given their expected spending, they would go from saving 12 percent of their annual incomes to spending 5 percent more than they earned. But the lower-income spouse was also surprised to see that, by working half-time rather than full-time, their net savings would actually increase thanks largely to lower taxes, child-care, and work-related expenses.

In Chapter 3, I provide suggested categories for tallying your expenses — such as housing, clothing, auto, cable TV, furniture, insurance, telephone, utilities, education, and so on. You can adjust and create new spending and income categories to match your personal financial situation.

As you plan for your next life change, remember the limitations of quantitative analysis. It can't factor in the nonfinancial considerations such as how you feel about working more or less because of a life change. Crunching numbers may also mistakenly give you the illusion of control. Those expectant parents that I told you about earlier found out that they were getting three new additions to their family and not just one!

Here are some key things to recognize and do both before and after you begin your family:

✔ **Set your priorities: You can't do it all and have it all.** As with many other financial decisions, starting or expanding a family requires you to plan ahead. Set your priorities and structure your finances and living situation accordingly. Is having a bigger home in a particular community important, or would you rather feel less pressure to work hard, giving you more time to spend with your family? Keep in mind that a less hectic work life not only gives you more free time but it also often reduces your cost of living by decreasing meals out, dry-cleaning costs, day-care expenses, and so on.

✔ **Take a hard look at your budget.** If you had a hard time living within your means before having children, then you definitely should take an honest look at how your income and spending will change after your family grows. In addition to diaper changes and less sleep at night, having children requires you to increase your spending. At a minimum, expenditures for food and clothing will increase. But you're also likely to spend more on housing, insurance, day care, and education. On top of that, if you want to play an active role in raising your children, working at a full-time job isn't going to be possible. So while you consider the added expenses, you may also need to factor in a decrease in income.

No simple rules exist for estimating how children will affect your household's income and expenses. On the income side, figure out how much you want to cut back on work. On the expense side, government statistics show that the average household with school-age children spends about 20 percent more than those without children. Going through your budget category by category and estimating how kids will change your spending is a more scientific approach. (You can use the worksheets in Chapter 3).

✔ **Boost insurance coverage *before* getting pregnant.** Before you try to have a baby, make sure that your health insurance plan offers maternity benefits. (Ask about waiting periods that may exclude coverage for a pregnancy within the first year or so of the insurance.) With disability insurance, pregnancy is considered a preexisting condition, so women should secure this coverage before getting pregnant. And most families-to-be should buy life insurance. Buying life insurance *after* the bundle of joy comes home from the hospital is a risky proposition — if one of the parents develops a health problem, he or she may be denied coverage. You should also consider buying life insurance for a stay-at-home parent. Even though the stay-at-home parent is not bringing in income, if he or she were to pass away, hiring assistance could cripple the family budget.

✔ **Check maternity leave with your employers.** Many of the larger employers offer some maternity leave for women and, in rare but thankfully increasing cases, for men. Some employers offer paid leaves while others may offer unpaid leaves. Understand the options and the financial ramifications before you consider the leave and, ideally, before you get pregnant.

✔ **Update your will.** If you have a will, you'll need to update it. If you don't have a will, make one now. With children in the picture, you need to name a guardian who will be responsible for raising your children should you and your spouse both pass away. Although choosing a guardian is a daunting decision, the thought of letting the courts decide who should raise your children can be even more frightful.

✔ **Enroll the baby in your health plan.** After your baby is welcomed into this world, enroll him or her in your health insurance plan. Most insurers give you about a month or so to enroll. New parents tend to forget to do things amidst the whirlwind of time-consuming parenting responsibilities. You should also get Junior a Social Security number, which comes in handy for many occasions — especially when filing your next income tax return. Without a Social Security number, you can't claim your child as a dependent (and get that tax break).

✔ **Understand child-care tax benefits.** For every one of your children with an official Social Security number, you get a $3,000 deduction on your income taxes (tax year 2002). So if you're in the 25 percent federal tax bracket, each child saves you $750 in federal taxes. On top of that, you may be eligible for a $1,000 tax credit for each child under the age of 17. That should certainly motivate you to take the two minutes to apply for your kid's Social Security number!

If you and your spouse both work (full- or part-time), and you have children under the age of 13, you can also claim a tax credit for child-care expenses. Or, you may work for one of the increasing numbers of employers who offer flexible benefit or spending plans. These plans allow you to put away up to $5,000 per year on a pre-tax basis. You can then use this money to pay for child-care expenses. For many parents, especially those in higher income tax brackets, these plans can save a lot of taxes. Keep in mind, however, that if you take advantage of one of these plans, you can't claim the child-care tax credit that I mention earlier. Also, if you don't deplete the entire account every tax year, you forfeit any money left over.

✔ **Ignore saving in custodial accounts.** New parents often feel the weight of new responsibilities on their shoulders. One common concern is how to sock away enough money to pay for the ever-rising cost of a college education. If you start saving money in your child's name in a so-called custodial account, however, you may not only be harming your child's future ability to qualify for financial aid but you may also be missing out on the tax benefits that come with investing elsewhere (see Chapter 12).

✔ **Don't indulge the children.** Toys, art classes, sports, field trips, and the like can rack up big bills, especially if you don't control your spending. Some parents fail to set guidelines or limits when spending on children's programs. Others mindlessly follow the examples set by the families of their children's peers. Introspective parents have shared with me that they feel some insecurity about providing the best for their children. The parents (and kids) that seem the happiest and most financially successful are the ones who clearly distinguish between material luxuries and family necessities.

As children get older and become indoctrinated into the world of shopping, all sorts of other purchases come into play. Consider giving your kids a weekly allowance and letting them discover how to spend and manage it. And when they're old enough, having your kids get a part-time job can help teach financial responsibility, as well.

Starting a Small Business

Many people aspire to be their own bosses, but far fewer people actually leave their jobs in order to achieve that dream. Giving up the apparent security of a job with benefits and a built-in network of co-workers is difficult for most people, both psychologically and financially. Starting a small business is not for everyone, but don't let inertia stand in your way. Here are some tips to help get you started and increase your chances for long-term success:

- **Prepare to ditch your job.** Do you spend all or nearly all that you earn, and have you failed to accumulate a nest egg? Many people in such a situation never leave their jobs behind to pursue their entrepreneurial dreams, because they feel dependent upon their paychecks. To maximize your ability to save money, live as Spartan a lifestyle as you can while you're employed; you'll simultaneously be developing thrifty habits that will help you weather the reduced income and increased expenditure period that comes with most small-business start-ups. You may also want to consider easing into your small business by working at it part-time in the beginning, with or without cutting back on your normal job.

- **Develop a business plan.** If you research and think through your business idea, you'll not only reduce the likelihood of your business failing and increase its success if it thrives, but you'll also feel more comfortable taking the entrepreneurial plunge. A good business plan should be a blueprint for how you expect to build the business. It should describe in detail the business idea, the marketplace you'll be competing in, your marketing plans, and expected revenue and expenses.

- **Replace your insurance coverage.** Before you finally leave your job, get proper insurance coverage. With health insurance, employers allow you to continue your existing coverage (at your own expense) for 18 months. Individuals with existing health problems are legally entitled to purchase an individual policy at the same price that a healthy individual pays. With disability insurance, you want to secure coverage before you leave your job so that you have income to qualify for coverage. If you have life insurance through your employer, secure new individual coverage as soon as you know you're going to leave your job. (See Chapter 15 for more details.)

- **Establish a retirement savings plan.** After your business starts making a profit, consider establishing a retirement savings plan such as a SEP-IRA or Keogh. As I explain in Chapter 10, such plans allow you to shelter up to 20 percent of your business income from federal and state taxation.

Caring for Aging Parents

There comes a time for many of us when we reverse roles with our parents. Instead of being the one who is cared for, you become the caregiver. As your parents age, they may need help with a variety of issues and living tasks. Although it's unlikely that you'll have the time or ability to perform all these functions yourself, you may well end up being the coordinator of service providers who will perform these functions.

Here are some things to consider when caring for aging parents:

- ✔ **Get help where possible.** In most communities, a variety of nonprofit organizations offer information and sometimes even counseling to families who are caring for elderly parents. You may be able to find your way to such resources through your state's department of insurance, as well as through recommendations from local hospitals and doctors. You'll especially want to get assistance and information if your parents need some sort of home care, nursing home care, or assisted living arrangement.

- ✔ **Get involved in their health care.** Your aging parents may already have a lot on their minds, or they simply may not be able to coordinate and manage all the health care providers that are giving them medications and advice. Try, as best as you can, to be their advocate. Speak with their doctors so that you can understand their current medical condition and need for various medications, and how to help coordinate caregivers. Visit home care providers and nursing homes, and speak with prospective care providers.

- ✔ **Understand tax breaks.** If you're financially supporting your parents, you may be eligible for a number of tax credits and deductions for elder care. Some employers' flexible benefit plans, for example, allow you to put away money on a pre-tax basis to pay for the care of your parents. Also explore the dependent care tax credit, which you can take on your federal income tax Form 1040. And if you provide half or more of the support costs for your parents, you may be able to claim them as dependents on your tax return.

- ✔ **Discuss getting the estate in order.** Parents don't like talking and thinking about their demise, and they may feel awkward discussing this issue with their children. But opening a dialogue between you and your folks about such issues can be healthy in many ways. Discussing wills, living wills, living trusts, and estate planning strategies (see Chapter 16) not only makes you aware of your folks' situation but it can also improve their plans to both their benefit and yours.

- ✔ **Take some time off.** Caring for an aging parent, particularly one who is having health problems, can be time-consuming and emotionally draining. If you were already juggling the responsibilities of a job, marriage, and parenthood before your parents needed help, you may now feel completely overwhelmed. Do your parents and yourself a favor by using some vacation time to help get things in order. Although this time off may not be the kind of vacation you were envisioning, it should help you reduce your stress and get more on top of things.

Divorcing

In most marriages that are destined to split up, there are usually early warning signs that both parties recognize. Sometimes, however, one spouse may surprise the other with an unexpected request for divorce. Whether the divorce is planned or unexpected, here are some key things to consider when getting a divorce:

- ✔ **Question the divorce.** Some say that divorcing in America is too easy, and I tend to agree. Although some couples are indeed better off parting ways, others give up too easily, thinking that the grass is greener elsewhere, only to later discover that all lawns have weeds and crabgrass. Just as with lawns that aren't watered and fertilized, relationships can wither without nurturing.

  Money and disagreements over money are certainly contributing factors in marital unhappiness. Unfortunately, in many relationships, money is wielded as power by the spouse who earns more of it. Try talking things over, perhaps with a marital counselor. If you invest in making your relationship stronger, you'll reap the dividends for years to come.

- ✔ **Separate your emotions from the financial issues.** Separating your feelings from your finances is easier said than done. Feelings of revenge may be common in some divorces, but they'll probably only help ensure that the attorneys get rich at your expense as you and your spouse butt heads. If you really want a divorce, work at doing it efficiently and harmoniously so that you can get on with your lives.

- ✔ **Detail resources and priorities.** Draw up a list of all the assets and liabilities that you and your spouse have. Make sure that you list all the financial facts, including investment account records and statements. After you know the whole picture, begin to think about what is and is not important to you financially and otherwise.

- ✔ **Educate yourself about personal finance and legal issues.** Divorce sometimes forces non-financially oriented spouses to get a crash course in personal finance at a difficult emotional time. This book can help educate you financially. In terms of the legal issues of divorce, visit a bookstore and pick up a good legal guide or two about divorce.

- ✔ **Choose advisors carefully.** Odds are that you will retain the services of one or more specialists to assist you with the myriad issues, negotiations, and concerns of your divorce. Legal, tax, and financial advisors can help, but make sure that you recognize their limitations and conflicts of interest. The more complicated things become and the more you haggle with your spouse, the more attorneys, unfortunately, benefit financially. Don't use your divorce attorney for financial or tax advice — your lawyer probably knows no more than you do in these areas. Also, realize that you don't need an attorney to get divorced. As for choosing tax and financial advisors, if you think you need that type of help, refer to Chapters 6 and 17 for advice on how to find good advisors.

✔ **Analyze your spending.** Although your "household" expenses will surely be less when you go back to being single, you'll probably have to make do with less income. Some divorcees find themselves financially squeezed in the early years following a divorce. Analyzing your spending needs pre-divorce will help you adjust to a new budget, as well as negotiate a fairer settlement with your spouse.

✔ **Review needed changes to your insurance.** If you're covered under your spouse's employer insurance plan, make sure that you get this coverage replaced (see Chapter 15). If you or your children will still be financially dependent upon your spouse post-divorce, make sure that the divorce agreement mandates life insurance coverage. You should also revise your will (see Chapter 16).

✔ **Revamp your retirement plan.** With changes to your income, expenses, assets, liabilities, and future needs, your retirement plan will surely need a post-divorce overhaul. Refer to Chapter 2 for a reorientation.

Receiving a Windfall

Whether through inheritance, stock options, small-business success, or lottery winnings, you may receive a financial windfall at some point in your life. Like many people who are totally unprepared psychologically and organizationally for their sudden good fortune, you may well find that a flood of money can create more problems than it solves. You may be saying, "I should have such problems." Fair enough. Who wouldn't rather be rich than poor?

Here are a few tips to help you make the most of your financial windfall:

✔ **Take the time to educate yourself.** If you never had to deal with significant wealth, I don't expect you to know how to handle it. Don't rush and pressure yourself to invest it as soon as possible. Leaving the money where it is or stashing it in one of the higher-yielding money market funds I recommend in Chapter 11 is a far better short-term solution than jumping into investments that you don't understand and haven't taken the time to research.

✔ **Beware of the sharks.** You may begin to wonder if someone has posted your net worth, address, and home telephone number in the local newspaper and on the Internet. Brokers and financial advisors may flood you with marketing materials, telephone solicitations, and lunch date requests. These folks pursue you for a reason: They want to convert your money into their income either by selling you investments and other financial products or by managing your money. Stay away from the sharks, educate yourself, and take charge of your own financial moves. Decide on your own terms whom to hire, and then seek them out. Most of the best advisors that I know don't have the time or philosophical orientation to chase after prospective clients.

✔ **Recognize the emotional side of coming into a lot of money.** One of the side effects of accumulating wealth quickly is that you may have feelings of guilt or otherwise be unhappy, especially if you expected money to solve your problems. If you didn't invest in your relationship with your parents, and, after their passing, you regret how you interacted with them, getting a big inheritance from your folks may make you feel guilty. As another example, if you poured endless hours into a business venture that finally paid off, all that money sitting in your investment accounts may leave you with a hollow feeling if you're divorced and you lost friends by neglecting your relationships.

✔ **Pay down debts.** Paying off your debts is one of the simplest and best investments you can make when you come into wealth. I had a counseling client come to me because he was frustrated that he didn't know how to invest several million dollars. He was worried about losing money on investments partly because he had worked so hard to build his wealth. He had a decent-sized home mortgage, which made complete sense for him to pay off. We generally borrow money to buy things that we otherwise can't buy in one fell swoop. Getting rid of debts is an especially good move when you have plenty of money.

✔ **Diversify.** If you want to protect your wealth, don't keep it all in one pot. Mutual funds (see Chapter 9) are an ideally diversified, professionally managed investment vehicle to consider. And if you want your money to continue growing, consider the wealth-building investments — stocks, real estate, and small-business options — that I discuss in Part III of this book.

✔ **Make use of the opportunity.** Most people work for a paycheck their whole lives so that they can pay a never-ending stream of monthly bills. Although I'm not advocating a hedonistic lifestyle, why not take some extra time to travel, spend time with your family, and enjoy the hobbies you've long been putting off? And how about trying a new career that you may find more fulfilling and that may make the world a better place? Many people have little flexibility. Don't waste flexibility if you have it.

Retiring

If you spent the bulk of your adult life working, retiring can be a challenging life transition. Most Americans have an idealized vision of how wonderful retirement will be. No more irritating bosses and pressure of work deadlines. Unlimited time to travel, play, and lead the good life. Sounds good, huh? Well, the reality for most Americans is far different, especially for those who don't plan ahead (financially and otherwise).

Here are some tips to help you through retirement:

✔ **Plan both financially and personally.** Leaving behind a full-time career creates big challenges, such as what to do with all your free time — the opposite problem that new parents have. You can get too much of a good thing, which is why planning for your time and activities in retirement is even more important than planning financially. If the focus during your working years is solely on your career and saving money, you may lack interests, friends, and the ability to know how to spend money when you retire.

✔ **Take stock of your resources.** Many people worry and wonder if they have sufficient assets for cutting back on work or retiring completely, yet they don't crunch any numbers to see where they stand. Sometimes ignorance can be blissful, but this is a case where ignorance may cause you to misunderstand how little or how much you really have for retirement when compared to what you need. See Chapter 2 for help with retirement planning.

✔ **Reevaluate your insurance needs.** During your working years, you carry disability and perhaps some life insurance to protect you and your dependents should you not be able to earn an income. When you have sufficient assets to retire, you don't need to retain insurance to protect your employment income any longer. On the other hand, as your assets grow over the years, you may be underinsured with regards to liability insurance (refer to Chapter 16).

✔ **Decide on health care/living options.** Medical expenses in your retirement years (particularly the cost of nursing home care) can be daunting. Which course of action you take — supplemental insurance, buying into a retirement community, or not doing anything — depends upon your financial and personal situation. Early preparation increases your options. If you wait until you have major health problems, it may be too late to choose specific paths. (See Chapter 15 for more details.)

✔ **Decide what to do with your retirement plan money.** When you're set to retire, you may have to elect what to do with your retirement plan money and decide which of your employer's *pension options* (plans that pay a monthly benefit during retirement) you want to take. If you have money in a retirement savings plan, many employers will offer you the option of leaving the money in the plan rather than rolling it over into your own retirement account. Brokers and financial advisors clearly prefer that you do the latter, because it means more money for them, but it could also give you many more (and perhaps better) investment choices to consider. Read Part III of this book to find out about investing and evaluating the quality of your employer's retirement plan investment options.

✔ **Pick a pension option.** Selecting a pension option is similar to choosing a good investment — each pension option carries different risks, benefits, and tax consequences. Pensions are structured by actuaries, who based them on reasonable life expectancies. The younger you are when you start collecting your pension, the less you get per month. Check to see if the amount of your monthly pension stops increasing past a certain starting age. You obviously don't want to delay access to your pension benefits past that age, because you won't receive a reward for waiting any longer, and you'll collect the benefit for fewer months.

If you know that you have a health problem that shortens your life expectancy, you may benefit from drawing your pension sooner. If you plan to continue working in some capacity and earning a decent income after you leave your employer, waiting for higher pension benefits when you're in a lower tax bracket is probably wise.

At one end of the spectrum you have the risky single life option, which pays benefits until you pass away and then provides no benefits for your spouse thereafter. This option maximizes your monthly take while you are alive. Only consider this option if your spouse can do without this income. The least risky option, and thus least financially rewarding while the pensioner is still living, is the *100 percent joint and survivor option,* which pays your survivor the same amount that you received while still alive. The other joint and survivor options fall somewhere in between these two extremes and generally make sense for most couples who desire decent pensions early in retirement but want a reasonable amount to continue should the pensioner die first.

✔ **Get your estate in order.** Confronting your mortality is never a joy, but when you're considering retirement or you're already retired, getting your estate in order makes all the more sense. Find out about wills and trusts that may benefit you and your heirs. You may also want to consider giving monetary gifts now if you have more than you need. You can't take it with you, and if you're worried about estate taxes, giving money yearly to your heirs reduces your taxable estate.

Chapter 21

Ten Things More Important than Money

. . . .

In This Chapter

▶ Understanding what's really important

▶ Taking time to appreciate the good things in life

. . . .

Throughout this book, I provide information and advice that enable you to make the most of your money. Whether you've been sticking with me since Chapter 1, or you've simply been skimming a few chapters, you probably know that I take a holistic approach to money decisions.

Although I hope that my financial advice serves you well, I also want to be sure that you remember the many things in life (I chose my ten favorites) that are far more important than the girth of your investment portfolio or the size of your latest paycheck. Too often in our capitalistic society, we place too much emphasis on financial success and status, and too little importance on living with a higher purpose. I hope this chapter makes a small contribution to keeping you on the best path.

Putting your family first

In America's culture, men (and increasingly, women) see their primary role as being the financial provider for their families. Such a focus seems to permit people to feel comfortable making sacrifices for the sake of their work and careers. We also seem to psychologically justify placing work before family, because we're taught the virtues of a strong work ethic.

Some employees rightfully fear that their bosses may not be sympathetic to the needs of their families, especially when those needs get in the way of getting the job done as efficiently as an impatient boss would like. Others put their companies first because that's what their peers do, and because they don't want to rock the boat.

Your spouse, your parents, and your kids, of course, should come first. They're much more important than your next promotion, and you should treat them that way. Balance is key. If your boss doesn't respect or value the importance of family, perhaps it's time to find a new boss.

Making and keeping friends

The older some people get, the less time they seem to have for friends. People who are too busy climbing the career ladder may not even make time for friends.

So many items in our consumer-oriented society are disposable, and unfortunately, friends too often fall into that category. Many friends aren't really friends as much as they are acquaintances who can further our careers, and when that function has been fulfilled, they're tossed aside.

What friends do you really care for? Do you have friends you can turn to in a time of need who can really listen and be there for you? Take the time to invest in your friendships, both old and new.

Investing in your health

Stress, poor diet, lack of exercise, problematic relationships within your family — all of these bad habits can have adverse personal health consequences. People neglect their health for different reasons. In some cases, as with money management, people lack the knowledge of the keys to good personal health. Getting too caught up in your career and working endless hours also often lead to the neglect of your health.

Some people don't fully realize what the downside may be of neglecting their bodies. The worst case, of course, is your untimely demise. But plenty of people suffer from ongoing conditions that damage the body and can make them feel far less well than they *could* feel. Unless you believe in reincarnation, you only get one body — take care of it and treat it with the respect it deserves!

Caring for kids

Investing in your children is absolutely one of the best investments you can make. Understanding how to relate to and care for kids can help make you a better and more fulfilled person. (And I think that understanding kids can help you better understand what makes grown-ups tick, too!)

Our children are our future. You should care about children even if you don't have any. Why? Do you care about the quality of our society? Do you have any concerns about crime? Do you care about the economy? How about entertainment and the arts? What about your Social Security and Medicare benefits?

All of these issues depend to a large extent on our nation's children and what kind of teenagers and adults they will someday become. I know that many parents struggle to balance the demands of work and raising kids. I think that everyone benefits when parents find ways to work at their careers less and spend more time with their children. Find ways to make do with what money (and things) you have. When your children are grown, they won't remember — nor appreciate — whether you were able to buy them more computer software or Yu-Gi-Oh! cards by working harder at your career. They *will* remember — and won't appreciate — a lack of attention.

Knowing your neighbors

Your neighbors can be sources of friendship, happiness, and comfort. Too often, I see people getting caught up in their daily routines and neglecting their neighbors.

Of course, you may not want to get to know all your neighbors better. But give them a chance. Don't write them off because they aren't the same age or race, or because they don't have the same occupation as you. Part of our coherence with our greater society comes from where we live, and our neighbors are an important piece of that connection. Don't miss out on it.

Appreciating what you do have

In my work as a financial counselor and writer, I have the opportunity to interact with many people from all walks of life. Despite the overall level of affluence in our society, I continue to be struck by how many people focus on and lament the material things they lack (a bigger house, more costly cars, and so on) rather than appreciate the material and nonmaterial things they do have.

Right now, make a list of at least ten things you appreciate. Periodically (daily, weekly, or monthly), make a similar list. Our culture sometimes causes us to dwell on what we don't have (which is usually not nearly as important as what we do have).

Minding your reputation

What do you think of when I say William Jefferson Clinton, Ivan Boesky, or Michael Milken? All of these people can be deemed successful in a career and monetary sense, but is that what first came to your mind?

One of my professors once said, "It can take a lifetime to build a reputation but only moments to lose it." As people chase after more fame, power, money, and possessions, they often devalue and underinvest in relationships, and breach the other commandments along the way.

Think of the people you most admire in your life. Although I'm sure that none of them are perfect, I bet each has a superior reputation with you.

Continuing your education

Education is a lifelong process — it's not just about attending a fancy college and perhaps getting an advanced degree. Whether the education is related to your career or a newfound hobby, you can always find something to learn. As long as you have your mental capacities, you can keep learning and building on what you already know.

And, who knows, maybe someday you'll gain an understanding of the meaning of life. The older we get, the more we have to reflect on and learn from.

Having fun

In the quest to earn more, save more, and invest smarter, some people get so caught up in society's money game, that money becomes the purpose of their existence. Whether you call it an addiction or obsession, having such a financial focus will surely steer you from the good things in life. I've known plenty of people who realize too late in life that sacrificing personal relationships and one's health isn't worth any amount of financial success.

Therapists' offices are filled with unhappy people who spend too much time and energy chasing promotions and money. These same people come to me as well. Often, they seem to worry about having enough money. When I tell them that they have "enough," the conversation usually turns to the personal things lacking in their lives.

Solving social problems

Although the United States may well have the greatest economy on the face of the earth, and the highest per capita income of any country, by other more important measures, Americans have a good deal of room for improvement. Among industrialized countries, we have some of the highest rates of infant mortality, poverty, gun violence, divorce, and suicide. We have more than our fair share of problems.

Why not be part of the solution rather than part of the problem? You can find plenty of causes worthy of your volunteer time or donations, such as Big Brothers Big Sisters, which partners adults with children for informal mentoring, Mothers Against Drunk Driving (MADD), which works to reduce drunk driving accidents, and Habitat for Humanity, which helps build affordable housing.

Glossary

adjustable-rate mortgage (ARM): A mortgage whose interest rate and monthly payments vary throughout its life. ARMs typically start with an artificially low interest rate that gradually rises over time. The interest rate is determined by a formula: margin (which is a fixed number) plus index (which varies). Generally speaking, if the overall level of interest rates drops, as measured by a variety of different indexes, the interest rate of your ARM generally follows suit. Similarly, if interest rates rise, so does your mortgage's interest rate and monthly payment. Caps limit the amount that the interest rate can fluctuate. Before you agree to an ARM, be certain that you can afford its highest possible payments.

adjusted cost basis: For capital gains tax purposes, the adjusted cost basis is how the IRS determines your profit or loss when you sell an asset such as a home or a security. For an investment such as a mutual fund or stock, your cost basis is what you originally invested plus any reinvested money. For a home, you arrive at the adjusted cost basis by adding the original purchase price to the cost of any capital improvements (expenditures that increase your property's value and life expectancy).

adjusted gross income (AGI): The sum of your taxable income (such as wages, salaries, and tips) and taxable interest less allowable adjustments (such as retirement account contributions and moving expenses). AGI is calculated before subtracting your personal exemptions and itemized deductions, which are used to derive your taxable income.

after-tax contributions: Some retirement plans allow you to contribute money that has already been taxed. Such contributions are known as after-tax contributions.

alternative minimum tax (AMT): The name given to a sort of shadow tax system that may cause you to pay a higher amount in federal income taxes than you otherwise would. The AMT was designed to prevent higher income earners from lowering their tax bills too much through large deductions.

American Stock Exchange (AMEX): The second largest stock exchange in the United States; it typically lists mid-sized firms and many of the new exchange-traded stock funds.

annual percentage rate (APR): The figure that states the total yearly cost of a loan as expressed by the actual rate of interest paid. The APR includes the base interest rate and any other add-on loan fees and costs. The APR is thus inevitably higher than the rate of interest that the lender quotes.

annuity: An investment that is a contract backed by an insurance company. An annuity is frequently purchased for retirement purposes. Its main benefit is that it allows your money to compound and grow without taxation until withdrawal. Selling annuities is a lucrative source of income for insurance agents and financial planners who work on commission, so don't buy an annuity until you're sure that it makes sense for your situation.

asset allocation: When you invest your money, you need to decide how to proportion it (allocate) between risky, growth-oriented investments (such as stocks), whose values fluctuate, and more stable, income-producing investments (like bonds). How soon you will need the money and how tolerant you are of risk are two important determinants when deciding how to allocate your money.

audit: An IRS examination of your financial records, generally at the IRS offices, to substantiate your tax return. IRS audits are among life's worst experiences.

bank prime rate: See *prime rate*.

bankruptcy: Legal action that puts a halt to creditors' attempts to collect unpaid debts from you. If you have a high proportion of consumer debt to annual income (25 percent or greater), filing for bankruptcy may be your best option.

bear market: A period (such as the early 2000s) when the stock market experiences a strong downward swing. It is often accompanied by (and sometimes precedes) an economic recession. Imagine a bear in hibernation, because this is what happens in a bear market: Investors hibernate and the market falters. During a bear market, the value of stocks can decrease significantly. The market usually has to drop at least 20 percent before it is considered a bear market.

beneficiaries: The people to whom you want to leave your assets or, in the case of life insurance or a pension plan, benefits in the event of your death. You denote beneficiaries for each of your retirement accounts.

blue chip stock: The stock of the largest and most consistently profitable corporations. This term comes from poker, where the most valuable chips are blue. The list of these stocks is unofficial and changes.

bond: A loan investors make to a corporation or government. Bonds generally pay a set amount of interest on a regular basis. They're an appropriate investment vehicle for conservative investors who don't feel comfortable with the risk involved in investing in stocks and who want to receive a steady income. All bonds have a maturity date when the bond issuer must pay back the bond at *par* (full) value to the bondholders (lenders). Bonds should not be your primary long-term investment vehicle, because they produce little real growth on your original investment after inflation is factored in.

bond rating: See ***Standard & Poor's ratings*** and ***Moody's ratings***.

bond yield: A yield is quoted as an annual percentage rate of return that a bond will produce based on its current value if it makes its promised interest payments. How much a bond will yield to an investor depends on three important factors: the stated interest rate paid by the bond, changes in the creditworthiness of the bond's issuer, and the maturity date of the bond. The better the rating a bond receives, the less risk involved and, thus, the lower the yield. As far as the maturity date is concerned, the longer you loan your money, the higher the risk (because it is more likely that rates will fluctuate) and the higher your yield generally will be.

broker: A person who acts as an intermediary for the purchase or sale of investments. When you buy a house, insurance, or stock, you most likely do so through a broker. Most brokers are paid on commission, which creates a conflict of interest with their clients. The more the broker sells, the more he or she makes. But more is not necessarily better for you. Some insurance companies let you buy their policies directly, and many mutual fund families bypass stockbrokers. If you're going to work with a broker, a discount broker can help you save on commissions.

bull market: A period (such as most of the 1990s in the United States) when the stock market experiences a strong upward swing, usually accompanied and driven by a growing economy and increasing corporate profits.

callable bond: A bond for which the lender can decide to pay the holder earlier than the previously agreed-upon maturity date. If interest rates are relatively high when a bond is issued, lenders may prefer issuing callable bonds because they have the flexibility to call back these bonds and issue new, lower-interest rate bonds if interest rates decline. Callable bonds are risky for investors, because if interest rates decrease, the bond holder will get his investment money returned early and may have to reinvest his money at a lower interest rate.

capital gain: The profit from selling your stock at a higher price than the price for which it was purchased. For example, if you buy 50 shares of Rocky and Bullwinkle stock at $20 per share, and two years later you sell your shares when the price rises to $25 per share, your profit or capital gain is $5 per share, or $250. If you hold this Rocky and Bullwinkle stock outside of a tax-sheltered retirement account, you'll owe federal tax on this profit when you sell the stock. In addition to the federal government, many states also levy such a tax.

capital gains distribution: Taxable distribution by a mutual fund or real estate investment trust (REIT) created by securities that are sold within the fund or REIT at a profit. These distributions may either be short-term (assets held a year or less) or long-term (assets held more than one year).

cash value insurance: A type of life insurance that is extremely popular with insurance salespeople because it commands a high commission. In a cash value policy, you buy life insurance coverage but also get a savings-type account. Unless you're looking for ways to limit your taxable estate (if you're extremely wealthy, for example), avoid cash value insurance. The investment returns tend to be mediocre, and your contributions are not tax-deductible.

Certificate of Deposit (CD): A specific-term loan that you make to your banker. The maturity date for CDs ranges from a month up to several years. The interest paid on CDs is fully taxable, thus making CDs inappropriate for higher tax-bracket investors investing outside tax-sheltered retirement accounts.

closed-end mutual fund: A mutual fund that decides upfront exactly how many shares it is going to issue to investors. After all the shares are sold, an investor seeking to invest in the closed-end fund can only do so by purchasing shares from an existing investor. Shares of closed-end funds trade on the major stock exchanges and therefore sell at either a discount if the sellers exceed the buyers, or at a premium if demand exceeds supply.

COBRA (Consolidated Omnibus Budget Reconciliation Act): Name of the federal legislation that requires health insurers and larger employers to continue to offer health insurance, at the employee's expense, for 18 months after coverage would otherwise end — for example, when an employee is laid off.

commercial paper: A short-term debt or IOU issued by larger, stable companies to help make their businesses grow and prosper. Credit-worthy companies can sell this debt security directly to large investors and thus bypass borrowing money from bankers. Money market funds invest in soon-to-mature commercial paper.

commission: The percentage of the selling price of a house, stock, bond, or other investment that is paid to agents and brokers. Because most agents and brokers are paid by commission, understanding how the commission can influence their behavior and recommendations is important for investors and home buyers. Agents and brokers make money only when you make a purchase, and they make more money when you make a bigger purchase. Choose an agent carefully, and take your agent's advice with a grain of salt, because this inherent conflict of interest can often set an agent's visions and goals at odds with your own.

commodity: A financial instrument whose value is derived from the performance of an underlying security such as a stock or bond. Commodities are a form of derivatives. Raw materials (gold, wheat, sugar, and gasoline, for example) are commodities traded on the futures market.

common stock: Shares in a company that don't offer a guaranteed amount of dividend to investors; the amount of dividend distributions, if any, is at the discretion of company management. While common stock investors may or may not make money through dividends, they hope that the stock price is going to appreciate as the company expands its operations and increases its profits. Common stock tends to offer you a better return (profit) than other investments, such as bonds or preferred stock. However, if the company falters, you may lose some or all of your original investment.

comparable market analysis (CMA): A written analysis of similar houses currently being offered for sale and which have recently sold. CMAs are usually completed by real estate agents.

consumer debt: Debt on consumer items that depreciate in value over time. Credit card balances and auto loans are examples of consumer debt. This type of debt is bad for your financial health because it is high-interest and it encourages you to live beyond your means.

Consumer Price Index (CPI): The Consumer Price Index reports price changes, on a monthly basis, in the cost of living for such items as food, housing, transportation, health care, entertainment, clothing, and other miscellaneous expenses. The CPI is used to adjust government benefits, such as Social Security, and is used by many employers to determine cost-of-living increases in wages and pensions. An increase in prices is also known as inflation.

co-payment: The percentage of your medical bill that your health plan requires you to pay out of your own pocket after you satisfy your annual deductible. A typical co-payment is 20 percent.

credit report: A report that details your credit history. It is the main report that a lender uses to determine whether or not to give you a loan. You must generally pay the lender to obtain this report.

debit card: Although they may look like credit cards, debit cards are different in one important way: When you use a debit card, the cost of the purchase is deducted from your checking account. Thus, a debit card gives you the convenience of a credit card without the danger of building up a mountain of consumer debt.

deductible: You may be thinking that this is a new product from the Keebler elves. Unfortunately, a deductible is actually much more mundane. With insurance, the deductible is the amount you pay when you file a claim. For example, say that your car sustains $800 of damage. If your deductible is $500, the insurance covers $300 and you pay $500 out of your own pocket for the repairs. The higher the deductible, the lower your insurance premiums, and the less paperwork you expose yourself to when filing claims (because small losses that are less than the deductible don't require filing a claim). Take the highest deductibles that you can afford when selecting insurance.

deduction: An expense you may subtract from your income to lower your taxable income. Examples include mortgage interest, property taxes (itemized deductions), and most retirement account contributions.

derivative: An investment instrument whose value is derived from other securities. For example, an option to buy IBM stock does not have value in itself; the value is derived from the price of IBM's stock.

disability insurance: During your working years, you have a lot riding on your ability to earn an income. Without it, you'd be in big trouble (unless a wealthy relative, wife, husband, or friend can support you). Disability insurance replaces a portion of your employment income in the unlikely event that you suffer a disability that keeps you from working.

discount broker: Unlike a full-service broker, a discount broker generally offers no investment advice and has employees who work on salary rather than on commission. Using a discount broker helps you avoid the conflict of interest that will inevitably come up with a so-called full-service broker. In addition to trading individual securities, most discount brokerage firms also offer no-load (commission-free) mutual funds.

diversification: If you put all of your money into one type of investment, you're potentially setting yourself up for a big shock. If that investment collapses, so does your investment world. By spreading (diversifying) your money among different investments — bonds, U.S. stocks, international stocks, and so on — you ensure yourself a better chance of investing success and fewer sleepless nights.

dividend: Quotient, divisor, dividend? Forget elementary school math. The dividend is the income paid to investors holding an investment. With stock, the dividend is the portion of a company's profits paid to its shareholders. For example, if a company has an annual dividend of $2 per share and you own 100 shares, your total dividend is $200. Usually, established and slower-growing companies pay dividends, while smaller and faster growing companies reinvest their profits for growth. For assets held outside retirement accounts, dividends, except from tax-free money market and tax-free bond funds, are taxable.

Dow Jones Industrial Average (DJIA): A widely followed stock market index comprised of 30 large, actively traded U.S. company stocks. Senior editors at the *Wall Street Journal* select the stocks in the DJIA.

down payment: The part of the purchase price for a house that the buyer pays in cash upfront and does not finance with a mortgage. Generally, the larger the down payment, the better the deal you can get on a mortgage. You can usually get access to the best mortgage programs with a down payment of at least 20 percent of the home's purchase price.

earthquake insurance: Although the West Coast is often associated with earthquakes, other areas are also quake prone. An earthquake insurance rider (which usually comes with a deductible of 5 to 10 percent of the cost to rebuild the home) on a homeowner's policy pays to repair or rebuild your home if it is damaged in an earthquake. If you live in an area with earthquake risk, get earthquake insurance coverage!

Emerging Markets Index: The Emerging Markets Index, which is published by Morgan Stanley, tracks stock markets in developing countries. The main reason for investing in emerging markets is that these economies typically experience a higher rate of economic growth than developed markets. However, the potential for higher returns is coupled with greater risk.

equity: In the real estate world, this term refers to the difference between the market value of your home and what you owe on it. For example, if your home is worth $200,000, and you have an outstanding mortgage of $140,000, your equity is $60,000. Equity is also a synonym for stock.

estate: The value, at the time of your death, of your assets minus your loans and liabilities.

estate planning: The process of deciding where your assets will go when you die, and structuring your assets during your lifetime so as to minimize likely estate taxes.

Federal National Mortgage Association (FNMA): The FNMA (or Fannie Mae) is one of the best-known institutions in the secondary mortgage market. Fannie Mae buys mortgages from banks and other mortgage-lending institutions and, in turn, sells them to investors. These loan investments are considered safe because Fannie Mae buys mortgages only from companies that conform to its stringent mortgage regulations, and Fannie Mae guarantees the repayment of principal and interest on the loans that it sells.

financial assets: A property or investment (such as real estate or a stock, mutual fund, bond, and so on) that has value that can be realized if sold.

financial liabilities: Your outstanding loans and debts. To determine your net worth, you must subtract your financial liabilities from your financial assets.

financial planners: A motley crew that professes an ability to manage your money. Financial planners come with varying backgrounds and degrees: MBAs, Certified Financial Planners, and Certified Public Accountants, to name a few. A useful way to distinguish among this mixed bag of nuts is to determine whether the planners are commission-, fee-, or hourly-based.

fixed-rate mortgage: The granddaddy of all mortgages. You lock into an interest rate (for example, 7 percent), and it never changes during the life (term) of your 15- or 30-year mortgage. Your mortgage payment will be the same amount each and every month. If you become a cursing, frothing maniac when you miss your morning coffee or someone is five minutes late, then this mortgage may be for you!

flood insurance: "When the flood waters recede, the poor folk start from scratch" (Richard Wright). They start from scratch unless they have flood insurance. If there's even a remote chance that your area may flood, having flood insurance, which reimburses rebuilding your home and replacing its contents in the event of a flood, is prudent.

401(k) plan: A type of retirement savings plan offered by many for-profit companies to their employees. Your contributions compound without taxation over time and are usually exempt (yes!) from federal and state income taxes.

403(b) plan: Similar to a 401(k) plan but for employees of nonprofit organizations.

full-service broker: A broker who gives advice and charges a high commission relative to discount brokers. Because the brokers work on commission, they have a significant conflict of interest: namely, to advocate strategies that will be of financial benefit to them.

futures: An obligation to buy or sell a commodity or security on a specific day for a preset price. When used by most individual investors, futures represent a short-term gamble on the short-term direction of the price of a commodity. Companies and farmers use futures contracts to hedge their risks of changing prices.

guaranteed-investment contracts (GICs): Insurance company investments that appeal to skittish investors. GICs generally tell you one year in advance what your interest rate will be for the coming year. Thus, you don't have to worry about fluctuations and losses in your investment value. On the other hand, GICs offer you little upside, because the interest rate is comparable to what you may get on a short-term bank Certificate of Deposit.

home equity: See *equity*.

home-equity loan: Technical jargon for what used to be called a second mortgage. With this type of loan, you borrow against the equity in your house. If used wisely, a home-equity loan can help pay off high-interest consumer debt or be tapped for other short-term needs (such as a remodeling project). In contrast with consumer debt, mortgage debt is usually at a lower interest rate and is tax-deductible.

homeowner's insurance: Dwelling coverage that covers the cost of rebuilding your house in the event of fire or other calamity. The liability insurance portion of this policy protects you against lawsuits associated with your property. Another essential element of homeowner's insurance is the personal property coverage, which pays to replace your damaged or stolen worldly possessions.

index: (1) A security market index, such as the Standard & Poor's 500 Index, is a statistical composite that measures the performance of a particular type of security. Indexes exist for various stock and bond markets and are typically set at a round number such as 100 at a particular point in time. See also *Dow Jones Industrial Average*, *Russell 2000*, and *Wilshire 5000*. (2) The index also can refer to the measure of the overall level of interest rates that a lender uses as a reference to calculate the specific interest rate on an adjustable-rate loan. The index plus the margin is the formula for determining the interest rate on an adjustable-rate mortgage.

individual retirement account (IRA): A retirement account into which anyone with sufficient employment income or alimony may contribute up to $3,000 per year ($3,500 if age 50 or older). Based on your eligibility for other employer-based retirement programs and which type of IRA you select (regular or Roth), your contributions may or may not be tax-deductible.

inflation: The technical term for a rise in prices. Inflation usually occurs when too much money is in circulation and not enough goods and services are available to spend it on. As a result of this excess demand, prices rise. A link is present between inflation and interest rates: If interest rates do not keep up with inflation, no one will invest in bonds issued by the government or corporations. When the interest rates on bonds are high, it usually reflects a high rate of inflation that will eat away at your return.

initial public offering (IPO): The first time a company offers stock to the investing public. An IPO typically occurs when a company wants to expand more rapidly and seeks additional money to support its growth. A number of studies have demonstrated that buying into IPOs in which the general public can participate produces subpar investment returns. A high level of IPO activity may indicate a cresting stock market, as companies and their investment bankers rush to cash in on a "pricey" marketplace. (IPO could stand for It's Probably Overpriced.)

interest rate: The rate lenders charge you to use their money. The higher the interest rate, the higher the risk entailed in the loan. With bonds of a given maturity, a higher rate of interest means a lower quality of bond — one that is less likely to return your money.

international stock markets: Stock markets outside of the United States account for a significant portion of the world stock market capitalization (value). Some specific stock indices track international markets (see ***Morgan Stanley EAFE index*** and ***Emerging Markets Index***). International investing offers one way for you to diversify your portfolio and reduce your risk. Some of the foreign countries with major stock exchanges outside the United States include Japan, Britain, France, Germany, and Canada.

junk bond: A bond rated Ba (Moody's) or BB (Standard & Poor) and lower. Historically, these bonds have had a 1 to 2 percent chance of default, which is not exactly "junky." Of course, the higher risk is accompanied by a higher interest rate.

Keogh plan: A tax-deductible retirement savings plan available to self-employed individuals. Certain Keoghs allow you to put up to 25 percent of your self-employment income into the account.

leverage: Financial leverage affords its users a disproportionate amount of financial power relative to the amount of their own cash invested. In some circumstances, you can borrow up to 50 percent of a stock price and use all funds (both yours and those that you borrow) to make a purchase. You repay this so-called margin loan when you sell the stock. If the stock price rises, you make money on what you invested plus what you borrowed. While this money sounds attractive, remember that leverage cuts both ways — when prices decline, you lose money not only on your investment but also on the money you borrowed.

limited partnership (LP): These partnerships, which are often promoted in a way that promises high returns, generally limit one thing: your investment return. Why? Because they're burdened with high commissions and management fees. Another problem is that they're typically not liquid for many years.

load mutual fund: A mutual fund that includes a sales load, which is the commission paid to brokers who sell commission-based mutual funds. The commission typically ranges from 4 to 8.5 percent. This commission is deducted from your investment money, so it reduces your returns.

marginal tax rate: The rate of income tax you pay on the last dollars you earn over the course of a year. Why the complicated distinction? Because all income is not treated equally: You pay less tax on your first dollars of your annual earnings and more tax on the last dollars of your annual income.

Knowing your marginal tax rate is helpful because it can help you analyze the tax implications of important personal financial decisions.

market capitalization: The value of all the outstanding stock of a company. Market capitalization is the quoted price per share of a stock multiplied by the number of shares outstanding. Thus, if Rocky and Bullwinkle Corporation has 100 million shares of outstanding stock, and the quoted price per share is $20, the company has a market capitalization of $2 billion (100 million × $20).

Moody's ratings: Moody's rating service measures and rates the credit (default) risks of various bonds. Moody's investigates the financial condition of a bond issuer. Its ratings use the following grading system, which is expressed from highest to lowest: Aaa, Aa, A, Baa, Ba, B, Caa, Ca, C. Higher ratings imply a lower risk but also mean that the interest rate will be lower.

Morgan Stanley EAFE (Europe, Australia, Far East) index: The Morgan Stanley EAFE index tracks the performance of the more established countries' stock markets in Europe and Asia. This index is important for international-minded investors who want to follow the performance of overseas stock investments.

mortgage broker: Mortgage brokers buy mortgages wholesale from lenders and then mark the mortgages up (typically from 0.5 to 1 percent) and sell them to borrowers. A good mortgage broker is most helpful for people who don't want to shop around on their own for a mortgage, or people who have blemishes on their credit reports.

mortgage life insurance: Mortgage life insurance guarantees that the lender will receive its money in the event that you meet an untimely demise. Many people may try to convince you that you need this insurance to protect your dependents and loved ones. Mortgage life insurance is relatively expensive given the cost of the coverage provided. If you need life insurance, buy low-cost, high-quality term life insurance instead.

mortgage-backed bond (GNMAs and FNMAs): The Government National Mortgage Association (GNMA, or Ginnie Mae) specializes in mortgage-backed security. It passes the interest and principal payment of borrowers to investors. When a homeowner makes a mortgage payment, GNMA deducts a small service charge and forwards the mortgage payments to its investors. The payments are guaranteed in the case of a borrower failing to pay his or her mortgage. The Federal National Mortgage Association (FNMA or Fannie Mae) is a publicly owned, government-sponsored corporation that purchases mortgages from lenders and resells them to investors. FNMA mainly deals with mortgages backed by the Federal Housing Administration.

municipal bond: A loan for public projects, such as highways, parks, or cultural centers, that an investor makes to cities, towns, and states. The tax-exempt status of their interest is what makes municipal bonds special: They're exempt from federal taxes and, if you reside in the state where the bond is issued, state taxes. Municipal bonds are most appropriate for people in high tax-brackets who invest money outside of tax-sheltered retirement accounts.

mutual fund: A portfolio of stocks, bonds, or other securities that is owned by numerous investors and managed by an investment company. See also *no-load mutual fund*.

National Association of Securities Dealers Automated Quotation (NASDAQ) system: An electronic network that allows brokers to trade from their offices all over the country. With NASDAQ, brokers buy and sell shares using constantly updated prices that appear on their computer screens.

negative amortization: Although it may sound like a description of the cause of dinosaur extinction, negative amortization occurs when your outstanding mortgage balance increases despite the fact that you're making the required monthly payments. Negative amortization occurs with adjustable-rate mortgages that cap the increase in your monthly payment but do not cap the interest rate. Therefore, your monthly payments do not cover all the interest that you actually owe. Avoid loans with this "feature."

net asset value (NAV): The dollar value of one share of a mutual fund. For a no-load fund, the market price is its NAV. For a load fund, the NAV is the "buy" price minus the commission.

New York Stock Exchange (NYSE): The largest stock exchange in the world in terms of total volume and value of shares traded. It lists companies that tend to be among the oldest, largest, and best-known companies.

no-load mutual fund: A mutual fund that doesn't come with a commission payment attached to it. Because of the lack of a load and the generally lower management fees of these funds, they tend to have better returns than load funds. Some funds claim to be no-load, but they simply hide their sales commissions as an ongoing sales charge. You can avoid these funds by educating yourself and reading the prospectuses carefully.

open-end mutual fund: A mutual fund that issues as many shares as investors demand. These open-end funds do not generally limit the number of investors or amount of money in the fund. Some open-end funds have been known to close to new investors, but investors with existing shares can often still buy more shares from the company.

option: The right to buy or sell a specific security (such as a stock) for a preset price during a specified period of time. Options differ from futures in that, with an option, you pay a premium fee upfront, and you can either exercise the option or let it expire. If the option expires worthless, you lose 100 percent of your original investment. The use of options is best left to companies as hedging tools. Investment managers may use options as a hedging tool to reduce the risk in their investment portfolio. Like with futures, when most individual investors buy an option, they're doing so as a short-term gamble, not as an investment. For example: You have an option to buy 100 shares of Rocky and Bullwinkle Co. stock at $20 per share in the next six months. You pay $3 per share upfront as the premium. During this time period, R&B's share price rises to $30, and you exercise your right to buy at $20. You then sell your shares at the market price of $30; you make a $10 profit per share, which is a return more than three times larger than your original investment.

pension: Pensions (also known as defined benefit plans) are a benefit offered by some employers. These plans generally pay you a monthly retirement income based on your years of service with the employer.

performance: You traditionally judge an investment's performance by looking at the historic rate of return. The longer the period over which these numbers are tallied, the more useful they are. Considered alone, these numbers are practically meaningless. You must also note how well a fund has performed in comparison to competitors with the same investment objectives. Beware of advertisements that tout the high returns of a mutual fund, because they may not be looking at risk-adjusted performance, or they may be promoting performance over a short time period. Keep in mind that high return statistics are usually coupled with high risk, and that this year's star may turn out to be next year's crashing meteor.

pre-certification: A condition for health insurance benefit coverage that requires a patient to get approval before being admitted to a hospital for nonemergency care.

preferred stock: Stock that offers a guaranteed amount of dividend payments to investors. Preferred stock dividends must be paid before any dividends are paid to the common stock shareholders. Although preferred stock reduces your risk as an investor (because of the more secure dividend and greater likelihood of getting your money back if the company fails), it also often limits your reward if the company expands and increases its profits.

price/earnings (P/E) ratio: The current price of a stock divided by the current (or sometimes the projected) earnings per share of the issuing company. This ratio is a widely used stock analysis statistic that helps an investor get an idea of how cheap or expensive a stock price is. In general, a relatively high P/E ratio indicates that investors feel that the company's earnings are likely to grow quickly.

prime rate: The rate of interest that major banks charge their most credit-worthy corporate customers. Why should you care? Well, because the interest rates on various loans you may be interested in are often based on the prime rate. And, guess what — you pay a higher interest rate than those big corporations!

principal: No, I'm not talking about the big boss from elementary school who struck fear into the hearts of most eight-year-olds. The principal is the amount you borrow for a loan. If you borrow $100,000, your principal is $100,000. Principal can also refer to the amount you originally placed in an investment.

prospectus: Individual companies and mutual funds are required by the Securities and Exchange Commission to issue a prospectus. For a company, the prospectus is a legal document presenting a detailed analysis of that company's financial history, its products and services, its management's background and experience, and the risks of investing in the company. A mutual fund prospectus tells you about the fund's investment objectives, costs, risk, and performance history.

real estate investment trust (REIT): Real estate investment trusts are like a mutual fund of real estate investments. Such trusts invest in a collection of properties (from shopping centers to apartment buildings). REITs trade on the major stock exchanges. If you want to invest in real estate while avoiding the hassles inherent in owning property, real estate investment trusts may be the right choice for you.

refinance: Refinance, or refi, is a fancy word for taking out a new mortgage loan (usually at a lower interest rate) to pay off an existing mortgage (generally at a higher interest rate). Refinancing is not automatic, nor is it guaranteed. Refinancing can also be a hassle and expensive. Weigh the costs and benefits of refinancing carefully before proceeding.

return on investment: The percentage of profit you make on an investment. If you put $1,000 into an investment, and then one year later it's worth $1,100, you make a profit of $100. Your return on investment is the profit ($100) divided by the initial investment ($1,000) — in this case, 10 percent.

reverse mortgage: A reverse mortgage enables elderly homeowners, typically those who are low on cash, to tap into their home's equity without selling their home or moving from it. Specifically, a lending institution makes a check out to you each month, and you can use the check as you want. This money is really a loan against the value of your home, so it is tax-free when you receive it. The downside of these loans is that they deplete your equity in your estate, the fees and interest rates tend to be on the high side, and some require repayment within a certain number of years.

Russell 2000: An index that tracks the returns of 2,000 small-company U.S. stocks. Small-company stocks tend to be more volatile than large-company stocks. If you invest in small-company stocks or stock funds, this is an appropriate benchmark to compare your performance to.

Securities and Exchange Commission (SEC): The federal agency that administers U.S. securities laws and regulates and monitors investment companies, brokers, and financial advisors.

simplified employee pension individual retirement account (SEP-IRA): Like other retirement plans, a SEP-IRA allows your money to compound over the years without the parasitic effect of taxes. SEP-IRAs are relatively easy to set up, and they allow self-employed people to make annual contributions on a pre-tax basis.

Social Security: If you're retired or disabled, Social Security is a government safety net that can provide you with some income. The program is based on the idea that government is responsible for the social welfare of its citizens. Whether you agree with this notion or not, part of your paycheck goes to Social Security, and when you retire, you receive money from the program.

Standard & Poor's 500 Index: An index that measures the performance of 500 large-company U.S. stocks that account for about 80 percent of the total market value of all stocks traded in the United States. If you invest in larger-company stock or stock funds, The S&P 500 Index is an appropriate benchmark to compare the performance of your investments to.

Standard & Poor's (S&P) ratings: Standard & Poor's rating service is one of two services that measure and rate the risks in buying a bond. The S&P ratings use the following grading system, listed from highest to lowest: AAA, AA, A, BBB, BB, B, CCC, CC, C. See also *Moody's ratings*.

stock: Shares of ownership in a company. When a company *goes public,* it issues shares of stock to the public (see also *initial public offering*). Many, but not all, stocks pay dividends — a distribution of a portion of company profits. In addition to dividends, the other way you make money investing in stock is via appreciation in the price of the stock, which normally results from growth in revenues and corporate profits. You can invest in stock by purchasing individual shares or by investing in a stock mutual fund that offers a diversified package of stocks.

term life insurance: If people are dependent on your income for their living expenses, you may need this insurance. Term life insurance functions simply: You determine how much protection you would like and then pay an annual premium based on that amount. Although it is much less touted by insurance salespeople than cash value insurance, it is the best life insurance out there for the vast majority of people.

Treasury bill: IOUs from the federal government that mature within a year. The other types of loans that investors can make to the federal government are Treasury notes, which mature within one to ten years, and Treasury bonds, which mature in more than ten years. The interest that these federal government bonds pay is free of state taxes, but it is federally taxable.

underwriting: The process an insurance company uses to evaluate a person's likelihood of filing a claim on a particular type of insurance policy. If significant problems are discovered, an insurer will often propose much higher rates or refuse to sell the insurance coverage.

will: A legal document that ensures that your wishes regarding your assets and the care of your minor children are heeded when you die.

Wilshire 5000: Despite the name, this index actually tracks closer to 6,000 companies of all sizes on major U.S. stock exchanges. If you invest in stock or stock funds of companies of all sizes, this index is an appropriate benchmark.

zero-coupon bond: A bond that doesn't pay explicit interest during the term of the loan. Zero-coupon bonds are purchased at a discounted price relative to the principal value paid at maturity. Thus, the interest is implicit in the discount. These bonds do not offer a tax break, because the investor must pay taxes on the interest he would have received.

Index

• *Numerics* •

11th district cost of funds, 276
15-year versus 30-year mortgages, 278–279
457 plans, 212, 215
401(k) plans, 212–213, 225
403(b) plans, 212, 213–214, 228–231

• *A* •

A, AA, or AAA bonds, 174
accessory expenses, 109
addictions, 64, 86–87, 116–117
adjustable-rate mortgages (ARMs).
      See also mortgages
  adjustment period or frequency, 276
  complexity of, 273
  fixed-rate mortgages versus, 268–270
  future interest rate, 274–276
  indexes, 274–276
  lender fees, 271–272
  length of ownership and, 270
  negative amortization, 275
  prepayment penalties, 273
  rate caps, 276
  refinancing to change, 294
  risks, 268, 269–270
  start rate, 274
advertising, 15–16, 94
aggressive investors, 155–156
aggressive retirement accounts, 225,
      226–228
alcohol expenses, 102, 117
Allen, John (securities lawyer), 14
allocation
  of assets in investments, 154–155
  dollar-cost averaging, 157–159
  long-term, 155–157, 241
  of retirement account money, 221–228
alternative minimum tax (AMT), 122
American Arbitration Association, 163
amortizing loans, 275
analyzing savings, 28–30

analyzing spending, 66–72
annual reports for mutual funds, 200–201
annuities. *See also* insurance
  commission-free, 310
  inside other retirement accounts, 220
  investing in, 188–189
  long-term investments, 245
  as retirement accounts, 219–221
  tax-sheltered, 212, 213–214, 228–229
appraisal fees on homes, 272
arbitration consultants, 163
arbitration with brokers, 163
ARMs. *See* adjustable-rate mortgages
asset allocation. *See* allocation
asset allocation funds, 196
assets
  allocating in investments, 154–157
  calculating, 26–27
  defined, 25
  financial aid and, 251
  ownership investments and, 146
ATM cards, 78
audits
  of mutual funds, 192
  tax, 138–140
auto insurance, 128–129, 346–350
autos. *See* cars

• *B* •

bad debt danger ratio, 23–24
bad debt versus good debt, 22–23, 73
balanced mutual funds, 196, 223, 225
balancing your checkbook, 71–72
balloon loans, 272–273
bankruptcy, 10, 79–85, 193
banks. *See also* checking accounts;
      savings accounts
  ATM cards, 78
  charge offs, 83
  financial planners in, 370
BB or BBB bonds, 174
Bear, John (*Send This Jerk the Bedbug
      Letter*), 96

Better Business Bureau (BBB), 96
Beware icon, 6
bond mutual funds
  hybrids, 196
  inflation-indexed Treasury bonds, 243
  intermediate-term, 195, 242
  long-term, 195, 242
  operating expenses, 203
  overview, 194–195
  recommended funds, 203, 241–243
  retirement accounts, 222–223, 225
  short-term, 195, 241
  tax-free, 242–243
  U.S. Treasury, 242, 243
  uses for, 195
bonds
  asset allocation, 155–156
  callable, 175
  CDs versus, 244
  higher yield from, 151
  as lending investments, 144–146
  leverage, 182
  maturity, 194–195
  overview, 173–175
  ratings, 174
  return on investment, 149
  stocks versus, 150–151
  tax-free, 133, 220
Bortner, Deb (securities expert), 15
brand names, 94
brokers
  best firms, 160–161
  broker-dealer networks, 161
  commissions' impact on, 162
  conflicts of interest, 162, 164–166
  discount, 160–161, 222
  individual stock recommendations by, 179
  legal recourse for losses due to, 163
  load mutual funds from, 201–202
  mortgage, 280–281
  places to avoid, 161–166
  research by, 166
  wrap or managed accounts, 165
Brown, Eric (*Home Buying For Dummies*), 277
budgeting, 99
bullion, 188
businesses. *See* small businesses
buyer's brokers, 287

• C •

callable bonds, 175
cancer insurance, 307
capital gains distributions, 205, 208
capitalization of stocks, 176, 195
car insurance, 128–129, 346–350
career counseling deduction, 129
careers. *See* employment
cars
  buying, 106–107, 108
  insurance, 128–129, 346–350
  loans, 20, 22, 63–64
  reducing expenses, 106–109
  tax deductions, 128–129
cash value life insurance, 323
  borrowing against, 75, 322
  buying, 326
  defined, 321
  getting rid of it, 325–326
  investing in, 189
  retirement accounts versus, 41, 323
  tax breaks, 322–323, 354
  term insurance versus, 320–324
CCCS (Consumer Credit Counseling Service), 82, 84
cell phones, 105
certificates of deposit (CDs), 144–146, 174, 244, 275
Certified Financial Planning (CFP), 360, 361
certified public accountants (CPAs), 136
Chapter 7 versus Chapter 13 bankruptcy, 84
charge cards, replacing credit cards with, 85
charge offs, 83
charity deductions, 127–128
checking accounts, 71–72, 78–79, 172
children. *See also* educational expenses
  caring for, 420–421
  spending on, 65
  teen drivers, 347
  tips on having, 408–411
churning, 163
clothing expenses, 109
COLAs (cost-of-living adjustments), 329
collectibles, investing in, 189
college expenses. *See* educational expenses
College for Financial Planning, 361
comfort level for investing, 143–144

commissions
  conflicts of interest, 162, 164–165, 286
  financial planners, 162, 363–364
  impact on human behavior, 162
  insurance agents, 310–311, 364
  on investments, 364
  no-load investments and, 162
  real estate agents', 286, 296
commodities (investments), 147, 378–379
commuter passes, 108
computers. *See also* Web sites
  checkbook software, 385–386
  financial software benefits, 382
  legal document preparation on, 391
  organizing tax information on, 126
  retirement-planning software, 386–388
  software defined, 381
  tax-preparation software, 136, 388
  tracking investments on, 387
  tracking spending on, 70–71
  trading online, 389–390
condominiums, 283–284
conflicts of interest
  brokers, 162, 164–166
  financial planners, 360, 369–372
  health insurance agents, 334
  publications, advertising and, 15–16
  real estate agents, 286–287
conservative retirement accounts, 225,
    226–228
Consumer Credit Counseling Service
    (CCCS), 82, 84
consumer loans. *See also* credit cards
  avoiding, 20, 98
  bad debt danger ratio, 23–24
  bad debt versus good debt, 22–23, 73
  car loans, 20, 22, 63–64
  home equity loans and, 75, 127, 293
  investing in paying off, 152, 234
  paying with savings, 74–75
  refinancing mortgages to pay off, 293
Consumer Reports, 94, 106, 357
contact lens insurance, 306
contingency-fee basis, 163
contractor references, 95
Cook, Wade (investment guru), 13, 14, 15
cooperatives, 283–284
corporate commercial paper, 173

Costco, 100–101
cost-of-living adjustments (COLAs), 329
coupon, 173
CPAs (certified public accountants), 136
credit cards
  carrying a balance, 20
  credit life and credit disability policies, 305
  cutting up, 77–78
  debit cards versus, 78–79
  filing bankruptcy and, 80, 81
  grace period, 10, 24, 76
  invention of, 62
  investing in paying off, 152, 234
  limiting the influence of, 85–86
  low interest rate hypes, 77
  making minimum payments, 62
  no-fee cards, 110
  overspending and, 62
  playing the float, 24
  reducing costs of, 110
  reducing interest rates on, 76
"credit repair" firms, 88
credit reports, 81, 88–89, 272, 282
credit union accounts, 236–237

• D •

DA (Debtors Anonymous), 86–87
daily hospital insurance, 305–306
Davis, Leona (CCCS victim), 82
daytrading, 148
DCA (dollar-cost averaging), 159
debit cards, 78–79
debt. *See also* consumer loans; credit
    cards; mortgages
  avoiding bad debt, 73
  bad debt danger ratio, 23–24
  bad versus good, 22–23, 73
  filing bankruptcy, 79–85
  financial planners and, 371
  making minimum payments, 62
  paying off high-interest debt, 152, 234
  reducing costs of, 110
  reducing using savings, 74–75
  reducing when you lack savings, 76–79
  trading consumer for mortgage, 127
Debtors Anonymous (DA), 86–87

deductibles
  benefits of higher deductibles, 304
  car insurance, 348
  costs of low deductibles, 115, 304
  defined, 115, 303
  health insurance, 332–333
  homeowner's insurance, 345
  renter's insurance, 345
deductions on taxes. *See also* tax breaks
  15-year versus 30-year mortgages and, 279
  auto, 128–129
  charity, 127–128
  defined, 124
  health insurance and, 333
  high-income limitations, 128
  home equity loans, 75, 127, 293
  for homeowners, 126, 265, 279
  increasing, 124–132
  miscellaneous expenses, 129–130
  organizing, 125–126
  property taxes, 265
  real estate investments and, 183
  retirement accounts, 38–39, 123, 132, 133
  shifting or bunching, 126
  standard versus itemized, 125–126
  tax-free gifts, 353
defined-benefit pension plans, 49–50, 217
defined-contribution pension plans, 50
dental insurance, 305
derivatives, 147–148
Direct Marketing Association, 86
direct trustee to trustee transfer, 229–231
directories for mutual funds, 206
disability insurance, 305, 326–331
discount brokers, 160–161, 222, 389–390
discounts, 345
diversification
  asset allocation, 154–157
  benefits of, 152–154
  defined, 152
  in index funds, 197
  investing in individual stocks and, 178–179
  as investment insurance, 350
  lending investments and, 145
  mutual funds for, 153, 192
dividends, 180, 205, 207–208
divorce, 10, 414–415
Dodge & Cox funds, 227, 228, 242
dollar-cost averaging (DCA), 159

Donahue, Phil (talk show host), 14
Donovan, Nancy (fifth-grade teacher), 12
down payment on homes, 276–277
drug expenses, 114, 117
dry cleaning, 109
due diligence and book publishers, 398

• E •

early withdrawal (retirement accounts), 39
earthquake insurance, 344–345
EAs (enrolled agents), 136
eating out, 101–102
education
  continuing, 422
  in personal finance, 11–12
Education Savings Act (ESA), 250–251
educational expenses
  deductions on taxes, 129
  estimating college costs, 253
  financial aid system, 247–251
  investing educational funds, 256–258
  life insurance for, 256–257
  loans, grants, and scholarships, 254–256
  overspending and, 65
  prepaid tuition plans, 257
  qualified state tuition plans, 252
  saving for, 37, 42, 253–254
  Section 529 plans, 252
  strategies for, 251, 253–256
11th district cost of funds, 276
emergency reserves, 40–41, 74, 236–239
employment
  changing jobs or careers, 405–406
  deductions on taxes, 129
  disability insurance programs, 327
  employer insurance plans, 309–310
  employer theft of retirement money, 213
  employer-sponsored retirement plans,
    212–215, 371
  first job, 404–405
  investing in, 152
  retirement plans and, 54
  self-employment, 130–132, 215–221
  worker's compensation, 328
enrolled agents (EAs), 136
entertainment expenses, 111
equity funds. *See* stock mutual funds

equity (real estate)
  borrowing against, 75, 127, 293
  defined, 49
  financial aid and, 251
  as retirement income, 49, 53
  reverse mortgages and, 295
equity (stocks). *See* stocks
Eric's Picks icon, 5
ESA (Education Savings Act), 250–251
escrow charges, 292
estate planning, 351–354, 391
estate taxes, 323, 353–354
excess liability insurance, 350
expenses. *See* educational expenses;
    medical expenses; spending
extended warranty and repair plans,
    304–305

• F •

FAFSA (Free Application for Federal
    Student Aid), 248, 255
family. *See also* children
  down payment assistance from, 277
  education by, 257–258
  help in self-employment businesses, 132
  investing in, 152
  putting first, 419–420
  talking money at home, 11–12
Federal Deposit Insurance Corporation
    (FDIC), 172–173, 244
Federal Reserve Bank, 242
Federal Student Aid Information
    Center, 255
Federal Trade Commission (FTC), 15
fees. *See also* commissions
  bankruptcy costs, 83
  escrow charges, 292
  financial planners, 376–377
  on investments, 165, 169
  lender fees on mortgages, 271–272
  minimizing, 169
  on mutual funds, 192
  no-fee credit cards, 110
Fidelity funds
  bond funds, 242
  money market funds, 238, 239, 240
  in retirement account portfolios, 227

15-year versus 30-year mortgages, 278–279
financial administration, 71–72
financial aid system, 247–251
financial fitness
  bad debt danger ratio, 23–24
  bad debt versus good debt, 22–23, 73
  common problems, 20–22
  education at home and school, 11–12
  good habits for, 18–19
  home affordability and, 260–261
  insurance knowledge quiz, 32
  investing knowledge quiz, 30–31
  net worth, 25–28
  obstacles to financial success, 17–18
  savings analysis, 28–30
  unreliable information and, 12–16
financial illiteracy, 10–16
financial liabilities, 26–27
financial planners
  Alice's case history, 357–360
  associations, 375
  bankruptcy advice, 84–85
  in banks, 370
  broker-dealer networks and, 161
  client cultivation techniques, 373–374
  commission-based, 363–364
  commissions' impact on, 162, 369–370
  complications created by, 360
  conflicts of interest, 162, 164–166, 360,
      369–372
  credentials, 360, 361
  debts ignored by, 371
  dependency created by, 372
  doing your homework, 360
  employer retirement plans and, 371
  fees, 376–377
  finding, 373–375
  hourly-based, 365
  implementation of strategies, 380
  interviewing, 375–380
  investment gurus, 13–15, 167–169
  investment newsletters, 166–167, 179
  legal services, 372, 378
  liability insurance, 379
  money-management services, 371–372
  narrow view taken by, 370
  percentage-of-assets-under-management,
      364–365
  qualifications, asking about, 378

financial planners *(continued)*
  real estate investments and, 371
  reasons for hiring, 365–367
  reasons not to hire, 367
  references, 379
  regulatory problems, 368–369
  sales pitches, 21, 164, 165, 169, 374
  scare tactics, 372
  small businesses and, 371
  tax services, 378
  unreliable sources of information, 12–16
financial planning. *See also* goals
  doing it yourself, 362–363
  doing nothing, 362
  for educational expenses, 42
  hiring help, 363–365
  for home ownership, 37, 41
  need for, 20
  owning a business, 37, 41
  retirement planning, 43–57
financing homes. *See* mortgages
fixed-rate mortgages. *See also* mortgages
  adjustable-rate mortgages versus, 268–270
  balloon loans, 272–273
  interest rates and points, 270–271
  lender fees, 271–272
  length of ownership and, 270
  prepayment penalties, 273
  risks, 268
flight insurance, 306
float on credit cards, playing, 24
flood insurance, 344–345
following mutual funds, 209
food expenses, 100–102
457 plans, 212, 215
401(k) plans, 212–213, 225
403(b) plans, 212, 213–214, 228–231
Free Application for Federal Student Aid
    (FAFSA), 248, 255
FreeEdgar.com Web site, 389
FTC (Federal Trade Commission), 15
fun, having, 422
futures (investments), 147–148, 378–379

• G •

gambling expenses, 117
gambling investments, 147–148
Garzareli, Elain (market analyst), 167–168

gas expenses, 108–109
GICs (guaranteed-investment
    contracts), 223
gifts, 111, 353
Giszczak, Helen (investment loser), 14
Givens, Charles (*Wealth Without Risk*
    author), 13, 14
Glassman, James (journalist), 36
global mutual funds, 196–197
goals. *See also* financial planning
  balancing financial with other, 35–37
  building emergency reserves, 40–41
  buying a business, 42
  competing, 39–40
  creating your definition of wealth, 33–37
  educational expense savings, 42, 253–254
  financial planners' help with, 366
  home ownership, 37, 41
  ignoring when buying, 65
  for investing, 143–144
  for mutual funds, 205–206
  prioritizing savings goals, 37–40
  retirement planning, 37, 43–57
gold, investing in, 188
good debt versus bad debt, 22–23, 73
grace period on credit cards, 10, 24, 76
grants for educational expenses, 254–256
Greenberg, Herb (business journalist), 168
group insurance plans, 309–310
Growth Multiplier, 51–52
growth stocks, 195
guaranteed renewability, 325, 329, 334
guaranteed-investment contracts
    (GICs), 223

• H •

hair care expenses, 112
happiness, wealth and, 34
Harbor Bond funds, 228, 242
health
  investing in, 152, 420
  retirement planning and, 44
  taking care of yourself, 338–339
health club expenses, 112–113
health insurance
  choice of health care providers, 332
  choosing the best plan, 331–334
  claims process, 335

co-payments, 332–333
deductibles, 332–333
denial of, 334–335
guaranteed renewability, 334
lifetime maximum benefits, 332
long-term care (LTC), 336–337
major medical coverage, 331
Medicaid, 336, 337–338
Medical Savings Accounts (MSAs), 333
Medicare, 336, 337
Medigap, 336
preexisting conditions, 335
reducing expenses, 114
retiree medical care, 336–338
shopping for, 334
taking care of yourself, 338–339
tax considerations, 333
hobbies, retirement income from, 53
Home Buying For Dummies (Tyson, Eric
    and Brown, Ray), 277
home ownership. *See also* mortgages;
    real estate
    advantages of renting, 266
    affordability, 260–261
    condominiums, cooperatives, and town
        homes, 283–284
    converting to rental property, 298
    costs of, 262, 263–265
    down payment, 276–277
    equity as retirement income, 49, 53
    escrow charges, 292
    financial fitness and, 260–261
    as financial goal, 37
    financing, 267–283
    finding out actual sale prices, 284–285
    finding the right property, 283–285
    homeowner's insurance, 341–346
    inspections before buying, 290–291
    maximum you can borrow, 261–263
    monthly expenses, 263–265, 267
    mortgage life insurance, 294
    negotiating, 289–290
    opportunity cost of owning, 263
    property taxes, 265
    real estate agents, 285–290, 296
    reducing expenses, 103–104
    refinancing, 292–294
    renting versus buying, 103, 181, 259–267
    researching neighborhoods, 285

retirement needs and, 45
reverse mortgages, 295
saving for, 40, 277
second homes, 185
selling your house, 260, 296–298
tax deductions, 126, 265
timeline for, 260
tips, 408
title insurance, 291–292
homeowner's insurance, 341–346
hospitalization insurance, 305–306
hybrid mortgages, 270
hybrid mutual funds, 196, 203

• I •

icons in book margins, 5–6
income
    growing rich on yours, 72
    mortgage approval and, 283
    retirement needs, 44–46
    shifting to reduce taxes, 124
    tax brackets and rates, 120–121
    tax deduction limitations and, 128
    taxable, 121–122
incorporation, 131
index mutual funds, 197–199, 203
Individual Retirement Accounts (IRAs).
        See also retirement accounts
    cash value life insurance versus, 41
    contribution limits, 218
    overview, 218–219
    penalty-free withdrawals, 39
    Roth IRAs, 218, 219
    SEP-IRAs, 216
    setting up, 221–222
    spousal, 218
    transferring accounts, 228–231
inflation, 145, 188
inflation-indexed Treasury bonds, 243
inheritances as retirement income, 54
inspections before buying homes, 290–291
insurance. *See also* annuities; health
        insurance; life insurance
    avoiding small potato policies, 304–306
    broad coverage, 306–308
    buying direct, 308–311
    car insurance, 128–129, 346–350
    claims process, 313–316

insurance *(continued)*
  commissions, 310–311, 364
  on contact lenses, 306
  credit life and disability policies, 305
  daily hospital policies, 305–306
  deductibles, 115, 303–304
  denial of coverage, 311–312
  dental insurance, 305
  disability, 305, 326–331
  employer plans, 309–310
  extended warranty and repair, 304–305
  for financial catastrophes, 302–303
  group plans, 309–310
  home warranty plans, 305
  homeowner's insurance, 341–346
  insurer ratings, 309
  investment risks and, 21
  laws of buying, 301–311
  measuring your knowledge, 32
  mortgage life insurance, 294
  need for, 317
  on packages in the mail, 306
  professional liability insurance, 131
  reducing spending on, 115
  renter's insurance, 341, 343, 345–346
  riders, 306, 343
  risk perception and, 307
  on savings accounts, 172–173
  shopping for, 308, 325
  state high-risk pools, 312
  taking care of yourself, 338–339
  tax-sheltered annuities, 214
  title insurance, 291–292
  umbrella insurance, 350
interest rates
  adjustable-rate mortgages, 274–276
  credit card, 76–77
  defined, 270
  fixed-rate mortgages, 270–271
  points and, 270–271
  refinancing mortgages and, 293
intermediate-term bond funds, 195, 242
Internal Revenue Service (IRS), 119, 135, 136
international mutual funds, 196, 203
international stocks, 176
Internet. *See* Web sites
interviewing financial planners, 375–380
Investigate icon, 6

investing. *See also* diversification;
    retirement accounts; risks of investing;
    specific types of investments
  in annuities, 188–189
  asset allocation, 154–157
  brokers' conflicts of interest, 162, 164–166
  in cash value life insurance, 189, 320–323
  in collectibles, 189
  comfort level, 143–144
  in commodities, 147
  daytrading, 148
  debit cards with accounts, 79
  deducting expenses, 130
  in derivatives, 147–148
  dollar-cost averaging, 157–159
  educational funds, 256–258
  in family and friends, 152
  final advice, 169–170
  in futures, 147–148
  gambling, 147–148
  goals, 143–144
  gurus, 13–15, 167–169
  investment firm differences for, 159–166
  investment newsletters, 166–167, 179
  lending investments, 144–146, 172–175
  long-term, 134–135, 155–157, 195, 240–245
  low-risk, high-return investments, 152
  making up for lost time, 53–54
  measuring your knowledge, 30–31
  in options, 147–148
  outside retirement accounts, 233–245
  ownership investments, 146, 175–187
  paying off high-interest debt, 152, 234
  in precious metals, 188
  reducing spending and, 99–100
  reducing taxes, 132–135
  return on investment, 148–149, 177, 207–209, 234
  sales pitches, 21, 164, 165, 169
  selling investments to reduce debt, 75
  tax consequences, 53–54, 132–135, 170, 235–236
  uncertain times and, 158
Investing For Dummies (Tyson, Eric), 229
investment banking, 166
Investment Company Act of 1940, 193
investment firms, 79, 159–166
Invisible Bankers (Tobias, Andrew), 308

IRAs. *See* Individual Retirement Accounts
IRS (Internal Revenue Service), 119, 135, 136

• J •

Jaffe, Charles (journalist), 361
job search deductions on taxes, 129
junk mail, reducing, 86

• K •

Keoghs, 217, 228–231

• L •

large cap stocks, 176
lender fees on mortgages, 271–272
lending investments, 144–146, 172–175
leverage, 181–182
liability insurance
  auto insurance, 346–350
  for financial planners, 379
  for homeowners, 343
  professional, 131
  umbrella (excess liability), 350
life changes
  buying a home, 408
  caring for aging parents, 412–413
  changing jobs or careers, 405–406
  divorce, 414–415
  first job, 404–405
  general tips for, 403–404
  getting married, 406–407
  having children, 408–411
  receiving a windfall, 415–416
  retiring, 416–418
  starting a business, 412
life insurance
  buying online, 390–391
  buying term life insurance, 324–325, 390–391
  calculating amount needed, 318–319
  cash value, 41, 75, 189, 320–324, 325–326
  credit life policies, 305
  for educational expenses, 256–257
  group plans, 310
  guaranteed renewability, 325
  mortgage life insurance, 294

other precautions, 320
people not in need of, 318
premium adjustment periods, 324
shopping for, 308, 325
taking care of yourself, 338–339
term versus cash value, 320–324
limited partnerships (LPs), 184, 220, 378–379
list billing, 331
living trusts, 352–353, 391
living wills, 352, 391
load mutual funds, 201–202
loans. *See also* consumer loans; credit cards; debt; mortgages
  access to credit, 62
  bad debt danger ratio, 23–24
  bad debt versus good debt, 22–23, 73
  against cash value life insurance, 322
  for educational expenses, 254–256
  filing bankruptcy, 79–85
  financial fitness, 84–85
  home equity loans, 75, 127, 293
  for reducing consumer debt, 75
long-term care insurance (LTC), 336–337
long-term investments
  allocating assets for, 155–157, 241
  annuities, 245
  bond funds, 195, 241–243
  certificates of deposit (CDs), 244
  defined, 241
  emergency reserves and, 240
  real estate, 245
  retirement accounts and, 240
  small businesses, 245
  stock mutual funds, 245
  tax breaks for, 134–135
LPs (limited partnerships), 184, 220, 378–379
LTC (long-term care insurance), 336–337

• M •

Malkiel, Burton (A *Random Walk Down Wall Street*), 14
managed or wrap accounts, 165
management of mutual funds, 177, 191–192, 204
marginal tax rate, 120–121, 236

market capitalization, 176
marriage
  advice, 406–407
  divorce, 10, 414–415
Master's Select International fund, 228
meat, expense of, 101
media. *See also* publications; Web sites
  alarmists, 394
  financial illiteracy and conflicts in, 14–16
  poor values in, 394–395
  profound influence of, 393
  pundits worshiped in, 395
  radio and television programs, 395–396
mediation by financial planners, 367
Medicaid, 336, 337–338
medical expenses. *See also* health
    insurance
  auto insurance and, 346–348
  car insurance and, 349
  reducing spending on, 114–115
  retiree medical care insurance, 336–338
medical information file, 334–335
medical power of attorney, 352
Medical Savings Accounts (MSAs), 333
Medicare, 336, 337
Medigap insurance, 336
middle-of-the-road investors, 155–156
Modern Bride magazine, 15–16
money
  getting your money back, 94–97
  happiness not guaranteed by, 34
  more important things, 419–422
  overemphasizing, 21
  relationship to, 35
  talking at home, 11–12
money market funds
  asset allocation, 155
  emergency reserves in, 237–240
  operating expenses, 203, 238
  overview, 172–173, 194
  recommended funds, 203, 238–240
  as retirement accounts, 222
  "sales" by, 238
  savings accounts versus, 194, 237
  taxable, 238
  tax-free, 133, 239–240
  U.S. Treasury funds, 238–239
money-purchase Keoghs, 217
Morningstar fund directory, 206

Morningstar.com Web site, 389
mortgage brokers, 280–281
mortgages. *See also* home ownership;
    real estate
  adjustable-rate, 268–270, 273–276
  backup loans, 283
  balloon loans, 272–273
  deducting interest on, 126, 265, 279
  down payment, 276–277
  15-year versus 30-year, 278–279
  financial fitness and, 260–261
  finding the best lender, 280–281
  fixed-rate, 268–269, 270–273
  fixed-rate versus adjustable-rate, 268–270
  home equity loans, 75, 127, 293
  hybrid loans, 270
  increasing approval chances, 281–283
  interest rates, 270–271, 274–276
  lender fees, 271–272
  maximum you can borrow, 261–263
  monthly housing costs, 264–265
  mortgage life insurance, 294
  negative amortization, 275
  points, 271
  preapproval or prequalification, 282
  prepayment penalties, 273
  refinancing, 104, 292–294
  reverse, 295
  risks, 268, 269–270
  trading consumer debt for mortgage
    debt, 127
MSAs (Medical Savings Accounts), 333
municipal bonds inside retirement
    accounts, 220
mutual funds. *See also* bond mutual funds;
    money market funds; stock mutual
    funds
  advantages, 177, 191–192
  annual reports, 200–201
  asset allocation funds, 196
  balanced, 196, 223, 225
  capital gains distributions, 205, 208
  costs, 192, 201–203
  directories, 206
  diversification and, 153, 192
  dividends, 205, 207–208
  fees, 192
  following, 209
  funds of funds, 197

hybrid funds, 196, 203
index funds, 197–199, 203
individual stocks versus, 177–179
international, worldwide, or global,
    196–197, 203
investment breakdown for, 193–194
loads, eliminating, 201–202
management of, 177, 191–192, 204
needs and goals for, 205–206
no-load, 160, 192
operating expenses, 202–203
performance, 192, 198, 204, 206–209
prospectuses, 164, 200, 358
rankings, 206
recommended funds, 203
rise of industry, 193
risk levels, 192
selecting, 200–206
selling, 209
share price changes, 208
socially responsible, 199
specialty (sector) funds, 199–200
tax-friendliness, 205
total return, 207–209
transferring retirement accounts, 228–231
types of, 193–200
Mutual Funds For Dummies (Tyson, Eric),
    209, 229
Myers, David (*The Pursuit of Happiness*
    author), 34, 37

• N •

Nader, Ralph (consumer advocate), 96
National Association of Insurance
    Commissioners, 315, 346
National Association of Personal Financial
    Advisors (NAPFA), 375
negative amortization, 275
negotiating
    buying a home, 289–290
    insurance claim payment, 314
    real estate agent commissions, 296
    rental increases, 102–103
    returning items, 96–97
neighborhoods, researching, 285
neighbors, knowing yours, 421
net worth, 25–28
New York Times, The, 113

newsletters, investment, 166–167, 179
newspapers, 397
Newsweek, 113
no-load investments
    annuities, 245
    brokers on commission and, 162
    for educational funds, 256
    for 403(b) plans, 213
    mutual funds, 160, 192
nonprofit organizations, retirement
    plans in, 214

• O •

opportunity cost of owning a home, 263
options (investments), 147–148, 378–379
overspending, 20, 61–65, 92–93. *See also*
    reducing spending
ownership investments, 146, 175–187

• P •

Parent Loans for Undergraduate Students
    (PLUS), 255
parents
    caring for aging parents, 412–413
    education by, 257–258
    talking money at home, 11–12
peer pressure, overspending and, 64
pension plans. *See* retirement accounts
periodicals. *See* publications
personal care expenses, 112–113
personal development, investing in, 152
Personal Finance For Dummies (Tyson, Eric)
    icons in book margins, 5–6
    new in this edition, 2–3
    organization, 3–5
    uses for, 1–2, 3
personal property coverage of insurance,
    342–343
phone expenses, 104–106
play-it-safe investors, 155–156
PLUS (Parent Loans for Undergraduate
    Students), 255
points on mortgages, 271
power of attorney, medical, 352
preapproval or prequalification for
    mortgages, 282

precious metals, investing in, 188
prepaid tuition plans, 257
prepayment penalties on mortgages, 273
price-earnings ratio, 175
private pension plans, 216
privately held companies, 175
probate, 352
professional expenses, 113–114
professional liability insurance, 131
profit-sharing Keoghs, 217
property taxes, 104, 126, 265
prospectuses, mutual fund, 164, 200, 358
psychological health and retirement, 44
publications
  advertising conflicts in, 15–16
  Consumer Reports, 94, 106, 357
  due diligence and, 398
  individual stock recommendations in, 179
  IRS, 135
  newspapers and magazines, 397
  online periodicals, 390
  recommended financial books, 398–399
  reducing spending on, 113
  retirement planning booklets, 51
  tax guides, 135, 136
publicly held companies, 175
Pursuit of Happiness, The (Myers, David), 34

qualified state tuition plans, 252

radio financial programs, 395–396
Random Walk Down Wall Street, A (Malkiel, Burton), 14
rate caps for ARMs, 276
real estate. *See also* home ownership; mortgages
  agents, 285–290, 296
  best investments, 182–183
  financial planners and, 371
  hidden values, 182
  leverage, 181–182
  limited partnerships (LPs), 184
  limited supply of land and, 181
  long-term investments, 245
  overview, 180–185

  as ownership investments, 146
  real estate investment trusts (REITs), 183
  retirement accounts versus, 55–56, 183
  return on investment, 149
  second homes, 185
  stocks versus, 183
  time shares, 184–185
  uniqueness of, 181–182
  usability of, 181
  worst investments, 184–185
  zoning and, 181
reducing spending. *See also* spending
  on addictions, 116–117
  avoiding brand names, 94
  avoiding consumer credit, 98
  budgeting, 99
  on clothing, 109
  by debt repayment, 110
  eliminating fat, 97
  on entertainment and recreation, 110–112
  finding the best values, 93–97
  on food, 100–102
  funding retirement accounts by, 123
  on insurance, 115
  investing the money saved, 99–100
  living within your means, 92–93
  on medical expenses, 114–115
  on personal care, 112–113
  on phone bills, 104–106
  on professional expenses, 113–114
  responsibility for, 92
  returning items, 94–97
  on shelter, 102–104
  strategies, 98–117
  on taxes, 115–116
  on transportation costs, 106–109
references
  for contractors, 95
  for financial planners, 379
referrals for financial planners, 373–374
refinancing mortgages, 104, 292–294
refunds
  returning items, 94–97
  on taxes, 119–120
Remember icon, 6
renter's insurance, 341, 343, 345–346
renting, 345–346
  advantages, 266
  converting home to rental property, 298

long-term costs of, 266–267
owning versus, 103, 181, 259–267
reducing costs, 102–103
renting-to-own, 98
a room in your home, 104
reputation, importance of, 421–422
retirement
  as financial goal, 37
  nonfinancial aspects, 44
  preparing for, 43–57
  retiree medical care insurance, 336–338
  tips, 416–418
retirement accounts
  15-year versus 30-year mortgages and, 279
  advantages, 38–39
  aggressive portfolios, 225, 226–228
  AGI and tax credits for contributions, 124
  allocating money in, 221–228
  annuities, 219–221
  balanced mutual funds, 223, 225
  bond mutual funds, 222–223, 225
  borrowing against employer's, 75
  brokers not recommending, 164
  calculating your needs, 44–46
  cash value life insurance versus, 41, 323
  conservative portfolios, 225, 226–228
  defined-benefit pension plans, 49–50
  defined-contribution pension plans, 50
  delaying saving for, 20, 54–55
  early withdrawal, 39
  employer theft, 213
  employer-selected investments, 222–225
  employer-sponsored plans, 212–215, 371
  financial aid and, 249
  457 plans, 212, 215
  401(k) plans, 212–213, 225
  403(b) plans, 212, 213–214
  funding by reducing expenses, 123
  guaranteed-investment contracts
      (GICs), 223
  inappropriate investments, 220
  IRAs, 39, 41, 218–219
  Keoghs, 217
  limited partnerships (LPs), 220
  money market funds, 222
  objections to, overcoming, 54–57
  prioritizing contributions, 221
  private pension plans, 216
  real estate investments versus, 183

real estate versus, 55–56
recommended firms, 226–228
relative simplicity of investing in, 211
Roth IRAs, 218, 219
savings accounts, 222
self-employment and, 131
self-employment plans, 215–221
SEP-IRAs, 216
setting up accounts, 221–222
statistics, 10
stock mutual funds, 224, 225
stocks, 224–225
tax breaks, 38–39, 123–124, 132, 133,
    211, 235
transferring, 228–232
types of, 211–221
retirement planning
  booklets on, 51
  calculating your needs, 44–46
  early retirement dreams, 43
  Growth Multiplier, 51–52
  making up for lost time, 52–54
  nonfinancial aspects, 44
  overcoming objections, 54–57
  pension plans, 49–50
  savings/investment strategy, 49
  Social Security and, 46–49
  worksheet, 50–51
return on investment, 148–149, 177,
    207–209, 234
returning items, 94–97
reverse mortgages, 295
riders on insurance, 306, 343, 349
risk perception and insurance, 307
risks of investing
  controlling, 151
  diversification and, 152–154
  dollar-cost averaging and, 159
  insurance coverage and, 21
  for lending investments, 145
  low-risk, high-return investments, 152
  money market funds, 173
  mortgages, 268, 269–270
  mutual funds, 192
  overview, 149–152
  rate of return and, 234
  savings accounts, 172–173
  stocks versus bonds, 150–151
Roth IRAs, 218, 219

• S •

sales pitches, 21, 164, 165, 169, 374
Sam's Club, 100–101
satellite television, 105
savings. *See also* retirement accounts
  15-year versus 30-year mortgages and, 279
  analysis, 28–30
  balanced approach to, 35–37
  for big purchases, 42–43
  to buy a business, 41
  competing goals, 39–40
  for educational expenses, 37, 42, 253–254
  emergency reserves, 40–41, 74
  for home ownership, 40, 277
  outside retirement accounts, 56
  paying consumer loans with, 74–75
  prioritizing goals for, 37–40
  savings rate calculation, 29–30
  statistics, 10, 20
savings accounts
  emergency reserves in, 236–237
  Medical Savings Accounts (MSAs), 333
  money market funds versus, 194, 237
  overview, 172–173
  as retirement accounts, 222
  return on investment, 149
Scheiber, Anne (miser), 35–36
scholarships, 254–256
schools, teaching personal finance in, 12
Section 529 plans, 252
sector mutual funds, 199–200
securities. *See* bonds; stocks
self-employment, 130–132, 215–221.
    See also small businesses
selling mutual funds, 209
selling your house, 260, 296–298
Send This Jerk the Bedbug Letter
    (Bear, John), 96
SEP-IRAs, 216
shelter expenses, 102–104
shifting deductions on taxes, 126
shifting income, 124
short-term bond funds, 195, 241
silver, investing in, 188
Silverman, David J. (*Taxes For Dummies*),
    136, 265, 354

small businesses
  buying, 186–187
  financial planners and, 371
  home equity loans and, 293
  investing in someone else's, 187
  long-term investments, 245
  overview, 185–187
  as ownership investments, 146
  saving to own your own, 37, 41
  self-employment deductions, 130–132
  self-employment retirement plans,
      215–221
  starting your own, 185–186
  tips on starting, 412
small cap stocks, 176
small claims court, 97
smoking expenses, 116
social problems, solving, 422
Social Security, 46–49, 319, 327
socially responsible mutual funds, 199
software. *See* computers
specialty mutual funds, 199–200
spending. *See also* reducing spending
  addiction to, 64, 86–87
  analyzing, 66–72
  on brand names, 94
  on children, 65
  eliminating fat, 97
  to feel good, 64
  finding the best values, 93–97
  ignoring financial goals during, 65
  to keep current, 64–65
  keys to success, 92–98
  overspending, 20, 61–65
  peer pressure and, 64
  questioning, 52
  renting-to-own, 98
  returning items, 94–97
Standard & Poor 500, 197
state disability programs, 328
state high-risk insurance pools, 312
stock mutual funds
  hybrids, 196
  long-term investments, 245
  operating expenses, 203
  overview, 195
  recommended funds, 203
  retirement accounts, 224, 225

stocks. *See also* mutual funds
  asset allocation, 154, 155–156
  bonds versus, 150–151
  capitalization, 176, 195
  daytrading, 148
  dividend reinvestment plans, 180
  international, 176
  investing in individual stocks, 178–180
  leverage, 182
  mutual funds versus, 177–179
  overview, 175–180
  as ownership investments, 146
  real estate versus, 183
  as retirement investments, 224–225
  return on investment, 149, 177
  short-term trading, 13–14
survival guide. *See* life changes

• *T* •

T. Rowe Price, 51, 228, 245
tax attorneys, 136
tax audits, 138–140
tax breaks. *See also* deductions on taxes;
    retirement accounts
  annuities, 189
  cash value life insurance, 322–323, 354
  long-term investments, 134–135
  tax-free investments, 133, 239–240,
    242–243
  tax-friendly investments, 134, 205
Tax Guide for Small Businesses (IRS
    Publication 334), 135
tax preparers, 130, 136
taxes. *See also* deductions on taxes;
    tax breaks
  alternative minimum tax (AMT), 122
  audits, 138–140
  daytrading and, 148
  estate taxes, 323, 353–354
  hiring professional help for, 130
  income brackets and rates, 120–121
  income shifting to reduce, 124
  investment consequences, 53–54,
    132–135, 170, 235–236
  on investment distributions, 235
  marginal tax rate, 120–121, 236
  obtaining forms, 119

professional help for, 130, 136–138
property taxes, 265
reducing, 115–116, 122–124, 132–135
refunds, 119–120
resources for help with, 135–138
taxable income, 121–122
total taxes paid, 120
transferring retirement money and, 232
Taxes For Dummies (Tyson, Eric and
    Silverman, David J.), 136, 265, 354
tax-free gifts, 353
tax-sheltered annuities, 212, 213–214,
    228–231
TD Waterhouse, 228, 325, 326
teaching personal finance in schools, 12
Technical Stuff icon, 5
telephone expenses, 104–106
television financial programs, 395–396
television, satellite, 105
term life insurance, 320–325, 390–391
time shares, 184–185
Tip icon, 5
title insurance, 291–292
Tobias, Andrew (*Invisible Bankers*), 308
total cost, 85
total return on mutual funds, 207–209
town homes, 283–284
transferring retirement accounts, 228–232
transportation expenses, 106–109.
    See also cars
Treasuries. *See* U.S. Treasuries
TV financial programs, 395–396
Tweedy Browne Global Value fund, 228
Tyson, Eric
  Home Buying For Dummies, 277
  Investing For Dummies, 229
  Mutual Funds For Dummies, 209, 229
  Personal Finance For Dummies, 1–6
  Taxes For Dummies, 136, 265, 354

• *U* •

Unsubsidized Stafford Loans, 255
USAA
  bond funds, 242
  disability insurance, 330
  homeowner's/renter's insurance, 346
  life insurance, 325, 326
  money market funds, 238, 239, 240

U.S. Treasuries
  bond funds, 242, 243
  buying direct, 242
  as indexes for ARMs, 275
  inflation-indexed, 243
  inside retirement accounts, 220
  as lending investments, 144–146
  money market funds, 238–239
utility expenses, 104

• V •

vacations, 111–112, 184–185
Value Line fund directory, 206
value stocks, 195
Vanguard funds
  for aggressive retirement accounts,
    226, 227, 228
  annuities, 245
  bond funds, 241–242, 243
  for conservative retirement accounts,
    226, 228
  index funds, 198, 199
  money market funds, 238, 239, 240
  stock mutual funds, 245
  Web site, 389

• W •

warehouse clubs, 100–101
Warning! icon, 6
warranties, 304–305
wealth, 33, 34, 72
Wealth Without Risk (Givens, Charles), 13
Web sites
  Alliance of Claims Assistance
    Professionals, 335
  American Arbitration Association, 163
  annuities, 245
  auto insurance, 350
  biased financial advice on, 384
  bond funds, 241–243
  car buying guides, 106
  credit bureaus, 282

Debtors Anonymous, 87
Direct Marketing Association, 86
discount brokers, 228, 389–390
Federal Student Aid Information
    Center, 255
Fidelity Investments, 227
financial planner associations, 375
Gamblers Anonymous, 117
Internet access expenses, 105
Internet defined, 382
investment firm "checking accounts," 79
investment research sites, 388–389
IRS, 119, 136
life insurance online, 390–391
money market funds, 238–240
mortgage information, 280
National Association of Insurance
    Commissioners, 315, 346
periodicals, 390
short-term thinking on, 384–385
Social Security, 48–49, 319
sources of information on, 383–384
"sponsored" content, 384
tax preparation help, 136
telephone service shopping, 105
tips for using, 383–385, 396–397
Treasury Direct program, 242
Vanguard, 199, 226, 228
wholesale superstores, 100–101
wills, 351–352, 391
windfalls, receiving, 415–416
worker's compensation, 328
worldwide mutual funds, 196–197
wrap or managed accounts, 165

• Y •

yield, 172
Your Federal Income Tax (IRS Publication
    17), 135

• Z •

zoning, real estate value and, 181

FOR

DUMMIES®

The easy way to get more done and have more fun

PERSONAL FINANCE & BUSINESS

0-7645-2431-3

0-7645-5331-3

0-7645-5307-0

Also available:

Accounting For Dummies
(0-7645-5314-3)

Business Plans Kit For Dummies
(0-7645-5365-8)

Managing For Dummies
(1-5688-4858-7)

Mutual Funds For Dummies
(0-7645-5329-1)

QuickBooks All-in-One Desk Reference For Dummies
(0-7645-1963-8)

Resumes For Dummies
(0-7645-5471-9)

Small Business Kit For Dummies
(0-7645-5093-4)

Starting an eBay Business For Dummies
(0-7645-1547-0)

Taxes For Dummies 2003
(0-7645-5475-1)

HOME, GARDEN, FOOD & WINE

0-7645-5295-3

0-7645-5130-2

0-7645-5250-3

Also available:

Bartending For Dummies
(0-7645-5051-9)

Christmas Cooking For Dummies
(0-7645-5407-7)

Cookies For Dummies
(0-7645-5390-9)

Diabetes Cookbook For Dummies
(0-7645-5230-9)

Grilling For Dummies
(0-7645-5076-4)

Home Maintenance For Dummies
(0-7645-5215-5)

Slow Cookers For Dummies
(0-7645-5240-6)

Wine For Dummies
(0-7645-5114-0)

FITNESS, SPORTS, HOBBIES & PETS

0-7645-5167-1

0-7645-5146-9

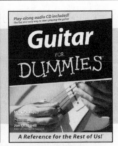

0-7645-5106-X

Also available:

Cats For Dummies
(0-7645-5275-9)

Chess For Dummies
(0-7645-5003-9)

Dog Training For Dummies
(0-7645-5286-4)

Labrador Retrievers For Dummies
(0-7645-5281-3)

Martial Arts For Dummies
(0-7645-5358-5)

Piano For Dummies
(0-7645-5105-1)

Pilates For Dummies
(0-7645-5397-6)

Power Yoga For Dummies
(0-7645-5342-9)

Puppies For Dummies
(0-7645-5255-4)

Quilting For Dummies
(0-7645-5118-3)

Rock Guitar For Dummies
(0-7645-5356-9)

Weight Training For Dummies
(0-7645-5168-X)

Available wherever books are sold.
Go to www.dummies.com or call 1-877-762-2974 to order direct

 **WILEY**

FOR DUMMIES

A world of resources to help you grow

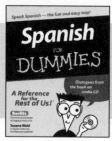

FOR DUMMIES®

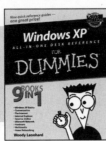

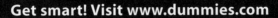

FOR DUMMIES®